Explorations in
cognitive
dissonance

Explorations in
cognitive
dissonance

Jack W. Brehm, Duke University

Arthur R. Cohen, New York University

John Wiley & Sons, Inc., New York · London · Sydney

To the memory of *Carl Iver Hovland*

Preface

The publication in 1957 of Festinger's *Theory of Cognitive Dissonance* stimulated widespread interest among psychologists in the issue of cognitive discrepancies and their motivating effects. Since then, investigators concerned with dissonance theory have utilized it in studying a broad range of phenomena, such as attitude change, decisional processes, social interaction and mass behavior, among other things. The particular interest in dissonance theory seems to us to be the result of a number of factors. For one thing, there exists a paucity of even moderately elegant and clearly stated theoretical models in social psychology. Secondly, the generality of the theory and its seeming applicability to a wide range of significant psychological problems have made investigators take note immediately. Also, a special virtue of the theory is that it has implications for numerous nonobvious effects that do not appear to be easily predictable from either common sense or from other current psychological formulations. And, finally, the operations for testing derivations from the theory appear to be clearly specifiable within an experimental framework, making the theory an attractive one for experimentally oriented psychologists.

Dissonance theory is becoming more widely used and with wider usage inevitably must come some imprecision in its application. Thus the theory may be overextended to explain the motivating effects of *any* perceived discrepancy, to understand *all* decisional conflicts, or to deal with the *entire range* of interaction processes. In effect, the success of any one formulation in predicting complex behavior stimulates a tendency to apply it to the entire spectrum of social psychology. We feel, therefore, that after five years of research occasioned by Festinger's book, it is time to take a close look at the theory. Thus, in view of the amount of published and unpublished research deriving from dissonance theory, we believe it is useful to try to evaluate the adequacy of the present theoretical formulation, to assess its generality and predictive power, to specify its limits, advantages and disadvantages, and to indicate its possible extension to new problems and areas in psychology. In sum, we shall attempt to discuss the theory from the vantage point of five years of intensive research evolving from the theory.

We had an additional aim in writing the present book. In the course of the past few years, the authors, separately, together, or in collaboration with associates and assistants, have completed a number of experimental studies that derive from dissonance theory. Some of these experiments bear directly on the present formulation of the theory as it now stands; some attempt to indicate possible lines of reformulation of the theory; and some represent extensions of the theory into heretofore unexplored theoretical territory. We felt that, rather than scatter these experiments throughout a number of technical journals, they could be better presented, evaluated, and brought to bear on the theory within the context of the present book, juxtaposed to one another and to the general body of studies in the area. Each of these new experiments will be fully presented; the procedures and methodological details will be clearly laid out, and the experiments will be clearly identifiable in the text.

We present first a brief description of the theoretical statement as it appeared in Festinger's book. In so doing, we shall attempt to indicate what we consider the most valid sort of evidence for the theory and to indicate what we take to be the basis for its success in delineating nonobvious or paradoxical aspects of behavior. In Part II we review the evidence bearing on dissonance theory; in Chapters 3, 4, 5, and 7 we present the research published to date and raise a number of theoretical and methodological points in connection with the evidence discussed. In Chapter 6 we present a number of new and unpublished experiments bearing directly upon straightforward derivations from the theory. Part III is devoted to a presentation of a number of extensions of the theory into new problems and areas in psychology. Here, too, a number of new and unpublished experiments are given in detail: Chapter 8 discusses the implications of dissonance for theories of motivation and Chapter 11 deals specifically with new evidence relevant to basic problems and assumptions of the theory and presents this evidence within the context of speculations concerning the possible directions of theoretical reformulation. In Part IV we discuss the relationship of dissonance theory to other theoretical and empirical models in psychology; in Part V the theory is viewed in the light of its potential application to some important social issues, and we summarize our main points and indicate some future perspectives.

We would like to express our gratitude to the National Science Foundation for generous and continued support of our work.

We are indebted to Farrar, Straus and Cudahy, to the University of Nebraska Press, and to the University of Minnesota Press for permission to use copyright material. Thanks are also due J. Stacy Adams, Jane Allyn, Elliot Aronson, Dana Bramel, Timothy Brock, Leon Festinger, Harold B. Gerard, Sidney Rosen, and Philip G. Zimbardo for making relevant materials available prior to publication.

It is a great pleasure to acknowledge our indebtedness to Leon Festinger for his long encouragement and support of our efforts, for the intellectual stimulation he has provided, and for his critical reading of the manuscript. Mary Lee Brehm, Charles N. Cofer, Harold B. Gerard, Charles W. Greenbaum, Harold H. Kelley, and Philip G. Zimbardo also read the entire manuscript, and their suggestions led to many corrections and improvements, for which we are grateful. We would like to stress, however, that the point of view represented in this book is strictly our own and that none of the above persons is responsible for it.

We have greatly benefited from discussions with Reuben Baron, Timothy Brock, Gerald S. Leventhal, and Nora Rosenau. Our debt is also considerable to the following student assistants and associates who worked with us: Kenneth Browne, Jon C. Crocker, James Hughes, Tom Leon, John Lukens, John Marth, Leslie Noller, Miles Novy, David Robertson, Vaida Thompson, and Charles Wilson.

We are happy to be able to thank our wives, Mary Lee and Barbara, for their help in proofreading and indexing but, more importantly, for their forbearance and constant encouragement.

The present book is truly a collaborative effort; it is unlikely that either of us could have written it alone. The order of authorship signifies only alphabetical precedence; we assume equal responsibility for both its strengths and weaknesses.

In dedicating this book to the late Professor Carl I. Hovland of Yale

University, we are expressing our appreciation for his support, critical appraisal, and friendship during the years we were at Yale.

JACK W. BREHM
ARTHUR R. COHEN

Durham, North Carolina
New York, New York
August, 1962

Contents

Why is "Thou Shalt Not Covet" the very last of the Ten Commandments? Because one must first avoid doing the wrong things. Then, later on, one will not desire to do them. If one stopped and waited until all the passions ceased, one could never attain holiness.

And so it is with all things. If you are not happy, act the happy man. Happiness will come later. So also with faith. If you are in despair, act as though you believed. Faith will come afterwards.*

I. B. Singer

* From *The Spinoza of Market Street*. New York: Farrar, Straus & Cudahy, 1961, page 144.

THEORETICAL
INTRODUCTION

part **I**

The theory and the role

of commitment

—1

Cognitive dissonance, according to Festinger (1957), is a psychological tension having motivational characteristics. The theory of cognitive dissonance concerns itself with the conditions that arouse dissonance in an individual and with the ways in which dissonance can be reduced.

The units of the theory are cognitive elements and the relationships between them. Cognitive elements or cognitions are "knowledges" or items of information, and they may pertain to oneself or to one's environment. Knowledge of one's feelings, behavior, and opinions as well as knowledge about the location of goal objects, how to get to them, what other people believe, and so forth, are examples of cognitive elements.

The relation that exists between two elements is *consonant* if one implies the other in some psychological sense. Psychological implication may arise from cultural mores, pressure to be logical, behavioral commitment, past experience, and so on. What is meant by implication is that having a given cognition, A, leads to having another given cognition, B. The detection of psychological implication is frequently possible by measurement of what else a person expects when he holds a given cognition.

A *dissonant* relationship exists between two cognitive elements when a person possesses one which follows from the obverse of another that he possesses. Thus, if A implies B, then holding A and the obverse of B is dissonant. A person experiences dissonance, that is, a motivational tension, when he has cognitions among which there are one or more dissonant relationships. Cognitive elements that are neither dissonant nor consonant with each other are said to be irrelevant.

The amount of dissonance associated with a given cognition is a function of the importance of that cognition and the one with which it is dissonant. The magnitude of dissonance is also a function of the ratio of dissonant to consonant cognitions, where each cognitive element is weighted for its importance to the person. As the number and/or importance of dissonant cognitions increases, relative to the number and/or importance of consonant cognitions, the magnitude of dissonance increases.

In general, a person may reduce dissonance by decreasing the number and/or importance of dissonant elements compared to consonant, or he may reduce the importance of all relevant elements together. It should be noted that propositions about the magnitude of dissonance can be tested without there being any actual reduction of dissonance, since a state of dissonance leads to *attempts* at dissonance reduction rather than necessarily successful reduction.

How dissonance is reduced (or attempts at reduction are made) depends on the resistance to change of relevant cognitive elements. Those cognitions with relatively low resistance tend to change first. The resistance to change of a cognitive element comes from the extent to which such change would produce new dissonance and from some joint function of the responsiveness of the cognition to reality (what it represents) and the difficulty of changing the reality. Where the reality represented is ambiguous (e.g., a diffuse emotional reaction in oneself, a physical stimulus in the presence of considerable "noise," or the prediction of an uncertain future event), the cognitive element can be changed quite readily without any change in the reality. On the other hand, if the reality is quite clear, then the resistance to change of the corresponding cognitive element will generally be proportional to the difficulty of changing the reality. How difficult it is to change a given aspect of reality varies all the way from extremely easy to essentially impossible. For example, it is frequently quite easy for a person to change his behavior, as when one finds he has entered the wrong word in a crossword puzzle. Or, to take the opposite extreme, a person may find it impossible to change the fact that he has lost a gift having considerable sentimental value. It should be noted, however, that where the reality is difficult or even impossible to change, the corresponding cognitive element could still be changed by making it nonveridical with reality, though by and large there appears to be an overwhelming pressure for a person to keep his cognitions veridical with reality.

In order to be perfectly clear about how the theory works, we will give two hypothetical examples. The first illustrates how dissonance may be aroused and reduced when a person chooses between two attractive alternatives. Suppose that a person is going to buy a new car and is considering both sedans and station wagons. Since he cannot afford to buy both, and since he ordinarily buys a car only once every 3 or 4 years, he must choose carefully. Prior to making his final decision, he will carefully weigh the pros and cons of each kind of car. Let us suppose, then, that the person in our example has gone through this process and has finally decided to buy the station wagon. What can we say about him in terms of dissonance theory?

It should be clear that all of the good or positive aspects of the station wagon that the buyer knows about constitute cognitive elements that "lead to," or are consonant with, his knowledge that he has bought the station wagon and will be using it for the next 3 or 4 years. Other cognitions that are consonant are those knowledges of bad or unpleasant aspects of the sedan that he rejected. Still other cognitions, however, will almost inevitably be dissonant with—that is, follow from the obverse of—knowledge of this choice. These are the knowledges of bad or unpleasant aspects of the station wagon and good or favorable aspects of the sedan. Any of these latter cognitive elements would have led the person to buy the sedan rather than the station wagon. If the person holds any cognitions that would have led him to buy the sedan rather than the station wagon, he will experience dissonance consequent to choosing the station wagon.

The amount of dissonance experienced by the person depends on the ratio of dissonant to consonant elements, where each element is weighted according to its importance to him. Thus, if the only dissonant element is that the sedan has a softer ride than the station wagon, and if the individual really doesn't consider a soft ride to be an important quality of his car, then little dissonance will be created. It could also happen that a soft ride is considered very important, but the advantages of having a station wagon outweigh this factor so much that, again, little dissonance would be experienced. In sum, the magnitude of dissonance experienced depends directly on the number and/or importance of dissonant cognitions *relative* to the number and/or importance of consonant cognitions.

Many derivations follow from the above formulation. For example, with the attractiveness of the chosen alternative held constant, the greater the attractiveness of the rejected alternative, the greater the magnitude of dissonance. With the relative attractiveness of two alternatives held constant, the more attractive they both are, the greater is the magnitude of dissonance. And with the attractiveness of two alternatives held constant, the greater the amount of cognitive overlap (qualities in common) between them, the less the magnitude of dissonance. The extreme case of this latter derivation is that there will be no dissonance aroused by a choice between two identical alternatives, for there are no cognitions that lead to choosing one rather than the other.

Returning to our buyer who has just chosen a station wagon, let us see how he may try to reduce his dissonance. In general, of course, he may try to reduce the number and/or importance of dissonant, relative to consonant, cognitive elements, or he may try to reduce the general importance of all of these relevant elements. What this means specifically is that he may try to eliminate or reduce the importance of dissonant elements, such as the good or favorable aspects of the sedan or the unfavorable aspects of the station wagon. At the same time he may try to increase the number and/or importance of cognitions that are consonant with buying the station wagon, such as favorable aspects of the station wagon and the unfavorable aspects of the sedan. He might also try to eliminate dissonant cognitions and add consonant cognitions by trying to convince other people that station wagons are better than sedans and thereby gain social support for his selection. Similarly, he might seek out information, such as advertisements, that is expected to point out the benefits of owning a station wagon. These, then, are some of the consequences that we might expect from dissonance aroused by a choice.

Our second example concerns the induction of unpleasant behavior. In this case, let us suppose that we wish to induce a child to eat a disliked vegetable. Since a person does not ordinarily eat a disliked vegetable, one way to accomplish this would be to offer the child a reward for eating a serving of the vegetable. It is clear, of course, that the reward must be sufficiently attractive to overcome the child's reluctance to eat. Assuming that it is and that the child has been induced to eat, what can we say about the child's behavior in terms of dissonance theory?

Knowledge that one has eaten a vegetable clearly follows from the obverse of knowledge that one dislikes the vegetable, and we may say that these two elements are dissonant with each other. On the other hand, knowledge that one has received a reward for having eaten the vegetable is clearly consonant with the knowledge that one has eaten the vegetable. Since the child's dislike of the vegetable is dissonant with his behavior of eating it, the child will experience dissonance. The amount of the dissonance will be a direct function of the importance of the dissonant cognitive element (the amount of dislike for the vegetable) compared to the importance of the consonant cognitive element (the amount of reward obtained for having eaten the vegetable).

Again, clear implications follow from this dissonance formulation, and we will cite two: The greater is the initial dislike for the vegetable, the greater is the magnitude of dissonance; and the greater is the reward for having eaten, the less is the magnitude of dissonance.

The dissonance experienced by the child could conceivably be reduced in a number of ways, and we will mention the most obvious. The child might try to reduce dissonance by increasing his liking for the vegetable, thereby making the formerly dissonant element consonant. He might also try magnifying the value of the reward and thereby make the dissonant element *relatively* unimportant. And, finally, he might try to reduce the relative importance of his dislike for the vegetable.

This brief outline should serve to remind the reader of Festinger's (1957) general theoretical statement. Given at this rather abstract conceptual level, the theory appears to be applicable to a wide range of phenomena. Nevertheless, most of the empirical work designed to test the theory, including that of the present authors, has dealt with a special case of the theory, namely, dissonance that occurs in conjunction with a commitment. We turn therefore to a discussion of the role of commitment in the arousal and reduction of dissonance.

THE SPECIAL CASE OF COMMITMENT

For the purposes of this discussion we assume that a person is committed when he has decided to do or not do a certain thing, when he has chosen one (or more) alternatives and thereby rejected one (or more) alternatives, when he actively engages in a given behavior or has engaged in a given behavior. Any one or a combination of these behaviors can be considered a commitment. If, for example, a person is watching a movie in a theatre, or if he has only decided to go to a movie, we may say that he is committed (albeit, more strongly in the former case than in the latter) to the behavior of watching a movie.

A major point about commitment is that it generally provides a clear specification of psychological implication. That is, it allows us to say, at least roughly, that certain cognitive elements are consonant with each other and that certain other elements are dissonant with each other. Thus if a person decides to chew gum rather than smoke cigarettes, his knowledge that gum-chewing helps to prevent tooth decay is clearly consonant with this commitment (i.e., commitment to chew gum follows from knowledge that gum-chewing reduces decay), and knowledge that a close friend is offended by gum-chewing is clearly dissonant with the commitment. What should be noticed in these examples is that without the commitment to one of the two behaviors, the various knowledges concerning the benefits or penalties involved in gum-chewing and smoking may have no power at all to arouse dissonance. Knowledge that gum-chewing is socially offensive does not lead either to the knowledge or its obverse—that gum-chewing reduces tooth decay. But when a person actually does chew gum, these cognitions become relevant and are either consonant or dissonant with the knowledge of the (committed) behavior. *It should be noted that the specification of consonant and dissonant relationships in the above examples does assume that the individual in question is motivated to benefit himself and to avoid harm.* Thus there is always the implication that the individual does something incompatible with some need or desire.

In addition to facilitating the specification of what is consonant and what is dissonant, commitment increases the resistance to change of an element (or set of elements) and thereby affects the kinds of attempts to reduce dissonance that may occur. This resistance aspect of commitment may occur whether a person's decision to do or not do something or choose an alternative is private or public. Ordinarily, of course, we do not know if a commitment has been made unless it is public, that is, unless someone has been told about it. We would assume that a public commitment is usually more resistant to change than a private commitment. This assumption can be subsumed under another plausible assumption, namely, that the resistance to change of a commitment increases as strength of expectation by others increases that one will hold to the commitment. A further factor affecting the resistance due to commitment concerns whether or not it is physically possible to change the commitment. Thus, when a person is already engaging in, or has engaged in, a given behavior, it may be quite impossible to change that fact (though change in *knowledge* of the behavior could still occur). If, for example, a person has smashed his automobile beyond repair, he is committed to that event beyond recourse. In summary, then, commitment, which we consider to occur when a person engages in an activity or when he decides on one thing rather than another, increases the resistance to change of the corresponding cognitive element, for it increases the resistance to change of the reality to which the element corresponds. According to our earlier discussion this effect of commitment would tend to be reduced to the extent that the reality involved was ambiguous, since in that case the resistance against making the cognitive element nonveridical with reality would be lessened and would be the controlling element for total resistance to change of the cognition in question.

It has been noted that when a person experiences dissonance, he will tend to change those dissonant cognitive elements that are least resistant to change. Hence dissonance aroused in connection with a commitment is likely to be reduced by change in elements other than those involved in the commitment. If a person chooses A of two attractive alternatives, A and B, he is not likely to reduce the resulting dissonance by saying that his choice was wrong and that he should have chosen B.

The role of commitment, then, in the theory of cognitive dissonance is, first, to aid the specification of psychological implication and hence the determination of what is consonant and what is dissonant and, second, to aid in the specification of the ways in which a person may try to reduce dissonance.

Because commitment provides relatively clear specification of consonant and dissonant cognitions, it also provides rather readily a condition under which many aspects of the theory can be tested. Where a person can be clearly committed to a given behavior or decision, information that is unambiguously inconsistent with that commitment should create dissonance and the individual should manifest attempts to reduce that dissonance. In the absence of other forces, a failure to find attempts at dissonance reduction under these conditions would be clear evidence against the theory.

But the problem of obtaining unequivocal evidence for a theory must also take into account alternative explanations for a given set of empirical evidence. Here again, however, the condition of commitment provides us with an interesting test, for other general theories about behavior have had relatively little to say about the effect of commitment. We do not mean to imply that the absence of an alternative explanation makes dissonance theory "right" but rather that the theory, to the extent to which it is "right," provides us with an understanding of "unique" and "nonobvious" behavioral phenomena.

Let us consider, for example, a person who has committed himself to listening to the political views of another. From a "common sense" point of view, we might expect that if the communicator's views differed from those of the listener, the latter might show some shift in his own view in the direction of that held by the communicator. It would also be "common sense" to say that the less the listener liked the communicator, the less he would change his own views in the direction of those held by the communicator. But analysis in terms of dissonance theory provides us with at least one quite different expectation, namely, that the listener's change toward the position held by the communicator will *increase* as his liking for the communicator decreases. This "nonobvious" prediction depends, however, on the fact that the listener is *committed* to listening to the views of the communicator. Under commitment conditions it is unequivocal that the expressed views are dissonant (inconsistent with having to listen to them), and it is difficult for the individual to reject the communicator or his views, for that would be inconsistent with having committed himself to listening to him. The listener will therefore tend to reduce his dissonance by changing his own views toward those expressed by the communicator. Since the magnitude of dissonance will vary inversely with the listener's liking for the communicator (a cognition consonant with the commitment), the amount of change in his views will tend to increase as his liking for the communicator decreases. What we wish to stress, however, is that in the absence of a commitment to listen, the arousal of dissonance would depend on whether or not having one view implied not being exposed to another, and the reduction of any dissonance aroused could conceivably take the form of change toward the communicator, change away from the communicator, rejection of the communicator, and so on. In short, it would be less clear that dissonance would be aroused, and it would be impossible to predict the likely effects of any such dissonance without information about the resistance to change of the relevant cognitive elements.

In summary, our position is that commitment is a condition under which: (1) The specification of dissonance and the manner in which it is likely to be reduced are relatively unequivocal; and (2) The implications are relatively unique in comparison with other theoretical approaches and frequently nonobvious in terms of common sense. This volume, then, will be primarily devoted to consideration of various implications of dissonance theory where commitment is involved. In the following pages we shall review the published evidence, raise a series of questions concerning theoretical implications, report new research bearing on some of these questions, review extensions of the theory, speculate on the conditions necessary for the arousal of dissonance and report some relevant evidence, discuss the way in which dissonance theory relates to other models of cognitive balance decision, interaction and social influence, and indicate some implications for applied social change.

Inconsistency between cognitions

— 2

Before beginning our review of the evidence relevant to dissonance theory, it might be profitable to discuss some of the problems inherent in the present statement of the theory insofar as it attempts to be precise about the determinants of dissonance arousal. This discussion will center around the major issue of inconsistency between cognitions. We shall consider how the theory might view opinions and attitudes. This discussion of conceptual problems will not delve deeply into what we consider basic theoretical issues in the theory; we shall discuss some of these issues in Chapter 11.

A fundamental condition for the creation of dissonance in a person is that he have two cognitions which are somehow discrepant with each other. As we have indicated, Festinger's statement of this condition is that one cognition "follows from the obverse of the other" (1957, p. 13). Since Festinger has already noted that the "follows from" relationship can sometimes be determined empirically but is limited by our abilities to specify and measure cognitions and the relationships among them, there is no point in our carrying this particular problem further. The variety of supportive research to be presented in the next chapters will show amply that the "follows from" relationship can be specified to a sufficiently precise degree for the gathering of evidence relevant to the theory. Nevertheless, the "follows from" relationship is not always clear and specifiable, and it is to one particularly ambiguous aspect that we now turn.

DISCREPANCY SIZE

Strictly speaking there is no concept of *degree* of a dissonant relationship: One cognition follows from another cognition, follows from the opposite of another cognition, or is irrelevant to it. While the total magnitude of dissonance associated with a given cognition varies as a function of the importance of the relevant cognitions and as a function of proportion of relevant relationships which are dissonant, the relationship between any two cognitive elements must be consonant, dissonant, or irrelevant. How, then, can one speak of *discrepancy size* as a variable related to the magnitude of dissonance?

The answer to this question may be divided into two major parts. The first part concerns the conceptualization of knowledge in general; the second concerns the conceptualization of opinions and attitudes.

It is presumably true that the objective events about which we have knowledge vary along a dimension from discreteness to continuousness. For example, it is generally quite clear whether or not a person owns a car; either he owns one or he doesn't, and there are no degrees in between. Similarly, a person's location is easily ascertainable in terms of gross characteristics, such as the city or state he may be in at a given time. On the other hand, some knowledge is frequently or nearly always in terms of a *location* on a continuous dimension, such as a person's weight, the color of an object, the annual rainfall in the state of North Carolina. In regard to the latter kinds of information, objects are not always heavy or light, one color or another, and the amount of rainfall is not "nothing" or "something"; weight is continuous, colors mix, and rainfall varies from one year to the next.

Efficient adaptation to one's abilities and one's environment requires that a person make relatively fine discriminations when they are possible. Thus while a person may operate as if his house either is on fire or is not, he cannot grow a garden on the two-valued discrimination that there is or is not rain. Crops in need of considerable moisture must be watered in direct proportion to the lack of rainfall. A half-inch of rain in a month is not the same as 4 inches.

It seems fairly safe to assume that a person does make relatively fine discriminations when they are possible and when they are instrumentally valuable. But if this assumption is correct, then it will surely also be true that continuous variables will frequently be involved in discrepant or dissonant relationships with other cognitive elements. Thus we are confronted with the likelihood that one cognitive element may be clearly consonant with one *value* of a continuous variable and may be clearly dissonant with another value of that same variable. Since dissonance theory has not provided explicit statements concerning the effect of intermediate values on the magnitude of dissonance, we are here concerned with what might reasonably be expected to occur.

A simple possibility is that the magnitude of dissonance increases in an approximately linear manner as the discrepancy size varies from the completely consonant to the completely dissonant value. Suppose, for example, that a person buys a super sports car in the hope that it will reach a speed of at least 150 miles per hour. Actually, the performing speed of the car could range from over 150 miles per hour down to not running at all. It is certainly clear that a speed of 150 miles an hour or over would be consonant with purchase of the car, and that the car's not running at all would be dissonant. If the discrepancy between the hoped for and actual speed of the car arouses dissonance as an approximately linear function, then as the speed of the car falls below 150 miles per hour, the magnitude of dissonance should gradually increase until it reaches a maximum where the car fails to run at all.

A second though less likely possibility is that the magnitude of dissonance is a "step" function of the discrepancy size. Where the discrepancy size is small, no dissonance occurs; and where the discrepancy size becomes larger than some critical value, the magnitude of dissonance becomes maximal. Another way to say this is that when there is psychological implication of a dimension of information, the person reacts to values along that dimension as if they were either consonant or dissonant, there being no intermediate reactions.

Regardless of the precise function that may describe the relationship between variations of a given parameter and the magnitude of dissonance, it is apparent that the possibility of variation along a continuum must somehow be taken into account. Dissonance can be aroused in regard to a continuous variable, and the magnitude of the resultant dissonance will almost certainly be a monotonic function of the discrepancy size along the continuous dimension.

However, the concept of discrepancy size has not been confined to this case of a continuous, unitary variable. In fact, its use in connection with dissonance theory has been mainly in the general tradition of attitude and opinion research and theory. That usage assumes that attitudes or opinions may, by and large, be considered unidimensional variables based on complex information and having several covarying characteristics. As an attitude varies from favorable to unfavorable, it also changes in respect to such dimensions as "importance," "strength," "resistance to change," and "salience." One rather interesting covariant of position along the attitude dimension is the amount of relevant information that the person possesses. It is generally assumed that as a person's attitude varies from neutral in either direction, he is likely to have increasing amounts of relevant information about the issue. We hasten to point out, however, that this correlation does not necessarily hold, since it is perfectly possible for a person to have a "neutral" position because he possesses conflicting information. What can be said, then, is that the concept of opinion or attitude is somewhat ambiguous, especially in regard to its implications for the possession of relevant information. Let us now see how dissonance theory might view opinions and attitudes.

Many studies that have used dissonance theory to predict the effects of variations in opinion or attitude discrepancies (Allyn and Festinger, 1961; Cohen, 1959b; Cohen, Terry and Jones, 1959; Zimbardo, 1960) have depended on the assumption that as discrepancy size increases, the number and/or importance of dissonant relationships increase. But since none of these reports has been explicit concerning the translation of an attitude or opinion dimension into the terms of dissonance theory, the translation will be detailed here.

A basic assumption is that a person holds a set of cognitive elements or items of information which lead him to adopt a given position on the issue. The position is a derivative of the more primitive factors, namely, the relevant cognitions, weighted according to their importances to the person. It serves as a summary of this sometimes complex and diverse set of cognitive elements. However, other than serving as a summary of the relevant cognitive elements, the attitudinal position has no significance in the conceptualization of dissonance phenomena. In effect, the attitude position is a convenient tool for research but is not, strictly speaking, appropriate to the terms of dissonance theory unless the attitude or opinion is identical with the cognitive element involved in the relationship.

What *is* necessary from the point of view of dissonance theory is that for a cognition in question, all consonant and dissonant cognitions be detected and weighted for their importance. Only to the extent that such detection and weighting can be carried out, either element by element or in summary form, can the operations be said to conform to the terms of the theory.

One implication of these considerations is that the relationship between an "attitude measure" and any attempt to change the attitude by arousal of dissonance must be carefully conceptualized. It is theoretically possible to arouse dissonance in regard to some information relevant to a given attitude while failing to arouse dissonance in regard to other information that is consistent with the same attitude. When such is the case, a measure summarizing change in regard to all relevant information will be less than optimally sensitive to the change produced by the dissonance. It would reflect not only the dissonance-produced change but also the lack of change in other attitude-relevant but dissonant-irrelevant information. It will be clear that this general problem would be accentuated to the extent that the attitude measure was made of items representing the dissonant-irrelevant information rather than items confined to dissonant-relevant information.

Another way to view this problem is to note that the cognitive elements which are relevant to a given state of dissonance may not constitute what has traditionally been called an attitude. The relevant cognitions may, on the one hand, be quite specific and, on the other, completely irrelevant to each other. Consider, for example, Mr. Jones, who is at a ball game. The cognitive elements relevant to his being at the ball game may be quite specific or quite general, and they may have nothing to do with each other. That is, he may like one of the teams (general attitude), he might want to see if a particular player is as good as advertised (specific reason), he might want to see a given team lose, he might want to get some fresh air, he might be trying to get away from his nagging wife and screaming children, he might be going to please a friend who really wants to see the game, and so on. These reasons are not mutually exclusive, and hence two or more could be operating at the same time. With the possibility of heterogeneous elements being involved, the only attitude that might appropriately be invoked in our example is "Mr. Jones' July 12th attitude toward attending ball games." As conceptualized, it would hardly be called a typical attitude dimension.

The other facet of the problem is illustrated by an examination of the dissonance process from the point of view of initial attitudes. Suppose, for example, we measure a person's attitude toward the church and find it to be quite positive. Our attitude measure is made up of items concerning the church's role in local, national, and world affairs, including philosophical and practical values, personal benefits as from sermons, social events, and so on. Given an attitude based on this variety of phenomena, how might dissonance occur? It is clear that dissonance could occur in connection with any of these aspects of the attitude. However, unless many, if not most of them, were involved in the arousal of dissonance, then one could hardly expect that there would be a noticeable effect on the attitude measure as a function of dissonance reduction. On the other hand, how might one try to arouse dissonance in regard to the general attitude without recourse to the subdimensions? The answer, in this case, is not particularly clear. What is needed is some over-all cognitive element that clashed (or can clash) with this general "attitude toward the church." The conceptualization of the attitude dimension is crucial: For it to be cogently amenable to an analysis in terms of dissonance theory, it must consist of a set of cognitive elements that are relevant to a given element or cluster of elements. For it to be relevant to a given element or cluster of elements, it must have a precise definition patterned according to the requirements of the theory rather than according to cultural usage or definition. In the case in question, one's attitude toward the church is difficult to relate to any given cognition or cluster of cognitions and illustrates one problem of applying dissonance theory to previous findings about social attitudes. Approaching the subject of attitudes toward the church from the point of view of dissonance theory, one might ask, "What cognitions are relevant to joining a given religious organization?" (v. Zajonc, 1960; Brock, 1962). What is different about these formulations is that they focus on a given cognition (*attendance or joining*) and ask what other cognitions are relevant, rather than starting with a (heterogeneous) set of cognitions and casting around for a single cognition relevant to them all.

It should be clear from this discussion that the use of discrepancy size in the analysis of attitude change phenomena is for the sake of methodological convenience and is at the cost of rather complex assumptions about how attitudes relate to the theory. But it is also clear that the theory does need a variable of discrepancy size in order to deal adequately with the role of perceptually continuous variables in the arousal of dissonance. We would therefore suggest that the determining statement of dissonance, the "X follows from the obverse of Y" relationship, might be amended to "X *follows from any variation from Y in the direction of being obverse.*"

Some of the studies to be reviewed do involve attitude discrepancy as an independent variable. As we have seen, these studies assume that the manipulation of discrepancy size is equivalent to the manipulation of the ratio of weighted dissonant to weighted consonant cognitions. One benefit of talking in terms of attitudinal discrepancies rather than in terms of clusters of cognitions is in the simplification possible. We shall simplify things the same way.

It should also be noted that in the following review of research bearing on the theory, we shall use the general label of "attitude change" to include all those studies which are concerned with changes in opinion, whether they refer to evaluations of people, objects, or behavior or to specific beliefs. Evaluation is generally assumed to refer to the component of attitude which refers to the appraisal of something (object, person, event) as good or bad, harmful or beneficial, important or unimportant, and so on. Opinion generally represents the component of attitude having to do with the knowledge that something is true or untrue, correct or incorrect, probable or improbable, and so on (Hovland, Janis and Kelley, 1953). The latter term, opinion, signifies knowledge about the object, while the former, evaluation, indicates how one feels about it. A combination of evaluation and opinion may be termed an attitude.

These distinctions are not made within the framework of dissonance theory, and they are not clearly applicable to all of the studies to be discussed. Nevertheless, though we will generally term all statements referring to evaluative and opinion changes as "attitude change," the distinction will be made only where it is appropriate for a given piece of research. It is assumed that such a procedure will help in the organization of data and in relating the relevant evidence to other theory and research in psychology.

THE RATIO OF DISSONANT TO CONSONANT COGNITIONS

Before leaving the topic of discrepancy it may be well to focus for a moment on one of the central assumptions of the theory, namely, that the magnitude of dissonance is a direct function of the proportion that is dissonant of all relevant cognitions. This assumption clearly differs from assumptions in most other theories of cognitive balance (e.g., Rosenberg and Abelson, 1960; Heider, 1958). It provides the basis for much of what is nonobvious about dissonance theory. Generally speaking, without this or a similar assumption, theories of cognitive balance have little to say about the magnitude of motivation aroused by any given situation, except insofar as they postulate increased tension with increased importance of the relevant cognitions. From dissonance theory, however, one may not only predict something about the magnitude of dissonance as a function of the ratio of dissonant to consonant cognitions, one can make derivations that are unique to the theory: that, for example, the amount of attitude change following forced compliance is an *inverse* function of the amount of reward given for compliance.

A more extensive discussion of the relationships between the dissonance formulation and the other balance or incongruity models will be presented in Chapter 12.

REVIEW OF
THE EVIDENCE

part II

Positive alternatives

—3

In this and the following chapter we shall review the existing research relevant to a wide range of derivations from dissonance theory. It will be clear that the bulk of this research concerns the consequences of dissonance for attitude change most broadly conceived; but, in addition, the effects of dissonance upon exposure to information and upon behavior have also been explored.

The experiments discussed represent three general kinds of investigations: (1) those that can be viewed as "free-choice" situations, (2) those that involve situations of "forced compliance," and (3) those that involve "exposure" to information.

The "free-choice" situations generally involve a choice between attractive or potentially attractive alternatives which differ along the dimension of attractiveness or some other dimension. The subject in these experiments presumably wants to make a choice because of the benefits or potential benefits accruing to the choice, and little or no external pressure is needed to produce the choice. Dissonance in these studies is usually conceived of as a function of the relative number of cognitions favoring the unchosen alternative.

The "forced-compliance" experiments usually involve a choice between engaging in a discrepant act (i.e., an act that one would not voluntarily have done) or not engaging in it. In order to get the subject to engage in the discrepant act, some kind of inducing force is applied to him. Dissonance is conceptualized here as a function of the degree to which the act is inconsistent with the subject's position and the number of cognitions favoring the discrepant act beyond the minimum necessary to get the subject to engage in it at all.

In the "exposure" studies, subjects generally are faced with, or work on, some bit of information that is inconsistent with their existing attitudes or cognitions. Here the specification of dissonance has to do with the inconsistency between the prior cognitions and the new information, and with the conditions under which the exposure occurs.

In discussing the range of experiments relevant to the theory we shall indicate which of the three general paradigms the particular experiment fits. However, the present review will organize the relevant research somewhat differently. This review will be organized according to different kinds of dissonance-arousing operations and, within these, will highlight different methods of reducing dissonance. There are a number of advantages in such an organization: (1) It permits the reader to gain a clear grasp of the empirical variables studied and manipulated in the various experiments and allows him to assess for himself the range of empirical problems and issues to which the theory has been directed; (2) It makes for a more flexible arrangement whereby studies which have manipulated more than one variable or combine, for example, exposure and choice situations can be multipally classified; (3) It is consistent with our general point of view, which stresses the theoretical centrality of choice and discrepant commitment rather than the specific content area of a particular experiment; and (4) It lays the groundwork for a general conceptual summary of the phenomena with which the theory has dealt.

Anticipating our later discussion, it should be noted that we conceptualize, and hence organize, dissonance-arousal situations somewhat differently from Festinger (1957). Where he has distinguished "choice" and "forced-compliance" situations as differing conditions for dissonance arousal, we view forced compliance as one kind of choice situation and therefore consider it together with other kinds of choices. At the same time we explicitly separate all nonchoice situations and, later, in our theoretical discussion, make certain distinctions within this class of events.

Among choice situations, we distinguish between those involving positive alternatives and those involving negative alternatives. With any alternative viewed as having both positive and negative attributes, a positive alternative is one in which the positive attributes outweigh the negative, and a negative alternative is one in which negative attributes outweigh positive. An attribute is, of course, a way in which the alternative can please or benefit the person, on the one hand, or displease or harm him on the other. These attributes are equivalent to cognitive elements.

We also distinguish between four ways in which the magnitude of dissonance may be affected in choice situations. In regard to the chosen alternative, dissonance is a direct function of the number and/or importance of negative attributes and an inverse function of the number and/or importance of positive attributes. In regard to the rejected alternative(s), dissonance is a direct function of the number and/or importance of positive attributes and an inverse function of the number and/or importance of the negative attributes. In addition, dissonance is a direct function of the general importance of the choice alternatives.

In the following review of the evidence relevant to the theory, we would like to caution the reader to give particular attention to the issue of dissonance arousal. As we have noted, the defining statement in this regard has to do with the conditions under which *one cognition follows from the obverse of another.* In the exposure experiments this assumes that, given the expression of an opinion, information which follows from its obverse is dissonance producing. In the "free-choice" situations, the fact that one chooses an alternative may follow from the obverse of the attractiveness of the characteristics of the other alternative. In most "forced-compliance" experiments, engaging in a task is consistent with its being pleasant, but follows from the obverse of its being an effortful, painful, unpleasant, boring task or one contrary to one's attitudes or values.

In the theoretical discussion in Chapter 11 we shall attempt to characterize the motivational implications of the defining statement, "follow from the obverse of." We hope to be able to indicate that the issues of choice and commitment to a situation which is discrepant with existent cognitions have consequences for a state of motive dissatisfaction and that their relevance for dissonance arousal lies in this sphere. For the present, however, we shall try to be as explicit as possible in the review section about the locus of dissonance and where we assume that the statement "follows from the obverse of" applies. This should enable the reader to pinpoint the conditions of dissonance arousal in each experiment.

We shall also attempt to be explicit about the possible modes of dissonance reduction and why reduction goes one way or the other. Many of the experiments reported do not try to block off alternative modes of dissonance reduction and instead pick an obvious mode that they assume will be affected by dissonance in any case. Other experimenters may be specifically concerned with one mode of dissonance reduction and will direct their entire experiment toward showing the particular avenue through which dissonance is reduced. We shall attempt to indicate where one or the other experimental strategy is utilized. In all cases, however, it will be clear where commitment to one or another course of events sets limits on the available modes of dissonance reduction and provides for greater specification of the avenue of dissonance reduction that will be used.

Let us now examine the data relevant to dissonance theory within the present schema. In this review we shall attempt to present a picture of the applicability of dissonance theory to a broad range of psychological problems. We will thus hope to indicate the usefulness of the theory by the specific derivations that have been made from it. Many of these derivations, we shall see, are contrary both to "common sense" and to what one would expect from other theoretical formulations.

POSITIVE ATTRIBUTES OF THE CHOSEN ALTERNATIVE

When a person is confronted with choice alternatives having predominantly positive attributes, he will, in the absence of other forces, choose one (or more) of them. If such a choice requires the person to give up or reject one or more alternatives, then the positive attributes (cognitions) of the rejected alternatives will be dissonant with the knowledge that one has rejected them. At the same time, negative attributes of the chosen alternative will create dissonance, but positive attributes of the chosen alternative will tend to *reduce* the dissonance associated with the choice. Hence it will generally be true that, with other factors held constant, *the greater the number and/or importance of positive attributes (consonant cognitions) associated with the chosen alternative, the less the magnitude of dissonance resulting from a choice.*

This proposition has been tested by a variety of studies designed specifically for that purpose. Most have utilized a choice between a person's saying what he believes to be true and his saying something quite different from what he believes to be true. These studies therefore assume that saying what one believes to be true carries positive attributes, such as being honest, benefiting others by telling the truth, and benefiting oneself by being truthful. To make the alternative of saying something untrue attractive, money or arguments in favor of other benefits have been offered. Thus, in general, these studies have required persons to choose between giving their honest opinions and giving a discrepant opinion in order to gain money, to please the experimenter, and so on.

The general characteristic of these studies is that they have induced the individual to make a statement which is discrepant with what he privately believes. Thus one way the person can reduce the consequent dissonance is by changing his private opinion so that it more nearly coincides with what he has said. Change in the person's private belief or evaluation has therefore been taken as evidence for the existence of dissonance, and it has been further assumed that the greater the change, the greater the dissonance prior to the change.

A "forced-compliance" study by Festinger and Carlsmith (1959) is typical of this paradigm. They had college students perform a boring and tedious task and then asked each to tell the "next subject" that the task was interesting and enjoyable. The positive attribute attached to making this false statement was varied in magnitude by offering to pay some subjects $1.00 and others $20.00. Subsequent to making the discrepant statements, all subjects were interviewed in order to measure their evaluation of the boring and tedious task about which they had made the false statements. To ascertain that the task really was unpleasant, a third group was interviewed after it had performed the task and without having been asked to make a discrepant statement. It was assumed that *dissonance aroused by making the statement discrepant with one's private evaluation of the task* would tend to result in a more positive evaluation of the task. The results for the three groups confirmed that: (1) The task was unpleasant; (2) Making a statement discrepant with one's true evaluation tends to produce change in evaluation toward the position of the statement; and (3) The amount of change in evaluation decreases as the amount of money offered for the discrepant statement increases. These results thus confirm the theoretical expectations.

A second "forced-compliance" study in which the positive aspects of the chosen alternative were varied was reported by Cohen, Brehm and Fleming (1958). They asked college students, in a classroom setting, to *write an essay supporting the side opposite to their private view* on an issue of current interest. Manipulation of positive incentive for taking the discrepant stand was accomplished by giving some of the students minimal reason for doing it while giving other students several additional reasons—for example, it would help the experimenter, the school administration, and science. Again, attitude change toward the induced position was taken as an index of dissonance. The obtained changes in attitudes, as measured by pre- and postexperimental questionnaires, revealed a trend in the expected direction. Those students who were given few reasons for adopting the discrepant stand showed somewhat more positive attitude change than did those who were given many reasons. The results of this study are consistent with those from the study described above by Festinger and Carlsmith, although because of sampling problems and reduced effects they may not by themselves constitute unequivocal support for the theory.

Stronger support for the notion that dissonance varies inversely with justification of the chosen alternative comes from "forced-compliance" studies by Rabbie, Brehm and Cohen (1959) and Brock and Blackwood (in press). Under the guise of a survey for the University administration, Rabbie, Brehm and Cohen asked college students to *write essays supporting the elimination of intercollegiate athletics. Pretest data had shown that the students held almost uniformly extreme positions against elimination.* Variation in justification for writing the discrepant essay was effected by giving minimal reasons to some students, multiple reasons to others, as in the experiment described above (Cohen, Brehm and Fleming, 1958). The postexperimental attitude toward elimination of intercollegiate athletics, as measured by a questionnaire, was more positive among those given little justification than among those given great justification. These results, then, are also consistent with the theoretical derivation that dissonance varies inversely with the positive attributes of the chosen alternative.

In Brock and Blackwood's (in press) study, also, subjects were told that they were participating in a "survey" being conducted at the University (of Pittsburgh). The opinion issue had to do with attitudes toward "increasing tuition by $10 per credit." The design was an "after-only" design. It was assumed that all students would be uniformly opposed to a tuition increase, and, in fact, the student newspaper had published a series of articles attacking a $4.00 per credit increase that had been instituted several months before the experiment. To produce dissonance, subjects were asked to *write essays against their own private opinion on the tuition issue.* To create low dissonance, half the subjects were given a series of reasons for writing the discrepant essay; and to create high dissonance, minimal reasons were given. This manipulation was essentially the same as that used in the two experiments discussed above. The outcome shows an identical trend: On a questionnaire given after the subjects had committed themselves, but before they actually wrote their discrepant essays, the low justification groups were more positive toward the notion of tuition increases than the high justification groups or than control subjects who were merely given the attitude measure without the attitude-discrepant commitment. The data provide additional support for the proposition that dissonance and consequent attitude change are inversely related to the positive attributes of the chosen alternative.

It may be noted here that, though the evidence is quite consistent within itself and with the theory, other explanations have been offered. For example, it has been suggested that attitude change from making discrepant verbal statements should increase as reward (or the positive feelings of the person) increase. But *very* large rewards, it is asserted, may cause interfering responses, such as suspicion and hostility, and thereby result in the negative relationship between reward and attitude change.

This kind of alternative explanation for the effects of increased incentive on attitude change stems, it would seem, from a learning theory point of view. It assumes that the reward or incentive reinforces the attitude-discrepant response up to a point where reward is too great to believe or consume. Thus, if sufficiently small rewards were offered to the person for making a statement discrepant with his private attitudes, attitude change would increase as reward increased. This alternative view of "forced-compliance" experiments indicates the necessity for further research where rewards offered for discrepant compliance are varied over a wide range. Evidence on this issue is presented in Chapter 6.

NEGATIVE ATTRIBUTES OF THE CHOSEN ALTERNATIVE

Just as increased positive attributes of the chosen alternative decrease the magnitude of dissonance consequent to a choice, so *increased negative attributes (dissonant cognitions) of the chosen alternative increase postchoice dissonance.* In this section we shall review studies designed to demonstrate the effect on dissonance of changes in the number and/or importance of negative attributes of the chosen alternative.

A "free-choice" experiment reported by Festinger (1957, pp. 126–131, 162–176) shows the effect of negative aspects of the chosen alternative quite clearly. College students were given $2.50 with which to play a card game against the experimenter. In describing the rules of the game, it was clearly implied that one side was much more likely to win than the other, and that the subject should easily be able to pick the winning side for himself. After the subject chose which side he would play, 12 hands were played, with the subject being able to bet a small amount of his money on each trial. Unknown to the subject, the deck was stacked in such a way that the subject was likely to lose a moderate amount over the 12 trials. The prediction was that after the choice, *the greater the loss, the greater the dissonance.* Since the cards were actually shuffled for each hand, some subjects were, by the end of the twelfth trial, winning a little, while others were losing anywhere from a little to a lot. At the twelfth trial the experimenter announced that before going on, the subject could look at a graph from which the true probability of winning could be computed. The subject was then allowed to look at the graph for as long as he liked. It was assumed that subjects who were, at the twelfth trial, either winning or losing only slightly would expect the graph to indicate they had chosen the correct side, while those who were losing moderately to a lot would expect the graph to indicate they had chosen the wrong side. Thus subjects who were winning only slightly or were losing slightly and were therefore experiencing little dissonance would tend to study the graph carefully, with the expectation that the information would reduce their dissonance by informing them that they had chosen the correct side. On the other hand, subjects who were losing moderate to large amounts would be experiencing greater dissonance and would also expect that study of the graph would simply raise that dissonance by disclosing that they had chosen the losing side. In short, those who were winning or losing slightly would be motivated to study the graph carefully, while those who were losing moderately or greatly would tend to avoid study of the graph. This expectation was confirmed by a measure of the amount of time that subjects spent looking at the graph.

This experiment illustrates the proposition that because the magnitude of dissonance is a function of the ratio of dissonant to consonant cognitions, it can be reduced not only by change in the dissonant cognitions *per se* but also by the addition of consonant cognitions. Conversely, a person who is experiencing dissonance will tend to avoid attending to cognitions that will increase the magnitude of that dissonance.

An interesting further aspect of this study concerns behavioral change as a mode of dissonance reduction. In addition to attending selectively to the graph, the subjects also changed sides when there was extreme dissonance over losing and they were given an opportunity to change.

This "free-choice" study was replicated by Cohen, Brehm and Latané (1959), with the addition of a questionnaire check on subjects' expectations in regard to what the graph would say about whether or not they had chosen the winning side, and a variation of importance through publicity. The results of this replication confirmed the assumptions and findings of the original study as reported above. It was also shown that when their winnings were to be made public, the subjects' tendencies toward both selective exposure and selective avoidance were more pronounced than under private conditions.

Both studies may be interpreted as supporting the proposition that dissonance increases as the negative aspects of the chosen alternative increase and that this dissonance can be reduced by selective attention to relevant information. However, it is difficult in these experiments to separate the expectation versus the dissonance determinants of the time spent looking at the graph, and they should not, therefore, be taken as entirely unequivocal evidence for the assertion that dissonance varies directly with the negative aspects of the chosen alternative.

More evidence on the relationship between negative attributes of the chosen alternative and consequent dissonance comes from a series of studies concerned most broadly with the amount of "effort" expended on or negative consequences of a task to which one is committed. An example of such a study is the "forced-compliance" experiment performed by Aronson and Mills (1959). Specifically, they tested the proposition that when a person decides to engage in an activity, the dissonance consequent to that decision increases as the number or importance of the reasons against engaging in the activity increase. In their experiment, *dissonance was induced by requiring female college students to take an "embarrassment" test in order to join a sex discussion group* for which they had volunteered. Each subject in the low dissonance condition was required to read a list of sex-related words to the male experimenter. Each subject in the high dissonance condition was required to read a list of obscene sex-related words to the same experimenter. Subsequent to the test the subject was allowed to audit a purported group discussion, which was actually tape recorded, and designed to be dull and uninteresting. Finally, subjects were asked to indicate how good they thought the discussion and how much they liked the group members.

Having a favorable attitude toward the discussion and the group constitutes cognitions consistent with joining the group: Hence, dissonance created by engaging in the embarrassment test in order to get into the group can be reduced by *increased* favorable attitude toward the discussion and group members. The more embarrassing or painful the test to get in the group, the more dissonance is created and the more favorable should be the attitude.

The results showed that attitudes of subjects in the mild embarrassment conditions did not differ from those of control subjects who took no test, while attitudes of subjects in the severe embarrassment condition were more favorable than those of either the control or mild test groups.

A "forced-compliance" experiment by Aronson (1961) lends further support to the hypothesized dissonance-producing effect of negative events. He was interested in demonstrating that the degree of effort a person expends in attempting to obtain a reward has an effect on the relative attractiveness of stimuli associated with rewarded versus unrewarded trials. The hypothesis was that *as effort increases, dissonance will increase*, and there will be a corresponding increase in the relative attractiveness of stimuli associated with unrewarded trials.

To test the hypothesis subjects performed a task that involved fishing for containers in order to obtain money that was inside some of them. For some subjects, the task was made easy; for others, the task was made effortful. The rewarded containers were of a different color from those of the unrewarded containers. Subjects were asked to rate the relative attractiveness of the two colors before and after performing the task. The results were in accord with the prediction. In the easy condition there was an increase in the relative attractiveness of the rewarded color. In the effortful condition, however, there was no change in the relative attractiveness of the two colors. Thus the direct effect of reward (possibly through secondary reinforcement) tends to be reversed to the extent that effort, and presumably dissonance, is involved.

Further evidence relevant to the effect of negative aspects of the chosen alternative comes from an "exposure" experiment by Cohen (1959b). He had subjects *work on a communication supporting a view opposing their own,* informing some of them that understanding of the arguments would be easy and informing others that understanding would be difficult. Measurement of subjects' attitudes subsequent to their having read the communication revealed that those who initially held a rather extreme view showed positive attitude change in proportion to the amount of difficulty they were led to expect in understanding the communication. Those subjects whose initial position was moderate and who therefore would have experienced little or no dissonance showed less change with greater effort. Thus subjects who had a strong initial position and who presumably expended relatively great effort in trying to understand the communication opposing their private attitude apparently experienced more dissonance, as indicated by their greater attitude change.

An "exposure" experiment by Zimbardo [1] provides additional support for the present derivation. Zimbardo solicited the opinions of undergraduates at New York University on a number of important issues. He chose 20 subjects who rated the "adoption of a numerical grading system" as the most important issue presented and who were all very

[1] Zimbardo, P. G. Self-persuasion: improvisation or dissonance. Unpublished manuscript, New York University, 1961.

strongly in favor of adopting a numerical system. Several weeks later the subjects individually participated in a study of "verbal behavior under various experimental conditions." They were told that as part of the study *they would have to read a report which was in fact a series of arguments against the numerical grading system which they favored.* To create variations in dissonance, half the subjects read the report under conditions of high effort, while half read the report under conditions of low effort. Effort was manipulated by having the subjects read the report aloud under varying conditions of delayed auditory feedback: In the high effort condition subjects received a delay interval of .3 seconds; in the low effort condition, their delay interval was .01 seconds. Pretesting had shown that the .3 second delay, compared with the .01, would create more disruption of the subject's speech, make comprehension more difficult, and hence increase the effort necessary to perform adequately. Immediately after reading the report opposing his own stand on the grading system, the subject was given the postquestionnaire regarding his opinions on the grading system. The data show that the effort manipulations were entirely successful, and though the effort conditions did not differ in recall of the information given in the report or in change on irrelevant attitude issues, they did differ in the amount of relevant attitude change obtained: The high effort subjects became significantly more opposed to the numerical grading system than the low effort subjects.

Finally, an experiment by Yaryan and Festinger (1961) also bears on the effort issue. They consider the situation of *a person who has expended considerable effort preparing for some future event and who also knows many things that indicate to him that the event will not actually occur.* Thus, *the information that he did expend effort in preparation is dissonant with the information he has that the event will not occur.* At least one way the person can reduce dissonance in such a situation is to persuade himself that the possible future event is indeed likely to occur. Yaryan and Festinger therefore hypothesized that after a person engages in effortful preparation for a future event, he should believe the event is even more likely to occur than he had previously believed.

In this experiment all subjects were given a standard set of instructions concerning the exact probability of their having to take an examination in the future. Subjects in the high preparatory effort condition had to commit to memory a list of difficult symbolic definitions in preparation for the aptitude test they might have to take. Subjects in the low preparatory effort condition merely had to look them over in order to get some idea of what they were all about. After each subject finished with the list of symbols (either memorizing it or familiarizing herself with it), she was asked on a six-point scale whether she believed that she was one of the people selected to take the test. The results showed that subjects in the high effort condition clearly had a stronger belief that they would have to take the test.

The Aronson and Mills (1959), Aronson (1961), Cohen (1959b), Zimbardo (pp. 30–31) and Yaryan and Festinger (1961) experiments, then, all provide evidence for the assertion that an increase in the negative aspects of the chosen alternative through the manipulation of "effort" involved in commitment to a discrepant position affects dissonance and consequent attitude change. In all five studies, increases in the unpleasant aspects of the discrepant situation to which the subjects were committed produced greater dissonance for them, leading to greater attitude change supporting the discrepant behavior.

Four additional studies supply further evidence on the effects of variations in the negative aspects of chosen alternatives. These studies, however, deal with variations in the cognitions supporting or disconfirming commitment to engage in unpleasant behavior. In the first experiment, a "forced-compliance" study by Brehm (1960a), junior high school students were induced to *commit themselves to eating different amounts of disliked vegetables.* Brehm found that the tendency to increase liking for the disliked vegetables was in proportion to the amount of the unpleasant behavior (eating) to which the person was committed only when there was negative information about the food. Thus greater dissonance and greater consequent attitude change in the direction of liking the disliked vegetable occurred as a joint function of the amount of negative behavior to which the subject was committed, and additional negative information.

Another relevant experiment that explores the effects of amount of negative behavior to which the subject is committed is the shock experiment of Brock and Buss (in press). In their "forced-compliance" study, they showed that attitude change, as determined by changes in evaluation of a subjective experience, is affected by dissonance. Their study dealt with the evaluation of aggression by examining the effects on *individuals who choose to deliver noxious stimulation when they are on record as opposing such punishment.* After such a choice, the greater the intensity of the aggression, the greater should be the dissonance and consequent tendency to reduce dissonance. The aggressor may reduce dissonance by evaluating the stimulus as less noxious, saying, in effect, "The pain I administered was really rather mild." Thus a main hypothesis of the study was: When dissonance is great (under the high choice condition), the greater the intensity of the aggression delivered, the greater the minimization of its painfulness.

Subjects who were opposed to the use of electric shock on humans in scientific research were induced to administer mild or extreme electric shock to a "subject" (victim). They were given either high choice or no choice about whether to administer the shock. Before and after these manipulations they were given mild shocks, and they rated the painfulness of those shocks. Change in evaluation of the painfulness of their shocks from before to after the experimental delivery of the shock to the victim was the principal dependent variable.

In the high shock condition, subjects were instructed to use only shocks at levels 6 to 10, nothing below. In the low shock condition subjects were instructed to use only the shock values 1 to 5, nothing above. Subjects in the no choice condition then proceeded with the experiment. In the choice condition, before proceeding with the administration of the shock, the experimenter gave the subjects option to leave and stressed the subjects' choice in whether or not they wanted to continue with the research.

Thus subjects presumably experienced dissonance as a function of behaving in a manner contrary to their values: They shocked others when they were against the use of shock. The more they experienced a choice in this and the more shock they had to deliver, the more dissonance and consequent revaluation of shock as less painful were expected. Seeing shock as less painful than it is reduces the dissonance between prior cognitions and behavior.

The data show that for the subjects placed in the high choice condition, the greater the magnitude of aggression they delivered, the greater the dissonance and consequent minimization of the painfulness of the shock.

An interesting sidelight in this experiment is that the greater revaluation of shock so as to minimize its painfulness occurred only when the "victim" was a male. When the victim was a female, the effect was reversed. When the victim was a female, rather than changes in evaluation of the painfulness of shock, the preferred avenue of dissonance reduction for the aggressor was evidently an increase in feeling of obligation; the subject saying, in effect, "I gave pain but I was obliged to do so."

It is clear that when the victim is a girl, the barriers against reducing dissonance via attitude change (minimization of shock) are greater than when the victim is a man. It is more difficult to feel that a girl is not being hurt by the shock than it is to believe that a man is not being hurt. Since there was a great deal of resistance to attitude change where there were girl victims, the subjects chose another available avenue that had not been experimentally blocked off: They increased their felt obligation to comply with the request to deliver shock. This study, then, shows that where resistance to change via one mode of potential dissonance reduction is great, dissonance reduction may occur via another avenue. In this case, having committed themselves to delivering shock, subjects can reduce their dissonance by attitude change or, if that mode is difficult, by increasing their felt obligation.

Thus, in addition to highlighting attitude change as a mode of dissonance reduction, the Brock and Buss (in press) study illustrates another rather esoteric avenue: the retroactive increase of felt obligation to perform the discrepant act, which serves to increase the relative number of cognitions supporting discrepant commitment, thereby reducing dissonance. This novel avenue of dissonance reduction has not generally received much attention; further evidence for it will be given in Chapter 6 and Chapter 8.

In summary, the Brock and Buss study shows that from dissonance theory one can predict the direction of an aggressor's revaluation of the pain he has delivered when his aggression is contrary to his beliefs. The results of this experiment indicate that, at least under high choice conditions, the greater the magnitude of the aggression delivered, the greater the minimization of its painfulness. It is clear, then, that dissonance can affect attitude change regarding the evaluation of the meaning or consequences of an aggressive act as well as attitude change involving the evaluation of persons or groups.

The other studies dealing with negative aspects of the chosen alternative were done by Smith (1961) and Raven and Fishbein (1961). In his "forced-compliance" experiment, Smith varied the characteristics of the communicator (i.e., experimenter or authority figure) at whose behest the person commits himself to the dissonance-producing discrepant act. The subjects were Army reservists undergoing training at an Army Reserve Center who, under the guise of a study of survival in food-emergency situations, *were induced to eat grasshoppers.* They were told by the experimenter, who was introduced to them as someone doing research for the Army Quartermaster, that in the "New Army," smaller units would have to be more mobile and possibly live off the land more. Therefore the researchers were going to find out "what your attitudes and reactions are toward an unusual food that you might have to eat in an emergency. This food is grasshoppers."

All subjects were then given a prequestionnaire, which included an attitude scale on their liking for grasshoppers as a food. Then, with half the subjects, the experimenter acted in a friendly, warm, permissive manner throughout the experimental period (the positive communicator condition). He smiled frequently, referred to himself by nickname, sat on the counter, said that the subjects could smoke if they wished, that they should relax and enjoy themselves. The other half of the subjects (the negative communicator condition) were treated throughout in a formal, cool, official manner. The men were ordered rather than requested; they were told that they could not smoke; the experimenter never smiled; he stood in a stiff pose and replied in a sharp manner to all questions.

After the subjects in both conditions had been induced to eat at least one grasshopper (encouraged by the offer of fifty cents), they were permitted to go ahead and eat as many as they liked. Subjects in the two conditions ate almost exactly the same mean number of grasshoppers. After eating, the subjects filled out the attitude measure again.

When the change scores in liking for grasshoppers were examined, it was found that the subjects in the negative communicator condition showed more increase in liking for grasshoppers than those in the positive communicator condition. Although this evidence is not entirely unequivocal because of the different numbers of subjects complying with the request to eat,[2] it does show that for those complying with the discrepant request, the more negative the characteristics of the inducing agent, the fewer the cognitions supporting commitment and the greater the dissonance. Having once eaten, one can reduce dissonance by changing one's attitude to be more consistent with the behavior.

Finally, the study by Raven and Fishbein (1961) dealt with variations in punishment for failure to report belief in extrasensory perception (ESP). They expected that subjects who consistently denied receiving ESP images would be especially likely to reduce the *dissonance between the knowledge that they had reported "no reception" of ESP and the knowledge that they had thus accepted punishment*, by reducing their belief in ESP. They gave subjects either shock or no shock for denying the reception of ESP images. It was found that the greater the punishment for denial of ESP, the greater was the subjects' disbelief in ESP. In this experiment, the subjects presumably reduced dissonance aroused by denying ESP when it would bring on punishment by making their belief in ESP more consistent with their commitment to accept a punishing shock.

In summary, then, the data from these experiments bear out the hypothesis from dissonance theory that the magnitude of dissonance will increase as the number and/or importance of negative attributes

[2] The problem of subject self-selection will be discussed in greater detail in Chapter 7.

of the chosen alternative increase. This dissonance, we have seen, can be reduced by selective attention to relevant information, by attitude change (evaluative and opinion change), by behavioral or decisional change, and by change in the perception of the force propelling the discrepant commitment.

POSITIVE ATTRIBUTES OF REJECTED ALTERNATIVES

Although there have been no studies designed to show the specific effect of variations in the positive aspects of rejected alternatives, there are four studies that approximate this condition. Each is a study of the effect of choosing between attractive choice objects. In each of these studies there was an attempt to manipulate the amount of post-choice dissonance by variation in the attractiveness of the rejected alternative. The over-all attractiveness of an object is not, of course, purely a function of positive attributes: It also varies with the number of negative attributes, such as disliked color, size, and brand name. But when an object is definitely attractive rather than neutral or disliked, large variations in attractiveness are likely to be due primarily to variation in the positive rather than the negative attributes. It will be assumed, in describing the following studies, that variations in the attractiveness of the rejected alternatives are essentially variations of the number and/or importance of positive attributes of the rejected alternatives.

The first relevant study involved a "free choice" and was done by Ehrlich, Guttman, Schonbach and Mills (1957). It was concerned with the consequences of an important decision for selective seeking of and attention to information bearing on the choice alternatives. It revealed that owners of brand new cars read advertisements of their own car more often than of cars they considered but did not buy and of other cars not involved in the choice. These selective tendencies were much less pronounced among old car owners who had made no recent decision. Thus this finding supports the derivation from dissonance theory that persons seek out supporting or consonant information after an important decision in which they have rejected an alternative having positive attributes.

The study by Ehrlich et al. (1957) also illustrates a secondary determinant of dissonance and consequent exposure having to do with the number of choice alternatives. Consistent with the assumption that the positive characteristics of unchosen alternatives are related to dissonance, it might be expected that the more alternatives involved in the choice, the more cognitive elements there are corresponding to desirable features of the rejected alternatives and the greater the resulting dissonance. The results show that there is a tendency for new car purchasers, who named two or more cars as ones they considered but did not buy, to read more "own car" ads than those who considered only one other car or none; the former thus show greater activity oriented toward reducing dissonance.

Stronger support for the derivation regarding the positive aspects of rejective alternatives comes from a "free-choice" experiment reported by Brehm (1956). The major purpose of the study was to provide evidence that *postchoice dissonance increases as the attractiveness of the rejected alternative increases.* To that end college students were asked to rate the desirability of eight different consumer articles, to choose between a specified two of them, and then to rate them all again. One of the two articles involved in the choice was always highly attractive while the other was made to vary from nearly equally attractive to relatively less attractive. As noted in our discussion above, this variation in the attractiveness of the rejected alternative may be assumed to depend primarily on variation in the positive attributes. It was expected that the highly attractive rejected alternative would create more postchoice dissonance than would the slightly attractive rejected alternative, and that whatever dissonance was created would manifest itself in pre- to postchoice changes in the desirability of the alternatives. The dissonance could be reduced by increases in desirability of the chosen alternative, and by decreases in desirability of the unchosen alternative. The actual changes in the pre- and postchoice desirability ratings confirmed these theoretical expectations: Enhancement of the chosen alternative and devaluation of the rejected alternative were directly proportional to the manipulated attractiveness of the rejected alternative.

Change in the number or importance of positive attributes in the rejected alternative can be effected not only through change in the attractiveness of the rejected alternative but also through variation in the amount of "cognitive overlap" of the chosen and rejected alternatives. What is meant by "cognitive overlap" is simply the extent to which the alternatives have attributes in common. It is obvious that *as the proportion of common attributes increases, the proportion that can be dissonant with the choice decreases,* and, hence, the amount of dissonance created by the choice will tend to decrease. That is, the number of positive attributes lost or negative attributes avoided by rejection of one alternative decreases as the chosen alternative includes more and more of the same attributes, other things being equal. When the two alternatives have the same attributes—that is, they are identical—nothing is given up or avoided by choosing one over the other.

And, conversely, as the number of common attributes decreases, and with attractiveness of the alternatives held constant, the magnitude of postchoice dissonance increases.

Two studies have been designed and conducted specifically to test the effect of overlapping cognitions on postchoice dissonance. As with the above studies on the attractiveness of the rejected alternative, they were not concerned with the rejected alternatives' positive attributes *per se* but rather with the degree of attribute similarity, regardless of whether the attributes involved were positive or negative. Since the alternatives were highly attractive, we again assume that variations in similarity are essentially variations in similarity of the positive attributes.

In the first "free-choice" experiment (Brehm and Cohen, 1959a), grade school children were individually asked to indicate on a scale how much they liked each of 16 toys both before and after being allowed to choose one. Some were given *a choice between qualitatively similar toys* (e.g., between metal crafts sets, or between sets of table games) and others were given *a choice between quite dissimilar toys* (e.g., between swimming fins and a ship model). It was expected that the magnitude of dissonance would be reflected in pre- to postchoice enhancement of liking for the chosen alternative and decrease in liking for the rejected alternative. The obtained liking changes confirmed not only the expected direction of change but also the theoretical derivation of particular interest here, namely, that dissonance reduction (and presumably dissonance) is greater with dissimilar than with similar choice alternatives.

An experiment by Brock (in press) also bears on the derivation regarding the similarity of alternatives. As part of a larger experiment, children aged 3 to 12 were given a choice between similar objects (two bags of crackers or two toys) or dissimilar objects (a bag of crackers and a toy). Dissonance and consequent revaluation of the chosen objects from before to after choice were greater for those children choosing between dissimilar objects: They increased their liking for the chosen alternatives and decreased their liking for the rejected alternatives more than in the case of the children who chose between similar objects.

The Brehm and Cohen (1959a) choice experiment provides additional evidence consistent with that in the Ehrlich et al. (1957) study regarding the effect of number of choice alternatives on dissonance. Some subjects were allowed to choose one of two alternatives while other subjects were allowed to choose one of four alternatives. The data show that those subjects who chose from among four alternatives increased their liking for the chosen alternative and decreased their liking for the next most attractive unchosen alternative more than those who chose between two.

These four "free-choice" studies all strongly support the hypothesis concerning the effects on dissonance of variations in the positive attributes of unchosen alternatives. Whether persons reduce dissonance occasioned by choice among alternatives through selective attention or through attitude change, the evidence is consistent with the derivation that the greater the positive attributes of the rejected alternative, the greater the dissonance.

An issue raised by the above "free-choice" experiments is whether or not such an analysis of the dissonance-arousing consequences of choice among alternatives has any implications for situations beyond those created in the laboratory. That is, does the revaluation that occurs after choice have any meaning for important real-life situations or is it confined only to "artificially produced" experimental settings? The Ehrlich et al. (1957) study suggests that it does, and in Chapter 6 we shall present further evidence on this point.

A second important issue here concerns whether or not avoidance or reduction of prechoice conflict could account equally well for the revaluation process demonstrated in these choice experiments. That is, it could be argued from a conflict theory point of view that conflict has motivational properties because it is unpleasant, and that in order to avoid the conflict, the person reduces it by revaluating the choice alternatives so as to make one clearly more attractive than the other. Further evidence regarding this issue will also be presented in Chapter 6.

Another way to vary the positive attributes of rejected alternatives is seen in a study by Gerard (1961). Subjects were first convinced by false feedback that they were either high or low in the ability to make accurate judgments about a series of perceptual stimuli. They were then placed in an Asch-type situation in which the objectively correct response to a set of perceptual stimuli was quite clear, but the other two persons judging apparently gave unanimous though frequently incorrect responses. An electrode was then placed on the forearm of each subject, and he was told that it measured the implicit movement of his muscle. In this way the subject was led to believe that his "first impulse" for each of the next series of judgments would automatically register on a signal panel in front of him and on signal panels in front of two other subjects who were to judge the same stimuli.

The subject was allowed to make his judgment only after learning the judgments of the other two. After eight trials he found that his first impulse, according to the signal panel, was either to conform to others' judgments regardless of whether or not they were correct or to make the correct choice regardless of the others' responses. In short, the subject was led to believe that he was a conformer or a deviate after having received information that he was either high or low in the ability to make similar kinds of judgments.

It should therefore be expected that *the greater the ability of the subject, the greater the dissonance experienced on conformity; in Gerard's experiment, a "conforming response" is dissonant with high ability* when conformity is not veridical with perception of the physical stimulus.

Gerard was interested in the subject's attitude toward the group as a means of reducing dissonance in this situation. He measured attraction to the group by a projective "test" given to the subjects after the conformity manipulation. In this case, having "conformed," the subject can reduce the dissonance between his "behavior" and his cognitions about himself by increasing his attraction to the group to which he presumably "conformed." The higher the subject's ability, the greater the dissonance and consequent attraction. Thus one's behavior is made consistent with one's attitudes; behavior and cognitions are seen to be consonant when conformity to a group to which one is attracted occurs.

For those subjects who were made to feel that their first impulse was to deviate, it is not clear that dissonance was aroused in the same manner, for they did not behave in a fashion discrepant with their perceptions of the physical stimulus. In their case, dissonance may have been aroused through behavior discrepant with their needs to be accepted by the others, so that the expected relationship between ability and subsequent attraction would not necessarily be a clear one. Also, having "deviated," they may have been able to reject the group which presented them with the discrepant information. The data show that they became less attracted, the higher their ability.

In any case, for those who experienced some discrepant commitment (i.e., conformed), the Gerard experiment shows that they changed their evaluations of the group as a function of their ability. Thus the rejected alternative of accuracy of perception arouses dissonance to the extent that the person has high ability to make accurate judgments (positive attributes). In all cases, new evaluations of the group were made consistent with conforming behavior toward the group.

Altogether, the evidence from the five studies described above lends considerable support to the proposition that dissonance increases as the number and/or importance of positive attributes of the rejected alternative increase.

NEGATIVE ATTRIBUTES OF REJECTED ALTERNATIVES

Relatively little attention has been paid to the specific effects on dissonance of variations in the negative attributes of rejected alternatives. One relevant study, however, was carried out by Aronson and Carlsmith (in press b). In their "forced-compliance" experiment they were concerned with the degree to which coercion used to force the rejection of a desirable alternative would produce attitude change regarding that alternative. Their subjects were nursery school children who were shown five toys and asked which toy in a given pair they would like to play with. By presenting the children with all ten pairs, a ranking was derived for the most preferred toy to the least preferred toy.

The experimenter then placed the second-ranked toy on a table and introduced the experimental manipulations. Half the children, those in the mild threat condition, were given a mild admonishment not to play with the toy on the table; in the severe threat condition, the children were strongly admonished not to play with the toy on the table under threat of the experimenter's anger, annoyance, and rejection of the child. The experimenter then left the room. After the children were allowed to play with the other four toys, the experimenter returned and the children re-ranked the toys in the same manner as earlier. The dependent variable in this study was the change in the child's relative ranking of the crucial toy from before to after the threat was administered.

Aronson and Carlsmith expected that a mild threat of punishment for playing with a desired toy would lead to greater dissonance than a severe threat. That is, having committed themselves to the discrepant behavior of *not playing with something they found desirable,* the children would experience greater dissonance, the fewer the cognitions supporting the discrepant commitment. Severe threat is a cognition more consistent with giving up a desirable object than is a mild threat. Thus the subjects in the mild threat condition would experience greater dissonance and could reduce it by devaluing the crucial toy more than those in the severe threat condition.

The results strongly support the hypothesis: The toy decreases in attractiveness more in the mild threat condition than in the severe threat condition. Thus the children who refrained from playing with the toy in the absence of a severe threat reduced the dissonance between not playing with the toy and the cognition that it was attractive by derogating the toy.

Although the Aronson and Carlsmith study appears to be the only one bearing on the problem of negative attributes of the rejected alternative, it does provide support for the notion that as they increase, dissonance decreases.

It should be mentioned that there is one study that bears simultaneously on all four categories we have mentioned: It deals with positive and negative attributes of chosen and rejected alternatives. This is Mills' (1958) "forced-compliance" study, which is concerned with the effects of cheating on attitudes toward cheating. Mills offered prizes to grade school children for good performance on simple tasks. Three experimental conditions were created: high temptation to cheat, with low restraints against doing so; low temptation with low restraint; and high temptation with high restraint. Temptation was manipulated by offering or not offering a prize either for an outstanding score or for improvement from a preliminary practice session. Restraints against cheating were manipulated by giving the subjects differential opportunity to cheat while scoring their own work. Attitudes toward cheating were measured before and after this procedure. In terms of dissonance theory, a restraining force against the behavior engaged in by the individual has the same dissonance-creating effect as does a negative attitude toward the behavior. Thus *an individual who cheats will experience dissonance in proportion to the strength of restraint against cheating.* And as with other induced discrepant behavior, *the amount of dissonance created will decrease as the inducing force (temptation to cheat) is increased.* Whatever dissonance is produced by cheating in the presence of cognitions inducing and restraining cheating can be reduced or eliminated by attitude changes favoring cheating.

The attitude change scores indicate that cheaters tended to become more lenient toward cheating and honest subjects tended to become more critical of cheating. The expectations that the magnitude of dissonance and consequent amount of attitude change would vary with the importance and magnitude of restraint were only partially confirmed. Nevertheless, the evidence is generally in accord with the theory and lends support to derivations in each of our four categories of dissonance arousal: positive and negative attributes of chosen and rejected alternatives.

COMPLEX CHANGE IN ATTRIBUTES OF CHOICE ALTERNATIVES

There is a series of studies that does not fit into our classificatory scheme because positive and negative attributes in the independent variable are not separable. In these studies, decrease in positive attributes is considered equivalent to increase in negative attributes so that variation in either or both positive and negative attributes may actually occur. Thus the distinction is sometimes lost between change in positive attributes only or change in negative attributes only. However, we continue to assume in this section that the general character of the alternatives is positive rather than negative.

Several of the following studies have attempted to affect the magnitude of postchoice dissonance by a direct manipulation of the degree of choice. Although we will have more to say in Chapter 11 about the role of choice in the creation of dissonance, we will assume here that low choice is equivalent to the bulk of relevant attributes being consistent with choosing a given alternative and that high choice is equivalent to approximately equal distribution of relevant cognitions consistent with choosing one alternative course of action rather than any other.

The attributes may, as noted above, be positive or negative. What is most important is that the direct choice manipulation may affect alternatives of both the chosen and rejected alternatives, thus preventing classification into our previously outlined schema. Suppose, for example, that the subject is to be induced to support an opinion position discrepant with what he privately believes, where the alternative is to support the position of his private belief. A low choice condition might be one in which the subject is told that subjects are assigned by chance to support one position or the other. Some of the attributes specifically associated with the alternative he is supposed to take are that choosing it will please the experimenter and help science, refusing to choose it means no participation at all (and the subject has volunteered to participate), and so forth. The high choice condition might, on the other hand, consist of the subject's being told that he can support the opposing side, but that he does not really have to, and that it is completely up to him whether or not he does. (However, the subject *is* pushed into taking the opposing side just as in the low choice condition.) In the high choice condition there is the implication that the subject would still be helping the experimenter and science no matter which side he chose—though his taking the opposite side to his private belief would be more helpful. Thus, compared to the low choice condition, the positive attributes of the chosen alternative are shared to some extent by the rejected alternative, and the negative attribute of no participation that was associated with the rejected alternative disappears altogether. In sum, a direct manipulation of choice is likely to involve change in attributes of both chosen and rejected alternatives.

The direct manipulation of choice was first used in an "exposure" experiment by Cohen, Terry and Jones (1959). Subsequent to an initial attitude measurement, college students were given high or low choice about whether or not to *listen to a communication characterized as upholding a position counter to their own*. All subjects were then exposed to the communication, and, finally, their attitudes on the issue were measured again. Analysis of attitude-change scores according to the subject's initial position on the issue revealed that choice had little or no effect on those who were initially moderate but had a great effect on those who were extreme in their opposition to the position of the communication. Among extreme subjects, high choice produced greater change toward the position of the communication than did low choice. Thus these data support the notion that dissonance is a direct function of choice.

Another example of a direct choice manipulation is an experiment on "forced-compliance" by Davis and Jones (1960). They induced dissonance *by having college students make derogatory remarks to a person who was presumably a student being evaluated on several personality dimensions.* All subjects were informed that this "student" was to hear either a positive or negative evaluation. But some were told that they were assigned to give one of the two kinds of evaluation according to whether they were an odd- or even-numbered subject, while others were told they could give either the positive or negative evaluation, but what was really needed was the negative evaluation. It was expected that dissonance engendered by the choice to rate a person negatively would tend to be reduced by negative shifts in real evaluations of the person. Postexperimental ratings by the subjects of the person they had falsely rated were, in fact, more negative in the high choice condition than in the low, thus supporting the specific experimental hypothesis and the more general formulation that dissonance increases with choice.

The Davis and Jones study also shows the role of commitment in the choice paradigm which we have been discussing. While some of their subjects in each of the high and low choice conditions were told that they would be unable to inform the target person of the false nature of their negative evaluation, others were led to believe that they would confront the target person and could dispel any belief he might have in their negative evaluation. The latter group of subjects, relative to the former, were not committed to the negative evaluation. And, as one would expect, the relatively noncommitted subjects showed no evidence of evaluating the target person more negatively in the high than in the low choice condition. Of course, it is not clear whether the effect of the revokable commitment is to eliminate the arousal of dissonance in the first place or to change the way by which dissonance is reduced. Additional evidence regarding the direct effect of commitment on dissonance arousal and reduction will be presented in following chapters.

A "forced-compliance" experiment by Brock (1962) provides further evidence on the effect of choice on dissonance. Giving non-Catholic college students either high or low choice in whether or not to comply, he induced them to write an essay on "Why I would like to become a Catholic." Change in attitudes toward Catholicism, as measured by pre- and postexperimental questionnaires, supported the expectation that dissonance and consequent attitude change toward the position of the essay would increase as choice increased. These results, in addition to supporting the hypothesized effect of choice on dissonance, show that dissonance can affect attitudes on a strong social issue.

The Brock and Buss (in press) shock experiment described earlier also provides some supporting evidence for the assertion that the direct manipulation of choice in agreeing to engage in discrepant behavior affects dissonance and consequent attitude change. In their experiment, for subjects confronting male victims, those given a high degree of choice in whether or not they would participate in the shock-deliverance task changed their attitudes so as to evaluate the shock as *less* painful after delivering it than before, whereas those in the no choice condition, having experienced little dissonance tended to increase the pain, perceiving the shock as *more* painful than before.

These experiments—the "exposure" experiment of Cohen, Terry and Jones (1959) and the "forced-compliance" experiments of Davis and Jones (1960), Brock (1962), and Brock and Buss (in press)—all show that attitude change supporting the inconsistent commitment increases as the degree of choice in making the commitment increases. Additional evidence regarding the relationship between manipulated choice and dissonance will be presented in Chapter 6.

Negative alternatives

—4

A person confronted with only negative alternatives will choose none of them. That is, a negative alternative is one that the individual will avoid if he can, and only if he is forced will he take one. Thus the character of a negative choice is that one alternative is taken because *any* other alternative is something worse.

It is, of course, assumed here that there must be some constraints or barriers against the subject's leaving the field, that is, some third factor must presumably focus the choice. Such "third factors" usually have to do with the general constraints of the experimental or institutional environment within which the test is being made. For the moment, however, we need only recognize the existence of such barriers that keep the subject fixed on a choice between the negative alternatives. In Chapter 11 we shall discuss the significance of such variations in the general constraining situation within the context of the effects of volition on dissonance arousal.

The studies concerning negative choice will not be divided under subheadings, for there are fewer studies than subheadings. We shall simply describe the relevant evidence and summarize the findings in terms of the classificatory scheme.

EVIDENCE ON NEGATIVE CHOICE

A "forced-compliance" study by Brehm and Cohen (1959b) was designed to show that *dissonance associated with choosing to do an unpleasant task* increases as the possibility of avoiding the task increases. They told introductory psychology students, in classes, that as part of a departmental program to evaluate student participation in research, all students would have to take part in a boring, tedious, and time-consuming task. The attempt to manipulate the coercive force to comply involved telling some classes that anyone who felt he could not participate would have to see the departmental director of undergraduate studies, while other classes were given no possible way of getting out of the situation. An additional attempt to manipulate the magnitude of dissonance consisted of telling all subjects that most students would be paid for their participation in the project but that a few, including the subject himself, selected by chance, would not be paid. Some students were told that others were being paid $1.00 (low relative deprivation condition) while the rest of the students were told that others were being paid $10.00 (high relative deprivation). It was expected that subjects who had little opportunity to get out of participation would feel less satisfaction with their assignment as relative deprivation increased. Subjects who had relatively high opportunity to be excused from participation (but who chose to participate) were expected to experience dissonance in proportion to the amount of relative deprivation. Since they could reduce dissonance by convincing themselves that their assignment was really quite satisfactory, it was expected that subjects in the high opportunity condition, compared to those in the low, would tend to feel more satisfied as relative deprivation increased.

The attempted manipulation of opportunity failed. Not only were there no between-condition differences in subjects' answers to a question on how difficult they thought it would be to get out of participation, but also the within-condition variation was almost significantly greater. Thus we may infer that the attempt to coerce the subjects cued off rather strong individual reactions to acceptance. For this reason, each of the five classes used in the experiment was split at the median according to how difficult subjects said it would be to get out of participation. Results of the satisfaction scores, obtained from the postexperimental questionnaire, supported the theoretical expectations that satisfaction would be an inverse function of relative deprivation under low (perceived) choice conditions, and a direct function of relative deprivation under high (perceived) choice conditions.

The data from this study support two propositions about the effect of negative choices: (1) The greater is the importance or number of negative attributes associated with the chosen alternative, the greater is the dissonance; and (2) The greater is the perceived importance or number of negative attributes associated with the rejected alternative, the less is the magnitude of dissonance. However, since the results are partly correlational, they do not yield unequivocal support. And, finally, the failure of the coercion manipulation itself is of interest and will be discussed at a later point, together with new evidence on the conditions under which coercion to perform an undesirable behavior may or may not produce dissonance and consequent attitude change in situations of discrepant commitment (see Chapters 6 and 11).

Other evidence relevant to the effect of a negative choice on dissonance comes from a "free-choice" study by Mills, Aronson and Robinson (1959) and a replication by Rosen (1961). In the original study, the investigators, under the guise of a departmental study, gave students in a psychology course *a choice between taking an essay examination and taking a multiple-choice examination.* An attempt was made to create choices of high or low importance by telling some students that *the examination would count 5% (low importance), and others that it would count 70% (high importance), toward their course grade.*

Since the subjects in this experiment did not choose whether or not to take the examination, but which of two examinations to take, the choice could have been perceived as having positive consequences, depending on the subject's expectations of how well he would do. Therefore this experiment might have alternatively been classified under the category of positive consequences. However, it seems reasonable to assume that the most salient feature of such a choice situation is the fear of potential failure on an examination the subjects had not sought.

To measure dissonance reduction tendencies, all subjects were given the instruction that the course instructor wanted them to learn something more about types of examinations; then they were asked to indicate, by a rank ordering, which one of six research articles they wanted to read. Each student was given a list of titles, three of which were about essay examinations and three of which were on multiple-choice examinations. All the titles of some lists implied that each article, whether about essay or multiple-choice exams, described the beneficial or positive aspects of the examination. Titles of other lists implied negative information. It was expected that subjects, to the extent they were experiencing dissonance from choosing one kind of examination rather than the other, would tend to choose positive articles and avoid negative articles about the exam they chose. Thus the tendency to choose positive articles and avoid negative articles about the kind of exam chosen should be greater in the high importance condition than in the low.

The average rankings given to the articles showed that the positive articles for the chosen kind of examination were preferred to those for the rejected kind of exam. However, there was no avoidance shown in regard to negative articles, nor was there any effect of the importance manipulation. Since the same behavior could have occurred because one hoped to get pointers on how to study for his chosen kind of examination, these data cannot be said to give strong evidence concerning the effect of negative choices on dissonance. It is argued by the investigators, however, that the instrumental value of negative articles is no less than of positive, and hence the difference between conditions must be due to an independent tendency to avoid negative information about one's chosen alternative.

The study by Rosen (1961) replicated the experiment just described. The major exception to the design is that article titles were counterbalanced and instead of being all positive or negative in character, three were for and three were against the chosen alternative, and one of the six was described as showing the advantages of essay over multiple-choice exams, while another was described as showing the converse. The importance manipulation again consisted of the examination counting either 5% or 70% toward the course grade. The resultant ranking of articles revealed a preference for those favoring one's own examination choice over that rejected, but with no significant effect from the importance manipulation. However, there was a *trend* consistent with the expected difference between importance conditions. Thus the tendency to choose supporting articles is probably an attempt to reduce dissonance but there is still a failure of the importance manipulation to affect the magnitude of dissonance materially. We shall discuss this issue in the next chapter.

It should also be noted that both experiments failed to find evidence confirming the theoretical derivation that subjects would avoid dissonance-producing information, the greater the dissonance aroused by choice. We shall discuss the evidence relevant to avoidance of dissonance in connection with a new experiment on the salience of dissonant information to be presented in Chapter 6.

On the whole, there is extremely little evidence relevant to negative choices. One reason for the lack of evidence is, no doubt, that a negative choice is difficult to create experimentally. Volunteers cannot easily be put into a negative choice situation, for, if they know what they are getting into, the choice cannot be more negative than their positive motivation to volunteer, and if they do not know what they are getting into, then other factors, such as the subject's hostility toward the experiment and experimenter, and the apparent plausibility of the situation, must be taken into account. In this connection we suspect that relatively little is known about the psychological consequences of coercive inducing forces.

EXPOSURE TO DISCREPANT INFORMATION

It frequently happens that a person, without making directly relevant decisions, is confronted with information inconsistent with his opinions, attitudes, beliefs, and so on—that is, with his "knowledge" of the world. If, as dissonance theory assumes, the person would ordinarily find such inconsistent information unpleasant, then he would generally avoid it if possible. But there are many instances where avoidance is difficult or impossible because the nature of the information is impossible to predict completely (as on news broadcasts), because indications about the nature of the information are misleading (as newspaper headlines sometimes are), because the information may be "forced" on one by a friend, and so on. And when such discrepant information is heard, it will, according to the theory, sometimes create dissonance and resultant attempts to reduce or eliminate the dissonance.

The factors that control the magnitude of such dissonance are the same as for cases involving decisions: the number and importance of cognitions consistent with holding a certain opinion, belief, etc., and the number and importance of cognitions inconsistent with holding that same belief, opinion, etc. Given the fact that a person holds a certain opinion, for example, the greater the number and/or importance of his cognitions inconsistent with that opinion, the greater will be the magnitude of dissonance that he experiences. It should be noted that if the individual receives new discrepant information of sufficient quantity and/or importance, he will change his opinion so that it conforms with the new information. Subsequent to such change, the old opinion and its consistent cognitions will now create dissonance in proportion to their relative number and importance compared to the new opinion and its consistent cognitions.

As with the choice paradigms discussed previously, the methods used to operationalize the theory are frequently "summaries" of the relevant cognitions weighted for their importances. In other words, the measure of a person's pre- and postexposure cognitions is at an abstract level; it represents, however, distinguishable items of relevant information, beliefs, and so forth that the person may have. Indeed, this measure is typically a global self-rating or judgment on some more or less complex opinion issue. Nevertheless, these gross measures are adequate to the testing of many derivations, as will be seen in the following review of relevant studies.

A final word about the criteria for selection of studies for this section is in order, since a review of "attitude change" literature is beyond the scope of this volume. The first criterion is that the study should have been done since the formulation of the theory, and the second is that it should *purport* to be a test of the theory. The reason for the latter, rather stringent rule is that many attitude-change studies which could be explained in terms of dissonance theory could just as easily be explained in some other way. Our primary concern is with evidence that bears on dissonance theory as a relatively *unique* explanation of behavior.

An "exposure" study by Adams (1961) was designed to demonstrate the basic notion that exposure to information discrepant with one's own opinion produces dissonance. He had home-visiting interviewers measure the opinions of mothers of first-grade children (who are presumably much concerned at this point with the behavior of their children) about whether a child's behavior is mostly inborn or mostly learned. Each mother expressed her opinion on an 11-point scale and then was asked to listen to a tape-recorded talk, purportedly by an expert, that upheld one side or the other of the issue. About half the mothers were *exposed to a view opposing their own*, while the remainder of them heard a view consistent with their own. When the message had been heard, the interviewer explained that there were other authoritative points of view on the subject, and these could be heard and discussed in the near future. The mothers were then given the opportunity to say they would come to the university to hear one of the following talks, both given by an expert: "The Importance of Inheritance and Maturational Factors in the Development of Children" or "The Role of Training and Environmental Factors in Child-Rearing." Finally, at the end of the entire interview session, which involved other research problems, each mother was again asked to indicate her opinion on the inborn-learned dimension.

It is clear that if exposure to information counter to one's own opinion creates dissonance, then mothers who heard the opposing view should experience more dissonance than those who heard the supporting view. The theory also states that one way of reducing dissonance is to seek out information supporting one's own view. Such information is presumably available to the mothers through further listening to one of the future expert talks: Thus the mothers who heard the opposing view should be more eager to choose to listen to the expert talk consistent with their own view than should the mothers who heard a talk consistent with their own view. Furthermore, mothers who heard the opposite side should show more interest in hearing their own side than in hearing the opposite side again.

The results of this study are not entirely confirmatory. Mothers who heard the opposite side do show more interest in hearing one talk or the other than do those who heard their own side, thus showing differential motivation to hear relevant information. But this differential motivation may simply be an arousal of intellectual curiosity on the issue, stirred by hearing previously unknown facts, arguments, conclusions. At the same time, those mothers who heard the opposite side do, as hypothesized, show more interest in the future talk supporting their own view than in the opposing talk, *but so do the mothers who heard the talk supporting their own view.* The results of this study, then, fail to support the idea that exposure to a view opposing one's own creates dissonance, at least insofar as their avoidance of dissonance-producing information is concerned.

A variation of the basic derivation that inconsistent information creates dissonance is the hypothesis that the magnitude of dissonance is a direct function of the *degree* of inconsistency. This variation is presumably appropriate whenever the issue contains more than two distinguishable positions ordered in respect to each other along a single dimension. Hence, if the person holds one of the extreme positions, he may be exposed to information representing the other extreme (high discrepancy) or to information representing an intermediate position (moderate or small discrepancy).

Evidence on inconsistency and issue importance as determinants of the magnitude of dissonance comes from an "exposure" study by Zimbardo (1960). In this study, both importance of the issue to the subject and the discrepancy between the subject's position and that of the communicator were manipulated. The design provided for experimental variation of the issue importance without covariation in resistance to change, relevant knowledge, and so forth. It also provided for manipulation of the discrepancy between the communicator and communicatee positions without necessary covariation in the communicatee's (subject's) position. Hence this experiment provides conditions for a test of the effects of these two factors—importance and discrepancy—on dissonance-produced opinion change.

Pairs of friends were led to believe that they disagreed either a little or a lot in regard to judgments on a case study of juvenile delinquency. Importance of the case study rating was varied by telling some pairs that their judgments represented basic values, personality, and outlook on important life problems and telling other pairs that their judgments did not mean much.

Any dissonance aroused by learning that the judgment made by one's friend disagrees with one's own judgment could easily be reduced or eliminated by changing one's own judgment. Hence, if dissonance increases as discrepancy and importance increase, then change in judgment toward the friend's most acceptable position should also increase. It was found that judgmental change toward the friend's position is directly proportional to the amount of discrepancy and to the importance of the issue. These results therefore lend support to the notion that exposure to information discrepant with one's own view creates dissonance.

Additional evidence for the effect of exposure to discrepant information should be mentioned. Allyn and Festinger (1961) conducted an "exposure" experiment to show that pre-exposure knowledge that a communicator will oppose one's own position results in dissonance reduction by avoidance and defensiveness rather than by opinion change. They had a communicator recommend to an audience of teenagers that the minimum age for driving an automobile be raised. *This position was, of course, opposed by most members of the audience for whom early driving is an important issue.* Prior to hearing the persuasive message, some subjects were informed that the purpose was to study the personality of the speaker, while other subjects were informed that the speaker was known to think teenagers a menace on the roads. Thus in the first condition subjects were given no clue about the position to be taken by the speaker and were also directed to pay attention to his personal characteristics, while in the second condition they were told the speaker would oppose their own views. Both two weeks before, and immediately after the communication, the subjects filled out a questionnaire that included four opinion items on the issue. The authors assumed that the presentation of a persuasive and attitude-discrepant communication creates dissonance, but that knowledge of the communicator's position would allow subjects to reduce dissonance through rejection of the communicator.

The obtained change in opinion toward the advocated position was indeed greater among subjects directed toward the speaker's personality than among subjects apprised of the speaker's bias. However, a statistically reliable difference was obtained only for subjects who showed a relatively large opinion change: 20% of the warned subjects and 43% of the unwarned subjects showing such change. These data do, then, lend additional support to the derivation that exposure to discrepant information creates dissonance.

Evidence providing somewhat stronger support for the effects of exposure to discrepant information on dissonance may be found in the aforementioned "forced-compliance" studies by Brock (1962) and Brehm (1960a) and in an "exposure" experiment by Cohen (1962). Brock had his non-Catholic subjects write essays supporting Catholicism under conditions of high and low choice in compliance. Within each of these conditions, however, he confronted half of the subjects with the request that they analyze their discrepant essays in terms of the meaning and implications of their discrepant position. The other half were asked to deal with their discrepant essays by focusing on the grammatical structure. In this manner the subjects might be said to have been differentially exposed to the implications of their discrepant acts.

Brock assumed that the greater the confrontation, the greater the dissonance and consequent attitude change in line with the discrepant stand. His results confirm this expectation in that, for those who were placed in the high choice condition, the more they were exposed (i.e., the more their attention and thinking were focused on the implications of their discrepant stand), the greater the attitude change. For the subjects in the low choice condition, where theoretically there should have been little dissonance created by compliance with the request to write the essay, the effects of confrontation were reversed.

Another bit of evidence on the effects of exposure to discrepant information is available from the "forced-compliance" food study by Brehm (1960a). He showed that junior high school students, committed to eating either a little or a lot of a disliked vegetable, tended, in proportion to the amount of eating, to accept a communication claiming that the vegetable was high in vitamin content and to reject a communication claiming that the vegetable was low in vitamin content. Thus, where the communication was dissonance decreasing, opinion change occurred, and where the communication was dissonance increasing, opinion change tended to be slight.

However, Brehm also showed in this experiment that attitude change as measured by direct liking of an object can also be affected by dissonance. He found that increased liking of the disliked foods was a function of the interaction of two dissonance-arousing variables: the amount of the disliked food which the person was committed to eat and the relative number of additional reasons for not eating that food (i.e., the degree to which information discrepant with eating or not eating was introduced after commitment). Increased liking was greatest where the amount of food was great and the number of reasons for eating were minimal, and where the amount was small but the reasons maximal.

An experiment by Cohen (1962) also bears on the effects on attitude change of exposure to discrepant information. This experiment is concerned with investigation of the "boomerang effect." We have seen by now that the typical model for effecting attitude change has been the presentation of a communication containing information, arguments, appeals, and so on, designed to produce change in the recipient in a given direction. While this paradigm might be understood in a variety of ways, one possible way is in terms of dissonance theory. What we wish to point out here is that the prediction of intended influence is not a simple matter in terms of the theory. Rather, the dissonance theory approach suggests a set of factors which can produce not only the intended shift in influence but also just the opposite, that is, a *boomerang* change in attitude.

Furthermore, dissonance theory allows the prediction not only of a boomerang attitude change but in addition suggests a somewhat broader view of the boomerang effect than for that in regard to attitudes. Let us then consider the problem of negative change rather broadly and see what dissonance theory has to say.

First of all, let us suppose that dissonance has been aroused in regard to some cognition, A, without specification of what that cognition might be. We know that the dissonance could be reduced by a change in that cognition so that it no longer followed from the opposite of some other element or cluster of elements, and we also know that cognition A will have some resistance to such change. Suppose, then, that A's resistance is great because the actual event to which it corresponds cannot be changed and because its meaning is unambiguous. When such conditions exist, the reduction or elimination of dissonance will certainly depend on other modes of reduction, such as change in the elements with which A is dissonant or the addition of consonant elements. It is the latter mode, the addition of consonant elements, that is of interest here, for it is through the addition of elements that we may have a negative effect.

When cognitions A and B are dissonant with each other and are highly resistant to change, a remaining mode of dissonance reduction is through the addition of elements consonant either with A *or with B*. In this way, the proportion of relevant elements which are dissonant is reduced.

The conditions we have specified provide the possibility of a negative reaction. That is, whenever a person is exposed to cognitions dissonant with one already held, and these various cognitions are highly resistant to change, then the individual may resort to bolstering the cognition he first held. If the initially held cognition were an attitude, and the dissonant cognitions were a persuasive communication discrepant with his attitude, then his bolstering of the initial attitude would be termed "boomerang" attitude change.

Cohen's experiment was specifically designed to bear on the problem of the "boomerang effect" from the perspective of the present discussion. It represents an attempt to test the dissonance formulation of the boomerang effect in a "mutual influence" setting. In this experiment a person was committed to convincing a susceptible second person of his position on an attitude issue by means of a persuasive communication. However, instead of the second person becoming persuaded to change his position toward that of the communicator, he became even more extreme in his initial attitude. According to the dissonance formulation, the more negative the reaction of the target person, the more dissonance experienced by the communicator. Since the communicator is committed to persuading the other of the worth of his position, dissonance can, in this situation, be reduced by the communicator becoming even more extreme in his own position. This serves to increase the proportion of cognitions supporting the initial stand and decrease the proportion of dissonant cognitions. Thus the hypothesis of the study was that subjects who were committed to persuading others of the worth of their own positions and instead succeeded in making them even more negative and extreme would experience dissonance; the more extreme the negative reaction, the greater the dissonance and consequent boomerang effect in order to reduce that dissonance.

The experimental design provided for the manipulation of dissonance by having subjects write strong persuasive essays to "partners" and having them discover that *instead of convincing their "partners," they had succeeded in causing them to strengthen their counterpositions somewhat (low dissonance) or very much (high dissonance).* The subject's reaction to this in terms of his own attitudinal response was then measured, and a change score from his initial position was taken. All communication and interaction between partners were controlled by standardized false feedbacks. It should be noted that in order to prevent the subjects from responding to their partners' rejection of their own positions by becoming extreme themselves as a stance preparatory to further negotiation, the subjects were assured that their own final position was terminal and that they would not have a chance to communicate again with their partners. The subject was also prevented from repudiating his partner's position by an assurance from the experimenter of the sincerity, credibility, and maturity of the partner. It was expected that with high commitment to their own position salient, and with other obvious modes of dissonance reduction closed off, the high dissonance subjects would show a boomerang effect.

The data strongly confirm the hypothesis. Subjects in the high dissonance condition changed back so as to strengthen their own initial positions more than those in the low dissonance condition. The data show that while 59% of the highs boomerang, only 19% of the lows do so. The fact that the highs actually changed toward becoming more extreme in their own initial attitude positions is shown by the fact that among the high dissonance subjects who changed in any direction, 19 out of 25 subjects became stronger in their own initial positions.

If this boomerang effect is indeed a manifestation of dissonance reduction on the part of the highs, we might expect from dissonance theory that the greater the importance of the cognitions surrounding the relationship between partners, the more dissonance would be experienced over the partner's negative reaction and the greater the resultant boomerang. Data relevant to this point were also gathered; they concern the subject's perception of his partner's likability and friendliness. Presumably the more friendly and likable the partner, the greater the importance of the situation. It should be noted that these data were collected *before* the partner's reactions were fed back, and that therefore we would not expect them to be contaminated by the subject's final attitude response. When the attitude-change scores are computed according to the experimental conditions and likability of the partner, the data show that the difference between experimental conditions in boomerang is largely confined to and exaggerated for those subjects who felt that their partners were relatively more friendly and likable.

A final piece of supporting evidence for the dissonance interpretation in this boomerang study concerns the degree to which the boomerang is accompanied by a lessened interest in and orientation toward the partner. If the subjects do strengthen their own positions as a way of reducing the dissonance occasioned by the "unintended effect" they produced, they should want very little to do with the partner afterward. The data show that the high dissonance subjects want less information about the partner, his motives, and his actions than the low dissonance subjects. Also, among the highs, those who boomerang desire less information about the partner than those few highs who change toward the partner.

We may say then that the dissonance formulation can provide a fairly general conceptualization of the boomerang effect. However, a number of important problems are worth discussing here. It should be noted that the addition of a new cognition in a boomerang reaction could just as easily bolster elements dissonant with A as consonant with A. Indeed, without some further understanding of the variables controlling dissonance reduction, we may be unable to predict a boomerang reaction. The variable of resistance to change does not help us in this particular experiment, since it must be assumed that both sides of the dissonant relationship are highly resistant to change: If either side is sufficiently low in resistance to change, then presumably it would change, and the dissonance would be reduced without a boomerang.

It is interesting to compare the Cohen boomerang experiment with Zimbardo's (1960) aforementioned experiment on communication discrepancy and attitude change. It should be clear that the two "exposure" experiments differ in that the Zimbardo experiment deals with attitude change on the part of the recipient of a communication, while the present experiment deals with change on the part of the originator of a communication. Nevertheless, such a comparison highlights the centrality of the factor of commitment in specifying the degree to which exposure to discrepant information will result in changes away from or toward the source of discrepancy.

In Zimbardo's experiment, the friend's discrepant opinion was clear and irrevocable and in Cohen's experiment, the responsibility of the subject in causing the partner's counter-move could not easily be denied. However, the resistance to change of the other pole of the dissonant relationship differs in the two experiments. In the Zimbardo experiment, the subject was committed to the close friend with whom she had come to the experimental session; in Cohen's experiment, the subject was strongly committed to convincing the other person of the worth of his own attitude position. Thus the subject's own attitude positions were differentially resistant to change in the two experiments. The result was that Zimbardo's subjects changed their attitudes toward the other person more, the greater the dissonance, while the subjects in Cohen's experiment strengthened their own attitudes more, the greater the dissonance. (It should also be noted that in both experiments, the greater the importance of the relevant cognitions, the greater the effect of discrepancy on attitude change, whatever the direction of change.)

It seems apparent, then, that what is needed for a boomerang dissonance reduction to occur is that the individual be relatively resistant to changing his own position. At the same time, the dissonance-arousing information to which he is exposed must also be resistant to change. With both sets of dissonant elements resistant to change, the individual can do little else to reduce dissonance except to add further consistent elements to one of the two sets of dissonant elements. The set that will tend to be strengthened, we submit, is the one that represents the person's "own" or initial position on the issue.

These considerations apply as well to dissonances that arise in conjunction with variables other than attitudes. Discrepancies that occur, for example, between one's self-concept and one's own behavior would presumably arouse dissonance and could produce negative changes. In this case, however, we cannot be sure which side holds prior commitment for the individual although a reasonable guess would be the self-concept. If prior commitment were to the self-concept, the dissonant behavior would tend to be denied, rationalized, and so on. However, where the behavior cannot be changed or misinterpreted, that is, where the cognition of behavior is also highly resistant to change, then the dissonance may well be reduced by a reaffirmation of that aspect of the self-concept with which the behavior is discrepant. In other words, the discrepant behavior may only strengthen the dissonant aspects of the self-concept.

Consider, for example, a person who believes himself highly religious but who fails on a given holy day to attend or support a church. The cognition about his behavior could be quite undeniable and explicit in signifying irreligiousness. Yet we would expect him to have prior commitment to his self-concept about how religious a man he was. Hence he would be expected to experience dissonance and to try to reduce the dissonance by building up the relevant parts of his self-concept. We would, in short, look for this person to increase the strength of his belief that he was highly religious. There is, of course, a limit to this kind of distortion. Nevertheless, this is an additional way in which negative reactions or boomerangs can occur from the arousal of dissonance.

The experiments by Brehm (1960a), Brock (1962), and Cohen (1962) demonstrate that whether in "forced-compliance" or "exposure" settings, the confrontation of the individual with discrepant information when he is committed in some way to the situation has consequences for the creation of dissonance and resultant attitude change. In summary of all the evidence, then, it can be seen that the data are consistent with the proposition that dissonance is created by exposure to information inconsistent with one's opinion. The data also support the further derivations that dissonance increases as importance of the issue and as discrepancy size increase. Nevertheless, much of the data can also be explained in other plausible ways and thus may not necessarily be considered clear support for the application of dissonance theory to this problem area. This discussion will be continued in Chapter 7.

This concludes our review of most of the extant evidence relevant to the dissonance formulation. We have tried to be as thorough as possible in presenting this evidence and have tried to make it as easy as possible for the reader to grasp the range of empirical phenomena covered in these studies.

It should be more than apparent by now that there are a number of very clear threads running through these experiments, whether they have been classified as "exposure," "free-choice," or "forced-compliance" studies. It should also be apparent that a number of problems are raised by the existing tests of the theory as well as a number of ambiguous or unresolved conceptual issues remaining in the dissonance formulation.

In the following chapters we shall take up some of the more immediate research problems and issues growing out of our consideration of the evidence. In Chapter 6 we shall present new experimental evidence bearing on rather straightforward derivations from the theory of the sort we reviewed here.

Related theoretical issues

— 5

THE EFFECTS OF IMPORTANCE OF COGNITIONS

Besides varying with changes in the positive and negative attributes of chosen and rejected alternatives, dissonance also varies with covariation in either the negative or the positive attributes of the chosen and rejected alternatives. What this means in effect is that the greater the general attractiveness or importance of the choice alternatives, the greater the magnitude of postchoice dissonance.

We have already seen, in the section on negative alternatives, two examples of attempts to manipulate importance (Mills, Aronson and Robinson, 1959; Rosen, 1961). These two attempts failed to show the hypothesized effects. Nevertheless, we can assume that importance has some effect if we consider as variations in importance the use of differential rewards or justifications for performing unpleasant tasks in the "forced-compliance" experiments.

In addition to its role in "forced-compliance" experiments, importance has been shown to operate in two "free-choice" studies and one "exposure" study. In all three experiments dissonance was shown to vary directly with the importance of the relevant cognitive elements. Zimbardo (1960) in his "exposure" study showed that opinion change from dissonant information increased as importance increased. Importance was varied by varying the degree of significance of performance on a case history for assessing the subject's basic social values, personality, and outlook on life. In their "free-choice" gambling experiment, Cohen, Brehm and Latané (1959) varied importance by varying the degree of publicity attached to the subjects' performance. They found stronger tendencies to attend to or ignore information relevant to a dissonance-producing choice under increasing publicity. In Cohen's (1962) boomerang study, importance, as determined by liking for the partner, produced greater dissonance and greater boomerang attitude change. This finding, however, was only correlational.

A possible factor in the failure of the importance manipulation in the Mills et al. and Rosen experiments may very well have to do with the specific operations used to induce importance. Both experiments were carried out in classroom settings in a context where examinations were a regular occurrence. Although it seems somewhat peculiar that such a seemingly powerful manipulation of importance as the "70% of grade" condition versus "5% of grade" condition did not have any great effect, it is plausible to assume that extrinsic forces like examination grades in a context where they are a common part of the routine are less powerful than forces having to do with the individual's self-concept or status. Perhaps the fact that the Cohen "exposure" study, the Zimbardo "exposure" study, and the Cohen, Brehm and Latané "free-choice" study did manipulate aspects of the person's self-concern was responsible for their success with the importance variable.

A "free-choice" experiment reported by Deutsch, Krauss and Rosenau (1962) is specifically directed toward the manipulation of importance through manipulation of the person's self-esteem. It therefore provides evidence on the validity of our line of reasoning. In their experiment female subjects rated six different kinds of jam on nine-point bipolar rating scales in terms of over-all taste and flavor. After the subjects had made their ratings, the experimenter selected for each subject a pair of samples that on the first scale had received equivalent ratings, if possible, at the center of the scale. The experimenter then announced that, "The company that's sponsoring the research would like to give you a sample jar of either brand, whichever you want." At this point a female experimenter was introduced as "an expert in the field of food selection factors" who was going to conduct a panel interview in which she would "probe for some of the reasons behind your food preferences." Half the subjects were given a high self-involvement manipulation; half were given a low self-involvement manipulation. The high self-involvement condition made the choice relevant to valued attributes of the self by stressing the relationship between peoples' ability to judge subtle differences in the quality of foods and their judgmental ability in other areas, such as leadership aptitude, executive potential, and artistic judgment. The low self-involvement condition was given no such self-esteem involving message. Subjects were then asked to select one or the other jam. After selection, the subject rerated all six of the samples, including the two from which she had chosen.

The major dependent variables of the study are the changes in the subjects' ratings of flavor and over-all taste from before to after choice. The data show that whether or not the choice involves the self is of consequence: In the high self-involvement conditions, the chosen alternatives increase in value, and the unchosen alternatives decrease in value more than in the low self-involvement condition.

We may thus conclude that importance does play a role in the arousal of dissonance, particularly when it involves the manipulation of central aspects of the person's self-esteem or self-concept. It is also possible that its role is different when viewed in terms of its effects on attitude change or other dissonance-reducing modes rather than in terms of its effects on selective exposure to dissonant information. Further evidence to be presented in the next chapter will also bear on the issue of importance insofar as it affects the salience and forgetting of dissonant information.

SOME NOTES ON DISSONANCE REDUCTION

We have seen in the review of the evidence that, just as there are distinguishably different situations that arouse dissonance, so there are distinguishable ways in which a person may try to reduce dissonance. The various methods of dissonance reduction were seen to be special cases of the general proposition that a person will attempt to reduce the number and/or importance of dissonant cognitions compared to the number and/or importance of consonant cognitions. Let us now briefly summarize the evidence in terms of the different modes of dissonance reduction investigated in the studies we have examined.

To begin with, dissonance can be reduced by (1) lowering the importance of all relevant cognitions and (2) lowering the number and/or importance of dissonant compared to consonant cognitions. It follows that a thorough understanding of reactions to dissonance requires some knowledge of the factors that control change in cognitions. This aspect of dissonance theory has been discussed by Festinger (1957) and need not be detailed here. We will simply refer to examples of each.

In his "free-choice" experiment on the effects of a choice between attractive alternatives, Brehm (1956) gave some subjects information about their alternatives after the choice was made. It was expected that the information, which consisted of good and bad facts about both the chosen and rejected alternatives, would be selectively judged by subjects and thus help them reduce dissonance. Whether subjects did or did not receive such information, they were exposed to high or low dissonance choices. Thus it was predicted that the amount of revaluation of alternatives would be greater in the high than in the low dissonance condition, and that the difference in amount of revaluation between high and low dissonance conditions would be greater with information than without. These predictions were supported by the pattern of results and therefore give tentative support to the notion that postchoice exposure to relevant information facilitates dissonance reduction.

Further relevant data are available from the previously mentioned study by Brock (1962). After his subjects had written attitude-discrepant essays, he had some of them indicate the grouping and bonding of relevant cognitions prior to measurement of their attitudes, while he reversed this sequence for others. It would be plausible to expect that those subjects who were first given the opportunity to consider the relevant cognitions would have their attitude change facilitated. However, the data show that the opportunity to mull over the attitude relevant cognitions is not sufficient to facilitate dissonance-reducing attitude change; in fact, such "mulling over" may very well facilitate dissonance reduction via other, uncontrolled modes. This issue bears on the general problem of repeated confrontation by dissonant experiences and whether or not people adapt or gain facility in dissonance reduction with repeated exposure. New experimental evidence dealing with this problem will be presented in Chapter 6.

There are many specific aspects of dissonance reduction which might ideally have been examined. An experimenter could have focused on the success of different methods, on how or why certain methods rather than other possible ones may be selected, on the substitutibility of different methods, and so on. At this point, however, we can throw little light on most of these problems and so have confined ourselves in our review to a description of the major kinds of variables that have been found to be affected by dissonance.

Aside from the magnitude of dissonance, we have seen that the most general factor controlling dissonance reduction is the resistance to change of relevant cognitions. This follows from the fact that once dissonance occurs, it can be reduced or eliminated only by elimination of dissonant cognitions, addition of consonant cognitions, or reduction of importance of relevant cognitions. The sources of resistance to change are at least two: the physical or psychological difficulty of changing a bit of "knowledge" (e.g., the extent of commitment), and the extent to which a given change would create further dissonance. Again, little explicit research has been done toward the careful delineation of the factors that control resistance to dissonance reduction, and there would seem to be little point in our reiterating Festinger's discussion at this point. However, we shall discuss certain aspects of this problem in the next chapter.

At this point we may note that the relevant elements in a dissonance will not always be easily changeable, and under these conditions one might expect dissonance reduction to take some form other than change in one or a cluster of dissonant elements. One such possible form, as we have seen, is the addition of further relevant cognitive elements. Of course, not all relevant elements would help to reduce a given dissonance. Such cognitions must be selected so that they are all consonant with a given element or cluster of elements. Only in that way will they reduce the proportion of relevant elements that are dissonant with each other.

The resistance of a cognitive element to change is a function of the difficulty of changing whatever reality it represents, on the one hand, and the ambiguity of its significance on the other; that is, from the difficulty of changing its physical source and from the difficulty of changing one's perception or judgment of it.

We do not mean to imply by the above discussion that only physical or social objects other than one's self are subject to these sources of resistance to change. Indeed, the same factors control the resistance to change of cognitions one has about one's self. Thus one's own behavior may be difficult or easy to change in actuality, or it may be difficult or easy to change in the way one judges it. The same will be true of one's opinions and attitudes and one's emotions and motivations: They all vary in the extent to which they are difficult to change in actuality, and they differ in the extent to which they are ambiguous in their significance or meaning. Unfortunately, however, there is little that can be said at present at the conceptual level about when such factors as one's own emotional reactions will be difficult to change in actuality or will be ambiguous in meaning.

In line with our emphasis, however, it is possible to point out some guidelines for the understanding of resistance to change. These guidelines are based on the notion of commitment, which we have stressed as being a distinctive aspect of dissonance theory and the perspective from which we have examined the relevant research material. Given the arousal of dissonance through engaging in discrepant behavior, the most immediate way of reducing such dissonance, and the way which takes perhaps the least psychological toll, would be to repudiate the behavior, that is, to "uncommit" oneself. The Davis and Jones (1960) experiment shows that when subjects could uncommit themselves, they did not change their attitudes. However, those subjects whose discrepant behavior was irrevocable became more negative toward the person they had derogated. Having chosen to commit themselves and with their discrepant behavior clear and unambiguous, they could only change their attitudes to come in line with their behavior as a way of reducing the dissonance engendered by that behavior.

Zimbardo's (1960) exposure experiment showed that subjects would change their attitudes toward a friend's position, the greater the dissonance. In his experiment, the subject may be said to have been committed to the friend she brought to the experiment. With other obvious modes of dissonance reduction, like leaving the field or repudiating the situation blocked, she could only change her attitudes in the direction of the discrepant position held by her friend. Cohen's (1962) exposure experiment also blocked obvious modes of dissonance reduction, such as repudiation of the situation. But here the subject was committed to convincing the other of his own position, and therefore he could not change in the direction of his partner. Being thus committed, and faced with unequivocal evidence of his discrepant behavior, he thus increased the strength of his own initial attitude position.

Finally, the Brock and Buss (in press) shock experiment provided another illustration of the relationship between commitment and mode of dissonance reduction. In this experiment, subjects chose to commit themselves to delivering shock to other people. With the impossibility of repudiating this behavior salient, they changed their attitudes so as to minimize the painfulness of shock, the greater the dissonance. However, where the victim was a girl, the resistance against minimizing shock was great, so that these subjects instead increased their perception of the force propelling them into the discrepant commitment, thereby reducing dissonance in a different way.

These experiments provide the most explicit examples of the relationship between commitment to one or another pole of the dissonant relationship (or facet of the dissonance situation) and the avenue used for dissonance reduction. However, in almost all of the experiments where subjects clearly take a stand with regard to some discrepant behavior—whether it is giving up one alternative for another, complying with an attitude-discrepant act, or involving themselves in some way with an attitude-discrepant communication—the particular commitment sets limits on the avenue of dissonance reduction. It thus provides the theory with predictive power in a number of nonobvious realms. Many of the relevant experiments do not specify the various modes of dissonance reduction very clearly nor do they set out explicitly to block off one or another mode in the interests of studying a particular mode. It should be clear, though, that this restriction is at least always implicit insofar as it is part and parcel of the experimental design. That is, any experimenter tries to make his experimental setting cognitively real and compelling for the subject, and to structure his inducements and manipulations so that they are unequivocal. This sort of procedure at once sets limits on dissonance reduction via "uncommitment," repudiation of the experimenter, repudiation of the situation, perception of great force used to induce discrepant compliance, and so forth. In this manner, there is some assurance that the particular reduction mode of interest, for example, attitude change, will occur with dissonance, and that the greater the dissonance, the more attitude change will be produced. Thus, while the four experiments we have cited bear directly on some of the problems associated with specification of dissonance-reduction modes, the general body of experimental work in the area, at the very least, implicitly does so when the dissonant situation clearly involves some attitude-discrepant commitment. Given commitment to the discrepant act, the subject can generally reduce his dissonance only by some realignment which makes his cognitions consistent with his behavior.

The research literature we have reviewed attests to the use of a number of dimensions of cognitions as avenues of dissonance reduction. As we have seen, opinions and attitudes, judgments and evaluations, perceptual distortion, and selective attention to information have been shown to serve in the reduction of dissonance. These modes of reduction have all been discussed in the preceding chapters. In addition, we have pointed out two relatively nonobvious modes of dissonance reduction: boomerang effects and obligation changes.

In the previous discussion of ways in which dissonance may be reduced, we have not always made a distinction between evaluation and belief or judgment but have generally referred to all such factors as "attitudes." It should be clear, however, that the "attitude" studies have dealt with a range of phenomenal measures of evaluation, liking, judgment, belief, opinion, attraction, and so forth.

We have seen that, just as a person may experience dissonance if one or more of his cognitions are inconsistent with a given evaluation of an object, person, or event, so he may reduce such dissonance by changing that evaluation so as to make it consistent. An occurrence that almost invariably involves a discrepant evaluation is a choice between attractive alternatives. Since the dissonance is a function of two or more choice alternatives, it follows that the dissonance may be reduced by change in their evaluations so that they become more consistent with the decision. Implied is increased attractiveness or value of the chosen alternative and decreased attractiveness or value of the rejected alternative(s). These implications have been tested in the "free-choice" experiments by Brehm (1956) and Brehm and Cohen (1959a): After choice, evaluations of the chosen object were raised, while those of the rejected alternative were lowered.

Another kind of evaluation was of persons, groups, and activities. The effect of dissonance on the evaluation of persons was studied in Davis and Jones' (1959) "forced-compliance" experiment, and changes in evaluations of groups and their activities by Gerard (1961) and Aronson and Mills (1959). Also, Brock and Buss (in press) showed that changes in the evaluation of a subjective experience are affected by dissonance.

Direct liking of an object was shown to be affected by dissonance by Brehm (1960a) and Smith (1961) in their "forced-compliance" studies of food preferences. Finally, liking for a given attribute of an object can also be affected by dissonance as Aronson (1961) showed. In his experiment, the direct effect of reward tended to be cancelled to the extent that effort, and presumably dissonance, was involved.

A number of studies were seen to demonstrate that general attitudes are affected by dissonance. Typical examples of such studies are the "free-choice" studies of Brehm (1956) and Brehm and Cohen (1959a) and the "forced-compliance" studies of Festinger and Carlsmith (1959) and Mills (1958).

Many of the studies described utilized a specific opinion dimension to measure attitude changes as a function of dissonance arousal. Evidence that opinion change may be used to reduce dissonance comes from the "exposure" studies by Cohen, Terry and Jones (1959), Cohen (1959b), Zimbardo (1960), Allyn and Festinger (1961), Cohen (1962), and Zimbardo (see pp. 30–31). The "forced-compliance" studies by Cohen, Brehm and Fleming (1958), Rabbie, Brehm and Cohen (1959), and Brock (1962) also illustrate dissonance reduction through change on specified opinion dimensions.

Studies by Festinger (1957, pp. 126–131, 162–176), Cohen, Brehm and Latané (1959), Ehrlich et al. (1957), Mills, Aronson and Robinson (1959), and Rosen (1961) have all shown that persons who experience dissonance will tend to be selective in attending to new information. In this manner dissonance can be reduced by the addition of consonant cognitions. Whether or not this generalization holds with regard to the avoidance of dissonant information, however, remains questionable.

A rather obvious and probably commonplace way for dissonance reduction to occur is through behavioral change. For example, whenever a person behaves in a way inconsistent with an attitude he holds, he may be able to reduce the resultant dissonance by change in that behavior. Conceptually, what is necessary is that the resistance to change of the behavior be less than the resistance to change of the attitude. That such behavioral change does sometimes occur has been demonstrated in the "free-choice" gambling studies reported by Festinger (1957, pp. 126, 131, 162–176) and by Cohen, Brehm and Latané (1959). It will be recalled that college students played a gambling game against the experimenter, having first chosen the side on which they wanted to play. Subjects were informed that they could change sides with the experimenter but only by paying a penalty of a certain amount of money. After the twelfth trial, subjects were given a chance to change sides without the penalty. It was found that the tendency to change sides was a direct function of the amount lost (hence, the magnitude of dissonance) under these conditions of lowered resistance to change in behavior.

In addition to overt behavior change, it is plausible to assume that dissonance could be reduced by changing one's cognitions about one's own behavior. Thus, under some conditions, dissonance might be reduced by some cognitive change about one's own behavior without change in the actual behavior itself. Generally speaking, one would expect a person to distort or change the cognitive aspects of his behavior to the extent that other methods of dissonance reduction were resistant to change and to the extent that the relevant dimensions of his behavior were ambiguous. Unfortunately, there are no data bearing directly on this aspect of dissonance reduction.

In one experiment (Brock and Buss, in press), we saw that dissonance aroused by discrepant commitment was accompanied by increased feeling by the subject that he had been compelled to comply with the discrepant request. By perceiving less choice in compliance, the subject increases the number of cognitions supporting the discrepant act and thereby reduces dissonance. Additional evidence on this avenue of dissonance reduction will be presented in Chapter 6 and Chapter 8.

Finally, there is evidence that the effects of dissonance are limited to cognitions that are directly relevant—that is, consonant or dissonant. In two of three experiments where attitudes on irrelevant issues were measured, variations in the magnitude of dissonance were found to have no effect. Mills' (1958) "forced-compliance" experiment measured the subjects' attitudes on attitude dimensions other than the dissonance-producing dimension of cheating. While the dissonance manipulations produced changes in attitudes toward cheating, they did not affect attitudes toward other aggressive acts unrelated to cheating. Similarly, Zimbardo's "exposure" experiment on effort found increased dissonance to produce increased attitude change toward a "numerical grading system" in regard to which the subjects had taken a discrepant stand, but no effect of the dissonance variation on unrelated attitudes. The fact that these "control topics" were also topics related to education (proportion of girls at school, honor system, municipal university in New York, etc.) makes even more significant the fact that they were not affected by the dissonance manipulation. In a third study (Rabbie, Brehm and Cohen, 1959), however, variations in the magnitude of dissonance did apparently affect an irrelevant attitude. While the dissonance-arousing issue was the "elimination of intercollegiate athletic competition," subjects' attitudes toward "compulsory Latin and Greek" were also affected. The irrelevant issue may, of course, have been seen as a lesser evil, and thus there may have been the implication that if the subject was willing to support the relevant proposition, then he was also willing to support the irrelevant proposition. Consequently, he may have experienced a separate dissonance in relation to the irrelevant issue. Nonetheless, there is a question as to whether the specificity of the effects of dissonance can be said to have been established empirically.

In conclusion, the reader will have noted from this brief summary of modes of dissonance reduction that empirical research has not been aimed specifically at exploration of the factors controlling dissonance reduction. This is in part because the unique aspect of the theory is the formulation concerning the magnitude of dissonance. However, it is also due to some lack of specification of factors involved in dissonance reduction. Although there has been little or no theorizing about such factors, we can at least make some issues more explicit. These issues center around the problem of the detection of dissonance.

It would certainly appear necessary to be as clear and specific about the effects of dissonance as about the conditions that arouse dissonance. For just as we cannot be sure a given set of conditions arouses dissonance simply by inserting some kind of "dissonometer" into the person, neither can we be sure that any given behavioral response is the result of dissonance. In what ways, we may ask, can one reasonably infer that a given effect is due to dissonance?

Most generally, this problem is that of alternative explanations. One always has to try to eliminate alternative explanations in order to make a given hypothesis or theory cogent. Nor can one ever eliminate all alternative explanations. However, there *are* certain characteristics of dissonance theory, particularly in experiments where commitment is ambiguous, that allow possible alternative explanations for certain research paradigms.

First of all, manipulation of the magnitude of dissonance will generally help determine whether or not a given effect is due to dissonance: The magnitude of the effect will covary with the manipulated magnitude of dissonance. Thus, to show that the attitude change resulting from discrepant self-persuasion is due to dissonance rather than to the arguments in the persuasion, one can hold the persuasive content constant and vary the inducing force used to obtain the persuasion. Since the inducing force can be manipulated without change in exposure to content on the issue, any consequent difference in the amount of attitude change can be attributed to change in the magnitude of aroused dissonance.

Secondly, it will usually be more compelling to show that a given variable changes from before to after dissonance arousal than to simply show the final effect. This is partly because the precision of the theory allows predictions of attempts to reduce dissonance more readily than predictions of end-states of affairs. But it is also true because of the interdependency between the relevant variables; variables that can serve as dissonance reducers also can generally serve to magnify dissonance. Consider again the case in which a person is induced to make persuasive statements discrepant with his private opinion. Instead of manipulating the inducing force, one might measure the amount of inducing force perceived and correlate that with the amount of attitude change shown. If the measure of perceived force is taken *after* the dissonance-arousing decision to comply, then it may undergo change that serves to reduce dissonance, that is, it may become magnified. Presumably, it would be magnified in direct proportion to the amount of dissonance experienced. But on the other hand, the amount of dissonance experienced would have been inversely related to the amount of perceived force at the time of arousal. Thus subjects who perceived relatively little force to begin with would experience relatively high dissonance and would tend to show relatively great magnification of the perceived force subsequently. With such complications, a correlation of final attitude (or even pre- to postarousal attitude change) with final perceived choice is often difficult to interpret. However, if the perceived force had been measured *prior* to dissonance arousal, as well as afterward, then the prediction that change in attitude would correlate positively with the initial perceived force would be no more equivocal than the usual set of correlational data.

The same principles apply to effects due to manipulations. Measurement of a dissonance-relevant variable after the arousal of dissonance is not always sufficient to show that the obtained effect is due to dissonance, even when there is a control condition to establish the direction of change. This will be true when the manipulation of dissonance allows a plausible alternative interpretation for the obtained difference between conditions. It will be particularly true where the alternative interpretation assumes an intervening process *dissimilar* to that of dissonance, that is, that the manipulation arouses differential psychological tension which produces proportionate changes in the dependent variable or variables. Alternative interpretations may assume, on the other hand, such processes as contrary motivational tensions, differential resistance effects, differential informational or judgmental effects, and so forth. The measurement of *change* in dissonance-relevant variables allows closer inspection of the assumed motivational process as it may be reflected both between and within experimental conditions. Thus, where one can make plausible assumptions about correlated changes (either positive or negative), one may also be able to rule out alternative explanations that assume either opposite effects or no effects. This problem will be discussed again in Chapter 8.

New evidence

— 6

The present chapter discusses a number of new experiments that bear on rather direct derivations from dissonance theory and that are designed to reflect on and add to the evidence presented in the preceding chapters. It is hoped that, together with the evidence described in Chapters 3, 4, and 5, a basis will be provided for an overview of the degree of support for the more direct derivations from the theory. This should allow an assessment of the utility of the theory for predicting behavior in a wide range of situations.

AN EXPERIMENT ON SMALL REWARDS FOR DISCREPANT COMPLIANCE AND ATTITUDE CHANGE

In reviewing the evidence on the manipulation of dissonance through the variation of consonant information, we saw that the data on the effects of rewards and justifications for discrepant commitment are quite consistent with the theory. However, the alternative explanation was raised that the inverse relationship between rewards and attitude change might disappear if rewards were small enough. This alternative explanation assumes that the obtained inverse relationship is due to the fact that large rewards engender suspicion and resistance and that subjects may say something of the order of, "It must be bad if they're paying me so much for it." The fact that high reward subjects show less change than low reward subjects could be due, then, to this resistance effect at the high end of the reward continuum, rather than to a dissonance effect at the low end of the reward scale, where cognitions supporting discrepant commitment are minimal. Therefore, this alternative reasoning goes, if sufficiently small rewards were given, the suspicion and resistance engendered would be reduced and the relationship between reward and attitude change would be a direct function of the magnitude of the incentive determining the response.

In order to explore further the effects of rewards associated with taking a discrepant stand and to gather information relevant to this alternative explanation, Cohen carried out a "forced-compliance" experiment in which rewards were varied at intervals over a wide range. This variation was accomplished by offering college students either $.50, $1.00, $5.00, or $10.00 to *write an essay against their private view on a current issue on campus.* Under the guise of a "general survey," 30 Yale students were asked to write an essay "in favor of the actions of the New Haven police." The attitude issue was chosen because in the spring of 1959, just prior to the study, there had been a student's "riot" at Yale with resulting accusations of police brutality toward the students. There was thus an assurance that (1) motivation and interest on the part of the students were maximal, (2) every student was on one side of the issue, that is, extremely negative toward the police and their actions and sympathetic toward the students, and, therefore, (3) any subject asked to write an essay in favor of the actions of the New Haven police *would be taking a position clearly inconsistent with his own attitudes.*

The students were approached in their dormitory rooms on a random basis; only one subject to a room was selected. The experimenter introduced himself as a fellow student who was a member of a research team from The Institute of Human Relations. He said that the researchers were "interested in and concerned with the recent riots" and that the subject knew that the "university administration and the public are very concerned with the issue." Thus the research group felt that the study had some "relevance and importance, especially in the light of recent events." The experimenter went on to say that, "It has been shown that one of the best ways to get relevant arguments on both sides of an issue is to ask people to write essays favoring only one side. We think we know pretty much how you feel about the students' rights in this matter." Here the experimenter paused for the subject's reaction, and after a usual indication of felt infringement on the part of the subject, the experimenter continued by saying, "What we really need now are some essays favoring the police side. I understand that you have very different views on the matter, but as you can see, it's very interesting to know what kinds of arguments people bring up in their essays if they have very different opinions about it."

The experimenter then went on to say that he would like them to write the "strongest, most forceful, most creative and thoughtful essay you can, unequivocally against your own position and in favor of the police side of the riots." The reward manipulation was then introduced. The experimenter said, "Now as part of our study, we have some funds available, and we are prepared to pay you \$_____ for writing the essay against your own position." All reward groups were told exactly the same thing, except that some were offered \$10.00 ($N = 6$), some were offered \$5.00 ($N = 10$), some were offered \$1.00 ($N = 6$), and some were offered \$.50 ($N = 8$). All groups were told that the decision to write the essay was entirely their own choice. However, in order to prevent their refusing to participate, they were also told that the experimenter *did* need their help in the study since he was a student and this was part of his research paper. Thus, while the latter "constraints" might reduce the absolute amount of dissonance occasioned by compliance, it prevented any considerable differential loss of subjects and therefore any self-selection bias. After the reward manipulations, the subjects were again reminded that they were to take as strong and unequivocal a stand as possible against their own position and in favor of the police.

After each subject wrote his essay on a blank sheet entitled, "Why the New Haven Police Actions Were Justified," the postmeasures were given. Subjects were told, "Now that you have looked at some of the reasons for the actions of the New Haven police, we'd like to get some of your reactions to the issue; you may possibly want to look at the situation in the light of this. So, would you please fill out this questionnaire." Subjects first filled out an opinion scale asking, "Considering the circumstances, how justified do you think the New Haven police actions were in the recent riot?" The scale used was an *a priori* 31-point scale, marked and labeled at every fifth point by the following terms: Completely justified; Very justified; Quite justified; Somewhat justified; Little justified; Very little justified; Not justified at all. This constituted the major dependent measure of the experiment. Checks were then made of the experimental inductions to clarify the possible effect of differential reward on attitude change. In order to check on the perceived amount of reward offered, the subjects were asked, "How much were you offered to write the essay?" Here the response was in terms of an 11-point scale, graded in tenths of a point, which ran from $0 to $10.00. The last item checked on the subject's perception of the degree of strength of the discrepant essay he agreed to write. On a seven-point *a priori* scale, running from "extremely moderate" to "extremely strong," he was asked, "How strong an essay in favor of the New Haven police did you agree to write?" This completed the experiment. It should also be noted, however, that though there was reasonable assurance that all subjects were extremely opposed to the police and that therefore we could assume some equivalent negative position in their initial attitudes, since the study made use of an "after-only" design, a control group was used. This group, consisting of 14 subjects, was given the attitude measure at the same time as the experimental subjects. The control subjects received none of the manipulations or other measures; they were simply given the attitude questionnaire regarding their opinions of the New Haven police actions. In effect, the control group may be said to have acted as a premeasure in this experiment.

Results

The check on the reward manipulations indicates that the subjects perceived accurately the rewards they were to receive for writing the essay. In all cases they checked the point on the scale reflecting the exact reward they were promised; in no case was there any overlap. It was also found that the subjects, in writing their essays, perceived that they were to take a strong and unequivocal stand against their own attitude position and that this perception was constant and high no matter what rewards they anticipated. On the scale where maximum strength of discrepant essay was seven, the mean for the $10.00 group was 5.72, for the $5.00 group it was 5.80, for the $1.00 group it was 5.58, and for the $.50 group it was 5.82. All of these means indicate strongly discrepant essays, and they do not differ reliably from one another. We may thus assume that the basic conditions for examining the effects of differential incentives in producing dissonance and attitude change have been fulfilled here: The subjects accurately perceived that they would be getting differential rewards, and any differences in attitude change as a function of reward would not be a function of the strength with which the subjects perceived that they had taken the discrepant stand.

The data on attitude change are entirely consistent with the notion that dissonance and consequent attitude change vary inversely with the amount of incentive for taking a stand discrepant with one's cognitions. The data in Table 1 show that as reward decreases, attitudes toward the police become more positive. Among experimental groups, the rank order of attitudinal effects is exactly what we might expect from the dissonance formulation; the linear trend is significant at less than the .01 level by F test.[3] When the range of scores, including the control group, is tested for differences by the Duncan Multiple Range Test (Edwards, 1960, pp. 136–140), the specific differences between experimental groups emerge. The $10.00 and $5.00 conditions are not

TABLE 1

MEAN ATTITUDES TOWARD THE POLICE ACTIONS

Control condition	2.70 *
$10.00 condition	2.32
$ 5.00 condition	3.08
$ 1.00 condition	3.47
$ .50 condition	4.54

* The higher the mean, the more positive the attitudes toward the New Haven police. Highest value equals 7.00, lowest value equals 1.00.

significantly different from each other or from the control condition, but the $1.00 condition is different from the control ($p < .10$) as is the $.50 condition ($p < .01$). Furthermore, the $1.00 condition and the $.50 conditions are both different from the $10.00 condition ($p < .05$ and $< .01$ respectively). Finally, the $.50 condition is itself different from the $1.00 condition ($p < .05$) as well as from the $5.00 condition ($p < .01$). These results are clearly in line with the derivation from dissonance theory regarding the effects of consonant information.

The alternative explanation for results concerning the effects of differential incentives thus does not appear to gain support from these data. The idea that at high incentive levels, subjects might feel that something is "wrong," and that the suspicion they experience could reflect itself in resistance against changing their attitudes, is not relevant for a comparison between, for example, $1.00 and $.50 conditions. No more suspicion can be attached to a $1.00 offer than to a $.50 offer. The other side of this general alternative explanation asserts that when subjects are given very little reward, they would have very little desire to change and might in fact show a resistance effect. The fact that

[3] Significance tests on all original experiments reported in this volume are two-tailed, unless otherwise reported.

the results show an inverse monotonic relationship between reward and attitude change over a wide range of rewards does not suggest that such a general alternative explanation is valid.

We may conclude, therefore, that the evidence continues to support the derivation from dissonance theory that decreasing cognitions consistent with the discrepant commitment increase dissonance. Whether rewards or justifications have been manipulated, throughout the empirical continua explored, dissonance and consequent attitude change are increased when cognitions consonant with the discrepant behavior are decreased.

A STUDY OF DISCREPANT INFORMATION IN BETROTHAL

An issue raised in connection with the "free-choice" studies of Brehm (1956) and Brehm and Cohen (1959a) concerns the adequacy of the dissonance formulation for understanding the consequences of decisions in important life situations. It might conceivably be argued that the effect of value of alternatives, cognitive overlap, and number of alternatives on revaluation, as well as stability of revaluation, is confined only to the rather "artificially" produced laboratory situations where persons are forced to choose between alternatives that are not of the highest importance for them. Therefore, a more demanding, real-life situation was sought for its advantages in testing the dissonance formulation of revaluation following choice.

The situation selected was one of marriage choice. In this study by Cohen, the magnitude of dissonance can be seen to vary as a function of change in various attributes of the chosen alternative. In a period prior to Christmas vacation, Yale College students were interviewed until 30 were found who were considering becoming engaged during the vacation. Each of the 30 was asked to answer the following six questions:

1. How many girls are you dating now while taking out your intended fiancee?
2. How important an issue is loss of freedom to you in considering engagement?
3. How much of a financial discrepancy is there between her family and yours?
4. How much religious disagreement is there between you and your fiancee?
5. How much difference in "social levels" would you say there is between you and your fiancee?

6. Being as honest as you can, how much difficulty have you had in making the decision to marry her?

These questions were intended to measure the extent to which certain dimensions relevant to marriage represented positive or negative (dissonant) aspects of the choice alternative of engagement. These aspects are relatively objective and clear and, hence, not easily changeable. Thus they would not be expected to change much as a consequence of postchoice dissonance.

Subjective feelings of need or devotion, on the other hand, are not clearly tied to reality and hence may be changed in order to reduce dissonance. Thus it was expected that a measure of need and devotion both before and after actual engagement would tend to reflect attempts at dissonance reduction consequent to the decision. To measure subjective change in need, the following three questions were asked both before and after the vacation:

1. How much does your future seem empty without your fiancee?
2. In general, being as frank as possible, how much would you say you love your girl?
3. How much do you feel that you were "meant for each other"?

Both the "objective" and "subjective" questions were answered on 71-point response scales with eight identified points, which varied from "Not at all" to "Extremely," except for the first objective item, which went from "None" to "Eight or more" in six categories (0, 1, 2, 3–4, 5–7, 8 or more).

It was expected, then, that the less positive was an objective aspect of the engagement prior to the actual decision, the greater would be the dissonance afterward. Since the dissonance would be difficult to reduce by distortion of the objective differences, it would more likely be reduced by magnification of the subjective need or love. Hence it was expected that, for all subjects who actually became engaged, the more negative the measure of objective conditions prior to engagement, the greater would be the amount of increase in need and devotion from before to after engagement.

After vacation the 30 students were again asked to answer the questions concerning devotion and need. Of the 30 students who had considered engagement, 20 actually did become engaged, and they constitute the sample for the following results.

Subjects' scores on each of the six pre-engagement objective questions were added in order to obtain an over-all index of the degree of pre-engagement conflict. These over-all scores were then divided at the median; subjects thus were divided into those with relatively good reasons (low conflict) for engagement versus those with relatively poor reasons (high conflict). For each of the three devotion items, change scores from before to after engagement were taken. It was expected that those with High Dissonance (high pre-engagement conflict) would be expected to experience greater postengagement dissonance and consequent increase in devotion and need.

Results

Table 2 gives the mean initial scores as well as the mean changes on the devotion and need measures as a function of the over-all positiveness of the objective attributes. From these separate scores, an over-all index of change was taken for each subject across all three measures of devotion. Table 2 also contains the pre-engagement conflict index for the sample as well as for the 10 subjects who did not become engaged. The latter group's initial devotion and need scores are also listed in Table 2.

It may be seen in column four that the High Dissonance subjects show a greater over-all positive change on the need and devotion index

TABLE 2

MEAN INITIAL SCORES AND CHANGES IN NEED AND DEVOTION AS A
FUNCTION OF PRE-ENGAGEMENT OBJECTIVE VARIABLES

	Need and Devotion						
	1. Meant for Each Other		2. Emptiness of Future		3. How Much Love		4. Over-all Index
Over-all Pre-Engagement Dissonance	Initial	Change	Initial	Change	Initial	Change	Initial	Change
No Decision (Mean pre-engagement conflict index = 8.04) (N = 10)	4.78		5.14		4.96		4.95	
High Dissonance (Mean pre-engagement conflict index = 10.30) (N = 10)	5.04	.70	5.03	1.23	4.88	.46	4.93	.79
Low Dissonance (Mean pre-engagement conflict index = 5.00) (N = 10)	5.28	−.32	5.83	.05	4.62	−.11	5.23	−.13
p-value of difference	<.10		<.001		ns		<.001	

than the Low Dissonance subjects; the subjects with relatively more reason against engagement show an increase in need and devotion from before to after engagement, while the subjects with relatively more reason for the engagement show some slight decrease. The pattern is clear for the over-all change index ($p < .001$ by t test), and the trends are clear for each of the separate need and devotion measures. It should be mentioned that there are no reliable differences between either of the sample groups and the No-Decision group in the initial pre-engagement need and devotion scores. Also, the No-Decision group falls midway between the two sample groups on the pre-engagement conflict index. Therefore it is difficult to attribute failure to become engaged to any special characteristics of the No-Decision group: it appears to contain as many persons with high pre-engagement conflict scores as those with low pre-engagement conflict scores. It would seem that some other, perhaps adventitious, factor was at work in determining their decision not to become engaged. In any case, this pattern of results lends confirmation to the hypothesis that dissonance is a function of the relative attractiveness of the choice alternatives.

These results are not, of course, unequivocally supportive of dissonance theory. On the one hand, they are correlational and are subject to alternative causal interpretations, and, on the other hand, they involve a problem of subject selection. In respect to the latter point, for example, it might still be that the 10 subjects who failed to become engaged as planned are simply those who, while having moderately large differences with their fiancee in regard to the objective variables, also became less attracted to them, and therefore decided not to become engaged. Those who became less attracted but had small differences on the objective variables would still have been motivated to become engaged as planned. Whether or not this interpretation is more or less valid than our dissonance interpretation cannot, of course, be ascertained without further study. Nevertheless, this study does illustrate the kind of practical implication that dissonance theory should have and how the theory may be applied to real-life situations as well as laboratory studies.

A STUDY OF CONFLICT AVOIDANCE

It has been assumed by at least some investigators (e.g., Miller, 1944; Berlyne, 1960) that a conflict situation produces motivations capable in turn of producing behaviors similar to those involved in dissonance reduction. The reasoning is not unlike the straightforward analysis of the effect of a choice between attractive alternatives on the arousal of dissonance. When a person chooses between attractive alternatives, there is high prechoice conflict just as there is high postchoice dissonance. One may suppose that the prechoice conflict is unpleasant and that the individual will try to reduce it. Presumably conflict can be reduced in much the same way as dissonance can: The more attractive alternative is increased in attraction while the less attractive alternative(s) is decreased. Thus, if one assumes that prechoice conflict has motivational properties similar to those of dissonance, one may explain much of the evidence relevant to dissonance theory as pre- rather than postdecisional phenomena.

Although we would not necessarily expect dissonance to occur in a prechoice situation, there remains the possibility that conflict does have motivational properties which produce effects similar to those produced by dissonance (the assumption that conflict is an unpleasant, drive-producing state is generally accepted). More specifically, if conflict is unpleasant, it should result in tendencies to avoid high conflict situations. As a simple check on this notion that conflict is unpleasant and will be avoided, the following study was designed and conducted by Brehm.

The purpose of this study was to demonstrate that a person will tend to avoid a choice in proportion to its potential for creating conflict. To that end, students in a class in introductory psychology were recruited to participate in a "consumer research project." When the student arrived at the experimental room (a professor's office), he was met by the experimenter (a professor) who explained that he was engaged in some research for a consumer research organization. The experimenter said that he was being paid by the consumer organization to find out what college students thought about various consumer articles, such as hotplates, swimming fins, binoculars, and so on. He pointed out that this project, unlike the usual basic research carried out in the department, was applied and was for the sole purpose of helping manufacturers sell more of their products.

The subject was then led to a table on which were the following items: lady's train case, man's electric razor, hot plate, lady's cigarette lighter, man's billfold, binoculars, steam iron, man's cigarette lighter, swimming fins and mask, hair dryer, and desk lamp. The retail value of these items ranged from about $7.00 to about $18.00. The subject was asked to look at each item carefully and then to rate it on an "Evaluation Sheet." The subject was told to take 10 to 12 minutes in making his ratings.

The evaluation sheet listed the 11 items in the order given above; each item included an 81-point rating scale, labeled each tenth point with *Not at all, Very slightly, Slightly, Somewhat, Moderately, Pretty, Quite, Very,* and *Extremely.* The subject was instructed to rate each item according to how inclined he would be to buy it at that moment. The higher the inclination, the higher should be the rating. When it was clear that the subject understood his task, he was asked to make the ratings and given about 10 minutes.

After the ratings had been finished, the experimenter said that he needed people to return to make several additional ratings, but that, because the research was applied rather than basic, he could not give additional experimental "credit points" (toward the course grade) for the additional sessions. He said that he had therefore arranged with the manufacturers of the products to give the sample items away at the end of the testing session. The subject was assured that there were duplicate items, though not an unlimited supply of each, and that there would be a choice of one from three or four chosen at random. If the subject agreed to continue, the experimenter pretended to look at a schedule of choices and then informed the subject that he could make his choice from either of two pairs and that he could make his choice very shortly but that first it was simply necessary to know which pair the subject preferred to choose between.

Unknown to the subject, the experimenter selected the pairs to make one of them high conflict and the other low. It was expected that if a person tends to avoid high conflict choices, the subjects would tend to select the low conflict pair over the high conflict pair.

Initially four subjects were given a choice between two completely separate pairs of items. But since the more attractive items of the two pairs seldom were equal in attractiveness, there was an additional factor influencing the choice between pairs. Nevertheless, each of these four subjects chose the pair representing the higher conflict choice.

To avoid differential attractiveness of the more attractive items in the two pairs, the system was changed to include the same attractive item in both pairs. Thus in one pair a highly attractive item would be included with one only slightly less attractive, while in the other pair the same highly attractive item would be included with one considerably less attractive.

Twelve more subjects were run with this revised system. Two of them refused to continue with the experiment because they needed to participate in a project giving "credit points." A third subject was deleted because, while he chose the high conflict pair, he chose the less attractive item of that pair, indicating low validity of his ratings. A fourth subject, who also chose the high conflict pair, was deleted because his ratings were generally very low, and he seemed to have little or no interest in the whole study.

Each of the eight remaining subjects chose the high conflict pair. In view of the attempt on the part of the experimenter to make the situation and choices important to the subjects, all of which should have maximized the amount of conflict in the choices, the results suggest that people *do not* tend to avoid high conflict situations, at least under these conditions.

In evaluating whether or not the conflict reduction hypothesis may then account for results of other studies on dissonance theory, it may be noted that the present situation is not unlike those in which dissonance reduction has been claimed (Brehm, 1956; Brehm and Cohen, 1959a). Thus situations which do in fact produce pre- to postchoice revaluations of choice alternatives may fail to produce sufficient conflict to cause them to be avoided. It may be, then, that conflict has little or no motivational property here, and that the explanation of pre- to postchoice revaluation of choice alternatives in terms of conflict reduction is not very compelling.

Our interpretation of these data is not, of course, unequivocal. For one thing, it is possible to argue that other factors are obscuring any conflict avoidance tendencies that may exist. Subjects may be preserving their opportunity to choose the second most attractive alternative or they may be trying to avoid ending up with the least attractive alternative, although there was nothing to indicate that that could happen. It might even be argued that subjects *were* avoiding conflict by choosing the pair in which their final choice was least obvious or determined. But the plausibility of this latter argument assumes that there would be a significant amount of conflict involved in choosing between the attractive item and the relatively unattractive item, which seems rather implausible. At a minimum, then, these data, though not entirely unequivocal, suggest that conflict, at least in this kind of choice, has little or no motivational property of the kind that might produce revaluations of the choice alternatives. This issue will be discussed again in Chapter 13.

AN EXPERIMENT ON COERCION AND ATTITUDE CHANGE

Generally speaking, the occurrence of cognitive dissonance has been shown in situations in which at least one of the choice alternatives open to the person is essentially positive rather than negative in character. That is, even when a person is confronted with the threat of punishment for choosing something to which he is attracted, the choice to avoid the punishment, along with the attractive goal, is not negative in character in the sense that the individual must be forced to make any selection at all. No additional constraint or force need be placed on the person to make him choose one of the two alternatives—that is, to take the attractive object and punishment or to reject both.

A choice in which both alternatives are primarily negative in character differs in that it does require some additional force to insure that any choice will be made at all. It is obvious that this type of choice may arouse negative reactions on the part of the chooser and may also involve less feeling of choice on the part of the chooser. Because of these characteristics, which are absent for choices among positive alternatives, it seems necessary to show that a choice between negative alternatives does create dissonance with consequent attitude change. Although we indicated in Chapter 4 that there is evidence which may be considered as demonstrating dissonance from negative choices, neither our classification nor the obtained results in those studies (Brehm and Cohen, 1959b; Mills, Aronson and Robinson, 1959; Rosen, 1961) are completely convincing.

Let us now look at a "forced-compliance" study by Brehm, which was patterned after an earlier study by Cohen and Brehm (see Chapter 11). Brehm's study was designed to provide experimental evidence that increased magnitude of negative attributes in the rejected alternative results in decreased magnitude of postchoice dissonance. The idea was to *make people choose to perform an unpleasant task by threatening them with differing amounts of punishment.*

The experiment was conducted in a fraternity house by a student who was a fraternity member. The subjects were 20 pledges for this particular fraternity. They were individually contacted by the experimenter. It was explained to each pledge that the experimenter was taking a class in psychology, in which he had to collect some research data. His project, he said, was to get normative data on the copying of random numbers. He also explained that what he wanted the pledge to do was copy random numbers for a 3-hour stretch. He admitted that the participation would not be fun, that it would indeed be boring and tedious, but he insisted that he had to get it done. The pledge was then presented a schedule sheet on which he was to indicate the period when he would perform the task. At this point, prior to the pledge's filling out the schedule sheet, the manipulation of coercion was introduced by the following instructions:

Low Coercion: "I realize that you don't want to do this task. However, I need the results for a term project. I'm afraid I'll have to paddle you if you don't sign up."

High Coercion: "I realize that you don't want to do this task. However, I need the results for a term project. You realize that I have the authority to call a tribunal on you or even keep you out of the fraternity. I'm afraid I'll have to use it if you don't sign up."

The 20 subjects were divided between these conditions, and none of them refused to participate in the copy task. After the pledge had filled out the appointment sheet, he was handed a questionnaire and given the following explanation and instructions.

"The I.F.C. (Interfraternity Council) has prepared this questionnaire to determine the advisability of using pledges as subjects in psychological research. Please be completely frank and honest in filling it out. Do not put your name on it. When you have finished, put the questionnaire into this envelope and seal it. Remember that I will not see it, so you can fill it out exactly as you feel."

The questionnaire was conspicuously labeled, "I.F.C. Questionnaire" and contained instructions reiterating that no one in the fraternity would see the answers. The envelope was addressed to the Interfraternity Council on campus. When the questionnaire was completed, the experimenter gave a full explanation to the pledge of the purpose of the experiment and the reasons for the procedure.

Results

One of the questions on the questionnaire asked: With how much punishment were you threatened if you did not agree to take part? The subject was instructed to check one point along a 41-point response scale, labeled at every tenth point by "None at all," "A little," "Moderate," "Quite a bit," and "Very much." The mean answer for each of the conditions provides evidence on the success of the coercion manipulation. With responses scored from 0.0 for "None at all" to 4.0 for "Very much," the mean of the Low Coercion condition was 1.44; the mean for the High Coercion condition was 3.40. The difference between these means is significant by a t test at beyond the 1% level. Thus perceptions of the severity of possible consequences for noncompliance were in accord with the experimental instructions.

Although perception of the threat is accurate, it could happen that the pledges would feel that the severe threat is less likely to be carried out than the mild threat, for tribunals are serious occurrences and relatively infrequent compared to paddling. To check on this possibility, another question asked: How likely is it that the punishment would have been carried out if you did not take part? Responses were indicated by marking a point along an 81-point scale, labeled at every twentieth point by "Not at all likely," "25% chance," "50% chance," "75% chance" and "Completely certain." Responses were scored from 0.0 to 8.0, respectively. The mean response for the Low Coercion condition, 5.20, was somewhat *lower* than the mean response for the Higher Coercion condition, 6.85. This difference, significant by a t test at about the 5% level, indicates that pledges confronted with threatened paddling considered the paddling less likely than those confronted with the tribunal and being excluded from the fraternity. Apparently, then, we have guessed wrong, and paddling is normally perceived as less likely than a tribunal. Thus any difference in the magnitude of dissonance could be explained as due to the difference in perceived probability of punishment as much as it is due to the difference in severity of punishment. This interpretation, however, would be essentially consistent with the derivation that dissonance is an inverse function of coercion.

The major indicator of dissonance reduction here was a single question, which asked: Considering what you will get out of this research project (interest, enjoyment, learning, etc.), how satisfied are you with having to take part in it? Answers were indicated by marking a single dot along an 81-point response scale, labeled at every twentieth point by "Extremely satisfied," "Moderately satisfied," "Neither," "Moderately dissatisfied," and "Extremely dissatisfied," and were scored from +4.0 to −4.0, respectively.

The theoretical expectation, it will be recalled, is that dissonance, and hence satisfaction, increases as the magnitude of the coercive force decreases. This derivation is clearly supported by the mean satisfaction scores, which are −2.59 for the High Coercion condition and −.80 for the Low Coercion condition. The difference between these means is significant at better than the 5% level by a t test.

These results are clearly consistent with the assumption that dissonance is aroused by negative choices just as it is where one or more of the alternatives is positive in character. Hence the constraints involved in a negative choice do not necessarily preclude the expected kind of dissonance arousal and attempted reduction. At the same time there may well be differential implications of negative and positive choice alternatives for the arousal of dissonance. It is also possible for a negative choice to create quite different dissonance effects from those reported here, as will also be seen in Chapter 11.

This study, then, supports the derivation that dissonance increases as the magnitude of the coercive force to comply decreases (where compliance is obtained) and provides further confirmation of the general proposition that increase in the number and/or importance of cognitions supporting a discrepant commitment produces less dissonance and attitude change.

AN EXPERIMENT ON CHOICE IN COMMITMENT TO COUNTERATTITUDINAL BEHAVIOR

In the section in Chapter 3 where we reviewed the evidence relevant to complex change in the attributes of choice alternatives, it was seen that all of the studies described manipulated choice in taking a discrepant stand in connection with some other dissonance-relevant variable, either premeasured or manipulated. However, it is always possible that the inferred or presumed effects of choice on dissonance are as much due to the other variables studied as to the choice manipulation alone. For this reason it seemed necessary to gather additional evidence on complex changes by observing the effects of the direct manipulation of choice without its interaction with another variable. This might provide more unequivocal evidence on the effects of choice on dissonance in situations of discrepant commitment.

A "forced-compliance" experiment by Cohen and Bibb Latané utilized a direct verbal manipulation of choice and examined the effect on attitude change of differences in perceived choice in taking a discrepant stand. In this experiment 60 Yale undergraduates were chosen at random from four residential colleges and were seen individually in their rooms; no more than one subject to a room was selected. The experimenter introduced himself to each subject as a student taking a survey as "part of a research course" and asked the subject to indicate his opinion on 10 issues pertaining to student life at Yale. Embedded in the questionnaire was the relevant attitude dimension: an item concerning the institution of a compulsory religion course at Yale. The subject responded to this item and all the others by means of an *a priori* 10-point scale that ran from "Strongly agree" to "Strongly disagree," with a neutral midpoint. When the subject had completed the questionnaire, the experimenter left. Three weeks later another experimenter interviewed all subjects in their rooms. He approached only those subjects opposed to the institution of a compulsory religion course at Yale as measured by the preliminary questionnaire. Most subjects were strongly opposed to the idea: of 60 students interviewed at the first session, only nine (those who were in favor of the religion course or neutral toward it) were dropped from the experiment and did not participate in the second experimental session.

The experimenter introduced himself as a student working for the Yale News Bureau who had been given the subject's name by the bureau. Subjects were told that the "Chicago Yale Alumni Board" was very much interested in the question of a compulsory religion course at Yale, but before going ahead with any action, they wanted to get some ideas on the issue. Subjects were then asked if they would help by tape recording a statement giving their views. They were told that a program was to be put together which would represent a collection of ideas on the proposal rather than an opinion poll. The taped statements would be edited and a final program of ideas made up on both sides of the issue.

The subjects were then told that, "We have many statements against the compulsory religion course, and now we need some ideas on the other side of the issue—a strong, convincing argument *in favor of* the compulsory religion course at Yale."

However, before speaking into the microphone, which was ostensibly to record the speeches to be presented to the Chicago Alumni Board, subjects were given the *choice* manipulation. Half the subjects (those assigned to the *Low Choice condition*) were simply asked to make the discrepant speech. The microphone was practically pushed into their hands, and they were given no chance to decline or to have any say in the matter. The other half of the subjects, assigned to the *High Choice condition*, were told, "We need some people to speak in favor of the proposal, but, of course, the matter is entirely up to you." In effect, the experimenter attempted to create the illusion that the subject was entirely free to refuse, at the same time that the experimenter reopened the issue (of the subject's participating by giving a speech in favor of the proposal) every time the subject appeared to be vacillating and on the edge of refusal. In this manner the experimenter and subject sometimes "argued" back and forth as much as three times, but in all cases agreement was finally reached. Furthermore, after agreement was reached, the experimenter emphasized that he did not want to force the subject into anything he did not want to do, and he made certain the decision was again seen by the subject as his own decision.

Of the 51 subjects, 26 were placed in the Low Choice condition and 25 in the High Choice condition. In summary, an attempt was made to engender the maximum amount of dissonance involved in forced compliance: The subject was again told that it was necessary to take a strong stand for compulsory religion at Yale; he gave his name, address, and class at Yale; he spoke into a tape recorder which was apparently taking down everything he said; and he assumed that his speech, identified as his statement, would be played before an important group of Yale alumni. Thus subjects in this experiment who varied in the amount of choice given them *took a strong public stand on an issue they opposed, producing a situation in which differential dissonance and attitude change could be expected.*

After finishing his speech, the subject filled out the postquestionnaire. He was asked for "some of his reactions to this business, before continuing." The subject first filled out an opinion scale identical with the premeasure. The subjects also answered an item checking on the choice manipulation. They were asked: Considering that you agreed to participate in the survey, how much choice do you feel you really had in choosing which side of the issue to speak on? The scale used was a 10-point scale which ranged from "Complete choice" to "No choice at all." The last section of the postquestionnaire contained an item designed to measure the degree to which the subject felt that he "presented a sincere, organized, and convincing speech." The scale used here was a six-point scale, varying from "Very good" to "Very poor."

When the subjects had completed the postmeasures, they were told about the experiment and cautioned not to speak about it for an appropriate time. This concluded the experiment.

Results

The check on the choice manipulation indicates that it was very effective in creating differing perceptions of choice in taking the discrepant stand. The mean perceived choice for the Low Choice condition was 3.71, for the High Choice condition, 8.54; these differences are significant at well beyond the .001 level by t test. The data also show that all subjects were extremely and almost identically opposed to the compulsory religion course at Yale at the outset. On a scale where 10 indicates the most extreme opposition, the mean attitude toward the proposal at the time of premeasure for the Low Choice condition was 9.05; for the High Choice condition it was 9.34. Furthermore, the check on the subjects' perceptions of whether they actually made a sincere, organized, and convincing speech indicates that the commitment to discrepant behavior was strong and uniform among them. The mean for the High Choice condition is 3.50; for the Low Choice condition, it is 3.53, indicating that subjects in both conditions felt that they had made speeches of good quality and felt this to an equal degree. Thus it may be assumed that any differences in attitude change appearing between the choice conditions are not due to any differences in initial attitude position or differences in strength of commitment, and that taking a positive stand in the face of such negative attitudes constitutes a state of strong potential dissonance.

The change in subjects' attitudes toward the acceptance of the compulsory religion course at Yale from before to after taking the discrepant stand constitutes the main data of the present experiment. The data show that the mean change for the Low Choice condition is 1.82, whereas for the High Choice condition it is 2.66, though this difference does not reach statistical significance. Upon inspection of the distribution of change scores within each of the two choice conditions it was found that a few extreme change scores in the Low Choice condition are responsible for the reduced significance of the difference between conditions. Thus, when a chi-square test is performed on the data after splitting change at the exact median, the choice groups are now seen to be significantly different in the predicted direction ($x^2 = 7.07$, $p < .01$). Table 3 presents the change data.

TABLE 3

DISTRIBUTION OF SUBJECTS BY ATTITUDE CHANGE SCORE
AND CHOICE CONDITION

	Low Change (0 to 1.4 on scale)	High Change (1.5 to 8.0 on scale)
Low Choice	18	8
High Choice	8	17

In general, the data support the assumption that variation in choice in taking a stand discrepant from one's attitudes produces variations in attitude change toward that discrepant position, so that the greater the choice, the greater the attitude change.

Thus the evidence from this experiment is entirely consistent with evidence from the experiments by Cohen, Terry and Jones (1959), Davis and Jones (1960), Brock (1962), and Brock and Buss (in press). They all support the derivation from dissonance theory that the more equal the distribution of relevant attributes consistent with choosing each alternative (the higher the choice), the greater the dissonance and consequent attitude change in line with one's discrepant commitment.

AN EXPERIMENT ON RECALL
OF DISCREPANT INFORMATION

If it is true, as seems apparent, that dissonance is psychologically unpleasant, then it would be plausible to expect a person to avoid dissonance just as he would avoid physical pain. One might then also expect that if a potentially dissonance-arousing situation faced an individual, and that situation also contained some means by which the dissonance could be avoided, a person would avail himself of those means and exhibit no signs of attempting to reduce dissonance (having already avoided its arousal).

The clearest relevant evidence comes from the "forced-compliance" study by Davis and Jones (1960) described earlier. It will be recalled that they asked students to give a negative evaluation to another student under high and low choice conditions and found that ratings of the target student were more negative under high—than low—choice. In another pair of choice conditions, subjects were told ahead of time that they would have a chance to talk with the evaluated student after the experiment was over. It was made clear that they would be able to say anything they wanted, including the fact that their negative evaluation was really false and asked for by the experimenter. Thus subjects in this condition could avoid dissonance by deciding (implicitly) to tell the evaluated person that the evaluation was actually false and had no meaning (i.e., by "uncommitting" themselves). Subjects in this condition would therefore be expected to rate the evaluated person the same regardless of whether or not they had had some choice in making the negative evaluation. This expectation was confirmed by the results. Of course, it is also possible that these subjects experienced dissonance and simply reduced it by "uncommitting" themselves rather than by changing their evaluation of the target person. Thus it is not entirely clear whether those who knew they could explain themselves actually avoided dissonance or simply reduced it in a different way from subjects who had little opportunity to dispel the target person's impressions.

Also concerned with avoidance of dissonance was the "exposure" study of Allyn and Festinger (1961). In this study, it will be remembered, subjects either were or were not apprised that a speaker would advocate *an opinion in disagreement with their own*. As was expected, those led to expect the disagreement showed less opinion change than the ones not expecting the disagreement. This outcome can be interpreted as dissonance avoidance by those apprised of the speaker's position.

On the other hand, the "free-choice" studies by Ehrlich et al. (1957), Mills, Aronson and Robinson (1959), and Rosen (1961), and the "exposure" study by Adams (1961), all failed to find evidence confirming the derivation that dissonant information will be avoided in proportion to the amount of dissonance produced. In each of these studies, while subjects sought out dissonance-*reducing* information, they did not necessarily *avoid* dissonance-*increasing* information.

These findings on avoidance were all obtained in situations where exposure to information was assumed to be affected by dissonance. Where attitude change was studied, as in the Davis and Jones (1959) and Allyn and Festinger (1961) experiments, avoidance can be inferred. However, the consistency of the negative findings on exposure, and the fact that selective exposure is a more direct reflection of avoidance of dissonant cognitions than attitude change, should make us somewhat skeptical of the validity of the derivation regarding the avoidance of dissonant information.

A possible reason for the failure to confirm the dissonance-avoidance derivation concerns the salience of dissonant information immediately after the dissonance-producing commitment. For it is plausible to assume that dissonant information would be salient, that is, would stand out and seem more significant than would irrelevant and, perhaps, consonant information. This effect would make it difficult for a person to reduce dissonance by minimizing the presence or importance of dissonant information, at least within a short period after the arousal of dissonance. Furthermore, the increased attention value of dissonant information could tend to obscure successful dissonance reduction if the measure of reduction involved exposing the subject to dissonant information, as was done, for example, by Ehrlich et al. (1957) when they asked car owners to inspect advertisements of cars they had considered but rejected. That a salience effect could also produce a tendency to expose oneself voluntarily to dissonant information (e.g., Adams, 1961; Mills, Aronson, and Robinson, 1959) is not so clear. There is also the possibility, of course, that the opportunity of exposing oneself to dissonant information is, at least under some circumstances, accepted as some sort of challenge.

The immediate salience of dissonant information has been noted previously (Brehm, 1955). Subjects who had made a choice between consumer articles were allowed to read "research reports" that gave both good and bad information about the articles. Asked a few minutes later what seemed most important to them about the research reports, the subjects most frequently mentioned bad, or dissonant, points about the chosen alternative.

To explore further the issue of whether or not dissonant information tends to be salient or avoided after dissonance is produced, Brehm performed an experiment on the recall of discrepant information. Brehm designed the study to show that *dissonance results from a person's receiving information discrepant with his own recently given, explicitly stated views,* and that the magnitude of this dissonance increases as the importance of the issue increases. The presence of dissonance was measured in two ways: by the immediate salience of dissonant information and by the selective forgetting of the dissonant information over a period of time.

College students recruited from introductory psychology classes were asked to bring a friend to their experimental session, and both served as subjects. When the pair of friends arrived at the experimental room, they were informed by the experimenter that they were to take part in a survey for a nationally circulated magazine devoted to television. The survey's purpose was stated to be a study of the relationship between the personality types of television stars and of the individuals who watch them. The friends were then placed in separate rooms for the remainder of the session.

Each subject was given a list of 40 personality traits, some desirable (e.g., intelligent, kind) and some undesirable (e.g., sly, lazy). Each trait was accompanied by the following scale responses: "Not at all," "Moderately," "Very," and "Extremely." Issues of high and low importance were created by having all subjects rate both themselves (high importance issue) and their favorite television star (low importance issue).

The introduction of discrepant information was accomplished by having each subject rate his friend or his friend's favorite star, as well as himself, and then showing some subjects fictitious ratings of themselves (High Importance condition) and other subjects fictitious ratings of their favorite star (Low Importance condition), purportedly made by the friend. The ratings on 30 of the 40 traits were made identical with those of the subject, while the remaining 10 ratings were made to differ from those of the subject by two points on the four-point scale. The same traits were made discrepant for all subjects, whether referring to the subject himself or to his favorite star.

In showing the subject the ratings made by the friend, the experimenter said, "Now we are interested in your ability to remember the items as they are checked on your friend's inventory. I will give you your inventory, your friend's inventory, and a blank inventory. I will

94 / *Explorations in Cognitive Dissonance*

give you 10 minutes to look over the two inventories that have been filled in, and then I will collect them. You may take as much time as you like to fill in the blank inventory, but it should not take you more than five minutes." The purpose in these instructions was to insure that the subject would look closely at the friend's rating in the Low Importance condition as well as the High, so that exposure to the discrepant information would be about equal between conditions.

When the blank inventory had been completed, the subjects were asked to return exactly one week later in order to fill out some additional questionnaires. They were asked not to talk about the study to each other during this interval. On returning, they were again instructed to indicate their friends' ratings on a blank inventory. When finished, they were apprised of the true purpose of the study and the reasons for the deceptions.

It was expected that discrepancies on the High Importance (self) issue would create more dissonance than those on the Low Importance (television star) issue. The index of dissonance in this study was *salience*, or relatively good recall, immediately after testing, and *forgetting*, or relatively poor recall, one week after testing, of the discrepant information compared to the nondiscrepant.

Results

The results of the immediate recall test, seen in Table 4, yielded clear support for the theoretical expectations. While subjects in the Low Importance condition recalled a smaller proportion of discrepant than nondiscrepant ratings, subjects in the High Importance condition recalled a larger proportion of discrepant than of nondiscrepant ratings; this interaction being significant by a *t* test at the 5% level. However, the expected salience of discrepant information in the High Importance condition is not very strong, probably because of a ceiling for recall, since five of the ten subjects in the High Importance condition recalled all 10 of the discrepant ratings, though only two of them recalled all of the nondiscrepant ratings. Because of this ceiling effect, the salience of discrepant information can be seen more clearly by counting the number of subjects who recalled a greater proportion of discrepant than nondiscrepant ratings, six in the High Importance condition and one in the Low. This difference is significant by an Exact test at the .05 level, *one tail.*

It was also expected that, by one week later, the discrepant information would be less well recalled than the nondiscrepant and that this differential effect would be greater for High Importance subjects than for Low. Again referring to Table 4, it may be seen that the proportions of correctly recalled items fall off more sharply for the discrepant than for the nondiscrepant information (significant at better than the 5% level by t tests), but that this effect does not differ between the High and Low Importance conditions. Thus the data indicate that dissonant information does tend to be forgotten more rapidly than does consonant, although they fail to show that the rate of forgetting is a function of the importance of the information. We can only speculate that the failure to find greater forgetting of dissonant information in the High Importance condition is due to the salience of the dissonant informa-

TABLE 4

RECALL OF DISCREPANT AND NONDISCREPANT INFORMATION

TIME OF RECALL	Average Per cent of Items Recalled Correctly	
	Nondiscrepant	Discrepant
Immediate		
Low Importance	82.3	71.0
High Importance	89.4	93.0
Delayed		
Low Importance	64.1 *	31.0
High Importance	74.8	57.0

* Delayed percentages are based on the total number of items. Use of the number correctly recalled immediately as the base line yields a similar pattern of results.

tion, as shown on the immediate recall test. That is, if one finds that a close friend has given one a rating of "unintelligent," that knowledge may be so dissonant, and consequently so salient, that a very long time is needed to forget it. Indeed, it may even be that the forgetting of highly dissonant information is extremely difficult, and that when one is exposed to such information, the resulting dissonance can be reduced only by methods other than forgetting of the information itself.

The notion that dissonant information may be salient immediately after dissonance is produced—although not having been explicitly derived from the theory—is an entirely plausible phenomenon and quite consistent with the theory. Immediately after dissonance is produced through exposure to discrepant information or as a result of a choice, the dissonant information may be most salient for the person as he is confronted with the consequences of his discrepant act. It is only over a period of time, as the person attempts to reduce his

96 / *Explorations in Cognitive Dissonance*

dissonance, that he may manage to change the dissonant information from being salient to being forgotten. In effect, the individual must suppress that which is initially salient. It should be clear, however, that while the present speculations about the immediate salience of dissonant information are grounded to some extent in acceptable data, the need to provide more valid evidence should stimulate more explicit and carefully defined research on the problem.

A "FORCED-COMPLIANCE" EXPERIMENT ON REPEATED DISSONANCES

It is apparent that many dissonances are situationally aroused and, to the extent that such situations tend to be repeated in the normal course of events, it becomes meaningful to inquire into the effects of repeated dissonances. At least two kinds of effects may be distinguished: (1) the summation of different dissonances on the same behavioral attempt to reduce dissonance; and (2) changes in reactions to dissimilar dissonance-arousing situations.

One effect of repeated dissonances concerns those situations in which the dissonance and available methods for reducing it remain the same from one situation to the next. Under these conditions, we would expect that the pressure to reduce dissonance would summate on one or more of the possible methods of dissonance reduction, thus increasing the magnitude of apparent attempts to reduce dissonance. Relevant evidence for this conjecture comes from the "forced-compliance" study by Aronson (1961) in which subjects fished for containers that had specified colors and amounts of money in them. Though Aronson does not present data on liking for the colors of the items fished for after each effortful trial, if we can assume that dissonance is distributed over trials and that more dissonance is thus accumulated in the high effort condition, the results of this study provide some support for the present conjecture. The results show an increasing effect in line with the dissonance-reduction hypothesis as a function of the amount of effort engaged in.

Another case of repeated dissonances concerns that in which the specific form of dissonance reduction appropriate to each situation differs. We have no precise theoretical formulation to predict what the effect of such repetitions might be, but we can indicate the logical possibilities and describe relevant evidence. The logical possibilities are, of course, that the occurrence of a given dissonance has no effect on reactions to subsequent unrelated dissonance, that it reduces the reaction to a subsequent unrelated dissonance or that it increases the reaction to a subsequent unrelated dissonance. Increased reaction might occur if the psychological tension involved has aspects that are not specific to the arousing situation, thus allowing the accumulation of dissonance where there is insufficient opportunity to reduce it from one situation before another is presented. Increased reaction could also occur from increased sensitivity to all dissonances from the occurrence of a given one, or from behavioral dissonance reduction sets or practice effects that could carry over from one dissonance to another. On the other hand, decreased reaction could occur from avoidance tendencies aroused by previous dissonances, from learning to tolerate dissonance, and so forth. In the absence of any further theoretical knowledge about these and other possible mechanisms, we will simply describe a relevant study by Cohen.

General Design

A group of 48 Yale College students were used, all of whom were on the same side of each of five different current issues on campus. The issues were: (1) compulsory chapel for all students at Yale; (2) compulsory coats and ties at Yale, at all times, at all places, for all activities; (3) language requirement of compulsory Latin and Greek; (4) elimination of all cuts at Yale, that is, compulsory attendance at all classes; and (5) complete elimination of all intercollegiate athletics at Yale. The subjects indicated their positions on each of these issues on a 51-point scale with six positions defined at equal intervals: "Extremely in favor," "Very much in favor," "Somewhat in favor," "Somewhat against," "Very much against," and "Extremely against." The subjects were all at the negative end of the scale on all five issues.

Three weeks after the initial attitude measure on these issues, each student was asked to write an essay supporting one side or the other on each of the issues. This was done under the guise of a survey being carried out by a student for his honors research project under the auspices of "The Institute of Human Relations." It was "aimed at obtaining a clear and objective view of students' opinions for and against these proposals." All subjects were told that essays supporting both sides of each issue were being requested, though certain kinds of essays were then needed more than others. Some subjects were then asked to write an essay *supporting* their own position on each of the first four topics (the Preconsonance condition); *other subjects were asked to write an essay opposing their own position on these four topics* (the Predissonance condition). Thus some subjects engaged in behavior consonant with their attitudes; others engaged in behavior dissonant with their attitudes.

For the fifth topic, the elimination of all intercollegiate athletics, *all subjects were told that essays in opposition to their private attitudes were needed.* This topic was selected as the subject of the standard discrepant essay as a result of the following information gathered in the prequestionnaire. Subjects, after giving their opinions on the five topics, were asked to rank the issues from 1 to 5 in terms of "whether you feel strongly about them, that is, would most want to discuss or debate them at length." Since Cohen was interested in selecting a topic that would have some real importance for the subjects but, on the other hand, would not be so involving that it would be impervious to change, the intercollegiate athletics issue, which had received an average ranking of 2.4, was chosen.

Thus, for all subjects, the fifth essay was inconsistent with their attitude. In addition, the subjects who had engaged in consonant or dissonant behavior were divided into two further groups: Some were given low justification for writing the discrepant fifth essay while others were given high justification.

Procedure

The subjects were approached by the experimenter in their dormitory rooms and interviewed one at a time. The experimenter introduced himself as a student working on his honors research paper on a series of problems important to the university administration.

The subjects were requested to write the first four essays in the following manner:

"It is our experience that the best way to get all the relevant arguments on both sides of an issue is to ask people to write a strong essay favoring only *one* side."

In the *Preconsonance* condition, subjects were then told:

"We already have enough essays *favoring* compulsory chapel, coats and ties, language requirements and elimination of cuts. What I really need are more essays against these."

Subjects in the *Predissonance* condition were told:

"We already have enough essays *against* compulsory chapel, coats and ties, language requirements, and elimination of cuts. What I really need now are more essays favoring these."

All subjects were then told:

"I understand that you may have very different views on the matter, but, as you can see, it is very interesting for us to know what kinds of arguments people bring up in their essays if they have very different opinions about it. Now go ahead and write the best essays you can (for) (against) these issues."

After the subjects had completed the first four essays, they were halted and given the following instructions:

"The last issue, having to do with the elimination of intercollegiate competition, is one on which we already have enough essays in support of continuing athletic competition. Here (here too) we need essays in favor of eliminating intercollegiate competition."

Manipulation of the magnitude of dissonance

Approximately half the Predissonance subjects and the Preconsonance subjects were given the high justification manipulation; half were given the low justification manipulation. In the *High Justification* condition, the experimenter said:

"By writing against athletic competition you will help the Institute in its scientific study of such problems and their solutions. It is also important to see both sides of an issue—objective thinking is a great asset in later life. And you will help me a great deal since this experiment is a vital part of my grade, and I have to obtain more essays against athletic competition between schools in order to use it for my honors research. I am completely dependent on you."

In the *Low Justification* condition, these instructions were largely omitted; the experimenter merely said that the subjects would be helping him out by writing the discrepant essay.

The subjects were given 5 minutes to write the fifth and discrepant essay (as they were for each of the previous four essays), and after completing this they were handed the postexperimental questionnaire. This questionnaire measured only their attitudes toward intercollegiate athletics and contained a scale identical to the one on the prequestionnaire. After they indicated their attitudes, the subjects were given measures designed to check on the success of the experimental manipulations and to gather data on modes of dissonance reduction other than attitude change. The items were 51-point scales with six points identified. To measure changes in perceived obligation as a mode of dissonance reduction, the subject was asked, "To what extent did you feel obliged to write the *fifth essay* on athletic competition against your initial position?" This scale ran from "Extremely obliged" to "Not at all obliged." It was assumed that this obligation measure could also serve as a general indication of the degree to which the justification manipulation was successful. To check on the Predissonance and Preconsonance manipulations, subjects were asked: How were your first four essays written? on a scale which ran from "Very strongly *against* own position" to "Very strongly *in favor of* own position." After the subjects had filled out these items, the experiment was terminated, and they were told about it in as much detail as was deemed feasible.

In summary, then, some students wrote consonant essays and were then given high or low justification for writing a dissonant essay; other students wrote dissonant essays and were then given high or low justification for writing another dissonant essay.

Results

The postexperimental questionnaire checks on the manipulations indicate that they were highly successful. In regard to the first four essays, subjects in the Preconsonance condition felt that they had written essays strongly in favor of their own positions, and subjects in the Predissonance condition felt that they had written essays strongly against their private attitudes. With one indicating an essay very strongly in favor of own attitude and six an essay very strongly against own attitude, the means for the Preconsonance conditions are 1.87 and 1.72; for the Predissonance conditions they are 4.87 and 4.91. The difference between practice conditions is significant at less than the .001 level by t test. If the obligation measure can be taken to indicate the degree to which subjects felt compelled to participate in writing the fifth discrepant essay, it can provide some information on the success of the justification manipulation. With a score of one signifying low obligation and a score of 6 high obligation, the means for the Low Justification conditions are 3.41 and 2.85; for the High Justification conditions, they are 4.14 and 4.21. The difference between justification conditions is significant at less than the .01 level by t test.

The major concern in this study is with the effect of the repeated consonant and dissonant experiences (Preconsonant and Predissonant conditions) on reactions to the final dissonance-arousal situation. Since the latter involved the writing of an essay discrepant with private attitudes, it would ordinarily be expected that subjects would show some attitude change toward the position supported in the essay. Furthermore, such change would be expected to be inversely proportional to the force inducing the discrepant essay. Hence attitude change should be positive and greater in magnitude in the Low Justification condition than in the High. This expectation applies directly to subjects in the Preconsonance condition, for they are, theoretically, in a situation that has been shown by previous research to produce dissonance and consequent attitude change. The interest, then, centers on the comparative reactions of subjects in the Predissonance condition. These subjects may, as noted before, react either more or less strongly because of having experienced a series of situations that presumably created dissonance.

In Table 5 are presented the Ns,[4] initial scores, and attitude change scores for each of the experimental conditions on the intercollegiate athletics issue, the one on which all subjects wrote discrepant essays.

TABLE 5

MEAN INITIAL SCORES AND ATTITUDE CHANGE ON THE FIFTH (DISCREPANT) ISSUE

	High Justification			Low Justification		
	N	Initial	Change	N	Initial	Change
Predissonance	15	1.00	.28 *	10	1.25	−.07
Preconsonance	10	1.63	.13	13	1.39	.62

* A positive value indicates dissonance-reducing change.

The premeasure of attitudes indicates that there was no reliably large difference between any two conditions prior to the experimental treatment: The means for the four experimental conditions are extremely negative, and none of them is reliably different from another. An analysis of variance performed on the data in Table 5 indicates that while there was no main effect of the justification manipulation ($F = .08$), the main effect of practice and the interaction between practice and justification were both significant (Practice $F = 4.73$, $p < .05$; Practice $\times$ Justification $F = 8.53$, $p < .01$).

As was expected for the Preconsonance condition, there is greater positive attitude change among those subjects receiving low justification than among those receiving high justification. In the Predissonance condition, however, there is essentially no effect of the justification ma-

[4] This experiment was run by two Es working simultaneously. Although they each contributed approximately equally to each experimental condition and although there were no reliable differences between Es, a procedural error over the number of subjects in each condition halfway through the experiment was responsible for the unequal Ns in the experimental conditions.

nipulation (the only difference being a slight trend in the negative direction), nor is there evidence of any attitude change consistent with attempts to reduce dissonance. As was said, the analysis of variance test of the interaction indicated that the justification manipulation had less of the predicted inverse effect in the Predissonance condition than in the Preconsonance condition. Thus, at least under the present conditions, repeated but essentially unrelated dissonances minimize the effect of a subsequent dissonance.

It should also be noted that within the Low Justification condition (high dissonance) there is a difference in perceived obligation to take the discrepant stand: The Predissonance subjects perceived that they were obliged more than the Preconsonance subjects (3.41 vs. 2.85; $p < .05$). The fact that the Predissonance subjects were requested to write four discrepant essays prior to the central attitude issue, while the Preconsonance subjects had only to write the last one in a discrepant manner, may have increased their sense of being forced.

On the other hand, change in obligation may be viewed as a potential mode of dissonance reduction, either complementary to or substitutive for attitude change. In the present experiment, given this difference in obligation, it may be assumed that the Predissonance subjects reduced their dissonance in this manner more than the Preconsonance subjects and therefore did not use the avenue of attitude change. Thus the differences in attitude change ($-.07$ for the Predissonance subjects; .62 for the Preconsonance subjects) may be comprehensible not only in terms of differential prior experience in reducing dissonance but perhaps even more because of the differential use of the avenue of perceived obligation as a mode of dissonance reduction. Once having reduced dissonance by increasing their perception of obligation, they may have had less need to do so via attitude change. It is also possible, of course, that increased perception of obligation is a more facile mode of dissonance reduction than attitude change, which demands a more complex reorganization of cognitions.

In any case, it may be well to dwell for a moment on the conditions under which this test occurred, particularly since there are no other data to help clarify the problems. First of all, it should be noted that the dissonance-arousal situations are not entirely dissimilar. They all involved writing an essay discrepant with one's private attitude, the only difference being the issue on which the essay was written. Although this relative similarity of dissonance-arousal conditions may make no difference conceptually, since the theory would not treat them as similar, it may make a difference in terms of the setting in which the study was done. That is, the issues all concerned possible actions about regulation of student activities by the school administration. Thus, if a student experienced dissonance on writing the first essay, he might have tried to reduce it by convincing himself that the administration is probably correct about such issues. Once he had convinced himself of this, he would experience little or no dissonance nor need to change his attitude on subsequent issues. Similarly, a student might have experienced dissonance on the first essay or two but reduced it by convincing himself that college life should be hard and full of unpleasant regulations. Again, once convinced of this tenet, he would experience little or no dissonance in regard to the final test issue. In short, as far as dissonance theory is concerned the dissonance-arousal situations are similar in that they have some cognitive elements that can overlap, especially in regard to reduction of the dissonances.

A second general characteristic of this test is that the separate dissonance-arousal situations were presented one right after the other. If the obtained phenomenon of reduced reaction to a dissonance-arousal situation depends on a defensive reaction, or even perhaps a tolerance buildup, then it might also depend on this quick succession of events. Where dissonance-arousing situations are more widely spaced, defensive reactions and tolerances might have time to wear off between dissonances.

A third characteristic of this test is that the dissonance aroused by the preliminary essays should have been relatively slight, since there was little or no choice involved in taking the discrepant stand. What might happen with more intense preliminary dissonances is unclear, though the trends in the obtained results would indicate a possible reversal of the ordinary effect of justification.

In conclusion, it remains an open question whether the Low Justification subjects in the Predissonance condition changed less as a result of less dissonance arousal or whether they reduced dissonance via the mode of obligation increase, thereby obviating the need to change their attitudes. The fact that both obligation change and attitude change are inversely related within the practice conditions suggests that the repeated use of attitude change may not be a means of reducing dissonance for the Predissonance subjects but, rather, that they increase their perception of being forced to comply with the discrepant request. Different experiences with dissonance-arousal may make a difference in the particular mechanism of dissonance reduction used by the person. Such a point of view highlights the issue of obligation change as a general response to dissonance arousal.

Theoretical and methodological problems

─7

PROBLEMS IN THE ATTITUDE CHANGE PARADIGM

The discussion of exposure studies in Chapter 4 raises the general question of the value of experiments in the area of communication and opinion change as tests of dissonance theory. Experiments in this area are frequently highly ambiguous because just as they can easily be interpreted in dissonance terms, they can also easily be interpreted in terms of, for example, judgmental processes. Thus we have to contend with the plausibility of other theoretical views.

As we said in Chapter 1, while it is reasonable to speak of dissonance as aroused by any discrepancy between cognitions, the conditions that result once commitment to some discrepant position has occurred provide the most valid tests of the theory, give it its nonobvious flavor, and permit a specification of modes of dissonance reduction. When both judgmental processes and dissonance processes can compete in explaining phenomena, as is the case where commitment is absent, dissonance theory enters a shadowy area insofar as its ease of confirmation is concerned.

It is pertinent here to specify exactly what we mean when we speak of "judgmental processes." Most generally, we refer to the notion of information processing. From such a point of view, any incoming bit of information is given its due, and the individual makes some compromise judgment between the information and his existing cognitions or between bits of information inconsistent with each other and with his existing cognitions. The analogy here is to some estimate he makes of all the various cognitions, to some arithmetic average of his cognitions.

On the other hand, an unequivocal dissonance process exists, it seems to us, when there is some commitment to a given position. Once this occurs, the person cannot process information and make some compromise judgment; he must accommodate his cognitions to his commitment. In effect, one pole of the inconsistency is now fixed. The person then either defends the new position to which he is committed and, for example, rationalizes in the face of discrepant information, or, if he can, he may uncommit himself, that is, say he was wrong. However, if he cannot do the latter, then he may have to show some change in his cognitive alignments.

The point here is that dissonance processes have the flavor of an either-or phenomenon; judgmental processes, on the other hand, admit of compromise all along the information continuum. Dissonance implies a distortion or discontinuity due to the commitment; the person may go too far and may overestimate change from one extreme position to another, end up advocating what he has disliked, and so forth. The judgmental process, unlike the dissonance process, implies a more "rational" assessment of different pieces of inconsistent information in terms of existing cognitions, and a resultant compromise solution.

The usual attitude change paradigm in many cases allows an interpretation of data in terms of judgmental processes. An interpretation in terms of dissonance theory, is, in this light, equivocal, unless certain special dissonance-reduction effects are shown. Thus studies in this area are equivocal, not because they do not involve discrepant cognitions but because they often do not present any effects that are not amenable to reinterpretation by means of judgmental assumptions.

The question we may ask here is, what could dissonance theory say about attitude change that a judgmental approach could not? The answer to this question centers on what one wants to do with a given study. If one merely intends to demonstrate a phenomenon, such general attitude-change studies may be adequate. But, if the goal is to test the theory, to rule out plausible alternative explanations, then attitude-change experiments must be created in such a way as to enable one to rule out judgmental explanations.

The typical paradigm for the study of attitude-change phenomena utilizes one or more experimental conditions (and perhaps one or more controls) to see what changes in the communicator, communication, or communicatee affect the amount of attitude change in the communicatee. When such a paradigm is used, the results can often be understood quite plausibly in terms of a judgmental or rational response to the experimental situation. Thus Hovland and his associates (e.g., Hovland, Janis and Kelley, 1953; Anderson and Hovland, 1957; Hovland, Harvey and Sherif, 1957; Sherif, Taub and Hovland, 1958) have suggested various implications of judgmental processes to explain attitude-change phenomena. Not only have considerable supporting data been collected, but this approach is rather straightforward in its simple form. That is, if a person is exposed to facts and arguments presented by a credible communicator, it is entirely plausible to assume that he will somehow crank this information into what he knows about the issue and then come up with a judgmental, compromise view between what he initially thought and what the communicator advocated. Furthermore, the extent of his change will clearly be a function of how sound is the communication to which he is exposed: The facts and arguments must be clear and cogent; the source must be expert, honest, and fair.

This judgmental view of attitude change can easily be applied to almost all phenomena of attitude change. We do not imply that it is always, or even most of the time, the most convincing interpretation, but it is one with which the investigator of attitude-change phenomena must contend. However, before we see how this view applies to research on dissonance theory, let us inspect the special problems of making an unequivocal interpretation from the dissonance-theory point of view.

As with the foregoing discussion of ambiguous conditions, one way we can proceed is to establish the conditions of *commitment*. In regard to much attitude-change research, however, we will have difficulty in establishing whether or not these conditions obtain. In the first place, a person's having an opinion or attitude on an issue is not enough to guarantee any kind of commitment. Indeed, just as the judgmental view assumes attitudes to be judgmental phenomena, so dissonance theory has to assume that they are *commitment* phenomena. But it seems unreasonable to assume that either assumption is always correct. Furthermore, it is not particularly clear exactly when having a given position on an issue will carry some commitment. Thus the establishment of commitment in attitude-change research is difficult, if not impossible, without some explicit attempt on the part of the investigator to measure or manipulate it.

Clearly many of the attitude-change researches provide little or no opportunity for the person to make some discrepant commitment, thereby endowing with some equivocality the identification of dissonance arousal in these experiments. Included here would be much of the research conducted by Hovland and his associates (e.g., 1949, 1953) in military and school settings, for their typical setting is that of a completely captive audience (see Hovland, 1959). With no choice about whether or not to expose oneself to the communication either beforehand or during exposure, the subject has no experience of choice in committing himself. Hence we would expect little or no dissonance arousal in this latter type of setting.

In this light let us examine some relevant research. The first example of a study in the attitude-change framework is Zimbardo's (1960) experiment on involvement and communication discrepancy. In this experiment, attitude change increased with increasing involvement and discrepancy. However, the point we wish to make here is that the effect of the discrepancy manipulation on judgmental change can be interpreted plausibly in terms of a purely judgmental effect. It can be argued that subjects in the high discrepancy condition received stronger or more compelling information in support of a different position from their own than did those in the low discrepancy condition. The discrepancy variation is thus likened to the difference between compromise judgments for two different sets of information: one set consisting of relatively homogeneous data, the other of heterogeneous data. For example, a person asked to average values of two and six will say something in the neighborhood of four. The process is purely judgmental and neither requires nor benefits from an explanation in terms of motives aroused by the size of discrepancy between the values.

At the same time, the effect of the importance manipulation on change in judgment provides some evidence that dissonance does occur in this type of situation and produces at least part of the change in judgment. For the difference in judgmental change as a function of importance implies a motivational effect and at the same time includes no differential information. However, another kind of explanation could be invoked. It may be that the high and low importance conditions are simply high and low relevance issues for the highly cohesive two-person group (the pair of friends). Thus the tendency for the subject to change her judgment toward the position held by her friend could be due to the perception that such change would aid group locomotion, to a desire to please the friend in order to remain close to her, to a desire to be like the friend because she is admirable in other ways, and so on. Although Festinger has asserted that many such group-influence processes can be explained in terms of dissonance theory

(1957, pp. 230ff), it can also be argued that there are group-influence processes distinct from dissonance. Only further research can settle this ambiguity. Until such data are forthcoming, the acceptance of the above experimental data as support for dissonance theory can be made only with due caution.

A second example of a study utilizing the attitude-change paradigm in relation to dissonance theory is the previously cited study by Allyn and Festinger (1961). Allyn and Festinger conclude that their results are consistent with dissonance theory; when forewarned that a speaker has views clearly discrepant from their own views on an issue, subjects will reduce dissonance through rejection of the communicator, but when not forewarned, subjects will reduce dissonance through opinion change.

But let us consider whether or not the conditions of this study really meet the conditions necessary for the arousal of dissonance. It is clear that the subjects *may* have been committed to their own positions. However, it is equally clear that they had no opportunity to commit themselves one way or another in regard to listening to the talk. Thus we would expect that little or no dissonance would be aroused in this experimental situation. How, then, might one explain the obtained effects? There is, of course, considerable ambiguity about the interpretation of these data, for the results appear to be readily understandable in terms of a judgmental process of attitude change. Subjects who were forewarned were told, in effect, that the communicator had a strongly biased position. Therefore, it could be, for example, that the communicator was seen as less trustworthy to those subjects who were warned that he had an extreme position than to the subjects told to note his personality. This could be true simply because one learns to distrust people who have an axe to grind: One suspects their facts, their arguments, their conclusions, and their fairness in presentation of both sides. Hence the same persuasive communication will have less effect to the extent that the communicator is seen as untrustworthy. As shown in previous research (e.g., Hovland and Mandell, 1952), the amount of opinion change produced by a communication is directly proportional to the credibility of the communicator.

In the study under discussion, if the subjects who were warned did indeed see the communicator as less trustworthy than did the other subjects, then they would presumably have been less influenced by his persuasive effort, as, in fact, they were. While a postexperimental question shows that a greater percentage of the warned than of the unwarned subjects thought the communication was biased, this effect is consistent with both the dissonance and the judgmental interpretations.

Without further clarification, the present data can be taken as consistent with dissonance theory but not as strongly supportive.

However, while the major results of this study can be interpreted in terms of a judgmental view as well as in terms of dissonance theory, let us see whether, through further exploration, we can find data to distinguish between the two. Allyn and Festinger analyzed their data according to the subjects' initial position on the issue on the assumption that this would reflect differences due to the importance of the relevant cognitions. They found a greater difference between experimental conditions for those who were extreme (thought the issue relatively important), but a judgmental view would also hold that opinion change can be proportional to the importance of the issue. On the other hand, this same breakdown of subjects failed to show differential rejection of the communicator, which is clearly inconsistent with dissonance theory and is, at the same time, *precisely what one would expect in terms of the judgmental interpretation.* A judgmental interpretation may therefore be more cogent than a dissonance interpretation.

The relevance of the issues of commitment and choice in this general area can be further illustrated by the exposure studies of Cohen (1959b), and Cohen, Terry and Jones (1959). In both studies, subjects experienced a good deal of choice in "exposing" themselves to information that they knew to be discrepant from their own attitude positions. In the first study, choice in exposure to a discrepant communication was manipulated directly. Under low choice conditions, a direct resistance effect seems to be able to account for the results: Subjects changed less toward the communicator, the more discrepant his position. Under conditions of high choice, however, we would expect dissonance when the subject commits himself to exposure; the more discrepant the information, the greater the dissonance over exposure. We would thus expect the subjects in the high choice conditions to change more toward the communicator, the greater the discrepancy between their own positions and that of the communicator. The results bear out this expectation from dissonance theory.

In the second exposure study, subjects agreed to work on a communication they knew to be discrepant from their own positions. It would be expected that the more effort they expended to "understand" it, the more dissonance should have been produced through commitment to exposure to the contrary information. When dissonance was produced through effort, the subjects were expected to show more dissonance and consequent attitude change, the more discrepant their own initial opinions from those of the communicator. When there was little effort and no resultant dissonance, subjects were expected to show a resistance effect: They were expected to change less, the more discrepant they were from the communicator. The results are consistent with these hypotheses.

What these studies illustrate is that when subjects commit themselves to exposure to a piece of discrepant information, dissonance is aroused by the *inconsistency between their commitment behavior and their initial attitudes* and not by the inconsistency between the communication and their initial attitudes. They can then only change their attitudes in line with the communication to which they have exposed themselves, and do so differentially, depending on the amount of dissonance they have experienced. It is this sort of situation that is entirely closed to the judgmental interpretation and rather unequivocally explainable by the dissonance formulation.

If one adopts this particular perspective in regard to the Allyn and Festinger experiment, it is possible to indicate just how an unequivocal dissonance effect could have been produced in a way contrary to the expectations of Allyn and Festinger. Had the situation been arranged so that the subjects, after being forewarned about the speaker's discrepant views, could choose to hear the discrepant information, or agree to work over it, or get involved with it in some way, they would have been committed to exposure to it to one degree or another. Under these conditions, dissonance theory would say that the fewer the cognitions supporting this commitment (the more negative the communicator in the forewarning condition), the *greater* the dissonance experienced and the greater the resultant attitude change. Thus an entirely nonobvious derivation from the theory is possible once the variable of commitment is specified, at least concerning exposure to discrepant communications. The generalization that the more negative, incredible, or disliked the communicator is, the more will persons change toward his position when they have committed themselves to exposure to it is entirely consistent with the host of evidence from the "forced-compliance" studies (e.g., Smith, 1961). Though this generalization has not been tested directly and may be difficult to operationalize, it does indicate the difference between the approach we have taken and that taken by Allyn and Festinger in their "exposure" study.

In general, it seems to us that the Allyn and Festinger study did not provide the conditions necessary for an unequivocal test of dissonance theory. In particular, it failed to give the subjects some degree of opportunity to commit themselves with regard to the dissonant information; it also failed to insure that the subjects were committed to their initial positions (though we may fairly safely assume they were).

Hence, though its results are largely consistent with a dissonance-theory analysis, it cannot be considered as unequivocal evidence for the theory in this problem area. It does, however, serve to show the difficulty of applying dissonance theory in the area of attitude-change phenomena. At the risk of being repetitive, then, we repeat that if the condition of *commitment* is clearly provided, then we may consider an empirical test unequivocally relevant to the arousal of dissonance.

Gerard's (1961) conformity experiment provides an illustration, within the framework of a single study, of the manner in which discrepant commitment may aid in separating and distinguishing dissonance effects from judgmental effects. For the subjects who were led to believe that they conformed to the group (i.e., acted in a manner inconsistent with their perceptions of the physical stimulus), dissonance was aroused; the higher their ability, the more the dissonance and consequent attraction and conformity to the group. On the other hand, those subjects who were led to believe that they had not conformed (i.e., had acted in a manner consistent with their perception of the physical stimulus) experienced no dissonance over their perceptual judgments (which were presumably related to the ability dimension), though they may have experienced some to the degree that they sought approval from others (presumably related to factors other than ability). For the non-conformers, the higher their ability, the *less* attractive they found the group that communicated the discrepant information and the *less* they were influenced by this group on a subsequent conformity trial. These results for the nonconformers may perhaps be interpreted as instances of the straightforward effect of judgment on attitude change and the conformity process: Those subjects who felt themselves more able discounted the source of discrepant information more than those with lesser ability. Thus commitment to a discrepant position will clearly produce dissonance; mere exposure to discrepant information may only produce a judgmentally determined effect.

The main point of our present discussion is that if one is trying to collect evidence in support of dissonance theory, it is difficult to do so with the conventional attitude-change paradigm. These attitude-change studies generally do not provide strong support for the theory. It may not be enough simply to say that dissonance will lead to attitude change when someone is presented with a persuasive communication. This is a fact with which all social psychologists are familiar, and many different theoretical models have been mobilized to explain it. To make a strong test of the theory it is necessary to point out more subtle implications, which are not covered by other views of the attitude-change process.

Our position is that one of the implications of dissonance theory that does not overlap with other models of attitude change concerns the role of commitment to a discrepant position. It is with commitment that the either-or response to incoming information so characteristic of dissonance theory is produced. Such a response is not what one might expect from other models of the attitude-change process. When commitment is present, there are differential implications of dissonance theory and, for example, judgmental models of attitude change; when commitment is absent, it is not clear that there are differential implications of dissonance and judgmental theory or, perhaps, even that dissonance theory has anything special at all to say.

BEHAVIORAL COMMITMENT

As we have seen in the gambling experiments of Festinger and of Cohen, Brehm and Latané, dissonance is frequently reduced or eliminated by a change in one's behavior. That is, whenever one behaves in a way that follows from the obverse of one or more cognitions that one holds, a simple way to reduce the resultant dissonance may be to stop behaving in that manner. The behavior can either be eliminated or changed to its obverse.

However, another use of behavior to reduce dissonance is most relevant here. This use, though mentioned earlier (Rabbie, Brehm and Cohen, 1959; Brehm, 1960a), has not been made explicit in the literature. It concerns the reduction of dissonance by commitment to increased behavior of the same kind that arouses the initial dissonance.

Suppose, for example, that a person commits himself to saying something discrepant with his private attitude. The resultant dissonance could ordinarily be reduced by change in the private attitude toward the assumed position, by magnification of the rewards to be gained or punishments to be avoided, and so on. It is a noteworthy point, however, that, in general, the behavior in which this person has engaged may have manifold possible justifications or purposes. That is, there are numerous ways in which the individual can justify engaging in the behavior. Almost anything that he can make relevant to the particular behavior in which he has engaged can be used in justifying it. Thus the individual may reduce his dissonance by finding and/or changing the magnitude of one or more such justifications. Since it is essentially impossible to detect and measure all such dimensions in a given experiment on dissonance, there is no guarantee that the experimental data will reflect this kind of reduction in any way other than by measurement of the amount of behavior to which the individual is willing or desirous of committing himself. At the same time, however, the experimenter may well measure such relevant variables as change in the attitude with which the initial dissonance is aroused. If it happens that the experimental subject is resistant to change on that particular attitude, he may seek out other modes of dissonance reduction, such as those suggested above. Thus he would tend to show little or no attitude change *but would have an increased desire to engage in the discrepant behavior.*

Change in desire to engage in a dissonance-arousing behavior need not depend on obscure justifications for the behavior: It can arise from increased liking for the behavior itself. It must be clear, however, that even when liking for the behavior itself would be difficult, there will almost inevitably be other, possibly idiosyncratic, justifications that can be found.

One implication of this point is that experimental evidence on the effects of behavioral commitment may result in negative correlations within conditions between attitude change and amount of the dissonant behavior in which the individual is willing to engage. If, as in the verbal compliance studies (e.g., Rabbie, Brehm and Cohen, 1959), the individual is left free to engage in as much of the discrepant behavior as he wants, then those who are resistant to changing their attitudes may well reduce dissonance by justifying the behavior more directly (as would be true with increased liking for the behavior) and thus engage in more of the verbal behavior than those less resistant to attitude change. Hence, to the extent that the initial decision to engage in the discrepant verbal behavior creates dissonance, there will tend to be a negative correlation between attitude change and strength of verbal behavior. It must be noted, however, that this prediction of a negative relationship depends explicitly on individual differences in resistance to change of the attitude (or whatever other major mode of dissonance reduction that is available). Although there could easily be variations in the extent to which persons would reduce their dissonance by increased justification of the discrepant behavior itself, such variations would not necessarily correlate with change in the attitude around which the dissonance was aroused.

Another facet of cognitive change concerns one's future behavior. If a certain kind of behavior would help to reduce dissonance, but is difficult or impossible at the moment, the intention or implicit commitment to execute it in the future may serve the purpose of reducing dissonance. For example, the experiment by Davis and Jones (1960) found that the promise of changing the behavior in the future resulted in less attitude change toward support of the behavior.

Another test of the implications of dissonance theory for behavioral change can be found in Gerard's (1961) aforementioned "forced-compliance" experiment on ability and induced conformity. It will be remembered that the subjects were first fed information as to their ability and then were made to believe that their true impulses were either to conform to or deviate from the group in an Asch-type situation. The measure of evaluation of the group taken after the conformity trials showed, as we noted, changes in attraction to the group as a central mode of the reduction of dissonance in this experimental situation. However, after the measures of attraction were taken, subjects were then placed in a "free" conformity situation where they were allowed to respond freely over a series of trials to stimuli presented within the group context. The data show that those subjects who did not reduce the dissonance between their apparent conformity and their ability by increasing their attraction to the group *actually did conform more* in a series of free trials where they could have behaved in any manner they chose. Thus they actually made their subsequent free conformity behavior consistent with their prior apparent (manipulated) conformity; they reduced the dissonance between their prior apparent conformity and high ability by actually behaving in a manner that demonstrated their closeness to the group. This result may be interpreted as some form of dissonance reduction through justification of the conforming behavior itself. Since the behavior is justified directly, there is no need to reduce dissonance in less direct modes, such as through attraction to the group members. But the direct justification will lead the individual to engage in the behavior (of conforming) again when he is given the opportunity.

COMMITMENT WITHOUT BEHAVIOR

Dissonance theory is somewhat ambiguous on the point of whether or not discrepant behavior need actually be engaged in in order to produce dissonance. However, it would appear that mere commitment to a decision to take a discrepant stand may be sufficient to produce dissonance and consequent attitude change. Evidence for this comes from the previously mentioned "forced-compliance" experiments by Brehm (pp. 84–88), Brehm and Cohen (1959b), Brock and Blackwood (in press), Rabbie, Brehm and Cohen (1959). In the Rabbie et al. experiment, it will be remembered, all subjects under different conditions of inducement agreed to write an essay in favor of a position with which they strongly disagreed. After committing themselves, half the subjects were first given an attitude measure and then asked to write their essays; the other half, in the conventional procedure, were first asked to write their essays and were then given the attitude measure. The results indicated that greater attitude change was produced under the theoretically appropriate inducement conditions (i.e., greater change under low justification than high) even where subjects had not yet actually engaged in the discrepant behavior but had merely committed themselves to it.

In the Brock and Blackwood (in press) experiment, justification for compliance with the request to write an essay against one's position on an important issue was manipulated. Once the subjects had committed themselves to writing the discrepant essay and had written the essay title on a blank page and signed their names to it, they were asked to fill out a postexperimental questionnaire concerning their attitudes, *before actually going ahead with the essay.* The data showed that the subjects in the low justification conditions indicated more favorable attitudes toward the discrepant position than those in the high justification conditions, even though they had not actually engaged in the behavior itself.

The relative deprivation study by Brehm and Cohen (1959b) also showed the effects of commitment without behavior. Having agreed to spend 3 hours in a boring, tedious, and profitless task, the subjects were told that they would be deprived relative to others who were also to participate in the task. Their attitudes toward participation in the task were then measured before they actually engaged in the task. The results showed that under conditions where the subjects perceived some choice in participating in the task, they experienced greater dissonance and consequent attitude change, the higher the relative deprivation.

Finally, the coercion experiment by Brehm (see pp. 84–88) showed that subjects became favorable to participation in a boring, tedious, and profitless task in inverse proportion to the coercive force making them participate, even when they had not yet engaged in the task but had merely committed themselves to it.

These results serve to demonstrate that commitment to a discrepant, dissonance-producing stand, without the subsequent discrepant behavior, may be sufficient to produce dissonance and consequent attitude change. These findings, although not explicitly handled by the present dissonance formulation, are entirely consistent with the data from the experiments on "free choice" that we presented earlier. In some of these experiments, it will be recalled, revaluation due to dissonance reduction occurred as a function of choice, even where subjects had not yet had any experience with the alternatives they had chosen.

THE EFFECTS OF DISCREPANT VERBAL BEHAVIOR

Assuming that attitude-discrepant behavior need not actually be engaged in in order to produce dissonance and attitude change, it seems appropriate to turn now to an examination of the effects on attitude change when the person *does* actually engage in the discrepant behavior to which he has committed himself.

Two "forced-compliance" studies (Cohen, Brehm and Fleming, 1958; Festinger and Carlsmith, 1959), while they have supported dissonance theory to one degree or another, have also produced specific effects that apparently relate to discrepant behavior *per se*. Since one theoretical derivation is that (other things constant) the magnitude of dissonance will vary directly with the amount of discrepant behavior, we would not be surprised to find that within an experimental condition involving discrepant behavior there was a positive relationship between the number or variety of arguments given by a person and the amount of attitude change he exhibited. In fact, this type of relationship has been observed in these two studies: The greater the discrepant behavior, the greater the attitude change, so that one's private view becomes more consistent with the persuasion. On the other hand, there is no obvious theoretical reason to expect a *negative* relationship between amount of discrepant behavior engaged in and amount of attitude change, and it is therefore surprising to find that this relationship, too, has been observed (Rabbie, Brehm and Cohen, 1959).

In an attempt to throw light on the role of discrepant behavior in the dissonance-arousal and reduction process, Rabbie, Brehm and Cohen, in their "forced-compliance" study, had college students commit themselves to writing a discrepant essay and then measured some subjects' attitudes *subsequent* to writing and other subjects' attitudes *prior* to writing. The magnitude of dissonance within each of these two conditions was manipulated by giving subjects either high or low justification for writing the discrepant essay. Thus any of four general effects might be disclosed: (1) The writing of the essay increases the amount of attitude change over that from dissonance alone; (2) It decreases the relative amount of attitude change; and/or (3) There is an interaction between writing of the essay and the magnitude of dissonance in determining the amount of attitude change; and (4) A final possibility is that the actual writing of the essay has no effect on attitude change.

It will be recalled from our earlier descriptions of this study that the postexperimental measure of attitudes was affected as predicted where attitudes were measured prior to the writing of the discrepant essay: low justification produced reliably more positive attitudes than did high justification. Thus the decision to support the discrepant position produced dissonance and consequent attitude change. With this in mind, let us now explore the effects of engaging in the discrepant behavior prior to the attitudinal measure. The data in the Rabbie et al. study show that the mean attitudes of subjects who first wrote the essay hardly differed from the attitudes of those who first responded to the attitude questionnaire. Thus there is no evidence that discrepant behavior *per se* has either a general enhancing or depressing effect on dissonance and consequent attitude change. It was also shown, however, that the difference between the means of the high and low justification conditions for those who first wrote the essay, though in the same direction and of nearly as great magnitude, did not even approach statistical reliability. The reason is simply that the variability of attitudes was much greater among those who first wrote the essay than among those who first gave their attitude. The difference in variance between these two conditions was significant at beyond the 5% level with both low and high justification. We see, therefore, that while discrepant behavior has no *general* effect under these conditions, it does interact with individual differences to increase the variability of response. It seems, then, that discrepant behavior increases *and* decreases reactions to dissonance-arousing situations. We may draw the conclusion that this variability of response is due in some direct way to making discrepant statements but does not depend on the dissonance aroused by the commitment *per se*. The reason is that there is about the same amount of increased variance from writing the essay first regardless of the magnitude of dissonance aroused.

Inspection of within-condition relationships between strength of discrepant behavior and amount of attitude change, not only in this study but also in others using discrepant behavior, fails to reveal systematic effects. This lack of pattern may arise in part from the fact that some studies have used actual change measures while others have used only postexperimental measures in conjunction with control data. In addition, indices of "strength" of discrepant behavior have varied greatly, sometimes derived from subjects' self-ratings, sometimes from a simple count of arguments given, sometimes from a coding of the "quality" or "intensity" or "originality" of the arguments. But the fact remains that relatively strong relationships between strength of discrepant behavior and attitudes or attitude change, sometimes positive and sometimes negative, have been found. In the above "forced-compliance" study (Rabbie, Brehm and Cohen, 1959) there was a *negative* relationship between number of arguments and positiveness of attitude in all four experimental conditions. Although the relationship was not significant in the individual conditions, it was significant at beyond the 2% level when all four conditions were combined. And it should be noted that the negative relationship appeared whether the attitude was measured before or after the essay had been written.

A positive relationship between "original arguments" and amount of attitude change was reported by Cohen, Brehm and Fleming (1958), but in this case it appeared in a relatively low dissonance condition and failed to appear in a relatively high dissonance condition. On the other hand, data from the "forced-compliance" experiment by Festinger and Carlsmith (1959) [5] show that postexperimental attitudes are negatively related to a rating of "number and variety of arguments" in their low dissonance condition but positively related in their high dissonance condition. At the same time, a rating of how convincing the given arguments were failed to relate to the postexperimental attitude in the high dissonance condition and again showed a negative relationship in the low. It should be noted that while relationships from the latter study are fairly strong in magnitude, they are not statistically reliable, for the numbers of subjects within the subcells of the analysis are extremely small.[6]

It is apparent that making discrepant statements affects the amount of attitude change, but how it interacts with dissonance is not clear. Whether the effect is due to changes in the magnitude of dissonance, to changes in the reduction of dissonance through attitude change, or to some altogether extraneous process remains a major problem. Crucial questions arise in regard to why the relationship between strength of discrepant behavior and attitude change should be positive at times and negative at other times.

Another piece of evidence relevant to this puzzling question comes from the previously mentioned "forced-compliance" study by Cohen and Latané (see pp. 88–91), where subjects made speeches over a tape recorder against their positions on compulsory religion courses at Yale. In this experiment there are data relevant to the relationship between perceived strength of discrepant behavior and attitude change. It will be recalled that subjects were given differential choice in taking the discrepant stand. After they made their speeches, a measure

---

[5] These data have been kindly supplied to the authors by Leon Festinger.

[6] In an unpublished "forced verbal compliance" study, Brehm found a *negative* relationship between the number of discrepant arguments and amount of attitude change (as measured by pre- and postexperimental questionnaires) in some conditions but a *positive* relationship in others.

of attitude change was taken, and the subjects were then asked to rate the quality of their speeches. On a six-point *a priori* scale ranging from "Very poor" to "Very good," they rated the degree to which they "presented a sincere, organized and convincing speech."

The data show an interesting relationship between the subjects' ratings of the quality of their speeches and choice in determining the degree of attitude change obtained. When the scores on perceived quality of speech are broken into the best median split and the attitude-change scores are distributed according to both quality of speech and the manipulated choice conditions, there is a significant interaction effect. The data are in Table 6. In this table, the higher the mean value, the more the attitude change in scale points; corresponding Ns are in parentheses.

TABLE 6

MEAN ATTITUDE CHANGE ACCORDING TO CHOICE AND PERCEIVED QUALITY OF SPEECH

| | Quality of Speech | |
CHOICE CONDITION	Low Quality	High Quality
Low Choice	.99 (14)	2.53 (12)
High Choice	2.96 (17)	1.68 (8)

Table 6 shows that in the Low Choice condition, those subjects who said that their speeches were of superior quality tended to change their attitudes more in line with their discrepant stand than those who said their speeches were relatively inferior. However, in the High Choice condition, where more dissonance is experienced, this tendency reverses itself: The better the perceived quality of the speech, the *less* is the change in attitude toward the discrepant stand (interaction $F = 5.82$, $p < .05$). Although the difference between quality conditions is not significant for the High Choice subjects, the quality conditions differ at the .10 level for the Low Choice subjects.

These suggestive data are consistent with the notion that when little dissonance is created because of the relative lack of choice in taking the discrepant stand, the subject begins to experience dissonance when he *makes* his speech; the better his speech is, the more dissonance he is creating between his initial attitude and his behavior and, therefore, the more attitude change he undergoes in order to reduce that dissonance. However, for those subjects who are given a high choice, there remains a good deal of theoretical ambiguity. In this condition, dissonance could have been created by the very act of commitment itself, in which case subjects who changed their attitudes may have done so purely as a result of the decision. But why those subjects who changed more should have said that they made poorer speeches is not at all clear.

These correlational data provide some confirmation by self-report for the theoretically expected positive relationship between discrepant verbal behavior and attitude change found previously. They also provide such confirmation for the surprising inverse relationship between the two, also found previously. At this point, however, we can only recognize that the role of discrepant verbal behavior in the arousal and reduction of dissonance remains unclear.

PROBLEMS IN RESEARCH: SAMPLING, SUBJECT LOSS, AND UNRELIABILITY

In evaluating the adequacy of specific tests of dissonance theory and, by implication, the firmness of the general formulation, it may be helpful to note a number of general methodological problems common to experiments purporting to test dissonance theory.

Perhaps the most general and at the same time most serious problem concerns the loss of subjects that frequently occurs in the running of experiments and in the analysis of data. In "free-choice" experiments this selection takes the form of eliminating those subjects who choose the less attractive of the alternatives offered to them. In "forced-compliance" experiments this selection of subjects takes the form of losing from the experiment those subjects who refuse to commit themselves to whatever the experiment tries to induce. This loss of subjects in either type of paradigm has implications for both the interpretation of effects obtained and for the generalizability of findings. When the loss amounts to only a very small percentage of the total number of subjects, there cannot be much limitation to the usual generalizability of these kinds of laboratory studies (made, as they are, primarily with college undergraduates). But when the loss is of sizable proportions, and especially when the loss is greater in one experimental condition than another, it may constitute a serious weakness in an experimental chain of events said to support the theory.

The typical problem in a "forced-compliance" experiment is that in a low dissonance condition the subject is offered such an attractive reward or is threatened with so much punishment that all subjects comply, while in a high dissonance condition the subject is offered just enough to get him to comply; and for some subjects this "just enough" is not enough and they decide not to comply. Although a certain amount of cajoling by the experimenter has been used to keep disinclined subjects in the high dissonance conditions (e.g., Festinger and Carlsmith, 1959), the subject must be given the impression that he does not have to commit himself if he is to experience high dissonance. In other words, the experimenter is confronted with the problem of how to give subjects the impression that they do not have to participate and yet get all subjects to commit themselves to participation. Because this aspect of dissonance theory is unique among psychological theories that have been put to experimental test, there is no precedent on how to cope with this dilemma. The use of impromptu encouragement by the experimenter not only carries certain vagaries of its own but also has not even been completely successful in eliminating loss of subjects. Typically, then, even when the experimenter varies the number of his attempts to keep subjects in the experiment according to their resistance, more subjects will be lost in a high than in a low dissonance condition.

One consequence of this differential loss is that "certain kinds of persons" fail to get included in high dissonance conditions but remain in low dissonance conditions. Though this bias alone may not explain the usual effects of "forced-compliance" studies, it does allow the possibility that certain kinds of people would not react in the typical way. Thus where differential loss occurs, it forces a caution on generalizability, even though it may not permit the formulation of specific, theoretical limits to generalization.

A more serious possibility from differential loss of subjects is that dependent variables may be directly affected. Suppose, for example, that subjects are to be induced to write essays counter to their private opinions. Those offered a large incentive for doing so all comply, and then their opinions are measured. Those offered a minimal incentive (in order to create high dissonance) will split, with some complying and some not complying. But only those who comply are considered usable subjects, and so their postcompliance opinions are compared with those of the subjects given the high incentive. But which subjects are most likely to have been excluded from the high dissonance condition? The best guess is those whose opinions most strongly opposed the position taken in the essay. Since comparable subjects in the low dissonance condition are still included, the average opinion for this group would now be less favorable toward the position taken in the essay than would the average opinion in the high dissonance condition, in which the extreme subjects have been excluded. In short, the loss of more subjects from the high dissonance condition than from the low should automatically result in a difference between the two groups in where they stand on the opinion issue. This automatic difference is in the same direction as would occur if there were dissonance arousal and reduction by opinion change toward support of the compliant behavior. Hence a difference consistent with the dissonance hypothesis would appear whether there were any attempted dissonance reduction or not. And the greater the amount of differential loss of subjects between high and low dissonance conditions, the greater the danger that an automatic difference would occur. It may be noted, parenthetically, that a similar ambiguity may arise even without differential loss of subjects between conditions if there is considerable loss, since the loss in different conditions might be for different reasons.

But there are ways of combatting these problems. It may be possible, for example, to demonstrate that the final difference between conditions is greater than could reasonably be accounted for simply by loss of subjects. Furthermore, a measure of *change* on the dependent variable from before to after the presumed dissonance arousal eliminates much of the ambiguity, for it is less plausible to argue that elimination of the subjects with extreme opinions increases the amount of automatic change toward the opposing position. And with change scores as well as with final scores it may be possible to demonstrate that more has happened than is reasonable to expect from loss of subjects alone.

Similar problems beset the experimenter who uses a "free-choice" paradigm. And the problems are magnified because high dissonance is created by giving the subject a choice between two alternatives that are only slightly different in rated attractiveness. If the subject chooses the alternative he has rated as lower, then the experimenter is in the dilemma of not knowing whether the subject's preferences are inaccurately reflected by his ratings, his preferences have changed since the ratings were made, or the subject has made an error in his choice. To consider these possibilities in reverse order, if the subject has made an error, then his choice may make a good test of the theory or it may not, depending on how he decides to reduce dissonance. For he should experience very high dissonance from having chosen the less attractive alternative, and if he tries to reduce that dissonance through revaluation of the alternative, there would clearly need to be considerable and striking revaluation in favor of the chosen one. But he also may reduce dissonance by admitting the error of choice, in which case there would be little or no revaluation of alternatives. On the other hand, if the subject simply changed his preference between making his ratings and making his choice, we would not be surprised to find that his postchoice ratings were switched so that the chosen alternative was now marked as the more attractive. But this change in rating would not necessarily indicate attempts at dissonance reduction, for the switch would have appeared in the ratings just prior to the choice if the ratings had been obtained again at that time. So the experimenter does not know if a switch in ratings reflects change in preference or that plus dissonance reduction.

Furthermore, of at least equal concern is the possibility that the ratings are simply not well related to the preferences. That is, it can easily happen that the subject will rate alternatives according to how attractive they are to him, but then choose one because of reasons irrelevant to the ratings. The problem is one of defining and measuring the factors that guide choice. But given that a subject may and sometimes will choose on a different basis from his ratings, what problems are raised for the experimenter working with the "free-choice" paradigm? Theoretically the problem is that the subject's rating cannot be considered relevant to his choice behavior and will therefore not tend to reflect attempts at dissonance reduction if they occur. In addition, the magnitude of dissonance resulting from the choice cannot be estimated because the ratings on which estimates are based are irrelevant. Pre- to post-choice changes in these ratings, then, are not likely to furnish a good test of the hypothesis that a choice creates dissonance and consequent revaluations of the choice alternatives.

From the preceding discussion we can see that the subject's choice of the less attractive alternative creates multiple ambiguities about interpreting pre- to postchoice changes in ratings of the alternatives. Consequently, the usual practice in "free-choice" experiments has been to delete the data for those subjects who show such reversals of choice. Although this practice seems justified in light of the above considerations, it creates further problems of its own. The problems created are not unlike those involved in the loss of subjects in "forced-compliance" experiments discussed earlier. They include differential loss of subjects between conditions when the dissonance manipulation consists of varying the difference in attractiveness between the alternatives, since nearly equal alternatives are more likely to result in a reversed choice than are clearly unequal alternatives. In the "free-choice" paradigm, however, the differential loss of subjects does not necessarily have quite the same implications about the "kind of person" whose representation is lost in the high dissonance condition. For the losses occur not because a person has a strong set of cognitive elements that would be dissonant with the commitment, as is true in the "forced-compliance" paradigm, but rather because of one or more of the reasons discussed above: Ratings are invalid, preferences are unreliable, or the choice is in error. But loss of subjects for these reasons would not seem to place any severe limitation on the significance of findings in support of the theory. What does have serious implication for interpretation of supportive findings, however, is the same kind of automatic production of effects as was seen to occur in regard to the "forced-compliance" model: Included among those subjects who would tend to reverse their choice from their ratings are those whose preference for the initially more attractive alternative has fallen and/or whose preference for the initially less attractive alternative has risen. The greater loss of such subjects from a high dissonance condition than from a low would mean that the average postchoice rating of the initially higher alternative would automatically be higher, and the average postchoice rating of the initially lower alternative would automatically be lower, in the high dissonance condition than in the low. Hence, having solved some ambiguities by deletion of subjects who show choice reversals, the experimenter is faced with the dilemma of not being sure that pre- to postchoice evaluative changes consistent with the predictions of dissonance theory are really due to dissonance.

A solution to this problem may not always be obvious or readily available. The problem of differential loss of subjects may be attacked by comparing the variance of change scores in a low dissonance condition with that of change scores for *all* subjects (including those deleted for reversal of choice) in the high dissonance condition. The assumption is that if subjects' preferences changed, or if they made errors of choice, the rejection of the initially more attractive alternative would still produce dissonance, which, in these cases, would tend to result in lowered valuation of it. Since subjects who make the expected choice of selecting the alternative initially marked higher would be expected to raise their rating of that alternative, the change scores of this group would tend to go up. Hence the change scores for both selectors and rejectors would, if dissonance were operating, tend to diverge. It is possible that this divergence would be revealed by a comparison of the variance of change scores of the high dissonance subjects with that of the lows.

This particular attack on the problem of differential selection is not, however, completely satisfactory. In the first place, the power of this test to detect different reactions on the part of rejectors and selectors within the high dissonance condition depends closely on the proportion of subjects who reject (reverse their choice). A small proportion of rejectors can have little effect on the variance of change scores for the whole group. Unless the proportion of rejectors approaches half of the high dissonance subjects, this test would not be likely to reveal differences in rating changes even if they were there.

The second drawback for this attack on the problem of differential loss is that it assumes the ratings are valid. As previously noted, if the ratings are invalid, then they would not be expected to reflect attempted dissonance reduction, no matter which alternative were chosen. Of course, this consideration would be of little consequence if there were few subjects whose ratings were invalid. Unfortunately, however, it seems likely that invalidity of ratings can be a major cause of choice reversal. That is, at least with the kinds of ratings obtained in "free-choice" studies, it seems more plausible to assume that the ratings were of low validity than it does to assume that preferences change within the few minutes between ratings and choice or that actual errors in choice occurred. In summary, then, the technique of comparing variances of the rating change scores is likely to be a weak method for determining whether or not dissonance is operating, at least to the extent that the cause of choice reversal is low validity of ratings.

The "free-choice" studies reviewed in this book generally suffer from one or more of the ambiguities we have been discussing. A certain amount of tolerance for such ambiguities seems appropriate in the stages of early investigation of a novel theory. But continued research with the same types of ambiguities would hardly be excusable, and it is to be hoped that future efforts will manage to overcome the problems due to subject loss in both "free-choice" and "forced-compliance" paradigms.

Besides the methodological issue of subject selection there is the problem of obtaining adequate control conditions. This problem will be discussed later (Chapter 8) in connection with conflicting motivation and expectation. Here we simply wish to note that dissonance and attempted dissonance reduction are frequently created in connection with forces that operate in a direction either opposed to the dissonance reduction attempts or forces independent of them. In the latter case there may occur factorial design "main effects" that are not predictable or easily accountable for in terms of dissonance theory. In the former case, the more perplexing outcomes of cancellation may occur, so that nothing seems to happen under conditions of relatively high dissonance (as in Aronson's [1961] study on effort and secondary reinforcement in which the two opposing effects apparently cancelled each other out).

The correlated effects will not, of course, always oppose the predicted effects of dissonance. And when they operate in the same direction, they weaken the dissonance theory explanation by supplying an alternative interpretation for positive results. Let us consider, for example, a "forced-compliance" experiment in which subjects are offered either $1.00 or $10.00 to participate in an unpleasant task. In the absence of any further controls, the amount of money offered to the subject may directly influence his evaluation of the task, especially if the task is unfamiliar or ambiguous. To the subject, $1.00 may mean that the task is not likely to be terribly unpleasant; $10.00 may mean that the task is likely to be quite unpleasant. Hence, if the dependent measure is an evaluation of the pleasantness of the task, there may be a tendency for $10.00 subjects to evaluate the task as less pleasant than would the $1.00 subjects. This difference between groups is precisely what would be expected in terms of dissonance theory, though, as we see, it may occur independently of dissonance.

This problem can be attacked in at least three different ways. First, it might be shown that subjects who are not committed to perform the task, nor offered money for doing so (that is, they are simply presented the same information about the task itself as are experimental subjects), evaluate the task more nearly like subjects in the $10.00 condition than like subjects in the $1.00 condition. This would support a dissonance interpretation, which asserts that there is little pressure to change the evaluation in the $10.00 condition but much pressure in the $1.00 condition. A second way to handle the problem would be to obtain evaluations of the task both before and after commitment to (or execution of) the task. Although this method may not produce an unequivocal interpretation, it does allow one to see whether or not there is *positive* change in the $1.00 and little or no change in the $10.00 condition. A third possibility is to try to control the influential information about the task. This method is illustrated in Brehm's experimental study of thirst motivation (pp. 137–143), where the experimenter told all subjects that the deprivation task was worth $10.00 and then told them that a departmental regulation prevented paying more than either $5.00 or $1.00.

In summary, then, experiments on dissonance theory seem frequently to involve correlated psychological processes and thus may require carefully thought-out control conditions in order to provide unequivocal interpretations in terms of dissonance theory.

This completes our presentation of the issues bearing on the direct validation of dissonance theory as stated by Festinger (1957) and as outlined in Chapter 1. We have also presented a number of new studies bearing on one or another aspect of the theory. It is clear that the theory has received a great deal of support and that most of the important derivations from the theory that have been tested have been confirmed by experimental research. It should be apparent that in almost all the experiments we described and in all the new ones we presented, the subject has been committed to one or another discrepant alternative that produces dissonance. Where such commitment was clear, the specification of the mode of dissonance reduction was enhanced and the theory was seen to generate interesting and non-obvious predictions.

We presented evidence that gave additional support for the derivations regarding increase in consonant information, negative attributes, and complex alternatives. We also showed that the dissonance formulation of the process of revaluation following choice was relevant to an important life situation and that these revaluation processes are not compellingly explained in terms of "conflict reduction." Furthermore, some new light was shed on the derivation regarding salience of dissonant information and on the effects of repeated experiences with dissonance. Finally, we discussed a number of issues and problems growing out of the experimental research bearing on the theory. These concerned problems in the attitude-change paradigm, the problem of behavioral commitment as a mode of dissonance reduction, the effect of commitment to discrepant behavior without the behavior, the varied consequences of actually performing a discrepant act, and some general methodological and theoretical considerations involved in evaluating tests of dissonance theory. In the following part we shall consider various extensions of the theory into new problem areas.

EXTENSIONS OF
THE THEORY

part **III**

Motivational effects of dissonance

— 8

As we have seen, most tests of dissonance theory have concentrated on attitudinal effects of the psychological tension produced by cognitive dissonance. They may thereby have neglected motivation as a dimension around which dissonance can be reduced in any situation. In addition, Festinger's theoretical formulation does not clearly specify the motivational control of the arousal of dissonance. That is, it is not presently clear in his statement of the theory exactly what is the effect of frustration of certain motivational states (attendant upon engaging in discrepant behavior) on the creation and resolution of dissonance and what are the implications of such dissonance resolution for goal-directed behavior.

It seems reasonable to assume that cognitive aspects of motivation are affected by dissonance in much the same way as other types of cognitions, such as opinions. It has long been obvious that motivation as a force producing behavior has various cognitive components. These components are closely related to the verbal reports that an individual can make about his motivational state (e.g., statements about the type and magnitude of his desires). Given this view of motivation, the dissonance formulation, which is directed toward the study of cognitive change, should permit increased understanding of *at least* the cognitive side of motivation.

The occurrence of dissonance frequently depends on motivation insofar as the specification of "psychological implication" is concerned. If a person gets caught in the rain without an umbrella, the occurrence of dissonance in him will depend on whether or not he is motivated to remain dry. One who is motivated to get wet will certainly experience no dissonance as a result of getting caught in the rain without protection. We take the position here that, under at least some conditions, motivation is an integral part of a dissonance-creating situation.

While it is clear that motivation must sometimes be taken into account in the prediction of dissonance, an additional and perhaps more important implication is that change in motivation may sometimes *result* from dissonance. That is, motivational change is one more way in which dissonance can be reduced. To clarify this proposition, let us consider a hypothetical example. Suppose Jane Doe, typical American housewife, has decided she ought to lose some weight in order to keep her figure trim. Having decided to diet, she goes without breakfast on a certain day and eats only an apple for lunch. However, she and her husband are invited out for dinner and find themselves confronted with one of Jane's favorite dishes, exquisitely prepared. Jane will, of course, take some of the dish simply to be polite and also, in order to get some nourishment. But the question is: Will she maintain her diet by taking a minimal amount or will she give up her diet (at least temporarily) in order to eat more of the delicious food? Let us suppose that she decides to maintain the diet. What we propose is that her refusal to eat this food is dissonant with her liking of it, and that the magnitude of dissonance is a function of her initial hunger. But the main proposition we wish to present is that Jane Doe can reduce her dissonance by changing her motivation, that is, by reducing her own hunger. To the extent that she can manage to see herself as not hungry, the dissonance consequent to her self-denial will tend to be reduced.

In summary, what we propose is that motivational change will serve to reduce dissonance just as will attitude change, selective exposure to information, and so on. At the same time it should be clear that we are primarily concerned now with the cognitive aspects of motivation: Concomitant physiological or behavioral changes may or may not occur in any given situation and with any given motive. For the moment, however, let us skip over the relationship between cognitive and noncognitive aspects of motivation and simply look at some experiments designed to demonstrate the effect of dissonance on cognitive aspects of motivation.

AN EXPERIMENT ON HUNGER

The first study, a "forced-compliance" experiment designed and conducted by Brehm and Jon Christopher Crocker, was intended to show the effect of dissonance on hunger. The strategy was to ask hungry persons to agree to go without food for a further period, giving them differential rewards to create differing amounts of dissonance consequent to the commitment to deprivation. Self-ratings of hunger immediately before and immediately after the commitment served to measure change in motivation.

The subjects were male volunteers from an introductory course in psychology. When the subject signed up for participation in the study, he was asked to refrain from eating any foods from the time he got up in the morning until his testing session in the afternoon. He was also asked to keep the subsequent evening free in case further testing might be necessary.

Subjects were run individually and assigned alternately to one of the two experimental conditions. On arriving at the experimental room the subject was reminded by the experimenter that the study concerned the effect of food deprivation on certain kinds of intellectual and motor performances. His attention was then drawn to sandwiches, cookies, and milk—all lying at the side of the testing table—with the comment that he would be able to eat at the end of the testing session.

The procedure then consisted of four steps: (1) a self-rating by the subject of how hungry he felt; (2) motor and intellectual performance tests consisting of a pegboard task, naming objects made of wood, and problem solving; (3) the experimental treatment, designed to produce either high or low dissonance from commitment to go without food for several additional hours; and (4) a second self-rating on hunger, using the same scale as for the first.

The motor and intellectual performance tasks required about 15 minutes and were included simply because they fit the rationale of the experiment. Irrelevant to the true purpose of the experiment, they will not be discussed further.

Manipulation of dissonance

This part of the procedure was designed to create two cognitions dissonant with each other. The subject, having gone without breakfast and lunch and thus having judged himself as fairly hungry, was induced to commit himself to going without food until after his usual dinner time. This was accomplished by the following instructions, given immediately after completion of the motor and intellectual tasks:

"You will recall that we asked you to keep your evening free since some people were to be asked to return for further testing in the evening. You are one of the people being asked to return for the later testing. This is, of course, up to you, but let me explain what is involved. You will have to go without any food until about 8 or 9 o'clock this evening. Then we will give you some more tests of your intellectual and motor performances. There will be sandwiches, cookies, and milk for you to eat at the end of the testing session."

In order to create different amounts of dissonance from the agreement to go without food, different incentives were offered. To create *High Dissonance,* the experimenter said: "Unfortunately, we cannot give any more experimental credit points for the evening testing session. You get your point for having taken part this afternoon so don't think you have to come again this evening. But we would appreciate your help. If, however, you don't feel like doing it, that's okay because we can get someone else to do it." If the subject hesitated, he was given further encouragement to help out.

To create *Low Dissonance,* the experimenter said: "Unfortunately, we cannot give any more experimental credit points for the evening testing session. However, we can pay anyone willing to come back, since we do need your help. The amount is $5.00."

Measurement of Hunger
The before and after self-ratings of hunger were made on a 61-point scale, labeled each tenth point by "Not at all," "Very Slightly," "Slightly," "Moderately," "Quite," "Very," and "Extremely." The subject was asked on both ratings to make as careful and accurate a judgment as he could and then to mark the single dot closest to how he felt. In addition, the second rating was said to be necessary because people had been found to change in their hunger from one moment to the next, some persons changing one way, some another, and some not at all.

After making the second self-rating, the subject was asked how many sandwiches, cookies, and cartons of milk he would like brought for his meal at the end of the evening session. A simple count of these items would presumably offer another measure of hunger.

Summary of design

Subjects indicated their hunger both before and after committing themselves to going further without food. Of the 11 subjects in the Low Dissonance (high incentive) condition, one refused to continue, reducing the N in this condition to 10; and two of the 11 subjects in the High Dissonance (low incentive) condition refused, reducing the N in it to 9.

Results

The prediction is that cognition of hunger is a function of dissonance reduction: Subjects in the High Dissonance (low incentive) condition should decrease in hunger, from before to after the commitment to further deprivation, compared to subjects in the Low Dissonance (high incentive) condition. Change in hunger was computed by assigning numbers (0 to 61) to the self-ratings for each subject and averaging this change for each of the two experimental conditions.

This computation revealed that subjects in the High Dissonance condition decreased in hunger (-5.67) and those in the Low Dissonance condition increased (4.30), the difference between these changes being significant at well beyond the 1% level by t test. These data are clearly consistent with the hypothesis that the cognitive aspect of motivation is a function of dissonance and its reduction.

However, although the data are consistent with the hypothesis, our conclusion must be qualified, for there was a considerable difference between the two conditions in initial hunger level. The average initial hunger in the High Dissonance condition was 40.2, and in the Low Dissonance condition, 27.9. This difference, significant by t test at about the 2% level, suggests there may be other plausible reasons for the difference in hunger change. Among these are regression effects, personality differences among subjects, and differential behavior of the experimenter. Whatever the cause of the difference in initial hunger level, we can check the possibility that it accounts for the differences in hunger change by comparing the two conditions, using only subjects whose initial hunger level was about the same. Selection of the five highest from the Low Dissonance condition and the five lowest from the High Dissonance condition yields average initial hunger scores of 36.6 and 35.6, respectively. The average hunger changes for these two subgroups are 3.6 for the Low Dissonance condition and -5.8 for the High. Since the difference between these is nearly identical to that for the total groups, we may conclude that the initial difference in hunger score (or its cause) does not account for the obtained differences in change scores. Thus the qualification of our conclusion that the data support the hypothesis is not serious, though the interpretation remains slightly ambiguous.

Additional evidence for the hypothesis is available from a count of the number of food items ordered by subjects for the evening testing session. Again, if subjects in the High Dissonance condition have been trying harder than those in the Low to convince themselves that they are not hungry, then they should order fewer items. This expectation is confirmed by the obtained averages, 2.7 in the High Dissonance condition, 4.2 in the Low (significant by t test at beyond the 1% level).

The data are in support of the theoretical notion that the cognitive aspects of motivation are affected by dissonance in much the same way as are such types of cognitions as opinions. More specifically, they support the hypothesis that the dissonance aroused by the inconsistency between being motivated, on the one hand, and commitment to further deprivation, on the other, can be reduced by a decrease in the cognized intensity of the motivation. The knowledge that one has low motivation is consonant with the knowledge that one has agreed not to experience motive reduction for a relatively long period of time.

However, this study of the effect of dissonance on hunger can hardly be considered definitive. Aside from the fact that hunger is only one type of motivation, the experiment contained at least two somewhat dubious characteristics: There was an initial difference between conditions in the amount of motivation, and the manipulation could conceivably have created these effects without the help of dissonance. The differences in initial hunger have been discussed previously but the alternative interpretation suggested here has not. The notion is that the perceived severity of the deprivation may be affected by the manipulation of inducements so that persons offered nothing for further abstention perceive the deprivation to be of little consequence, while those offered $5.00 perceive the deprivation to be quite painful. If, then, the individual judges his own hunger in terms of the perceived painfulness of the deprivation ("If the deprivation is worth $5.00, then I must be quite hungry."), the self-rating of hunger will be directly proportional to the amount of the inducement. While this interpretation may not be entirely plausible, it is an alternative to the suggested explanation in terms of dissonance theory. Of course, what we need is additional empirical evidence.[7]

[7] Professor Kurt Back of the Duke Sociology Department and Dr. Morton Bogdonoff of the Duke Medical School recently performed an elaborated replication of this study on hunger. Their results are entirely consistent with the present findings

A second study was therefore designed to provide a further demonstration of the effect of dissonance on motivation and to extend our knowledge of the relevant variables and eliminate alternative interpretations.

AN EXPERIMENT ON THIRST

In this "forced-compliance" experiment by Brehm, dissonance was aroused in regard to thirst and could be reduced by decreases in the level of perceived thirst. The general plan was to induce thirsty people to continue to go without liquids for various amounts of inducements and with differing amounts of thirst-relevant stimuli present. Thirst was measured not only by self-ratings but also by amount of water drunk.

The subjects, volunteer male and female introductory psychology students at Duke University, were asked to forego any liquids from bedtime of the evening before until the experimental session in the afternoon. It was explained that the purpose of the study was to examine the effect of thirst on motor and intellectual functioning.

When the subject arrived for his experimental session, he was reminded of the purpose and asked if he had gone without liquids as required. He was then asked to indicate how thirsty he was on a questionnaire. After the thirst measure, he was put through a pegboard task, a digit-symbol task, and an object-naming task, all of which required about 15 minutes. At that point the subjects in the experimental (as opposed to the control) conditions were induced to continue going without liquids until the following afternoon, at which time they would return for further testing. This inducement will be described in detail below. All subjects were then given two intellectual problems to solve (e.g., getting cannibals and missionaries across a canyon) and finally were asked to indicate again how thirsty they were, using the same scale as for the initial measure of thirst. In giving the measure a second time, the experimenter said that research had shown that some people change one way, some another, and some not at all. After the second thirst measure, the experimenter said: "Now, although you will not be allowed to drink any liquids after you leave here, you may drink as much water as you like right now. I will be back in a moment and we will continue the tasks. You

---

and clearly lend further support to our supposition that dissonance can affect self-judgments of hunger.

may drink all the water you want right now." The experimenter then left the room for a few minutes. When she returned, she explained that the experiment was actually over and that the subject would not be returning for testing the next day. Finally, the true purpose of the experiment and reasons for the deceptions were carefully explained.

Relevant stimuli

One purpose of the present study was to examine the effects on dissonance and consequent motivational change of motivationally relevant stimulation. This was accomplished by having a pitcher of water with paper cups sitting on the testing desk throughout the experimental session. About half the subjects were exposed to these stimuli while the other half were exposed only to the materials necessary for the procedure of the experiment.

Deprivation inducement

The experimenter explained that further "credit points" (for course grades) could not be given for the additional deprivation and testing but that students would be paid instead. To avoid creating differential impressions about the painfulness or worth of the deprivation merely as a direct function of the differential inducements, it was necessary to create the impression that the task was worth a standard amount. This was managed by having the experimenter tell all subjects that the further deprivation and testing were actually worth $10, but that a departmental regulation prevented their being paid more than either $5.00 or $1.00—the former to create low dissonance, the latter to create high. If subjects hesitated or refused after the first request, the experimenter said: "Well, it would be very helpful if you would continue. Since you've already started, scheduling would be simpler with you. I find that other students are agreeing to do as I ask, since it does involve only one more day without fluids." If a subject still refused, he was given the next (problem solving) task. If the subject agreed, he was asked to sign a sheet that indicated the time at which he would return. He was also given a standard university pay form, made out in the amount he had been promised, and was told it would be redeemed when he returned.

Design

The design consisted of exposing subjects to low or high amounts of relevant stimulation (absence or presence of pitcher of water) and then inducing them with either low or high value rewards to agree to further abstention. Two additional conditions were run in order to reveal the effect of the high or low relevant stimulation and general experimental procedure on changes in self-ratings of thirst during the experimental session. Everything in those control conditions was the same except that the inducement to further deprivation was omitted.

In running the experiment it was found that not all subjects could be induced to commit themselves to further deprivation. This was partly because the subjects found the deprivation to be unpleasant, but also because the subjects had not been warned in advance that they would be asked to continue the deprivation, and many thus had interfering commitments, such as participation in an athletic event or being out of town. It was therefore decided to run enough subjects so that there would be 10 males and 10 females in each of the four experimental conditions. While the proportion of refusals was not different between the High and Low Dissonance conditions, there was a tendency for more subjects in the High Stimulation (19) condition to refuse than in the Low (10). This difference is clearly consistent with our contention that stimulation relevant to the motivational dimension is noticeable and may increase the motivational level.

Of the remaining 10 males and 10 females in each condition, a few were deleted from the final analysis because they indicated on the first thirst measure that they felt little or no thirst. These subjects had rated themselves as less than "Slightly" thirsty. Their data were deleted because these subjects could hardly be expected to experience dissonance from committing themselves to further deprivation as long as the initial deprivation had not made them thirsty. For these subjects, there was nothing dissonant with commitment to further deprivation.

Our theoretical expectations may now be summarized. The magnitude of dissonance is inversely proportional to the amount of payment and directly proportional to the amount of thirst. The subjective impression of thirst is directly proportional to the amount of relevant stimulation. A person will try to reduce dissonance by decreasing his thirst: The greater the dissonance, the greater is the reduction in thirst. Furthermore, since dissonance is greater under high than low relevant stimulation, the greater the amount of relevant stimulation, the greater the reduction in thirst.

Results

Before looking at change in thirst, let us see to what extent we have succeeded in creating the conditions necessary to test these hypotheses. Evidence concerning the effectiveness of the payment manipulation is available from a postexperimental question on the appropriateness of the amount of payment for the induced deprivation and second testing. This measure was introduced immediately after the second self-rating of thirst. It consisted of an 81-point scale, identified by nine equally spaced labels ranging from "Extreme Underpayment," through "Appropriate" at the midpoint, to "Extreme Overpayment." With answers scored from —4.0 to +4.0 for under- and overpayment respectively, the values in Table 7 were obtained. Corresponding Ns and variances are also included. It would be expected that subjects in the Low Payment (High Dissonance) condition would indicate they were underpaid and those in the High Payment (Low Dissonance) condition would indicate they were overpaid. This expectation is fulfilled for the male subjects, as Table 7 shows.

TABLE 7

MEAN RATINGS OF APPROPRIATENESS OF PAY FOR EACH
EXPERIMENTAL CONDITION

	Males			Females		
Conditions	Mean	N	Variance	Mean	N	Variance
High Diss—High Stim	—.14*	7	4.79	.27	9	1.44
High Diss—Low Stim	—.23	7	4.72	.90	10	5.43
Low Diss—High Stim	.39	9	.74	1.97	10	3.24
Low Diss—Low Stim	.41	9	1.13	.15	8	.15

* A minus figure indicates that pay is perceived as inappropriately low.

The females, however, show a considerably different pattern of response. In general, they indicate they are overpaid and those in the Low Stimulation condition seem to feel they are overpaid in *inverse* proportion to the amount of money given! It is apparent, then, that the males have reacted to the inducement manipulation as expected while the females have reacted in some altogether unexpected fashion. Before we consider the significance of these data, however, let us inspect the data concerning the success of the manipulation of relevant stimulation.

Evidence on the effect of the relevant stimulation is available from the initial self-rating of thirst. Although the effect of this manipulation on the thirst measure might not be strong, we would certainly expect a trend showing that subjects in the High Stimulation condition reported greater thirst than those in the Low Stimulation condition. The mean initial thirst scores, along with the Ns and variances, are shown in Table 8.

TABLE 8

INITIAL THIRST SCORES FOR ALL EXPERIMENTAL CONDITIONS

Conditions	Males			Females		
	Mean	N	Variance	Mean	N	Variance
High Diss—High Stim	3.81	7	1.08	3.16	9	.80
High Diss—Low Stim	3.40	7	1.01	3.30	10	1.22
Low Diss—High Stim	3.93	9	.44	3.66	10	.98
Low Diss—Low Stim	3.56	9	.36	3.11	8	.60
Control—High Stim	4.20	6	.66	3.96	7	1.14
Control—Low Stim	3.81	7	1.60	3.88	6	1.34

Here it is again evident that the male sample conforms to our expectations while the female sample does not. Though the difference between High and Low Stimulation males is only a nonsignificant trend, it is in the expected direction and of about the same magnitude in all conditions. Among the females there is a reversal in the High Dissonance condition.

The combined evidence on the success of the manipulations indicates that the males should show changes in thirst as predicted while the females may not. Let us now inspect changes in self-rating of thirst for the males alone; the females do not conform to the experimental conditions necessary for an adequate test of the present hypothesis. Why they do not conform is unclear, though it may relate to the fact that the experimenter was also a female. Or they may perhaps have a different attitude toward research or toward payment for participation. In any case, their data are reported without further discussion so that the interested reader can draw his own conclusions.

The thirst changes, presented in Table 9, show that the payment and stimulation variables have the expected effect on the males. The amount of decrease in thirst is an inverse function of payment and a direct function of stimulation. An analysis of variance indicates that the payment effect is reliable (p less than .05) though the stimulation effect is not nor is the interaction ($F = 2.14$). However, the only simple difference that is reliable is that between High and Low Dissonance conditions within the High Stimulation condition ($p = .05$ by t test). Thus the results give moderate support to our theoretical expectations. Self-judgments about thirst appear to be subject in part to cognitive dissonance.

Motivational Effects of Dissonance / 141

The thirst change among subjects in the control conditions raises questions about how the outcome for the experimental conditions should be interpreted. Subjects in both of these conditions show some decrement in thirst, with those in the High Stimulation condition (−.47) showing more than those in the Low Stimulation condition (−.09). These thirst changes, it will be noted, are not clearly different from the corresponding changes in the High Dissonance condition.

TABLE 9

MEAN CHANGES IN SELF-RATING OF THIRST

| | Self-Rating Changes | | | |
| | Males | | Females | |
Experimental Conditions	Mean	Variance	Mean	Variance
High Diss—High Stim	−.63*	1.00	−.07	.37
High Diss—Low Stim	−.19	.80	.04	.06
Low Diss—High Stim	.23	.15	.01	.19
Low Diss—Low Stim	.09	.39	.31	.69

* A minus figure indicates a decrease in thirst.

Should one conclude, therefore, that what really happened was that the Low Dissonance subjects became more thirsty whereas the High Dissonance subjects hardly changed at all? Unfortunately we cannot tell from the present data, for the control condition does not really control for all other factors except for the magnitude of dissonance. In particular, the control condition differs from the experimental conditions in terms of the subjects' expectations about when they will be able to drink liquids. It seems plausible to assume that this difference, along with other possible differences, may well account for the decreased thirst among control subjects. Or, it may plausibly be assumed that experimental subjects, in general, have a greater tendency to become more thirsty than do control subjects. In effect, then, the control condition is not really adequate as a baseline against which to compare the effects of dissonance. A further discussion of this point may be found later in this chapter.

A related question of considerable interest is whether or not dissonance-produced motivational changes extend to actual behavior as well as to cognitive realignments. In an attempt to collect relevant data, subjects in the present study were allowed to drink water immediately at the end of the experimental session. What we might expect is that the amount drunk would be less for those subjects who showed a sizable decrease in thirst, namely, those in the High Dissonance— High Stimulation condition. The figures in Table 10, which show the average number of cubic centimeters of water drunk, fit our expectation rather well. Although none of the differences is statistically significant, the subjects who drink the least are those in the High Dissonance—High Stimulation condition, who had also shown the greatest decrement in thirst.

TABLE 10

AVERAGE NUMBER OF CUBIC CENTIMETERS OF WATER CONSUMED FOR MALES

Experimental Conditions	Cubic Centimeters
High Diss—High Stim	244
High Diss—Low Stim	305
Low Dis—High Stim	303
Low Dis—Low Stim	313

Considered together, then, the results of this experiment provide some support for the proposition that motivation can be affected by dissonance. When we consider the evidence from the study on hunger as well, we can safely conclude that dissonance can indeed affect the cognitive aspects of motivation. These demonstrations are particularly interesting because they have shown the effects of dissonance in regard to relatively clear and physiologically concrete forms of motivation.

These two experiments would seem to open the way to an exploration of the effects of dissonance on social motives; certainly those motives dealing directly with cognition, such as achievement, social affiliation, and agreement with other people, should be less resistant to dissonance-produced changes than tissue needs like hunger and thirst. Because of the greater ambiguity and susceptibility to change of these social motives, it may be easier to demonstrate both cognitive and behavioral effects of dissonance with them.

AN EXPERIMENT ON AVOIDANCE MOTIVATION

A "forced-compliance" experiment by Cohen and Philip G. Zimbardo represents an attempt to deal directly with the effects of cognitive dissonance on the *behaviors* assumed to stem from social motivation. One of several important factors affecting the magnitude of dissonance in a situation where a person commits himself to deprivation of an important motive is the *amount* of deprivation to which he commits himself. According to the present theory, greater deprivation should result in a greater discrepancy between motivation and goal availability; we therefore assume that, holding constant initial motive strength and incentives for commitment, commitment to greater deprivation should result in greater dissonance and consequent reduction of motivation and thus in fewer responses directed toward satisfying the particular motive involved. By actually decreasing his motivation, the person reduces the dissonance created by the discrepancy between his knowledge of his motivation and his knowledge that he has committed himself to further deprivation.

If a person wants very much to achieve some success in an important task, he should, everything else being equal, desire to avoid performing the task in a situation that promises failure. However, if for some reason the person commits himself to a situation promising failure, he can reduce his dissonance by lessening his failure-avoidance motivation. That is, one way of making consonant the relationship between one's motivation to avoid failure (or achieve success) and one's commitment to failure is to reduce the motive to avoid failure (or to succeed).[8] A decrement in failure-avoidance motivation should then be reflected in less behavior guaranteed to promote success. Thus the greater the prospect of failure to which the person commits himself, the more dissonance he should experience and the more he should attempt to reduce that dissonance by a decrement in avoidance motivation, which will be reflected in less concern with changing the conditions so as to ensure a greater probability of success on a subsequent trial. We should also expect such a decrement in avoidance motivation to manifest itself in, among other things, less desire to change to another, different task, and, since subjects are less motivated to succeed and disadvantages of the task are therefore less relevant for them, a lesser emphasis on the negative characteristics of the task situation when they are asked to recall aspects of the task.

General Design

Subjects' needs for achievement were aroused, and they were then given a disturbing 5-minute failure experience with a task on which it was extremely difficult to conceive of the possibility of success.

[8] No explicit distinctions are made here between the motivation to achieve success and the avoidance of failure motivation. For our present purposes, these presumably separate motivational strands can be viewed within one framework, though they have of course, been explicitly separated and shown to have different implications for behavior (see Atkinson, 1957).

This was assumed to affect them so that their resultant motivation would be to avoid the task in the future. They were then asked to commit themselves to a further 50-minute session under the same conditions. This situation was supposed to produce dissonance, since subjects whose motives were to avoid a failure situation would then be committing themselves to experiencing further failure. The magnitude of the dissonance was manipulated by varying the subject's expectations of how well he would do in the next session. Half the subjects were told that they would probably do "very poorly," half were told that they would do "not too badly." Changes in the subject's behavior associated with approach or avoidance of the failure situation could then be taken as an index of the change in motivation serving to reduce dissonance.

Subjects

Twenty subjects were recruited from introductory psychology classes at New York University as part of their course requirement. Twelve were male and 8 female. They were distributed equally in the experimental conditions.

Procedure

Subjects were run individually and all were taken into a soundproof room where they donned earphones. They were first told that they were participating in an experiment on verbal behavior and memory under special experimental conditions. The procedure then consisted of the following steps:

1. Subjects were given instructions designed to create a high level of motivation to succeed. They were further told, through the earphones, that this was "a study of students' ability to memorize, interpret, and understand some materials under adverse conditions." These instructions stressed the creativity, sensitivity, and general ability needed to perform well under certain disruptive speech conditions.

2. The subjects were then given a poem to read aloud and 3 minutes to memorize it.

3. All subjects were then required to recite the poem from memory and to discuss its psychological implications under conditions of delayed auditory feedback. Specifically, a delay of .2 seconds was mechanically interpolated between their speaking and the return of their speech sounds over the earphones. Delayed auditory feedback (DAF) usually produces speech, emotional and thought disturbances, and, because of the novelty of the experience, subjects do not have established standards for "good" performance on this task.

4. As soon as the subjects indicated that they had finished with their interpretations of the poem, they were taken out of the cubicle and given the experimental treatment designed to produce either high or low dissonance from commitment to participate in a longer session with the DAF apparatus.

5. Measures of behavior assumed to reflect the strength of motivation to avoid the DAF procedure as well as cognitive measures of alternative modes of dissonance reduction were then taken.

Manipulation of Dissonance

This part of the procedure was designed to create two conditions dissonant with each other. The subject, having had his achievement motive aroused, was induced to commit himself to another longer session with the DAF apparatus, which, because of his prior 5-minute experience, he knew to be detrimental to ready success. All subjects were told that, "In a second session for which we are asking our subjects to volunteer, we will be studying the same phenomenon but for a full 50-minute period and not for only 5 minutes as in the initial session. Although participation in this initial session is part of your course requirements, volunteering for the second session is *entirely up to you*. Since it will be after the regular term is over, we are giving all of our subjects $2.00, a nominal fee for returning for the second session. Now, before I ask you whether you wish to return at a time convenient to you, let me tell you that from our experience and analysis of several response measures obtained from you today, we can tell you that, compared to all of the other students we have tested, next time you will:

(High Dissonance:) perform very poorly, among the worst subjects we have ever run.

(Low Dissonance:) perform not too badly, about average or a little less than the average subjects we have run. In spite of this, we would like you to return for a second session. Will you be able to come?" At this point the subjects' freedom of choice was stressed several times. If subjects agreed to return (and all experimental subjects did agree except for one additional subject in the High Dissonance condition), they were scheduled for the alleged second session, filled out a petty cash voucher, and committed themselves by signing their names.

Measurement of Motivation

DAF DIAL SETTING. After agreeing to return, subjects were told that the initial testing was over and they were brought into the "apparatus room" and shown the DAF equipment. They were shown the recorder and the dial indicating the delay interval. They were told that in the initial session the interval was extreme and constant at point 13 on the 15-point scale. *It was stressed that the size of the delay determined the amount of speech disruption and presumably the amount of failure the subject experienced and that a shorter delay would enable one to perform much better.* Subjects were then told that, since they knew their own subjective reaction to the situation, we would like *them* to choose the point on the dial with which they would like to begin the next session (and keep for at least half the session). The subject then adjusted the dial himself in response to the request that he select the interval he wanted to experience in the second session. The subject could see how the tape loop changed speed as a function of the direction and extremity of dial setting.

RECALL OF INFORMATION. After the subject had set the dial, he was taken out of the "apparatus room" and given an essay to read. This essay was a two-page article purportedly written by Hebb and dealing with the advantages of research on auditory feedback. After 5 minutes, subjects were asked to recall the advantages and disadvantages of research on auditory feedback by listing points specifically mentioned in the article as well as any others of which they could think. They did this on a sheet with two columns labeled "advantages" and "disadvantages." It was assumed that a count of the ratio of disadvantages to the total number of items would indicate the strength of the subject's avoidance motivation for the task.

CHECK ON THE MANIPULATION AND COGNITIVE AVENUES OF DISSONANCE REDUCTION. The subjects were then asked to indicate on 81-point scales:

(a) "When you were asked to return for an additional 50 minutes and told how well you would probably perform, *how well did you actually anticipate performing* in the 50-minute session to follow?" This scale ran from "Extremely poorly" to "Very well."

(b) "How well do you want to do when you go into the experimental room and speak into the earphones?" The scale varied from "Not at all well" to "Very well."

(c) "Considering that you had to participate in this initial session as part of the course, how much *choice* do you feel you had in whether or not you put in the additional time on the tape recorder feedback task?" The scale here ran from "No choice at all" to "Complete choice."

(d) "How *obliged* did you feel to participate in another session with the tape recorder feedback task?" The subjects rated their perception of the obligation on a scale that ran from "Completely obliged" to "No obligation at all."

CHANGE OF TASK ALTERNATIVE. When the subject sat in the sound cubicle, he had placed his finger on an electrode and was told that this was measuring autonomic responses. The procedure gave no data but was merely instituted as a device to measure change of task alternative. After the checks on the manipulations, the subjects were shown a typical PGR record and a scale used to measure deflections on the record. They were told that: "We have a great many such records to analyze and it is a somewhat tedious job, which has to be done." They could help out equally well during the next session by being a subject in the DAF experiment, as they were in the present session, *or* by spending the same amount of time for the same $2.00 in analyzing the PGR records. They indicated their wishes on a five-point *a priori* scale that ran from "Much rather be a subject in the DAF part of the study" to "Much rather assist in analyzing the PGR records."

Finally, all subjects were told of the deception, were assured that they would not have to return for another session, and were asked to maintain the secrecy demanded by the experiment.

Summary of Design

Subjects set the DAF dial after committing themselves to extreme (High Dissonance) or moderate prospect of failure (Low Dissonance). It was assumed that the more dissonance the subjects experienced, the more they would lower their failure-avoidance motivation, and therefore the *less* would they be expected to decrease the DAF interval. It was also expected that the recall of disadvantages of the DAF task and the desire to avoid the DAF task would be less, the greater the dissonance.

Results

The check on the prospect of failure manipulation showed that the mean of the High Dissonance subjects was 4.50, while the mean for the Low Dissonance subjects was 5.51. While the means are in the right direction, indicating a tendency for the High Dissonance subjects to expect more failure, the difference between conditions is not a very reliable one (p is less than .20). We can only tentatively conclude that the dissonance manipulations may have been effective, though they seem not to have been as clear as one might wish.

The major issue in the present experiment concerns the changes in actual behavior that are assumed to reflect dissonance-produced changes in motivation. When we examine the major dependent variable, we see a strong effect of the dissonance manipulation: Nine out of ten subjects in the Low Dissonance condition decreased the DAF interval, whereas only two out of ten in the High Dissonance condition decreased it. In fact, those in the High Dissonance condition kept the dial pretty much as it was set, while the Lows reduced the interval considerably, presumably as a function of their stronger avoidance motivation. The mean change for the High group is $+.03$; for the Low group, -3.42. The difference between the conditions, with an N of 10 in each condition, is significant at less than the .05 level by t test ($t = 2.35$).

The data on task change also indicate a lessened avoidance motivation on the part of the High Dissonance subjects. When the subjects are broken into those who want to change and those who want to remain with the DAF task, the High Dissonance subjects show a greater tendency to stay with the DAF task than the Lows. Not one of the Highs wants to change tasks, while four out of ten Lows prefer to change to the PGR task (p is less than .10 by chi-square test). The data on recall of disadvantages associated with the task also show a trend in the same direction. The difference is unreliable (p is less than .20 by chi square), but the High Dissonance subjects tend to list fewer disadvantages of the DAF task than the Low Dissonance subjects: 13.3% of the items listed by the Highs are disadvantages, while 22.8% of the items listed by the Lows are disadvantages.

Although the data on task change, and especially on recall, are rather weak, they are quite consistent with the DAF dial-set data. Thus the High Dissonance subjects decrease the DAF interval less, want to change tasks less and tend to recall relatively more positive qualities of the task. This consistent range of behaviors appears to be directly related to the amount of deprivation to which subjects committed themselves. When committing himself to failure, the greater the subject's promised failure, the more the dissonance and the more the consequent reduction in motivation to avoid the failure situation, so as to make his commitment consistent with his motivation. This greater decrement in motivation to avoid the situation is reflected in a greater behavioral involvement in the DAF situation.

In addition to providing some behavioral evidence for the effects of dissonance on motivational change, the present experiment also shows that dissonance can be reduced through cognitive change. The measure of the subject's desire to do well and the measures of choice and obligation are relevant here. The former measure indicates that, for subjects with greater dissonance, there is less cognized intensity of success motivation. Though the difference between conditions is not very reliable ($p < .20$), the mean for the High Dissonance condition was 5.0; for the Low, 6.1. The data also show that subjects in both conditions generally felt a great deal of choice and little obligation to commit themselves to further deprivation. However, the experimental groups differ in the degree to which the subjects felt they were "coerced." With high means indicating more choice and less obligation, the means for the High Dissonance condition on the choice and obligation items, respectively, were 4.94 and 5.02, while for the Lows they were 6.67 and 6.77 ($p < .10$, $p < .05$). These data tend to support the notion that the Highs reduced dissonance more than the Lows by increasing their feelings that they were "forced" into commitment and by saying that they have less motivation to succeed.

While the data tend to be consistent with the hypothesis about the effects of dissonance on the behavioral concomitants of motivation, there may be alternative interpretations of the present results that should cause them to be viewed with some caution. It could be said that the manipulation of prospective failure led the subjects to feel that they had actually done more or less poorly in the initial session. Those subjects in the High Dissonance condition could have inferred, from the promise that they would do very poorly next time, that they had actually done poorly *this* time, and as a result they may have felt that their adequacy was challenged. Thus they may have felt that they had to "prove themselves" on the next trial, and, given the choice, they chose to stay with the task and perform it under the same conditions. To say that they have "failed badly" may imply that the present DAF level is the minimum level of success for them; the information that they failed badly relative to others may only have indicated to them that they did poorly on an easy task and could not therefore settle for less than the initial DAF level. The Lows, however, according to this explanation, would only have experienced moderate failure. They could therefore have set the DAF dial at a lower level, ensuring a greater probability of success in the next session. Even if they lowered the dial, they would presumably still be in the range of acceptability for success. It should be noted, though, that the initial level of the DAF dial was almost as extreme as it could be (13 out of 15), making it difficult for the subject to assume that the task was easy. Furthermore, of all the subjects questioned afterward, not one indicated that he thought the task easy. This alternative explanation is a crude extrapolation of level of aspiration concepts (Lewin et al., 1944). Unfortunately the present experiment does not provide the data necessary (e.g., information concerning the subject's perception of an acceptable performance for himself and his comparison group) for an adequate application of level of aspiration formulas.

The present experiment suggests that dissonance-produced changes in motivation, which are reflected in behavioral change, can be accompanied by changes in cognition. On all three cognitive checks (the measure of cognized intensity of motivation and the measures of cognitions regarding the pressures toward discrepant commitment), the High Dissonance subjects tended to show more change as a function of their greater commitment to deprivation. The greater the prospect of failure, the more the subjects felt that they were coerced into committing themselves and the less resulting motivation they tended to have. Thus subjects can reduce dissonance by increasing the proportion of cognitions supporting their discrepant behavior (more obligation) and by decreasing the proportion of cognitions arguing against their discrepant behavior (less cognized intensity of motivation).

In this experiment, however, the clearest evidence consistent with the notion that dissonance can affect motivation is the actual change in behavior around the DAF task. Having committed themselves to greater deprivation (failure), the High Dissonance subjects reduced their avoidance motivation more, as indicated by their greater willingness to experience failure on the subsequent trial.

In summary, the discussion here has centered around three experiments, all of which assumed that motivation may be affected by dissonance. In the hunger, thirst, and avoidance motivation experiments, subjects chose to commit themselves to a situation promising deprivation of an important need. In terms of our framework, they chose to behave in a manner that followed from the obverse of some important motive they may have been assumed to have. In the one case, hungry as a result of having gone without food, they agreed to go further without food; in the second case, having gone without liquids, they committed themselves to additional deprivation of liquids; and in the case of the avoidance experiment, wanting very much to avoid failure, they agreed to participate in a situation that promised failure.

THEORETICAL ISSUES IN THE DISSONANCE ANALYSIS OF MOTIVATION

A general implication of our discussion of motivation concerns the role of cognition in a theory of motivation. It seems to us that most contemporary theories of motivation neglect cognitive components. We assume, on the other hand, that the individual's commitment to varying magnitudes and durations of deprivation and satiation may affect not only his cognitions about his motivational state but also the noncognitive aspects of his motivation. Thus accurate prediction of consummatory or other behavior accompanying or resulting from motivation may demand the analysis of commitment to deprivation as well as mere deprivation itself.

Traditional learning theory has not been concerned with the issue of commitment to deprivation because of its concentration on animal research. But for humans, who have to deny motive satisfaction in committing themselves to deprivation, cognitive factors become important mediating variables. In general, learning theorists have tended to regard cognitions as epiphenomena, but the position taken here is that cognitions associated with a given motive can affect the motive itself and consequent behavior. Thus specification of cognitive factors centering around commitment to deprivation can sharpen our understanding of the relationship between the antecedents and consequences of motivation.

What we suggest is that dissonance-produced change in the cognitive aspects of motivation can directly affect either the noncognitive components of motivation, including physiological states, or behaviors ordinarily thought to vary with motivation, such as goal consumption, perception, and performance. A dissonance-produced reduction in how hungry a person feels may be accompanied by reduced stomach contractions and may also be accompanied by reduced tendencies to eat food and, for example, to perceive food-related objects in a projective test.

The extent to which we may expect such ramifications of dissonance-produced change in motivation is not yet clear. As Brehm (1962) has noted, it may be ". . . that only noncognitive components of motivation affect such behaviors as learning and performance, in which case change in the cognitive component would be of consequence only when it produced a correlated change in the noncognitive component, or when it was used as an index of the strength of the noncognitive component."

"It could also be that both cognitive and noncognitive components of a given motivation have significant psychological effects, but on different dimensions of behavior. Thus, for example, cognitive components might affect performance but not learning, while noncognitive components might affect learning, but not performance."

It is perhaps even more interesting to consider the possibility that it is *only* the cognitive component of motivation that affects consummatory behavior and other psychological processes. That is, it may be that physiological states can affect consummatory and other processes only insofar as they have cognitive representation, or even that a state of deprivation, short of debilitating the organism entirely, would have to have cognitive representation in order to have any kind of psychological effect at all. In that case it may be possible under some conditions to bypass the physiological aspects of motivation and simply deal with the cognitive processes.

The implications of these suggestions may be relevant for a host of problems that heretofore have resisted analysis in terms of cognitive components. Though common-sense experience points to their importance in everyday life, we have had no theoretical guidelines to relate them to motivation. The notion that cognitive dissonance can affect noncognitive aspects of motivation suggests that physiological reactions of all sorts may perhaps be partly understood in terms of their cognitive accompaniments. For example, we might expect dissonance to affect noncognitive aspects of hunger, such as salivation, stomach contractions, and blood sugar, and it is plausible that any or all of these may be affected by the kinds of cognitive changes suggested by our research. In this connection, Brehm (1962) has cited a recently completed, unpublished exploratory study by Back and Bogdonoff. "Briefly, they patterned their experiment after the hunger study reported earlier, except that they also took blood samples at various points throughout the period of deprivation, which in their study was carried on for 24 hours. The changes they obtained in self-ratings of hunger were as expected: high dissonance subjects tended to decrease while low dissonance subjects tended to increase. But these investigators were particularly interested in the possible effects that such hunger changes might have on the mobilization of free fatty acids in the blood, and they had their blood samples analyzed for this effect. A preliminary analysis of the results indicates that there is a difference between experimental conditions in fat mobilization, with high dissonance subjects showing less than low dissonance subjects. Although it would be premature to conclude that dissonance, or even change in the cognitive aspect of hunger may have an immediate effect on the mobilization of fats, it is certainly fair to conclude that further investigation along these lines is justified by results so far obtained." Such investigation, we might add, could lead to novel insights in psychosomatic medicine.

In general, then, the present view implies that the understanding of motivational phenomena can be improved by taking into account those forces that affect the cognitive aspects. In particular, whenever dissonance is aroused in connection with motivation there may be consequent changes in consummatory and various psychological processes. The determinants of these changes are the determinants of dissonance arousal and reduction. We have already noted the role of: (1) the amount of incentive for committing oneself to deprivation, (2) the role of relevant stimuli under conditions of commitment, and (3) the amount of deprivation to which the person commits himself. All three serve to determine the size of the discrepancy between motivation and goal availability and therefore the amount of dissonance produced. Any theory concerned with motivation must also take account of, at least: (4) the strength of the initial drive.

The most broadly stated theory of motivation would probably say that the stronger the *initial* drive, and the more salient the relevant drive-related stimuli, the more will the person act in a fashion instrumental to achieving drive satisfaction. However, under conditions where the person agrees to postponement of his need satisfaction or to deprivation, dissonance theory, as we have seen, may lead to quite opposite expectations. It says that as all these forces toward need satisfaction and away from deprivation cumulate (i.e., the higher the drive, the higher the relevant stimulation, the less the incentive for commitment to deprivation, and the greater the anticipated deprivation), the greater will be the dissonance experienced upon deprivation. The greater the dissonance, the more the person must reduce it, and therefore the greater may be the consequent denial of motivation. Under such conditions we arrive at predictions that go counter to most generally accepted hedonistic assumptions about the effects of deprivation on motivation.

With the application of dissonance theory it is also clear that motivational change will depend in part on the resistance to change of the relevant cognitive aspects of motivation. Within the actual limits of deprivation in civilized life, and considerng the fact that there are additional determinants of motivation besides deprivation, actual deprivation may have relatively little effect on motivation. Rather, the level of motivation may be primarily controlled by cognitive factors. However, under extreme conditions of deprivation the effect of cognitive forces, such as dissonance, may be completely overridden. When extreme conditions occur, the cognitions about motivation are simply highly resistant to change by cognitive pressure. It may be expected, then, that the cognitive determination of motivation will be primarily of a situational and ephemeral nature, rather than having the presumably stable characteristics ordinarily associated with other kinds of psychological processes, such as attitude change.

In any event, the present emphasis on the effects of dissonance-producing commitments involved in motive deprivation and satiation, and the implications for motivational change and consummatory behavior, would appear to be relevant for contemporary theories of motivation. The degree to which motive strength and consummatory behavior remain strong under actual or approaching deprivation may be partly dependent on the incentives, coercions, choices, and justifications accompanying deprivation. In most of the research involving arousal of drive states through deprivation of physiological or social motives, the conditions of deprivation generally involve strong incentives; participation is ensured through desire to please the experimenter, earn money, or contribute to science (e.g., see the starvation studies on conscientious objectors reported in Guetzkow and Bowman [1946]). Thus we might expect drive state to be high in such studies and the consequent appearance of a host of strong consummatory behaviors and possible disorganization, fantasy, hallucinatory, and psychosomatic effects. Under such conditions we should expect a minimum of dissonance effects as alternate channels of drive reduction. However, when the forces propelling commitment are weak, cognitive dissonance may result, thereby modifying motivation and consummatory behavior or, in the extreme case, itself providing the mechanism by which motive reduction can be accomplished.

SEPARATING DISSONANCE FROM MOTIVATION EFFECTS: THE PROBLEM OF ADEQUATE CONTROLS

A somewhat tangential issue raised by the discussion of extension of dissonance theory to motivation concerns the identification in any given study of those effects that are attributable to dissonance and those that are attributable to the direct effects of motivation. If dissonance theory is to be of any use in uncovering unique aspects of behavior not easily referrable to conventional "naive" hedonistic paradigms of motivation, it becomes necessary to consider ways of gauging the respective contributions of dissonance processes and conventional motivational processes.

This problem can be illustrated with reference to Brehm's (1960a) experiment on commitment to eating disliked vegetables. From the dissonance formulation we would expect that persons committed to eating disliked vegetables would experience dissonance. The fewer the cognitions supporting their discrepant behavior, the greater the dissonance. Therefore the introduction of a communication indicating that the vegetables they were committed to eat lacked vitamins should have produced more dissonance and greater consequent attitude change toward liking the vegetables than a communication which said that the vegetables had high vitamin content. However, the communications themselves may be assumed to have a direct effect: The less the communication favors the vegetables, the more they will be disliked. Thus in the condition where we have the subjects exposed to a low vitamin communication, we might expect high dissonance and high liking through the introduction of dissonant cognitions, but also high dislike through the direct effect of the information about vitamin content. In this case, the two effects might be expected to cancel each other out, with the result that a good deal of ambiguity would remain concerning the processes of dissonance arousal and reduction.

Brehm solved this problem through the use of a control condition in which subjects did not experience any dissonance through commitment to eating. With these subjects the direct effect of the communications alone on liking was measured, and it was expected and found that the low vitamin communication did indeed produce greater dislike. This provided a baseline against which the dissonance effects of the communications could be evaluated when subjects had actually committed themselves to eating. Thus, although it was not necessarily expected that the dissonance effect of the low vitamin communication would overturn its direct effect on liking, the relative effect of the introduction of the communication after commitment could be assessed against what would have happened had there been no commitment (i.e., no dissonance). As it turned out, the direct effect of supporting information on liking tends to be reversed or minimized to the extent that there is dissonance introduced by behavioral commitment.

Another illustration of the interaction of dissonance and motivation effects is shown by Aronson's (1961) experiment. In his experiment, while it might have been possible that the dissonance effects of increased effort would surmount the direct motivational effects of secondary reward, there was no necessary reason to hope so in the face of the known powerful effects of incentive on evaluation. However, while the effects of secondary reinforcement on evaluation in the low effort (low dissonance) conditions was considerable, to the extent that there was dissonance present (high effort), there was an increasing tendency toward reversal of the effects of secondary reinforcement in line with the dissonance hypothesis. In this case, the low effort condition provided a baseline of straightforward effects of motivation on evaluation uncontaminated by any dissonance process. Against this, the effects of the introduction of the dissonant behavioral commitment could be measured.

Both experiments show what part dissonance processes can play when there is some behavioral commitment. However, more generally, they illustrate the broad problem of dealing with the presumed inverse effects of dissonance within the same framework as the conventional direct effects usually ascribed to motivational processes. Whenever, in attempting to test or extend the dissonance formulation, we use models drawing on the conventional operations and procedures for arousing motivation and measuring its effects, we must be especially wary of this range of problems. Antecedent conditions of deprivation by and large make people behave more in the interests of need satisfaction. When people commit themselves to further deprivation, they may very well experience dissonance and, as a consequence, reduce their motivation. But they also have a stronger need that must be satisfied. Without a measure of the effects on goal consumption which the need deprivation would have in the absence of a commitment to further deprivation (while also controlling for time of further actual deprivation), there is no way of assessing whatever effects dissonance processes can be presumed to have.

The problem of adequate control groups for obtaining such a baseline of direct motivational effects is by no means a simple one. An indication of the kinds of problems that arise in this connection can be found in Brehm's above-mentioned thirst experiment. In that experiment, a control condition was run in order to see whether or not thirst would change simply as a function of the experimental procedure when there was no induced commitment to further deprivation of liquids. It had been expected that the control subjects would show little or no change in thirst with the possible exception that those who were exposed to the relevant stimulation (pitcher of water) might increase somewhat in thirst. However, these control subjects, and especially those exposed to the relevant stimulation, showed a decrease in thirst. In fact, contrary to expectations, their behavior looked much more like that of the high dissonance subjects than that of the low dissonance subjects. One might therefore be tempted to conclude that the high dissonance condition had little or no effect on thirst, while the low dissonance condition increased thirst.

But, as with any experiment, differences in outcome may be due to any one or a combination of differences in independent conditions. In the case in question, the control condition does not eliminate every difference except that of the magnitude of dissonance created in subjects. (Of course, neither does this occur in any other experiment on dissonance theory, for the magnitude of dissonance is usually not varied except by manipulation of some such variable as incentive value, or effort, etc.) For in such a control condition not only is there no dissonance between a commitment to further deprivation and existent thirst but also there is no commitment to further testing and deprivation, or the possibility of obtaining a reward. Without a commitment to further deprivation, there is undoubtedly some expectation of immediate satiation after the experimental session. Furthermore, if the experimenter's instructions about the worth of the further deprivation do have some effect on the self-rating, then this alone might account for a difference between the experimental and control conditions, for the control subjects were not told this. In summary, several factors differ between the experimental and control conditions. Some of these factors might operate to increase the relative thirst of experimental subjects; others might operate to decrease it. In the absence of better theoretical and parametric knowledge about the operations of whatever factors may be relevant to thirst change, the value of this type of control is considerably diminished. It is unfortunate that the significance of this statement for the experiment on thirst has become evident only in retrospect.

But if the control condition used was inadequate to furnish a baseline against which thirst changes in the experimental conditions could be compared, then what condition would have been adequate? It seems apparent that in some studies, such as the thirst experiment, this question is not easy to answer. For it is not at all clear that to tell control subjects that others were being induced to further deprivation, and that such deprivation was worth $10 although that much could not be paid, would put the control subjects in the same psychological condition as the experimental subjects except for the existence of a state of dissonance arousal. Furthermore, as noted, the dissonance arousal in this case involves the creation of a certain expectancy in regard to motive reduction. It is entirely possible that control subjects in the thirst study actually anticipated the consummatory behavior to which they were so close and were forced to defend against it (perhaps from another kind of dissonance arousal) by trying to become less thirsty until they could actually have the water. Indeed, it seems quite plausible to assume that knowledge of being motivated may be dissonant with *any* condition other than availability of the goal object. A further complication arises from the fact that incentives were offered for deprivation. To offer the same incentive to control subjects as, for example, a payment for what they had already done would put them in an entirely different psychological situation from that of the experimental subjects.

Generalizing from this example, it can be seen that often there is no obvious way to obtain a baseline against which to compare experimental groups. This difficulty confronts the entire range of dissonance studies making use of "forced compliance" as well as those using the "exposure" paradigm. Under such conditions the detection of the direction of response change that is produced by the independent variables can only be inferred. When there is an expected pattern of effects, as in the present thirst experiment, little more can be done than to show that the pattern is obtained, even though absolute levels and directions of change among all groups may indicate that other factors besides dissonance are at work.

The discussion of the thirst experiment has carried us farther afield than we indicated in our opening discussion of the relationship between dissonance effects and motivation effects. It is clear that the general problem of assessing the relative contributions of dissonance effects and straightforward effects, whether of motivation, judgmental processes, expectations, and so forth, is at issue here. The problems encountered in selecting appropriate control conditions are common to situations in which dissonance and other general processes operate side by side.

In conclusion, we may say that there will always be an interplay between the forces assumed to stem from dissonance and those assumed to stem from the straightforward effects of motivation, judgment, or expectation. The specification of discrepant commitment to some state of need deprivation, whether it involves not eating, agreeing to fail, working over some unpleasant task, putting in effort for small recompense, exposing oneself to counter-communications, or whatever, allows for the prediction of effects that tend to reverse those stemming from conventional hedonistic behavior theory notions or simple notions of information processing. This does not mean that dissonance experiments demonstrate the incorrectness of assumptions about the straightforward effects of incentive, judgment, or expectation. It does imply, however, that the more dissonance that is produced, the more will assumptions about the simple and straightforward effects of these other psychological processes be inapplicable.

Dissonance theory and
the study of personality
— 9

An additional set of insights into the general usefulness of the dissonance formulation may be gained by exploring the implications of the theory for research in personality and clinical psychology. At least two facets of this problem are relevant to our general discussion: (1) Does dissonance theory provide some guidelines for a new perspective with regard to some of the classical personality problems like defense mechanisms, and, if so, what assumptions must be made in order to use the theory? (2) What assumptions must the theory make about individual differences, that is, how does the theory view the problem of individual differences? We will take these questions up in that order in the present section.

DISSONANCE AND DEFENSE MECHANISMS

In a paper aimed at clinical psychologists, Festinger and Bramel (1962) discuss in detail the use of defensive projection as a means of dissonance reduction. It will have been noted by now that there is a similarity between certain "defense mechanisms" discussed by psychoanalytic theory and certain avenues of dissonance reduction. Certain dissonance-reduction mechanisms appear to look very much like "rationalization" or "defensive denial," for example.

160

One reason for this similarity is that once ego-defenses become established as reactions to characteristic conflict-arousing situations as a means of handling inner impulses, they may become behavioral modes themselves and therefore may be used in a wide variety of situations (see Cohen, 1959a). Thus a given ego-defensive behavior, as a characteristic individual reaction to tension or conflict in discrepant situations, might reflect itself in a given mode of dissonance reduction. As Festinger and Bramel say, the concept of dissonance and the psychoanalytic concept of "inner conflict" may have overlapping meanings. They go on in some detail to distinguish between the two notions.

Their argument, paraphrased, runs as follows: Psychoanalytic theory is mostly concerned with situations in which the person's perception of some aspect of himself is discrepant from his internalized values (his superego). A person who considers homosexuality an extremely invidious trait and is suddenly made aware of the fact that he has homosexual tendencies may have a fear of disturbing and painful guilt feelings and punishment aroused in him. In order to avoid further anxiety and guilt, according to psychoanalytic theory, the ego will initiate defensive measures, of which the most pervasive appear to be various forms of denial of the threatening information about himself.

Dissonance theory, on the other hand, would first ask whether dissonant relations would be expected to exist among the cognitions involved. Is the cognition that one has homosexual tendencies necessarily dissonant with the belief that such tendencies are bad and that one should not have them? The answer, according to Festinger and Bramel, is no, except for those persons who believe that they consistently live up to their internal standards. For some people, the knowledge that a trait is undesirable may not necessarily imply in itself that one does not possess it. Thus some people who are threatened in the psychoanalytic sense may also experience considerable dissonance, whereas others will not. In other words, according to psychoanalytic theory, the conflict sufficient to produce defensive behavior does not necessarily include what would be defined as dissonance.

Festinger and Bramel do not say that dissonance would be completely absent from the cognition of the person who does not expect himself always to live up to his own standards. For example, when he discovers he has homosexual tendencies, this knowledge may be dissonant with his belief that he is really quite masculine, even though it may not be dissonant with his conviction that homosexuality is a bad thing. In any concrete case to which the psychoanalytic theory is applied, it is quite unlikely that dissonance will be completely absent. However, any contribution which dissonance might make to

Dissonance Theory and the Study of Personality / 161

defensive behavior would be in addition to the factors emphasized by psychoanalytic theory. They say that perhaps the key differences between the approaches are highlighted by the lack of concern for the self-concept in classical psychoanalytic theory. Dissonance theory would place more emphasis on the individual's concept of what he is rather than his concept of what he should be (superego).

Festinger and Bramel ask whether the Freudian defense mechanisms against anxiety could also be used to reduce dissonance in the type of situation we have been discussing. They consider as an example the defense mechanism of projection, which is especially interesting to social psychologists because of its interpersonal implications. A person who has high self-esteem (i.e., he has many cognitions favorable to himself) considers homosexuality a very bad thing and a matter of considerable importance. When such a person is suddenly confronted with information that he is sexually attracted to members of his own sex, this cognition will be inconsistent with his cognitions concerning what a good person he is and also inconsistent with his belief that he is actually quite a masculine person.

Can this dissonance be reduced by attributing homosexuality to other people? One possible way to do this, according to Festinger and Bramel, would be to attribute homosexuality to people who are liked and respected in order to be able to revaluate homosexuality as such. If liked and respected persons possess the trait, perhaps the trait is not so bad after all. Then possession of the trait would no longer be discrepant with high self-esteem and therefore dissonance would have been reduced. A further possibility is that the person, by attributing homosexuality to members of his reference or comparison group, may be able to convince himself that he does not deviate from the persons most important to him. If he is only average in his possession of the trait, then subjectively it does not so strongly disconfirm his favorable self-esteem.

In their paper Festinger and Bramel cite at length an experiment by Bramel (1962) designed to study the use of projection as a mode of dissonance reduction. In this experiment each subject was told that the first part of the experiment was designed to discover what kinds of people had insight into themselves. He was asked to take a number of personality tests that, he was told, would be carefully analyzed by members of the clinical psychology staff. After the tests were scored, he was to learn the "results" in an interview, during which time his self-insight would be measured.

At the beginning of the second session (about a week later), the subject was told that the second part of the experiment was concerned with forming impressions of personality and that he would be asked, in addition to other things, to make some judgments about another subject. The two subjects appeared simultaneously, and, prior to the reporting of the results of the tests, they were introduced to one another. The experimenter asked each in turn (in the presence of the other) a set of questions about himself and his attitudes toward certain current events in order to enable the two strangers to gain some impression of each other in preparation for a later measurement of their attitudes toward each other. The subjects were then separated, and the appropriate test report was communicated to each of them privately.

Unknown to the subject, the "results" that he received had been prepared with no reference to his actual performance. There were only two test reports, one very favorable (the *favorable* condition) and the other very unfavorable (the *unfavorable* condition). The tone was objective and the general favorability (or unfavorability) quite consistent throughout the report. One subject of each pair was assigned randomly to the *favorable* condition and the other to the *unfavorable* condition. Thus, experimentally, the self-esteem of one subject was enhanced, while the self-esteem of the other was reduced somewhat.

After receiving the "results" of their personality tests, the two subjects were brought together into a room and seated at a long table; in front of each subject was a box containing a dial that faced the subject. Two wires with electrodes on the ends issued from each box; each subject perceived his apparatus immediately in front of him and could not see the other subject's apparatus.

The subjects were first asked to make some judgments of each other, using 11 adjective scales that could be scored for general favorability. A self-concept measure followed, consisting of 16 polar adjective pairs similar to those included in the prior rating of the other person. This scale provided a check on the effectiveness of the experimental manipulation that had attempted to influence their level of self-esteem.

Next, the experimenter read a set of instructions to set the stage for introducing the undesirable cognition that, presumably, should create considerable dissonance for subjects in the "favorable self-esteem" condition but should not produce much dissonance for subjects in the "unfavorable self-esteem" condition. It was explained that psychologists were especially interested in whether or not people could estimate "deeper and more personal aspects of the personality" on the basis of a first impression, and that this part of the experiment would be concerned with the perception of sexual arousal. An elaborate explanation of the physiology of sexual arousal and the sensitive techniques for their measurement followed. Considerable emphasis was placed on the unconscious nature of sexual arousal and the impossibility of exerting conscious control over its expression in the "psychogalvanic skin response." The subject's task was to observe his own sexual-arousal response on his galvanometer for each of a series of photographs of men that would be projected onto a screen. He was to record this figure on a page of a small, anonymous booklet. After recording his own arousal level for the particular picture on the screen, he was to make an estimate of the dial indication of the other subject's apparatus for the same photograph. The subjects were explicitly told that movements of the dial indicated homosexual arousal to the photographs. As a precaution against excessive threat, the subjects were told that persons with very strong homosexual tendencies would consistently "go off the scale." Furthermore, the anonymity and privacy of the situation were carefully spelled out, with the intention of convincing the subject that no one but he would know what his own responses had been.

Unknown to the subject, the experimenter exerted complete control over the movements of the needles, which were identical for the two subjects. Each photograph had been assigned an "appropriate" scale value in advance, so that those depicting handsome men in states of undress received more current than did those depicting unattractive and fully clothed persons. Both subjects were thus led to believe that they were sexually aroused by certain pictures and not by others, according to a consistent pattern. In effect, they were made to believe that they had "behaved" in a manner contrary to their self-images by somehow producing homosexual responses, just as Gerard's (1961) subjects were made to believe that their first impulse was to "conform" or remain "deviate." According to the hypothesis, the subjects in the favorable condition should experience considerable dissonance when observing their needle jump in response to photographs of unclothed males. "Behaving" in a strongly undesirable manner is quite dissonant with believing one is an extremely fine person. Subjects in the unfavorable condition, on the other hand, would have more cognitions consonant with having produced homosexual responses and not so many dissonant cognitions. Discovering one has a very undesirable trait is less discrepant from believing one is an undesirable person. Thus, if projection of an undesirable trait is a positive function of the magnitude of dissonance, then subjects in the favorable condition should attribute more homosexual arousal to others than those in the unfavorable condition. The results showed clearly that subjects in the favorable condition evaluated their partners as having significantly higher arousal than did subjects in the unfavorable condition. The average subject in the favorable condition evaluated his partner as having had the same arousal level as he himself had; those in the unfavorable condition generally evaluated the other person as having had less arousal than they themselves had. This difference between the groups in change in evaluation was specific to the trait of homosexuality. There was no difference between conditions in the general favorability with which subjects rated their partners. In short, it would appear that projection occurred in order to reduce dissonance, for there was more projection where dissonance was high than where it was low, even though "threat to superego" was the same for both conditions.

Some of the results derived from internal analyses were especially interesting. It was found, for example, that an identifiable projection effect tended to occur mainly when self-esteem was exceptionally high —in other words, when the discrepancy between the self-esteem and the homosexual "behavior" and resulting dissonance was great. Even within the favorable condition, projection occurred relatively consistently only when measured self-esteem was above the average for that group.

It seemed plausible to Bramel that the major dissonance-reducing effects of projection would occur only if the person onto whom the trait was projected was liked or favorably evaluated. By projecting onto respected persons, an individual might succeed in making homosexuality appear a less undesirable trait, and by projecting onto his reference or comparison group he may conclude that he is no worse than average in the degree to which he possesses an undesirable trait. The data show that subjects in the unfavorable condition attributed more homosexual arousal to people they did not respect. Subjects in the favorable condition also attributed more arousal when their partner happened to be evaluated poorly or moderately. However, this simple halo effect disappeared when these subjects happened to be with a partner whom they respected. Considering only those subjects who rated their partner very favorably, there is a significant difference between the favorable and unfavorable conditions in the expected direction. Thus, subjects in the two conditions differed in their evaluation of their partner as homosexual only when their partner was rated favorably. This suggests that defensive projection occurred only when the available social object was favorably evaluated.

As Festinger and Bramel note, the finding that defensive projection occurred only when the available social object was favorably evaluated differs considerably from usages of the projection concept by writers in the psychoanalytic tradition. Such writers (e.g., Ackerman and Jahoda,

1950) say that projection is generally aimed at persons and groups who are disliked and considered noncomparable and inferior to the projector. It would seem, for example, that the projection concept may have indeed been used too freely in explaining hostility toward out-groups, without any clear specification of the conditions under which it represents defensive attribution or rationalizations of displaced hostility. The problem may be stated as: Under what conditions does dissonance produce projection onto out-groups and under what conditions does it produce projection onto in-groups? Additional research by Bramel (in press) has explored the possibility that self-ascription versus denial of the threatening information may control whether one projects onto persons similar or different from oneself. He has shown that the person who is forced to ascribe the dissonant trait to himself may try to get other people like him into the same boat; the person who is able to make a partial, though not completely successful, denial may, according to certain psychoanalytic assumptions, try to separate himself from the trait by throwing it out onto out-groups.

The issue of denial is relevant to an evaluation of Bramel's experiment and the entire notion of defensive projection. The subject, it should be noted, could not make an outright denial of the meaning of the needle movements so that the dissonance-producing information regarding his homosexuality "response" was clear, unambiguous, and consciously available to him. Under such circumstances the commitment to his "own homosexuality response" was very strong and therefore resistant to change. Thus one good way to reduce the remaining dissonance in the absence of refutation of the discrepant information was to try to see others as similar.

Festinger and Bramel's use of the dissonance formulation to explain the occurrence of projection raises the interesting issue of the place of dissonance theory vis-à-vis psychoanalytic theory with regard to such phenomena. Do they mean to put dissonance theory forth as an alternative explanation for understanding ego defenses, or, instead, do they visualize dissonance theory as a formulation existing side by side with psychoanalytic theory insofar as they both attempt to deal with defensive phenomena? It seems to us that theirs is the latter intention. What then would be the advantage of specifying a dissonance formulation of processes with which psychoanalytic theory has long dealt? The answer would seem to be predictive accuracy. If one assumes that the sorts of variables suggested by the dissonance application to these personality phenomena are more amenable to measurement and conceptualization than the sorts of variables classically identified by psychoanalytic theory, then dissonance theory can certainly be assumed to add precision to the understanding of defense mechanisms. In addition, these concepts are more clearly specified, more easily subject to empirical test, and more easily linked to other empirical operations. Such variables as the self-esteem of the individual or his patterns of liking and respect are different from the variables generally used by psychoanalytic theory to account for ego-defensive behavior. Because of this they may make for more accurate and controlled research into the determination of this kind of behavior.

It is true, however, that Festinger and Bramel make no attempt to join dissonance theory and psychoanalytic theory. The theories remain standing alongside one another, both assumed to have a great deal to say about the phenomena under scrutiny. But we may well ask if there would be any advantage in applying these theoretical models to ego defenses in a more integrated fashion. In order to discuss this point we must first raise the question of whether the person has to be consciously aware of the cognitive conflict he experiences in order for dissonance to be produced.

It should be clear that the dissonance formulation as it stands makes no assumptions about the need for a person to be conscious about commitment to discrepant behavior or about the resultant dissonance. However, all of the aforementioned experiments that we have considered to be rather unequivocal in their arousal of dissonance appear to make at least the implicit assumption that the processes under observation are concerned with some awareness of his own responsibility for his discrepant commitment on the part of the subject. In Gerard's (1961) experiment, for example, had the subject not felt some uncertainty and decisional conflict and even some twinges toward conformity when he saw the others making responses radically different from his, the manipulation of conformity through the identification of his "first impulse" might not at all have been successful. Thus, when he saw the needle indicating that he had "conformed," he may be said to have had some subjective awareness of having chosen to "commit" himself to the discrepant response.

The same point applies to Bramel's experiment. Even though the subjects were told that the sexual arousal was unconscious, similar processes of choice in commitment may be said to have been operative. Young men just having come into manhood are conscious of their identity and masculinity. When they look at pictures of men in various states of undress, we may assume that they possess a great deal of cultural foreknowledge about the impropriety of sexual arousal under such conditions. They are all eager to behave and feel in the right manner and may therefore feel a good deal of uncertainty and anxiety when viewing the pictures. Thus, when the experimenter feeds back the information that they have experienced some homosexual arousal, it must be seen against this baseline of uncertainty and conflict and the subject's knowledge that he could give either an acceptable "response" or an invidious one. Here also, then, the dissonance experienced is a function of the fact that he has "behaved" to produce an invidious response discrepant from his self-image, that is, his behavior "follows from the opposite of" his motivation to maintain a positive self-picture. In effect, he has "committed" himself in a manner that has created some conflict within himself between an important motive and its satisfaction.

In Chapter 1 we indicated that discrepant commitment may be a unique aspect of dissonance theory. This implies, then, that unequivocal dissonance arousal may be based on the choice to commit oneself to a discrepant situation. For choice to be present, it may be necessary that there be some perception of uncertainty, conflict, or the potentiality of alternative responses in the situation of discrepant commitment. To the degree that this is a valid position, and that manipulations like Gerard's and Bramel's are effective because of this, there seems to be some basis for assuming that some awareness of the individual's own responsibility for his discrepant commitment is a necessary condition for the unequivocal identification of dissonance arousal. However, because of the lack of any very direct evidence, the entire question of whether responses to inconsistency require awareness must remain an unresolved one at this time. We can only speculate, although with some degree of confidence, about whether the dissonance formulation demands a specification of the consciousness issue in terms of choice, responsibility, and commitment.

Now to return to our point about the juxtaposition of dissonance and psychoanalytic theory. The Festinger and Bramel model is not explicit on the role of the processes of choice and commitment that we have highlighted, and, as a result, it is difficult to see that they are generally speaking about a situation that probably demands some "conscious awareness" of a discrepant commitment. It is precisely this factor of choice in commitment, which may be unique to dissonance theory, that makes it difficult to see how the theory can interact with psychoanalytic theory in explaining, for example, defensive projection. It would seem that a much broader attack might be more valuable than one that permits the two theories to function side by side in dealing with ego-defensive processes.

Festinger (1957, pp. 235–243) himself has suggested that such a state of affairs as strong emotion without a conscious explanation of it produces dissonance and motivates the individual to invent reasons for his feelings. According to Festinger, Freud had recognized this phenomenon. From this lead, it would appear that, using the Festinger and Bramel argument as a starting point, a more detailed analysis of at least the processes of projection, homosexuality, and paranoia may be possible. Such an analysis would deal with the interplay between conscious and unconscious forces and may not necessarily assume the person's awareness of a discrepancy.

Berkowitz (1960), in a stimulating paper on the judgmental process in personality functioning, offers an explanation for the dynamics of paranoia and projection that illustrates the potential benefits to be gained by dealing more explicitly with the interplay between the more conscious forces central to dissonance theory and the unconscious forces postulated by psychoanalytic theory. His ideas, although somewhat different from the conventional psychoanalytic formulation, are based on it. Also, while they are not identical to the assumptions of dissonance theory, they are entirely consistent with it, at least as it has been discussed in the present book. As Berkowitz points out, the psychoanalytic concept of projection involves, among other things, lack of insight into (or the repression of knowledge of) the possession of undesirable traits that produce conflict. If this lack of awareness is motivated, it may be due to a perceived inconsistency between the given trait and the individual's self-concept. Also, according to the psychoanalytic formulation, reaction formation must be considered here. In projecting his own characteristics onto others, the person may not only repress awareness that he has those characteristics, but he may also lean over backward in denying them and insist to himself and others that he is just the opposite. This is shown by the paranoid: According to psychoanalytic theory, the paranoid's basic problem involves latent homosexualty, and, since this is threatening to him, he represses the drive and projects it onto important others. However, even the attribution of homosexual desires onto others provokes anxiety, so the idea is transformed from "he loves me" into "he hates me."

Berkowitz's explanation, on the other hand, runs as follows: Paraphrasing his argument, we may say that, as in psychoanalytic theory, the process commences when the person judges himself (his "real self," i.e., his "behavior") as being toward the homosexuality end of the continuum, whereas his "ideals" are anchored toward the extreme heterosexual end. This discrepancy produces dissonance, and, in defense, the person "represses real knowledge of his self-evaluation," and may believe that he is really the way he would like to be. Such a process could, of course, occur entirely below the level of conscious awareness, though the notion of "judgment" in fact denotes conscious experience of this by the individual at some level. In any case, the individual represses his homosexual attributes but also exhibits reaction formation in characterizing himself as nonhomosexual. Seeing himself as extremely heterosexual, the person may see important others as more homosexual than they actually are. But even this is dissonance-producing, since liked others cannot be characterized as having a trait of which one disapproves. The person may reduce such dissonance by increasing his dislike for the person possessing the evil trait. However, since the basis for the hatred is kept from awareness, some tension may still remain. The discrepancy between the tension and no conscious explanation for it motivates the individual to find reasons for his feelings. Thus Berkowitz proposes that to a considerable extent the paranoid's feelings of being persecuted are the reasons he invents to give conscious meaning to his hatred for others. And extrapolating from Festinger's observations, Berkowitz feels that the magnitude of dissonance and consequent projection and paranoia can be a function of the size of the discrepancy between the way a person behaves and feels and what he thinks of himself.

The major point we wish to make here is that although the mechanism of projection may have been established early in life as a mode of resolution of inner conflict, it can also be seen as serving to reduce the dissonance arising from discrepancies between aspects of the individual's self-concept (both conscious and unconscious) and his behavior. Thus projection might well be viewed as a consequence of the motivation to reduce discrepancies within the self produced by some choice to commit oneself to a stand that is incompatible with the satisfaction of some important motive, in some cases, the motive for a favorable self-evaluation.

If one followed this line of reasoning, numerous implications for processes characteristically viewed as within the province of personality theory might be uncovered and made amenable to a dissonance formulation. For example, aggression directed against the self and its concomitant of depression could be explored as a function of the exercise of aggression toward others. If a person for some reason hurts or is openly hostile toward some innocuous other person whom he does not necessarily want to hurt, he may be expected to experience dissonance. The higher his self-evaluation, the more would aggression be dissonance arousing, since his behavior is more discrepant from his self-concept, the more self-esteem he has. The person can reduce dissonance in this situation by increasing his dislike of the other person, thereby making his perception of the other person consistent with his behavior.

If, on the other hand, the other person is, for example, a good friend, and barriers to derogation exist, the person can reduce dissonance by increasing his feelings of dislike or hostility toward his self. A bad act is thus made consistent with the kind of person one is. The greater the dissonance, the more the dislike directed toward the self in order to reduce that dissonance. We thus arrive at a rather paradoxical prediction: The higher the person's self-esteem or the more favorable his self-evaluation, the more he will show aggression against the self when he commits a discrepant act of aggression. Such an analysis could conceivably be applied to other personality processes like regression or dependency, reaction formation, and repression or denial. When the motivations, either conscious or unconscious, can be specified, a dissonance-arousing discrepant commitment can be identified and often shown to have effects on perception, cognition, and behavior that might not be expected from other theoretical approaches.

The point here, as well as Berkowitz's argument, represents an attempt to deal explicitly with the interplay between the unconscious forces posed by psychoanalytic theory and the more conscious ones specified by dissonance theory. Such a scheme may permit a better specification of the interaction between the environmental stimulus events impinging upon the person and the inner constraints as they both serve to determine his daily behavior in the social world. In effect, a formulation of this sort might aid in elaborating a more subtle and differentiated view of the relationships between personality and social behavior than we have at present.

INDIVIDUAL DIFFERENCES

A second issue in evaluating the relevance of the dissonance formulation for the study of personality concerns the question of individual differences. In the previous section we attempted to present a dissonance theory view of processes traditionally explained by psychoanalytic theory. In the present section we shall assume that predictions to a range of effects from dissonance theory could be sharpened by taking into account personality variables that are widely considered to be important determinants of cognition, perception, and social interaction. Assuming that it is possible to insert these personality variables between dissonance arousal and reduction in order to increase predictive accuracy, what are the kinds of difficulties and problems that the investigator might run into? We shall discuss some of these problems, which deal for the most part with a rather abstract notion of "personality variables" as a general class of variables. We hope in this manner to pinpoint some of the problems of the interrelationship between personality and cognitive processes and thereby to help facilitate future research and theory.

It is obvious that people will differ in their reactions to dissonance-arousing situations. Such differences could occur for a variety of reasons. On the arousal side, people may perceive a situation differently; on the response side, people may try to reduce dissonance in different ways. In between these two, people may be differentially sensitive to, or tolerant of, dissonance when it does occur.

Each of these sources of difference between people might be understood in terms of historical (learning) processes or in terms of personality variables. That is, a person who is offered five dollars for saying something he believes to be untrue may perceive the five dolars to be of relatively low value or of relatively high value, thus experiencing high or low dissonance. We may try to understand the value placed on the money in terms of his past experience (e.g., money is easy to come by) or in terms of a personality variable (e.g., acquisitiveness). Whichever way one might try to understand the differences, the purpose would be to increase one's understanding of the processes involved in the arousal and reduction of dissonance.

While it is easy to suppose that there are personality factors that play a role in the dissonance process, it is difficult to demonstrate what they may be. The reason for the difficulty is that the criterion variable—dissonance—is not directly measurable. To illustrate what this means, let us consider again the aforementioned case in which a person accepts money to say something he believes to be untrue. This individual will, according to the theory, experience dissonance. How do we determine that he does in fact experience dissonance? Not by measuring the dissonance but by measuring the attempts to reduce dissonance. Now let us suppose that we wish to show how one's perceptual style affects the magnitude of dissonance. Having measured the perceptual style of several people, say, in terms of sharpening and leveling, we now put each person in the dissonance arousal situation mentioned above. Since we cannot measure the resultant dissonance directly, we measure some attempt to reduce dissonance. The reader will note that we are already on thin ice in that the extent to which a person *attempts* to reduce dissonance will vary not only with the initial magnitude of dissonance but also with the success of the attempts. In other words, if in this situation the person tried to reduce dissonance by justifying his discrepant persuasion, the success in reducing dissonance of each attempted justification would determine in part whether or not a further attempt would be made. At the same time, we have no way of assessing just how successful each attempt is;

all we can say is that if any given attempt is followed by another, then it was not entirely successful in reducing dissonance.

Added to our inability to assess the amount of dissonance reduction represented by any given attempt to reduce dissonance is the fact that there are likely to be several distinguishable ways in which dissonance can be reduced. There may be several different dimensions along which the individual can justify his discrepant behavior, and there are likely to be possible methods of reduction other than justification. If the only way to measure the magnitude of dissonance is to measure the amount of attempts to reduce it, then we must, of course, measure all attempts to reduce it. Thus, to measure the magnitude of dissonance that a person experiences in a given situation, it is necessary to measure the magnitude of *all* attempts to reduce the dissonance, and it is also necessary to control the effects of differential success that these attempts may have.

But even if we could accomplish all this, we would still not necessarily be able to relate our measures of perceptual style with our measures of dissonance reduction, for still other factors must be taken into account. To see what some of the various problems are, let us imagine the following diagram. At the left side of this diagram are the factors that create dissonance and control its magnitude, while on the right are some possible ways in which dissonance may be reduced. In the center is the relationship of central interest, that is, that between the magnitude of dissonance and a personality variable (here, for example, perceptual style). Recalling now that the magnitude of dissonance is measured by the magnitude of attempts to reduce dissonance, we see that what we really establish is a relationship between one or more measures of attempts at dissonance reduction and the measure of the personality variable. However, it is also clear that factors other than dissonance can produce a relationship between these measures. Now let us see how complicated is the problem of establishing a relationship between the magnitude of dissonance and a personality variable.

Suppose, for example, that we have found more attitude change in a high dissonance condition than in a low (as manipulated) and that the attitude change thus obtained correlates with our measure of the personality variable. What might account for this relationship? It will be seen immediately that aside from the assumed direct relationship between the personality variable and dissonance, there are several possibilities. The personality variable may relate, either directly or through some intermediary variable, to any of the variables controlling the magnitude of dissonance, to any of the variables involved in dissonance reduction, and to the *selection* of method by which dissonance is reduced. That is, the amount of attitude change will presumably vary with the amount of dissonance produced, which in turn will vary with each of the factors that control the magnitude of dissonance. If the personality variable should for any reason be correlated with any of the independent variables, then it will correlate with the amount of attitude change produced. This means not only that the personality variable may be related to dissonance through one of the controlling variables in terms of dissonance theory but also that numerous variables could be involved. Of course, the personality variable might just as well be related to one or more of the ways in which dissonance can be reduced. In this case, the relationship could be with: (1) the readiness to change on a given variable, (2) the resistance to change on a given variable, or (3) the preference for one method of reduction rather than another. For any of these cases it would be inappropriate to say that the personality variable was related to dissonance *per se*. In addition, it should be noted that the effect of selection of method of dissonance reduction depends on the extent to which *all* possible methods of dissonance reduction can be measured and compared and on the correlation between the various methods of dissonance reduction. The relationship between methods of dissonance reduction can be either positive or negative, as can be seen from previous research, although the conditions controlling the direction of this relationship are not known.

It is apparent, therefore, that the mere relationship between the magnitude of change in a given variable and a personality measure does not insure that the personality variable has any direct effect on dissonance. Indeed, it would not even be clear that the personality variable was related to dissonance rather than to some variable that controls dissonance reduction.

What with the ambiguity concerning an explanation of the relationship between a personality variable and the magnitude of dissonance, it becomes somewhat difficult to identify the theoretical significance of whatever personality variable may be found to relate. For example, Festinger has suggested (1957) that people may differ in their tolerance for dissonance and hence may exhibit differential amounts of attempts to reduce dissonance when confronted with a given situation. It could also be suggested that people differ in their sensitivity to dissonance or in their facility in reducing dissonance. However, it would seem that until we can isolate that aspect of the dissonance formulation to which the personality variable is related, we will be unable to understand its significance.

Although these considerations indicate that there may be consider-

174 / *Explorations in Cognitive Dissonance*

able ambiguity about the significance of personality variables in understanding dissonance processes, certain notions and evidence are worthy of mention. The first, consisting of an apparent phenomenon from the study by Brehm and Cohen (1959b), concerns a dimension that may affect the magnitude of dissonance. In this study, it will be recalled, college students were requested to participate in a boring and tedious task. Although an attempt was made to manipulate the magnitude of restraint against trying to escape from participation in the task, a postexperimental questionnaire check on the success of this attempt indicated that it failed to produce reliable effects. Instead, the difference between experimental conditions was *less* than the differences within conditions, as measured by variances. This greater variability within conditions approached statistical reliability.

While a relatively great variability within conditions (like any other effect) could result from chance alone, it is rather surprising here. Indeed, it seems so unlikely that it provokes speculation about what might cause it. We suggest that it is a meaningful phenomenon and that it reflects an important personality variable for dissonance theory. What it suggests is that individuals tend to react diversely to coercive forces. That is, when a person is told he must do something, he may comply without resistance or he may react with anything up to considerable resistance. The resistance is triggered by the coercive force, and the magnitude of the resistance is due in part to the personality makeup of the individual. We suggest that individuals vary in the extent to which they feel they control their own fate. The more a person feels he controls his own fate, the more he will tend to resist coercion. Given that the individual does comply with the coercive force, the greater his resistance, the greater his dissonance. Hence those who feel they control their own fate, compared with others, will tend to experience greater dissonance and exhibit greater attempts to reduce dissonance.

The results of the study were, of course, consistent with this explanation in that those who felt it would be relatively easy to get out of the task performance tended more to show a dissonance reduction pattern in their reactions: They were more satisfied with a high relative deprivation assignment than with a low.

Additional evidence on the effect of personality variables comes from a study by Rosen (1961), described earlier. It will be remembered that he replicated a study by Mills, Aronson and Robinson (1959) in which dissonance in college students was aroused by their choice between types of examination, and attempts to reduce this dissonance were measured by the students' selection of reading material relevant to the choice. Both studies found, as predicted, that the reading material selected tended to be that which supported the type of examination chosen. In the replication, Rosen also gathered information relevant to two personality dimensions that might plausibly be related to the magnitude of dissonance. Reasoning that dissonance (at least in this experimental situation) is a function of a risk of being wrong, he proposed that dissonance may then be a function of other factors related to risk avoidance. The variables he chose to investigate were decision certainty and width of categorizing. To measure these variables, he asked his subjects, 11 days subsequent to the experiment, to complete a ten-item abbreviated version of Pettigrew's (1958) Category Width Scale and also to indicate on a five-point scale their judgmental certainty of the range of each category of information. Category width scores were computed by summing the weights for the individual ranges given on each item. Certainty scores were similarly computed by summing the ten individual ratings.

The category width scale measures the degree to which subjects are broad, medium, or narrow in their estimated ranges of a number of varied categories; it gives the subjects' typical equivalence ranges for classifying objects. Category width is assumed to be related to risk taking: Those whose width is broad are assumed to have a tolerance for Type I errors where they risk negative instances in an effort to include a number of positive instances; those with narrow width are assumed to have a tolerance for Type II errors by excluding positive instances and thereby restricting category ranges in order to minimize the number of negative instances. Since the dissonance manipulations may have been related to risk avoidance, the specification of people of different risk-taking predispositions was presumed to affect dissonance arousal.

The results of this investigation showed that those who expressed a more extreme preference for reading articles that supported their decision about examinations (high dissonance reduction) also tended to use narrower categories. This effect was significant for males but not for females. No relationship was found between decision certainty and dissonance reduction. In keeping with our earlier discussion of the problems involved in relating personality measures to dissonance, we must note that the measure of category width has not been shown to relate to the manipulated magnitude of dissonance. That is, it has not been shown to relate to attempted dissonance reduction as a direct function of the magnitude of dissonance. Hence we must view any interpretation with considerable caution.

The role of personality variables in the understanding of dissonance is not well developed and offers a major challenge to further investigation. It is apparent that at least two kinds of variables must receive attention: those dealing with cognitive structure and change and those dealing with the involvement, motivation, concern, and so forth of the individual.

A serious attempt to explore the relationship between personality predispositions and dissonance arousal and reduction would involve an explicit search for personality variables that are theoretically coordinated to the specification of arousal and reduction. For example, if we take as a basic assumption of the theory as we define it the fact of discrepant commitment and the importance of prior choice in commitment, then the personality variables isolated ought to refer to differences between people in characteristic commitment tendencies or decisional ease or difficulty. Thus arousal would take place, the more that the people involved had certain personality predispositions related to the ease of commitment or decision. The same is true for variables on the reduction side. There may be personality predispositions that make for differences between people in the modes of dissonance reduction they characteristically use. This could be specified, for example, in terms coordinate with differences between people in the mechanisms by which they resolve unconscious conflicts. Thus different strengths of different ego-defenses might be related to different characteristic modes of reducing dissonance. Another example might involve differences between people in cognitive style or in flexibility or rigidity or extremity of attitudes; those who show certain kinds of cognitive control mechanisms or certain constellations of cognitive structure might very well change their attitudes more or less easily as a mode of reducing dissonance. We could go on to elaborate numerous examples, but in the absence of data this is somewhat unprofitable. All we mean to emphasize here is that a serious search for relevant personality variables would demand a clear description of their specific connection to specific dissonance-arousing variables and modes of reduction.

This concludes our discussion of the role of dissonance in the study of personality. We have tried to indicate, in our section on individual differences, that the problems of interrelating personality characteristics and issues of dissonance arousal and reduction are manifold. However, it should be clear that there are advantages to be gained by both personality theory and dissonance theory if such a coordination is made. The increased conceptual refinement of personality variables and the increased predictive precision of the dissonance model would each appear to be valid benefits.

Expectations and inequity:
a dissonance approach
—10

DISSONANCE AND THE PSYCHOLOGY OF EXPECTATIONS

An interesting extension of dissonance theory to the issue of expectations has been made by Aronson (1960). This extension of the theory is based on the assumption that the dissonance occasioned by commitment to a discrepant position, for instance, is due to the discrepancy between: (1) one's expectation that, as a rational man, he will behave with integrity and (2) the cognition that one did not behave with integrity. Aronson says that many of the research findings growing out of the dissonance formulation can be interpreted as attempts on the part of the individual to confirm expectancies. Taking account of the individual's expectancy is necessary in order to determine what is inconsistent with what; the events that confirm expectancies are consonant, sought out, while the events that disconfirm expectancies are dissonant, to be avoided, minimized, or cognitively distorted so as to render them more consonant.

Aronson's theory leads him to the position that the confirmation of expectancies is one of the central motivating forces in human behavior. Thus persons will at times seek out failure, punishment, frustration, and so on, in order to confirm expectations regarding the nature of their self-concept.

One obvious derivation from this position says that an event that is identical with an expectancy will be preferred to other events. The nonobvious extension of this point concerns a situation in which a person holds the firm belief that he has no skill in a given area and hence expects to perform poorly. Suppose, Aronson says, that a person performs superlatively. The person would not be expected to experience disappointment, frustration, misery, embarrassment, depression, and so forth, but he should experience dissonance. Thus the person should be made uncomfortable by success and should try to minimize it and perhaps even seek failure in order to reduce his dissonance. On the other hand, if the person expects failure and fails, or expects success and succeeds, there should be no dissonance and consequent denial or minimization of the event.

In an experiment designed to test this hypothesis, Aronson and Carlsmith (in press a) first gave subjects sets of photographs to judge. The subjects were told that one of three photographs on a card was that of a hospitalized schizophrenic and that the test was designed to measure their ability to judge accurately. There were 100 cards in all; they were grouped into five sets of 20 cards each. After the subject had made 20 judgments, the experimenter scored his performance, and the subject moved on to the next set. By false feedback, half the subjects were led to believe that they had scored consistently high on this "personality attribute"; half were made to believe that they had scored consistently low. Thus, when beginning the fifth section, some subjects expected to score high, while others expected to score low. On the fifth and final set, half the subjects in each condition had their expectancies confirmed by false feedback; half had their expectancies disconfirmed. Then, under a pretext, the experimenter allowed the subject to judge the fifth set again. The dependent variable was the number of judgments the subject made on the repeated fifth trial that differed from the ones he made the first time.

Aronson's theory leads him to expect that those subjects whose expectancies are confirmed will be content with their score, while those whose expectancies are disconfirmed will change their responses in an attempt to re-establish a consistent self-concept regarding their performance. For those whose performance is less than their expectation, the prediction is straightforward, but for those whose performance exceeds their expectations, the startling prediction is that they would prefer to believe that their sensitivity is low and thus change their responses, rather than have their expectations of failure disconfirmed. Aronson's data strongly support his contentions in this regard.

This derivation from expectancy assumptions is generalized by

Aronson to deal with the class of situations in which persons who expect a negative event to occur, who are set for it, and who have rehearsed their behavior in regard to it, will feel discomfort if it does not occur. Thus, if the subject is then offered his choice between the negative event and a neutral event, at least up to a limiting point, he will choose the negative event simply because he has expected it to occur. Going further, Aronson assumes that having an expectancy regarding an event confirmed results in a state of pleasantness and that this will generalize to the objects in the environment that are involved in the confirmation or disconfirmation. This is not true, he says, when the same state has been attained, but when there has been no prior expectancy. For example, expecting a given solution to taste sweet will make it seem sweeter after it has been tasted and judged sweet, whereas persons with no expectation regarding sweetness will not judge a solution to be sweeter after tasting it. In general, Aronson assumes that over a large class of events, there will be positive affect on the confirmation of expectancies, negative affect resulting from disconfirmation.

Even with regard to the powerful motive of achievement, the striving to confirm expectancies should result in persons showing decrements in performance and in self-judgment regarding ability in order to reduce discrepancies between expectations and performance. For Aronson, knowledge of prior expectations permits finer predictions concerning the way a person handles dissonance due to the discrepancy between, for example, his usual performance and a new performance. Having gone this far, he is able to generalize his notions so that they become relevant to level of aspiration phenomena; thus a person who has reduced dissonance between his performance and expectations by disparaging a task might even intentionally score lower than his usual level of performance on a next task in order to fortify his belief.

It should be clear that in the expectation model presented by Aronson, the motive to resolve the inconsistency between expectations and performance is seen as an overriding social motive, so strong, in fact, as to take precedence over such a powerful social motive as achievement. However, there remains some lack of specification in his model as to just why this occurs. Should one assume that under all conditions the confirmation of expectancies is the primary motive that demands satisfaction at the possible expense of other motives like pain avoidance, achievement of affiliation? Or should one assume that there are conditions under which these other motives will take precedence in determining behavior? Aronson's model takes for granted some anchoring of expectations so that they become the motive force to which the individual is most strongly committed. In so doing it does not entirely specify the conditions that produce striving for expectation fulfillment rather than for the achievement of success in task performance. Thus the dissonance arising from the discrepancy between expectations and, for example, successful performance, as in the Aronson and Carlsmith (in press a) experiment, is presumably resolved in favor of satisfaction of the expectation motive rather than the achievement motive on an *a priori* basis. But the central question here is: What are the relative strengths of the motives involved (i.e., expectancy-fulfillment and achievement) in relation to the discrepancy-producing behavior of the person? That is, if the person makes some commitment to a given behavior (succeeding) that is discrepant from his prior cognitions (the expectation that he will fail), why does he resolve that dissonance by failing on the next trial, in other words, by fulfilling his expectancy motive and frustrating his achievement motive?

The answer to this question, in the light of the dissonance model as we view it, may reside in the fact that the person has himself initiated some conflict between his two important motives by committing himself, that is, by performing successfully. He can reduce this dissonance by distorting his performance, but if the commitment is public, irrevocable, and based on physical reality, it will probably remain anchored. The person can then either change his expectations or reduce his achievement. He may choose to do the latter when the expectancy motive is stronger and takes precedence in satisfaction. If, on the other hand, he were strongly motivated to perform well, that is, if the satisfaction of his achievement motive was paramount, he would still experience dissonance, but the commitment to good performance could result in dissonance reduction by strengthening of the achievement motivation and/or behavior.

Thus a possible addition to Aronson's model might be a specification of the degree of commitment that produces the dissonance. Such a specification of the commitment variable might help to refine predictions about the avenues persons use to reduce the dissonance between their expectations and their performance, perception, or social behavior.

A DISSONANCE ANALYSIS OF DISCREPANCIES IN COMPENSATION: THE PSYCHOLOGY OF INEQUITY

The discussion of Aronson's notions regarding expectations raises the issue of the degree to which tensions arising from the discrepancies between a person's compensations and his performance (with regard to some internalized standards he has set for himself, or vis-à-vis others) motivates the individual to reduce those discrepancies. This issue is a central one in understanding the issue of equity. Inequity can, of course, result from either success or reward or recognition (i.e., outcomes) falling below the expectations the individual sets for himself or from outcomes greater than the individual's expectations. The problem of undercompensation is obviously the more common problem, and in attempting to understand the individual's efforts to increase an outcome we usually have recourse to numerous alternative explanations, for example, those centering around the obvious and general need to maximize rewards. It is the other side of the coin, however, the side dealing with the individual's reaction to inequity resulting from overcompensation, that is more interesting and that appears to be difficult for competing theories to explain, though it appears to be largely amenable to a dissonance theory analysis.

An experiment by Day (1961) will serve to illustrate this point in a clear and straightforward manner. In his experiment 50 boys and girls from 4 to 6 years of age were given a number of training trials in which they pushed the handle of a plunger mechanism to receive rewards. These rewards, M & M candies, were wrapped in clear plastic packages. During the training session six different levels of rewards were given. When the plunger was pushed down so that the dial read between 6 to 9 pounds, one wrapped candy was given. For 9 to 12 pounds, two candies were given; for 12 to 15, three candies; for 15 to 18, four candies; for 18 to 21, five candies; for 21 to 24, six candies. Pressure below 6 pounds was not rewarded. Since the pressure exerted by subjects in early trials tended to vary considerably, subjects were given trials until their response stabilized in the same pressure category for five trials in a row. After these five trials, an increased reward consisting of 25 M & Ms was given each subject for each of five consecutive trials regardless of how hard he pushed. The response pressures were recorded for the training and the increased reward trials. The general hypothesis, derived from dissonance theory, states that when a subject is trained at a certain reinforcement level for a number of trials, he comes to expect that reward for the amount of work performed. However, when the reward level is suddenly increased, the subject is faced with cognitions that are discrepant. On the one hand, there is the cognition of the physical effort actually expended, and, on the other hand, there is the reality of the increased reward. In this situation dissonance theory predicts that the subject will attempt to reduce the discrepancy between the two cognitions, and, given the reality bounds of the reward, one way he might do this would be to increase his "effort" so as to "earn" his reward.

The data show that significantly more subjects respond to the increased reward by increasing the mean response pressure from the last five training trials to the five overrewarded trials: 64% of the subjects significantly increase their response pressure over their training trials, while 36% of the subjects show a tendency to decrease their response pressure. When the data are further analyzed according to the age of the subjects, it appears that increases or decreases in response pressure are largely a function of age: When only the oldest third of the population is isolated (children between 5.2 years and 6.4 years), 80% of the subjects increase their response strength whereas only 20% decrease it. Thus the response to overcompensation by an increase in effort may be dependent on learning associated with maturation, but once the person is old enough, we may consider it to be a strong possible response to such inequity.

Day's experiment deals with at least one reaction to the problem of inequity involved in overcompensation. An attempt to evolve a more global theory has been made by Adams (1961). As we shall see, Adams' theoretical model seeks to extend the dissonance formulation to the entire range of inequities and particularly to those residing in the relationship between one's own inputs and outcomes and another's inputs and outcomes.

Adams defines inequity as follows: Inequity exists for a person whenever his perceived job inputs and/or outcomes stand psychologically in an obverse relation to what he perceives are the inputs and/or outcomes of another person. Though Adams attempts to deal with the varied possibilities for inequity resulting from the interaction between self and others, and input and outcome, what is particularly interesting about his analysis is what happens to the person when he is at "the top of the heap." Thus persons will feel that an inequity exists not only when their effort is high and their pay is low and others' effort is low and pay high, but also when their own effort is low and pay high and others' effort is high and pay low. In effect, a person will experience the discomfort of inequity when he is relatively overcompensated as well as when he is relatively undercompensated.

The dissonance formulation is invoked to deal with the inequity situation in the following manner. Adams assumes that the presence of inequity creates dissonance in the person and that the magnitude of dissonance is proportional to the magnitude of inequity present. This statement is, of course, the same as previous statements we have

Expectations and Inequity: A Dissonance Approach / 183

made concerning the dissonance occasioned by the discrepancy between expectation and outcome; here inequity results from this discrepancy. It is also assumed that the dissonance will motivate efforts to reduce the discrepancy, that is, to reduce the inequity or to achieve equity.

Adams then enumerates and illustrates a variety of means available to the person so that he may reduce the inequity.

1. The person may increase his inputs if they are low relative to others' inputs and to his own outcomes. He may do this by increased effort or productivity, as did the children in Day's experiment.

2. The person may decrease his outcomes if they are high relative to his own standards regarding the relationship between inputs and outcomes or high relative to another's outcomes. This might take the form of a person's lowering his pay. Adams feels that this is an improbable mode of reducing inequity, although theoretically possible. However, the Aronson and Carlsmith (in press a) experiment provides supporting evidence for the general point here: With inequity resulting from unexpected success, subjects increased their failure on a repeated performance trial, after they had first succeeded on it, when their expectations were that they would fail.

3. The person may distort his inputs and outcomes, increasing or decreasing them as required. Since most individuals are heavily influenced by reality, distortion is generally difficult, that is, it is not easy to distort one's ability or the objective factors in one's background.

4. The person may increase, decrease, or distort the inputs and outcomes of others. Thus, if the person's effort was too low compared to the other's and to his own pay, he might induce the other to decrease his effort instead of increasing his own effort. Or if his effort is high and his pay is low, whereas the other's effort and pay are low, he might induce the other to increase effort so as to stabilize their relative inputs and outcomes.

Adams discusses at length the means by which persons can reduce inequity and the various interactions that can take place around the question of establishing equity. Of course, not all means of reducing equity are equally satisfactory; the nature of the input and outcome discrepancies and situational circumstances make some means more available and stable than others. Whether or not persons involved in the inequity relationship have: (1) common perceptions, or (2) are both motivated to reduce the inequity, or (3) constitute a social system, or (4) communicate freely, or (5) perceive veridically their own and other's inputs and outcomes will affect the strength, mode, and success of attempts to reduce inequity. As Adams says, many possibilities of incompatible solutions exist. For example, after an attempt to reach an equitable solution, one person might reduce his effort to match his low pay, whereas another who receives high pay for less effort would be trying to reduce the inequity by obtaining a raise for the first person. If he were successful, the first person would be receiving a pay increment for less effort, a situation that would produce dissonance and might motivate further efforts toward discrepancy reduction.

Adams presents a series of case histories in support of a number of his major contentions. Although none of this evidence is conclusive in itself, it illustrates the implications of the model and possible ways of making more rigorous tests. For example, when a person is overcompensated and paid by the piece, he may decrease his productivity, whereas, when he is overpaid by the hour, his productivity may increase.

An experiment designed to test this hypothesis was carried out by Adams and Rosenbaum (1962). Nine subjects were assigned to each of four conditions: (1) where an hourly rate of $3.50 was paid and the subjects were made to feel overcompensated by stating that they were not qualified to earn the hourly rate of $3.50; (2) where the hourly rate of $3.50 was paid, but the subjects were made to feel that they were fairly paid by stating that they were very well qualified to earn the rate; (3) where a piece rate of $.30 was paid and the subjects were made to feel overcompensated as in the first condition; and (4) where a piece rate of $.30 was paid but the subjects were made to feel they had been fairly paid as above. The task was to obtain interviews with the general public for 2 hours, and subjects were under the impression that they were hired for an extended time period.

The data support Adams' hypothesis. They show a significant interaction such that subjects overcompensated by the hour show a higher productivity than comparable individuals earning the same pay but feeling equitably compensated, whereas overcompensated persons paid by the piece show lower productivity than comparable persons paid at the same piece rate but feeling equitably compensated. This is assumed by Adams to indicate an increase in performance among the hourly workers who are overcompensated in order to establish equity, whereas the piece workers who are also overcompensated reduce the amount they can earn when they are overcompensated in order to establish equity.

Adams and Rosenbaum checked out an alternative explanation that attributed the hourly overcompensation results to the fact that the dissonance subjects produced more in order to make their jobs more secure. They found that this explanation was not supported. Where public and private conditions were run, it was found that in the private condition (where the subject mailed his work to an office in another city) as well as in the public condition (where the subject turned his work in to the experimenter), overcompensation led to greater productivity than did no overcompensation.

Although these data are in line with Adams' hypothesis and are in accord with the equity model, they may not be entirely unambiguous. In both conditions subjects could possibly be attempting to convince the experimenter that they are more valuable than he believes them to be: in the hourly rate condition, by producing more interviews; in the piece rate condition, by doing each interview more carefully and therefore producing fewer. Thus results in both conditions could then conceivably be explained by a need to raise one's self in the eyes of the experimenter rather than to establish equity. Nevertheless, this experiment certainly does follow directly from Adams' theoretical notions and illustrates one of the possibilities for experimental test of the theory.

It should be mentioned that some subjective evidence for Adams' equity theory exists in Zimbardo's aforementioned "exposure" experiment where he manipulated effort through differential delayed auditory feedback. Zimbardo found that those subjects who felt that they were overpaid for committing themselves to the discrepant behavior perceived that they had actually exerted more effort in the delay apparatus than those subjects who did not feel that they were overpaid.

Adams hopes that his theory, through the application of the discrepancy model, will contribute much toward an understanding of inequity. However, there may be some ambiguities in the theory that should be mentioned here. As we said at the outset, the issue of undercompensation, insofar as it predicts attempts to raise outcome, is a somewhat obvious one in that the maximization of rewards may be the strongest motive. Insofar as lowering others' outcomes is concerned, the degree to which this mode of resolution is followed when there is undercompensation will probably be a function of at least the environmental barriers against increasing reward, against lowering effort, and the chances of lowering the others' reward to match one's own. Also important is the degree to which the person's motive structure makes salient not only the need for reward but also the degree to which the person can reduce inequity by seeing others in the same boat. That is, the person's motivation with regard to his relationship to others is central. The same is true with overcompensation. The general assumption of discrepancy reduction may not be enough to enable clear predictions of modes of reducing inequity. Persons could feel that financial or other outcomes are less important than (1) the social norms in which they have a stake, (2) their relationship to others in the same shop, (3) feelings of guilt because they are getting relatively more pay, (4) the stability of their self-images, which are tied to certain internalized standards regarding the relationship between reward and performance, and so forth.

In effect, what we are saying is that through some behavior the person may have produced some discrepancy between the satisfaction of one motive and another. The degree to which the response the individual has produced results in a discrepancy between motive satisfactions will determine the degree of dissonance aroused. And the dissonance can be reduced, depending on which of the relevant motives is strongest for the person. Thus the person may not be able to change his equity relationships to others if he is too committed to his particular social relationship or if he has some strong internalized standards about the appropriateness of certain rewards for certain effort. For example, having behaved, and under conditions where he cannot undo the particular behavior, he uses the more pliable mode of dissonance reduction, that is, he may lower his performance. Or, on the other hand, if his strongest motive in the situation is to earn a great deal of money and he does not want to lose the pay, but yet does not want to establish a relationship of inequity with his work mates, he may decide to increase his effort. He thus reduces the dissonance occasioned by the inequity between his input and outcome. Adams' equity model, then, might benefit from a specification of the notion of commitment; this might help in specifying clearly which of the alternative modes of dissonance reduction the person will use in a situation of inequity.

The present discussion of expectations and inequity should serve to broaden our perspective regarding the potential areas of application of the dissonance formulation. Aronson's and Adams' models represent important extensions of the theory; they suggest that the theory is readily applicable to various specific issues of aspiration, performance and interpersonal relationships.

Speculations about
dissonance arousal

— 11

Our review of the literature has shown the variety of research and empirical generalizations to which dissonance theory has led. It has also shown, however, that there are important ambiguities concerning various aspects of the theory. In this chapter we shall point out some difficulties concerning the specification of conditions under which dissonance occurs and suggest some theoretical solutions for these difficulties.

As already noted, the defining statement for a dissonant relationship is that one cognition follows from the obverse of another. The magnitude of dissonance associated with any given cognitive element can then be ascertained by comparing the number and importance of dissonant elements with the number and importance of consonant elements. In addition, the magnitude of dissonance is directly proportional to the importance of the relevant elements, other things held constant.

Although these statements seem rather abstract, they can be operationalized sufficiently well to provide empirical tests, as is shown in our review of the evidence. In particular, the studies involving "forced compliance" and those involving "free choice" seem to be particularly clear and successful in their demonstrations of dissonance. What is common to these studies is that *they all require the subjects to make a choice, either between choice objects or whether or not to engage in a given behavior.* As Festinger (1957) has noted, and as we have noted, it seems apparent that conditions involving choice almost inevitably result in dissonance.

At the same time there is at least one class of events in which the application of the theory is sometimes equivocal. This is the broad class of situations in which a person is simply exposed to information that is inconsistent with one or more cognitions he already holds. Although among these situations are cases in which the specification of dissonance is relatively unequivocal, there are also instances in which it is not clear whether or not dissonance would be aroused, and even instances in which it is entirely unlikely that dissonance would be aroused even though there are "inconsistent" cognitions.

Perhaps we can pinpoint some of the ambiguities by considering a hypothetical case. Suppose a person makes his living by farming and that he has a choice each year about whether to grow tobacco or corn. Let us also suppose that the conditions of weather, disease, and market prices that favor one crop will tend to be poor for the other crop. Knowing this, the farmer must make a careful choice about which crop he will grow. Subsequent to making a decision, the farmer will prepare the soil in a special way, acquire certain pest and disease preventatives or curatives, and so forth. The decision is followed by essentially irrevocable actions, including the actual planting of one crop or the other. Now let us consider where and how dissonance can arise.

The decision itself will, of course, result in some dissonance. If the farmer has decided to grow tobacco and has taken irrevocable action in that direction (such as having planted his seedlings in the fields), then knowledge that corn requires less fertilizer than tobacco, that corn requires less expensive insecticides than does tobacco, and so on, would be dissonant with the irrevocable decision. When these cognitive elements are held prior to the decision, they create dissonance as soon as the decision is made. In general, knowledge that is inconsistent with taking a given alternative becomes dissonant the moment the decision to take that alternative is made.

But all possible negative consequences of the decision to grow tobacco are not known at the time of the decision. Can *all* such negative consequences create dissonance? Let us consider each of two distinguishable types of postchoice negative consequence.

First, there is the consequence that is suspected, or known as a possibility, prior to the choice. That is, the farmer may know that the two possible crops, corn and tobacco, require two different weather conditions for optimal growth and that either could easily occur. Thus, while it is impossible for him to know ahead of time which crop will be favored by the weather, he knows that the weather can vary from quite good to quite poor for the crop chosen. The judged probability of favorable weather for each alternative is one of the cognitions that helps to determine the choice and thus plays a role in the determination of dissonance resulting from the choice *per se*. But unless the farmer counts on the worst possible weather for the crop he chooses, the actual weather conditions that obtain can be worse than he has counted on in making his decision. If such bad weather occurs, does it create dissonance?

It may be noted that a decision whose consequence is largely a matter of chance is ordinarily called a gamble. Thus we may pose the same problem in terms of gambling behavior: A gambler knows that when he bets on a horse he may lose, and he certainly would not place a bet he knew he would lose. But does such a loss create dissonance in the gambler?

The second type of postchoice consequence we wish to consider is that which is not suspected prior to the decision. Returning to our farmer, suppose that after he has his tobacco crop well under way, tobacco smoking is shown to be the direct cause of a deadly and prevalent disease. This knowledge would certainly have affected the farmer's decision if it had been available beforehand. But the knowledge was not only not available, it was quite unexpected. Does it, then, arouse dissonance?

Another way to look at the unexpected event is to view it as one over which the individual has no control. Consider, for example, a person walking along a street. If a tree branch falls on him, inflicting a painful wound, does this event create dissonance in the walker? In this case the person has been the victim of an unpleasant event over which he had no control. While he might have chosen the shady side of the street over the sunny, and thus had some control over his getting hit, he might also have found both sides of the street to have equally many and equally healthy-looking trees. Again, the choice, like that of the gambler, is made with insufficient information to guarantee the outcome. Does the victim then experience dissonance when the outcome is "bad"?

The general theoretical statement, which holds that one cognition, the obverse of which would follow from another, creates dissonance, can be interpreted to imply that any of these examples involves the creation of dissonance. But such an interpretation assumes that any event follows from the obverse of an already held cognition simply by virtue of being unpleasant or inconsistent in some sense. On the other hand, it could be argued that the occurrence of an unpleasant or inconsistent event does not *necessarily* follow from the obverse of cognitions already held.

In summary, we hold that it is not always clear when dissonance will occur. This unclarity arises from conceptual and theoretical ambiguities. Let us see, then, how this aspect of the theory might be clarified.

THE EFFECT OF CHOICE

We have held that the arousal of dissonance is unequivocal in situations that involve choice, whether it is the selection of one from multiple alternatives or the acceptance or rejection involved in a "forced-compliance" situation. The reason is that: (1) The act of choice is inconsistent with any information supporting the selection of only the unchosen alternative, and (2) The act generally implies a commitment. Thus the information inconsistent with the choice becomes dissonant. It is apparent that if a person did not have to give up one or more alternatives in making his selection, then the "choice" would create no dissonance. In effect, for the choice to create dissonance it must involve some commitment to one alternative rather than to another. Let us therefore give some further consideration to the role of commitment in the arousal of dissonance.

COMMITMENT

In spite of its apparently crucial role in the creation of dissonance, commitment has received little attention as an explicit variable in dissonance research. A study reported by Festinger (1957, pp. 55–61) showed that a person's feeling of confidence in the correctness of his judgment tends to be higher with final (committed) judgments than with tentative (noncommitted) judgments. It was presumed that committed judgments would produce dissonance (since the judged stimuli were ambiguous), which in turn might be reduced by the individual's convincing himself that the judgment was indeed accurate.

The previously described study by Davis and Jones (1960) showed that the commitment involved in a decision followed by overt behavior can be reduced by allowing the possibility of changing the meaning of the behavior. It will be recalled that they induced college students, under high and low choice conditions, to make a negative evaluation of another (target) person, presumably also a college student. High commitment to the negative evaluation was obtained by telling the subject that the target person would be left with the impression that the negative evaluation was true even after the experiment was over and that the subject and target person would not see each other again. Low commitment was obtained by telling the subject that the target person would be informed that the negative impression was false and, further, that the subject could say whatever he wanted to the target person at the end of the experiment. As was expected, the high choice condition produced a more negative evaluation of the target person in the high commitment condition but not in the low commitment condition. Thus the promise of changing the meaning of the choice and behavior served to eliminate the commitment aspect.

AN EXPERIMENT ON THE EFFECT OF COMMITMENT

What is needed, however, is a study explicitly designed to show the effect of inconsistent cognitive elements with and without the presence of commitment to a specific element. The following study was therefore designed and conducted by Brehm and Gerald S. Leventhal. It was set up so that the effect of the occurrence of a discrepant cognitive element could be examined under conditions of low and high importance as well as with and without commitment to a prior cognition. This was accomplished by letting a person build up an expectation from a series of informational items under conditions where that information served as the basis for a general judgment. The role of importance was revealed by making the accuracy of the over-all judgment instrumental to goals of greater or lesser importance.

The subjects in this study were students from classes in introductory psychology who had volunteered to participate in a study of "weight judgment." These students are required to participate in a certain amount of research and, furthermore, receive "credit points" for each hour they do participate. Thus their participation is not completely voluntary although they do have choice about which of various projects they will participate in. Nevertheless, the majority of them had been in little or no research prior to their participation in this study and were quite interested in doing well at whatever they might be asked to do. This genuine interest in the research interfered with attempts to manipulate importance: In general, subjects tend to attach high importance to an experimental task. For that reason an attempt was made to manipulate importance in two different ways. The first involved the derogation of the experimental task and its significance, and then the possibility of winning prizes of low or high value; the second way involved building up the personal and scientific significance of the task. Since the attempt to affect importance through prizes of differing value failed, at this point we will report the procedure only in terms of the personal importance manipulation.

Subjects were run individually. When a subject arrived for the experimental session, he was seated at a table facing a black curtain that prevented his seeing what was at the experimenter's side of the table. The experimenter reminded him that the study was concerned with judging weights. The manipulation of importance was then introduced.

Low Importance was created by the experimenter's making the following points: (1) that he was not concerned with how well the subject performed but only with how people in general behaved; (2) that the task was not very interesting; (3) that he was conducting the experiment simply as practice for a course he was taking; and (4) that the experiment was not working, and the present subject's results would therefore not be useful in any way.

High Importance was created by indicating that the study was a regular scientific experiment and by stressing that it would determine how well the subject would do on the task. Thus, instead of reducing the subject's natural ego involvement, the experimenter stressed it, and, in addition, instead of saying that the study was for practice, he said that it was a regular scientific experiment.

After the instructions for the Importance manipulation, the description of the weight judgment task was given. The task involved the subject's sitting at a desk, putting his hand under a curtain, lifting a small weight, assigning a value to that weight, and then predicting the average weight of a series of 15 weights. This routine was followed for each of 11 trials. The weights were identical in size and appearance and had the following gram values: 80, 90, 101, 113.7, 127.5, 144, and 291.6. The weights were given to the subject in the following order: 113.7, 80, 127.5, 90, 144, 101, 113.7, 80, 127.5, 90, and 291.6. It will be noted that the weights alternated between light and heavy. Subjects were told that there was a simple system that might help them in estimating the weights and the series average. Almost all subjects later reported having noticed the alternation between light and heavy weights. It will also be noted that the eleventh weight is much heavier than the subject is likely to expect. Thus *the eleventh weight serves as the inconsistent information.*

Prior to lifting any weights, the subject was told how to assign numbers and what was meant by an average. He was then told that to keep subjects interested and on their toes, a prize consisting of a $5.00 gift certificate would be given to anyone who reached a certain level of accuracy in his prediction of the average.[9] To make the prize seem within reach, the experimenter said that between one third and one half of the participants were expected to win one. He explained that near the end of the series of weights, the subject would be given one critical judgment that would determine whether or not he would win a prize.

The experimenter explained the weight value scale in the following way. He told the subject that any value between zero and 200 could be assigned to each weight. He also said that the values of the first two weights would be given to the subject and that, subsequently, it would be up to the subject to assign the values. The first two weights were then placed under the subject's hand, and the subject was instructed to lift them alternately. The subject was told that the value of the first and heavier weight was 50, the value of the second and lighter weight was 38. The subject was then given each of the other weights in the series, one by one.

The *Commitment* condition was inserted after the tenth weight and just prior to presentation of the discrepant weight. In the *Low Commitment* condition, the weight value and estimate of the series average were obtained in the same way as for all other weights. (There was a slight variation of this in the Low Importance condition in that subjects were instructed to consider this estimate of the average very carefully even though it would not be the estimate determining whether or not they won a prize. This was instituted to control for attention and care in making this particular estimate. Its effect should be to maximize the subject's motivation to be accurate, although it may also have raised the degree of commitment somewhat.)

High Commitment was obtained by telling the subject, after he assigned a value to the tenth weight, that his *estimate of the average at that point* was the crucial guess which would determine whether or not he would win a prize and, hence, how well he performed on the task.

After the weight value and prediction of average had been made following the last, discrepant, weight, a questionnaire was given to the subject. The questions, to be described later, were intended to check the success of the importance manipulation as well as other variables thought to be relevant in this test.

[9] The attempt to manipulate importance through the prize value consisted of varying the prize from $1.00 to $5.00 gift certificates.

Summary of Design

The subjects consisted of 8 males and 60 females, approximately equally distributed in the experimental conditions. Subjects were equally and randomly distributed to each condition of Low Importance and Commitment. Since the attempt to affect Importance through variation in the prize value failed, the subjects in these conditions were combined to constitute the Low Importance conditions, containing 20 subjects for each of the two levels of commitment. Then the High Importance condition was administered to 28 more subjects, equally and randomly distributed between the two levels of commitment.

Theoretical Expectations

Subjects in the Low Commitment conditions are oriented toward making an accurate estimate of the average weight for the series. Their concern with being accurate should be greater under the High Importance conditions than under the Low. Hence we might expect subjects in the High Importance condition, compared with those in the Low, to try harder to take the discrepant weight into account in making their estimates of the average. Thus the High Importance subjects should show more shift of their estimated average from before to after exposure to the discrepant weight than Low Importance subjects.

If it is true that commitment provides the condition necessary for inconsistent information to arouse dissonance, then subjects in the High Commitment conditions should behave differently from those in the Low Commitment conditions. Furthermore, since dissonance is also a direct function of the importance of the inconsistent cognitions, the effect of High Commitment should be greater in the High than in the Low Importance condition. The dissonance aroused in conjunction with the commitment might conceivably be reduced in a number of different ways. It could result in perceptual distortion that minimizes the inconsistency, selective exposure to further relevant information, and so on. However, perceptual distortion would, in this case, be difficult, for the inconsistency is large and clear and would thus require tremendous distortion for the elimination of dissonance. Exposure to further information was not a plausible response, since the inconsistent weight indicated that the remaining weights in the series might also be different from the preceding weights. However, the subject could quite easily engage in judgmental distortion. He could simply convince himself that the inconsistent weight was not representative of the series and that it was therefore not as important toward estimation of the average as were the previous ten weights. The result of such distortion would be a relatively small shift in the estimated average due to exposure to the inconsistent weight. Thus we would expect subjects in the High Commitment condition to show relatively little shift in their estimate of the average, and we would further expect this shift to be smaller as the importance of being accurate increased.

Results

The effect of the discrepant weight on the estimated average depends on the discrepancy between the estimated average just prior to exposure to the discrepant weight and the perceived value of the discrepant weight itself. The relevant data are presented in Table 11, where it may be seen that the estimated average prior to the discrepant weight is approximately the same in all conditions except in the High Importance—High Commitment condition, which shows a somewhat higher average. This somewhat higher average is not due, however, to either the Importance or the Commitment manipulations, since an inspection of the estimated average for previous trials shows that this group began with an estimate about eight points higher and maintained a higher estimate by about eight points through trial nine, the weight just prior to the one in question. Similarly, the perception of the discrepant weight (Table 12), is somewhat higher in the High Importance—High Commitment condition, and this difference corre-

TABLE 11

ESTIMATED AVERAGE PRIOR TO DISCREPANT WEIGHT

	Low Importance	High Importance
Low Commitment	54.2	53.3
High Commitment	51.0	63.6

TABLE 12

VALUE ASSIGNED TO DISCREPANT WEIGHT

	Low Importance	High Importance
Low Commitment	99.8	110.4
High Commitment	100.6	118.9

sponds quite well with differences that occur in regard to estimates of the individual weights for the previous trials. Thus the unreliable but consistent tendency for subjects in the High Importance—High Commitment condition to give higher estimates than do subjects in the other conditions is apparently due to a normal sampling error.

Since we are primarily interested in shifts in the estimated average, and such shifts are presumably a function of the perceived inconsistency, an appropriate measure is the ratio of the change in estimated average from before to after the inconsistent weight, over the discrepancy between the perceived value of the critical weight and the prior estimated average. We will call this measure the Corrected Shift Score. It has been multiplied by 100 to make it more comparable with the figures from which it was derived. The reader should note that the Corrected Shift Score takes into account the between-condition differences that appear in Tables 11 and 12, even though these differences are not reliable. Its major function, however, is to reduce within-condition variability on the assumption that the change in estimated average is positively correlated with the perceived discrepancy between the average and the inconsistent weight.

As may be seen in Table 13, the Shift Scores show that subjects in

TABLE 13

CORRECTED SHIFT SCORES

	Low Importance	High Importance
Low Commitment	18.5	28.1
High Commitment	19.8	14.0

the Low Commitment condition, presumably in an attempt to be more accurate, change their estimates of the average more under High Importance than under Low (significant by F test at the 5% level). And, as we would expect, subjects in the High Commitment condition tend to show *less* shift in their average in the High than in the Low Importance condition. Although this latter tendency is not statistically significant, it is significantly different from the opposing tendency in the Low Commitment condition (interaction F significant at 5% level). *Thus the effect of commitment is to reverse the rational, judgmental process.* That is, when a person is exposed to information inconsistent with a judgment he has made, the direct effect of the inconsistent information will increase with its importance so long as the individual is not committed. However, when the individual is committed prior to exposure to the inconsistent information, dissonance is created, and the pressure to reduce the dissonance may lead the individual to minimize the significance of the inconsistent information.

It might be argued that the present experiment shows the resistance effect of commitment and nothing more. Where High Importance without commitment tends to produce greater shift in the estimated average, the addition of commitment simply produces resistance to change in the estimated average. This explanation does not, however, fit the pattern of results. Under the High Commitment condition, the Shift Score is *lower* with High Importance than with Low. Although this difference is not reliable, it is certainly a trend in the wrong direction for the resistance hypothesis. Furthermore, there is no reason to expect an interaction from the resistance hypothesis: The effect should be about as large in the Low Importance condition as in the High. But as the data show, there is absolutely no evidence of any resistance to change in the estimated average in the Low Importance condition. Thus we conclude that a possible effect of commitment to a position prior to exposure to information inconsistent with that position is to arouse dissonance. This dissonance can be reduced by minimization of the significance of the inconsistent information.

It would be possible, of course, for the dissonance to be reduced in other ways. A person who is committed and has received inconsistent information may seek further information that would help minimize the importance of the inconsistent information directly, or information consistent with his commitment. Another possibility for reducing the dissonance would be to admit one was wrong. If, for example, the information inconsistency were extreme, and the importance of that information were great relative to other relevant information, then the easiest mode for dissonance reduction could be to admit to error and adopt a new position. Thus, in the present study, if the inconsistent weight were even more discrepant and if it were 1 out of 5 instead of 1 out of 11, subjects might well have tended to admit error and have consequently adopted a large shift in their estimate of the average. Indeed, we might expect a larger shift, when it does occur, under conditions of High Commitment than under Low. The reason, of course, is that under High Commitment the shift is motivational, whereas under Low Commitment it is essentially passive (rational or judgmental).

In summary, commitment appears to be an important variable for our understanding of dissonance phenomena. It can provide the psychological implication whereby inconsistent information becomes dissonant. It also helps in understanding how dissonance is reduced, since the increased resistance to change of the cognitions regarding the behavior to which the person is committed makes them unlikely to undergo change.

Although commitment is apparently an important aspect of choice, it sheds only a little light on the theoretical ambiguities with which we are concerned. For the question with which we must cope is whether or not the dissonance-arousing character of choice can be entirely attributed to commitment in the face of inconsistent information. The farmer we considered earlier may, for example, find himself exposed to events inconsistent with commitments other than those involved in immediately relevant choices. A sudden and relatively large increase in land tax would certainly be inconsistent with the commitment of owning a lot of land for which there was no buyer. Or, suppose it were suddenly decided to run a superhighway right where his home sits. Or, again, suppose his house were hit by lightning and burned to the ground. Any of these possibilities would ordinarily constitute an inconsistency between a commitment and some event. But would each necessarily involve the arousal of dissonance in the farmer?

More generally, we are concerned here with the conditions under which an inconsistency that exists between a commitment and some event or information is sufficient to arouse dissonance. We shall attack the problem first by asking the relatively simple question: Does inconsistent information arouse dissonance if it occurs *after* a choice? A forced-compliance study by Brehm (1959) was explicitly designed to bear on this issue.

Brehm's (1959) study was directed toward providing evidence for the notion that a postchoice event can create dissonance. In this experiment, junior high school students were induced to eat a small dish of a disliked vegetable in order to obtain a prize. Eating the vegetable follows from the opposite of disliking it, and thus we would expect all subjects to experience some dissonance. Then, to see whether or not a further inconsistent cognition would increase the magnitude of dissonance, the experimenter told some of the subjects, after they had nearly finished eating, that he would be writing a letter to their parents to indicate what vegetable they had eaten. The implication of such a letter was that the subjects would be expected to increase their eating of that vegetable at home. Prechoice knowledge of the letter would have militated against the decision to eat. But as the procedure was set up, the subject could neither escape from having agreed to eat nor from having the letter sent. In short, the letter constituted an event inconsistent with the commitment to eat and was outside the control of the subject.

The magnitude of dissonance was measured in terms of increased liking for the vegetable. Dissonance from having to eat the vegetable could easily be reduced by increased liking. If exposure to this event creates dissonance, then subjects exposed to it should show greater increase in liking for the vegetable than those not told about the letter. This expectation was clearly supported by the results.

This experiment suggests that a person need not know about something at the time of choice for it to create dissonance when he does learn of it. Thus exposure to information inconsistent with a prior commitment will sometimes create dissonance. It should be noted, however, that the commitment in the present study, that is, having taken part in the eating of the disliked vegetable, occurred by virtue of the subject's choice. He was not forced to eat; he *chose* to eat. A question may therefore be raised about whether or not exposure to inconsistent events creates dissonance *only* when those events, the exposure, or the commitment, result from a prior choice. A tentative answer to this question is supplied by the results of the experiment conducted by Brehm and Cohen (1959b).

This study, described earlier, involved an attempt to pressure college students into participating in a boring and tedious task. Once they agreed to participate, they were led to believe that others—but not themselves—were being paid either $1.00 (low relative deprivation condition) or $10.00 (high relative deprivation condition) for participation. *They were told that their selection as one not being paid was due completely to chance.* Thus they were not only given the relative deprivation information after commitment to the task, they were led to believe that it was a chance, or uncontrollable, factor.

Since an attempt to manipulate the pressure to participate failed, the reactions of subjects were analyzed in terms of their perceptions of how difficult it would be to get out of participation. It was assumed that the degree to which a subject was satisfied with being assigned to the study would reflect the degree to which he had tried to reduce dissonance.

The analysis showed an interaction between perceived choice (difficulty of escape) and the amount of relative deprivation: Under low choice, subjects felt satisfied in inverse proportion to the amount of relative deprivation; under high choice, subjects felt satisfied in direct proportion to the amount of relative deprivation. Thus it appears that dissonance created by the amount of relative deprivation was greater with high than with low perceived choice. Although these data are partly correlational and subject to other interpretations, they are consistent with the view that *inconsistent events will create dissonance even when they are due to chance, but only to the extent that they or the commitment occur as the result of prior choice.*

An interesting aspect of these results is that there was no evidence of dissonance reduction for those subjects who indicated they had little choice *even though they were committed*. In fact, we could interpret the results to mean that the lower the degree of felt commitment (the greater the perceived choice), the greater is the dissonance. Thus, while the evidence does indicate that prior (perceived) choice affects whether or not subsequent inconsistent events arouse dissonance, it also indicates that some factor in addition to commitment may be involved. To see if we can find a clue about what other factor might be involved, let us consider this study a little further.

It will be recalled that according to our measure of the perceived difficulty of getting out of participation, the attempt to manipulate the amount of the coercive force failed. There was no statistically reliable difference between the condition means. Indeed, it may be noteworthy that the means were not only similar, but their difference approached being significantly *small* compared to the within-condition variations in scores. While such an outcome could be due to chance, it could also be due to some factor that triggers individual differences in reaction. Is there any reason to believe that individual differences might have been triggered by our attempted manipulation? It seems that there is. Our attempt to force the college students to participate in a rather unpleasant and time-consuming study was probably unique at this institution. It therefore seems plausible that some of the students would have resented the coercion, and that this resentment would have increased their desire to get out of participation. We must assume, of course, that this reaction varied in magnitude among the subjects. To the extent that a person did feel resentful, he would entertain the idea of getting out of participation and would therefore tend to see the difficulty of getting out as relatively low. He would, in short, feel that he could get out if he really wanted to. What may be involved here is the individual's feeling of control over his own behavior. We suspect that what the attempted coercion produced was strong individual differences in concern with and feeling of personal control. We shall call this conscious control of one's own behavior *volition*.

THE EFFECT OF VOLITION

The degree of volition, then, is the extent to which a person feels that he controls his own behavior (including responses, emotions, motivations, etc.). Volition implies not only initiation and selection of behavior but also responsibility for its consequences. What we wish to suggest is that *volition provides another source of psychological implication*. Thus the ability of a cognitive inconsistency to arouse dissonance would be a function of the degree to which volition is involved in the occurrence of that inconsistency: Other things equal, the greater the volition, the greater the dissonance.

It is clear that all choice behavior involves volition to one degree or another. That is, the person making a choice generally does it quite consciously and purposively. He is not just assigned to an alternative; he *selects* an alternative. Since most dissonance experiments have utilized an explicit or implicit choice in arranging the commitment and the inconsistent information, they have also insured that subjects would experience some degree of volition. It is possible, then, that the successful demonstration of dissonance in these various studies is due to this implicit inclusion of volition.

The notion that volition is necessary to the arousal of dissonance would lead to somewhat different expectations, however, than an analysis in terms of dissonance theory as stated by Festinger (1957). For volition may be a function of factors other than the ratio of dissonant to consonant cognitions. While there will be volition in the ordinary choice situation, the amount of volition can *either* increase or decrease as the choice alternatives become more nearly equal in attractiveness. The magnitude of dissonance, according to the theory, would tend only to increase under such conditions. But if volition is necessary to the arousal of dissonance, as we are suggesting, when volition decreases, then the magnitude of dissonance could conceivably decrease. This might occur even though we might otherwise expect dissonance to increase as where the choice alternatives become more nearly equal in attractiveness.

A further implication of this suggested role of volition is that the occurrence of an event inconsistent with a commitment will arouse dissonance in the individual to the extent that he has some volition regarding the situation. Hence we would expect that if the individual felt that the occurrence of the inconsistent or unpleasant event was a consequence of his own volition, then it would arouse dissonance. On the other hand, if the inconsistent event is not a consequence of a volitional act, then it will not arouse dissonance. In summary, volition provides an important qualification of psychological implication. When the person gets himself into a situation, and therefore feels responsible for its consequences, inconsistent information should, no matter how it comes about, arouse dissonance. If the person was not responsible for getting himself into the situation, then inconsistent information should not arouse dissonance.

To return briefly to our hypothetical farmer, he should experience dissonance, according to our analysis, even when the unpleasant or inconsistent events are completely unexpected. Thus the sudden disclosure that tobacco causes a deadly disease would arouse dissonance insofar as the farmer really had considered planting corn instead. On the other hand, whether an increase in land tax, even when unexpected, would arouse dissonance depends on whether or not the farmer had exercised some volition and (perhaps recently) bought the farm. A recent purchase would clearly make the increase dissonance arousing. If, on the other hand, he had inherited the farm and had never considered doing anything else, he would not experience dissonance from increased taxes. Similar considerations would apply to his house being in the way of a superhighway or being struck by lightning. As can be seen, the notion of volition may allow some resolution of the questions we have posed for the theory.

There remains a crucial problem inherent in our suggestion that volition may determine whether or not dissonance is aroused. The problem is that we are not prepared to make an explicit theoretical statement about the determinants of volition. And rather than attempt a degree of specification that may be premature, we will simply describe some particular instances in which volition plays a part in the arousal of dissonance.

The fundamental condition is that a person must feel he has some control about whether or not to put himself into a situation in which inconsistent cognitive elements occur. We have held that such a feeling of control is an integral part of the typical dissonance experiment; that may be why dissonance is aroused by the inconsistent cognitions that are created. Furthermore, the degree of volition will frequently be positively correlated with the magnitude of dissonance as defined in terms of dissonant and consonant cognitions. Consider, for example, a two-alternative choice situation. As the two alternatives become more nearly equal in attractiveness, the proportion of cognitions dissonant with choice of the more attractive alternative increases, and, hence, the magnitude of dissonance should increase. But the same would be true of the degree of volition, since, as the choice alternatives become more nearly equal in attractiveness, the individual must become more concerned with which alternative he will choose. When one alternative is clearly more attractive than the other, the degree of volition would ordinarily be low, since the individual would select the attractive alternative without much consideration. The fact that he could choose the less attractive alternative would be of little consequence. In general, then, the degree of volition will frequently be positively correlated with the ratio of dissonant to consonant cognitions.

A similar analysis would apply to the "forced-compliance" paradigm.

We may say, for example, that the greater the force that produces compliance, the less is the ratio of dissonant to consonant cognitions, and, also, the less is the degree of volition.

If it is true that there is a subjective experience of volition which generally varies inversely with the amount of external force that obtains compliance, then we should be able to find evidence for it. Cohen's small rewards experiment is relevant to this issue. In this experiment, described in Chapter 6, the inducing force was manipulated and the perceived amount of volition measured. College students were requested to write essays counter to their private opinions on an issue of current concern. They understood they would be paid for writing the essay. The inducing force was varied by offering different amounts of pay. The amounts were $.50, $1.00, $5.00, and $10.00. It was expected and found that attitude change toward the assumed position decreases as amount paid increases.

Our interest at this point, however, is in the perception of volition as a function of the amount to be paid. Immediately after the subjects had finished writing their discrepant essays, they were given a post-experimental questionnaire, which included the following question: "Considering that you agreed to take part in the general survey, how much choice do you feel you really had in whether or not you could turn down the request to write the essay?" Answers were indicated along an *a priori* seven-point labeled scale having five unlabeled points between the seven. The labels ranged from "No choice at all" to "Complete choice." According to the above suggestion that volition is an intervening variable in the arousal of dissonance, it would be expected that perceived volition would decrease as payment increased.

The means for perceived volition in each condition, given in Table 14, show quite clearly that volition decreases as the inducing force increases, although there is a slight reversal under high dissonance ($.50). These data, then, support our contention that volition is, at least at times, an intervening variable in the arousal of dissonance.

TABLE 14

MEAN RATING OF VOLITION BY AMOUNT OF PAY

	$0.50	$1.00	$5.00	$10.00
Perceived Volition	5.78	6.37	4.04	3.83

While these data show that volition and dissonance covary as a function of force, they do not show that volition is anything but the inverse of the force that produces compliance. If the two variables are not separable, then there is no reason to add the notion of volition to the variables already used in the theory.

A stringent test of the significance of volition in producing dissonance would be to *create variations in volition in a way that goes counter to the theoretically expected relationship between force and attitude change*. That is, the creation of relatively high volition accompanying relatively high force would allow one to see which variable related in a theoretically meaningful way with evaluative change.

Dissonance theory leads to the derivation that the magnitude of dissonance from engaging in unpleasant behavior decreases as the inducing force increases. The same derivation holds whether the inducing force is positive or negative, that is, whether the force consists of the acquisition of benefits or the threat of punishment. Hence the greater the coercion obtaining compliance, the less is the magnitude of dissonance and the less is the amount of consequent evaluative change of the unpleasant behavior.

The use of coercion implies its exercise by some authority figure in order to obtain compliance by the individual to some undesirable or discrepant event. In the experiment on chance relative deprivation by Brehm and Cohen (1959b), there were large individual differences in perceived choice as a function of the attempt to coerce the subjects into participating in an unpleasant task. As we have noted, a plausible interpretation of this variability in response is that some subjects reacted to the attempted coercion negatively. Such negative reactions might occur if the coercion were seen as improper or illegitimate, which it might have been, for the attempt was to make *all* students participate in the unpleasant task. Thus the results of that study can be interpreted as dissonance arousal and reduction (through revaluation) as a function of *volition created by illegitimate coercion*. If this line of reasoning is correct, it should be possible to create an experimental situation in which volition *increases* as the magnitude of coercion increases.

One way in which coercion can be made illegitimate is to give the authority figure using the coercion a position or status inappropriate to the particular threats used. Thus, where coercive threats are inappropriate, there should be a negative relationship between the theoretically expected effects of these two variables on the magnitude of dissonance and consequent revaluation: If the objective force is the determinant, then revaluation should vary inversely with both coercion and volition; if volition is the determinant, then revaluation should vary directly with both volition and coercion. It is possible, then, that the effect of volition in arousing dissonance may be clarified through the use of illegitimate coercion.

AN EXPERIMENT ON ILLEGITIMATE COERCION, VOLITION, AND ATTITUDE CHANGE

Cohen and Brehm performed the following experiment in order to separate the hypothesized effects of the inducing force and those of volition. In line with the above reasoning, they used an illegitimate coercive force to make college students agree to participate in an unpleasant ask. A questionnaire measured the participants' perceptions of the coercive force, volition, and task valuation. The effect of the illegitimate coercion was made clear by having conditions of low and high threat as well as a control condition that involved no threat. Since the procedure itself is in large part identical to that used by Brehm in the study on coercion and attitude change reported in Chapter 6, it will only be summarized except where there were differences.

The subjects consisted of 30 Yale undergraduates—ten in each experimental condition—who were fraternity pledges recruited from four different campus fraternities. Arrangements had been made with the pledgemasters of the various fraternities to send pledges to the experimental room "to help out in some research for a short period of time."

The general condition of illegitimacy was established in the following way. First, the pledges were told by their pledgemasters that they were to report for a *short* project of 15 to 20 minutes duration, whereas the experimenter then demanded that they sign up for a boring and profitless task that would take 3 to 4 hours. Above all, however, the experimenter was a professor who had no connection whatsoever with any of the fraternities involved. To make the coercion completely illegitimate, then, the experimenter threatened to have the pledge's fraternity penalize him if he failed to participate in the unexpectedly long task. Since such an influence by a professor on a fraternity's business would be very unusual, it was expected that the attempted coercion would be seen by the pledge as illegitimate. The exact procedure follows.

When the subject arrived, he was told that he was expected to participate in 3 to 4 continuous hours of copying random numbers. It was emphasized that participation would be extremely dull and that there was nothing the subject would learn from it, but that his help was needed in order to "establish norms for other research." After being shown an example of the task, the subject was given one of the following coercion manipulations:

High Coercion. "Now we need your cooperation, and if you don't cooperate, I'm afraid we'll have to report you as uncooperative to your pledgemaster and the other fellows and really push for some severe penalties. This can have very bad effects; we'll try to see that it has very strong consequences for extending your pledge period considerably and even for keeping you out of the house permanently."

Low Coercion. "Now we need your cooperation, and if you don't cooperate, I'm afraid we'll have to report you as uncooperative to your pledgemaster and the other fellows and see that you get some hours of extra duty as a pledge."

In the *Control condition,* the subjects were told: "Now we need your cooperation." Nothing was said to them about any possible penalties for noncooperation.

After the manipulation, the subject was given a schedule sheet on which to indicate his free hours. All subjects with the exception of one in the Low Coercion condition agreed to participate and filled out a schedule sheet.

Perception of the coercive force, perceived choice about whether or not to participate (volition), and evaluation of the number-copying task were measured on a questionnaire given immediately after commitment to participation. The questionnaire was introduced as being purely for the use of the Interfraternity Council in evaluating the use of pledges in research, and its anonymity was stressed. A *priori* questions and multiple response scales were used to measure the variables of interest; these were also used in the Brehm experiment and are fully reported on pp. 84–88.

Here we may briefly note that measures of satisfaction, volition, and threat were all taken on *a priori* 81-point scales with nine identified points. The present experiment made use of one additional measure taken on the postquestionnaire. The subjects were asked, "How annoyed were you by the request that you participate in the proposed research?" This was answered on an 81-point *a priori* scale with nine identified points running from "Not annoyed at all" to "Extremely annoyed." Threat, volition, and annoyance were scored from zero to eight; the higher the number, the greater the respective response. The satisfaction measure was scored from -4 to $+4$; the more positive the figure, the greater the satisfaction.

Results

The test of whether dissonance depends on the coercive force itself or on volition arising from the coercion assumes that the experimental conditions have resulted in a direct relationship between coercion and volition: the greater the coercion, the greater the volition. The effect of the coercion manipulation was measured by a question on the severity of threat, and the mean responses to this question are presented in column 1 of Table 15. These data show that little or no threat was seen in the Control and Low Coercion conditions, and that considerable threat was seen in the High Coercion condition, which is significantly different from the Control condition at the 2% level.

Whether or not the threat was perceived as illegitimate can be inferred from the amount of annoyance reported by subjects. Although being given a choice may tend to minimize annoyance in experimental subjects compared to Control subjects, it should still be possible to compare the two experimental conditions. The relevant data, column 2 of Table 15, show that subjects in the High Coercion condition were more annoyed than were subjects in the Low Coercion condition (p less than .05).

Since subjects in the High Coercion condition perceived more threat and were more annoyed than subjects in the Low Coercion condition, according to our theoretical argument, they may reasonably be expected to have felt relatively more volition in regard to complying with the experimenter's request. Subjects' responses to the question on felt volition are shown in column 3 of Table 15. Although the only statistically reliable difference is that between the High Coercion and Control conditions (beyond the 1% level), there is a clear trend for High Coercion subjects to report feeling more volition than Low Coercion subjects.

TABLE 15

MEAN RATINGS OF POSTQUESTIONNAIRE ITEMS BY EXPERIMENTAL GROUPS

	1. Severity of Threat	2. Annoyance	3. Volition	4. Satisfaction
High Coercion (N = 10):	4.00 *	2.88	3.14	+1.09
Low Coercion (N = 10):	2.18	1.61	2.04	− .70
Control (N = 10):	1.46	2.64	.95	−1.58

* In all cases, the higher the mean figure, the greater the response in question.

Thus our coercion manipulation *has produced a difference in volition that is directly related to the amount of coercive force applied.* Since this is the condition necessary for distinguishing between the effects on dissonance of the coercive force *per se* and of volition, we may now proceed to an inspection of the data relevant to the questions of central interest.

If coercion is the controlling determinant of the magnitude of dissonance, then revaluation of the task should vary inversely with coercion (and volition) as has been demonstrated in other research. But if volition is the controlling determinant of dissonance, then revaluation should vary *directly* with coercion (and volition). The measure of revaluation—subjects' satisfaction with being assigned to the experiment—is given in column 4 of Table 15. It shows very clearly that subjects in the High Coercion condition are more satisfied than subjects in either the Low Coercion condition (p less than .05) or the Control condition (p less than .01). These results therefore support the contention that volition is an important determinant of the magnitude of dissonance.

There is at least one equivocality about our interpretation of these data in that we cannot be sure that the severe threat was judged to be as likely to be carried out as was the mild threat. It is possible that the fraternity pledges would think it plausible for a professor to get them some hours of extra duty, but implausible that a professor could get them excluded from the fraternity altogether. If this were true, it could mean that subjects in the High Coercion condition perceived the effective force on them as being quite low rather than as very high. Hence they would be expected to experience high dissonance compared to the Low Coercion subjects for whom there was a realistic threat, and the results of the study would therefore be understandable as a straightforward effect of the amount of force resulting in compliance. But, on the other hand, it is not clear why the High Coercion subjects would have felt relatively more annoyed if they really perceived that the threatened punishment would not likely be carried out. It seems more plausible, therefore, to assume that the High Coercion subjects took the threat quite seriously and reacted to it with feelings of high volition. On the whole, then, the data support the proposition that volition can affect the magnitude of dissonance *independently of the ratio of dissonant to consonant cognitions.*

An interesting implication of our view of the role of volition in the arousal of dissonance is that even though a person may choose between nearly equally attractive alternatives, if he is forced to make that choice, then the amount of resulting dissonance will be relatively low.

Speculations About Dissonance Arousal / 209

More generally, the magnitude of dissonance resulting from a choice is directly proportional to the degree of volition in making the choice. Thus we may hypothesize that *as the pressure to make a choice increases, the magnitude of postchoice dissonance and consequent revaluation of alternatives decreases.*

AN EXPERIMENT ON VOLITION OF CHOICE

A study specifically designed to test this proposition was therefore designed and conducted by Gerald S. Leventhal and Brehm. The strategy of the study was to induce persons into a choice situation with incentives of differing magnitudes that would presumably affect the extent to which they consciously chose to participate in the experiment. The procedure was as follows.

The subjects were male college students enrolled in a course in introductory psychology. Students in this course are required to participate in 3 hours of research and, in addition, are given "credit points" toward their final course grade for each hour they do participate, including those required. However, students are free to choose which of several research projects they will participate in. The subjects in the present experiment volunteered to participate in a study on work efficiency.

Each subject reported individually to the experimental room. He was placed at a table with the experimenter and reminded that the purpose of the study was to find out something about human work efficiency. The experimenter then told the subject that the first session was simply preliminary to the major part of the study, which consisted of a 5-hour testing session to be held within about a week. It was explained that if the subject decided to participate, he would put in 5 hours of continuous, nonstop work on rather unexciting tasks. The experimenter emphasized that the subject could choose for himself whether or not he wanted to participate as soon as he heard exactly what was involved. At this point the manipulation of volition was introduced through the instructions about the payment with credit points for participation.

Low Volition was established by offering 12 credit points for participation in the 5 hours of work. The normal payment would have been five credit points in addition to the one for coming to the preliminary session, and subjects were therefore expected to participate without making a careful choice.

High Volition was established by offering six credit points. Since this amount was only normal, and the 5-hour task was rather demanding, it was thought that subjects would consider the alternative and make a careful choice.

After explaining the reward, the experimenter said he would allow the subject to try out the tasks used in the 5-hour testing session in order to help him decide whether or not to participate. The subject was then given a 5-minute trial experience with each of the two following tasks.

Figure Recognition

For 6 seconds the subject was shown a 5″ by 7″ card with six abstract designs on it. Then, with no time limit, he was shown a series of five cards, each of which contained nine designs, four of which were repeats of designs shown on the first card. The subject indicated which designs he recognized but was given no indication of the accuracy of his performance. Three separate sets of cards were run through in the 5-minute practice period.

Syllable Memorization

The subject was presented with two eight-syllable lists of three-letter nonsense syllables. The syllables were presented one at a time for approximately 2 seconds each, and the subject was instructed to learn the lists, using the method of anticipation. The task was sufficiently difficult so that no subject learned the two lists perfectly. This task was designed to be approximately equally attractive to the Figure Recognition task and yet relatively unlike it, so that a choice between the two tasks would ordinarily create a measurable amount of pre- to postchoice revaluation. However, the subject did not know at this point that he would eventually have the opportunity to choose between these tasks.

When the practice was completed, the subject was asked if he was willing to participate in the 5-hour test session. After he agreed to take part, he was told that the experimenter needed some information concerning how he felt about the tasks, for this might affect his work efficiency. The subject then indicated his liking for each of the tasks on a rating scale to be described below. Immediately following this rating, it was explained that each subject would work on only one of the two tasks, and the subject was allowed to choose between them. A time was then agreed on for the 5-hour test session, and a reminder slip that included the name of the task on which the subject would work was made out. Finally, the experimenter mentioned the "well-known fact" that a person's feelings about something may change from one moment to the next and that it was important for the experimenter to take this into consideration. The subject was then asked to indicate again his liking for each of the two tasks. The experiment was then complete and the experimenter explained the deceptions and reasons for them to the subject.

Dependent Measures

Initial liking for each task was measured by the question "How much do you like the _____ task? Put a check at the place on the line which best indicates your feeling." Accompanying this question was a 6-inch line with identification marks each half inch and the following equally spaced labels: Dislike very much, Dislike a fair amount, Dislike a little, Neither, Like a little, Like a fair amount, Like very much. Responses were scored from zero to 6.0 respectively. The questions for both tasks were on the same sheet. The postchoice measure of liking was identical except that instead of naming the tasks, it asked about the "Task you chose" or the "Task you did NOT choose."

Summary of Design

Subjects were induced, with either a high or low incentive, to commit themselves to participation in an experiment. Their liking for each of the experimental tasks was then measured both before and after they were allowed to choose the task on which they would work. A third group was offered the low incentive for participation but was then simply assigned to one of the two tasks. Eleven subjects were offered the high incentive and 32 the low incentive. One subject in the high incentive group and three in the low incentive refused to participate. An additional eight subjects either rated the two tasks equally, making it impossible for us to know which task, if any, would be preferred or else they chose the task rated lower, indicating that their ratings or preferences were low in reliability or validity. The data for all eight were deleted from the final analysis, although their inclusion would not change the pattern of effects. In summary, there were 10 subjects in the Low Volition (high incentive) condition, and 21 in the High Volition (low incentive) condition, of whom seven were allowed to choose between the alternatives.

Theoretical Expectations

Before considering the effect of volition, let us see what might be expected from a straightforward analysis in terms of dissonance theory. First of all, it is clear that the experimental design and procedure through the initial ratings of the tasks are similar to the "forced-

212 / Explorations in Cognitive Dissonance

compliance" paradigm. Thus those subjects offered the small incentive for participation in the tasks, compared to those offered the large incentive, should experience more dissonance and evidence this dissonance through relatively greater attraction to the tasks. It may be noted, however, that strictly speaking we were not trying to arouse differential amounts of dissonance in the High and Low Volition conditions in regard to participation in the experiment. We shall have occasion to return to this point in discussing the results.

Let us also consider what dissonance theory might say about revaluation of the tasks as a function of the choice under high and low incentive conditions. The situation is analogous to a choice between, for example, washing the dishes and cleaning out the attic, where one will receive either $1.00 or $10.00, depending on which task is chosen. It is apparent that the reward may be considered an overlapping cognitive element whether it is large or small. Hence, while the nonoverlapping cognitions (having to do with the tasks themselves) remain constant, the number (or importance) of overlapping cognitions changes.

It will be recalled from Chapter 3 that, other things being constant, the magnitude of dissonance resulting from a choice decreases as the amount of cognitive overlap increases. But there are two ways in which the present situation does not conform to that particular derivation of the theory. First, other things are *not* constant, since the number (or importance) of relevant cognitive elements increases as the magnitude of the incentive increases. This increase in the number or importance of relevant cognitive elements could possibly serve to increase the magnitude of dissonance. On the other hand, the increase in proportion of weighted elements that overlap could possibly reduce the magnitude of dissonance. Or both factors might operate and tend to cancel each other out, resulting in relatively little difference in dissonance as the incentive increases. In the latter case, the prediction of whether or not the magnitude of dissonance would change with increasing incentives would depend on knowledge of metrical values of the opposing effects, information that would be difficult to obtain. Still another possibility is that the addition of overlapping cognitive elements would have no effect on the amount of postchoice dissonance. In any event, we do not feel that an unequivocal prediction from the theory regarding manipulation of the force to choose is readily available.

The second way in which this situation differs from the theoretical derivation concerning cognitive overlap has to do with the order of events. It is not obvious that the derivation about cognitive overlap applies to elements that occur *prior* to the choice between alternatives, though the present situation is specifically arranged in that way. In the present situation it is intended that the individual have some prior experience of getting himself into a choice. But it is not at all clear from the theory that cognitions relevant to having gotten into a situation affect the magnitude of dissonance aroused by subsequent events. If that position were to be taken, then surely the cognition corresponding to the individual's commitment to participate should be an important source of consonance and should tend to reduce the magnitude of dissonance from expected subsequent events to near zero. Having to choose between the two tasks that one had agreed to engage in would then surely not create dissonance unless both tasks were quite attractive. Since the tasks in the present experiment were designed to be slightly on the negative side, little or no dissonance would be expected. Such a prediction is clearly different from what the present experiment was designed to show.

It is our contention that the amount of dissonance created by a choice between two alternatives is a function not only of the relative attractiveness of the alternatives themselves but also of the degree of volition involved in the person's having to make a choice. If the degree of volition decreases as the magnitude of the incentive increases, then the amount of dissonance resulting from the subsequent choice should vary inversely with the incentive. In the present experiment, the dissonance-produced revaluation of choice alternatives should be greater in the High Volition (low incentive) condition than in the Low Volition (high incentive) condition.

Results

The effect of the volition manipulation on the revaluation of choice alternatives is seen in Table 16. Since dissonance from the choice can be reduced both by increased valuation of the chosen alternative and decreased valuation of the rejected alternative, the total amount of dissonance reduction is the combination of these two effects. It is apparent that the total amount of dissonance reduction is greater in the High Volition condition than in the Low ($p < .01$ by t test). This difference clearly supports our proposition that dissonance is a direct monotonic function of volition.

As noted earlier, some subjects in the High Volition condition were assigned one of the two tasks instead of being allowed to choose between them, so that the effects of volition on the pleasantness of consequent events might be assessed. Unfortunately, however, the initial ratings of the tasks in the two different assignment conditions were quite dissimilar, presumably due to sampling error, and therefore make interpretation of the changes in liking difficult. For this reason, these results are reported in Table 17 without further comment.

TABLE 16

TASK RATING CHANGES AS A FUNCTION OF VOLITION UNDER
CONDITIONS OF CHOICE

Volition About Being in Experiment	Task Rated	Initial Rating	Change	Total Dissonance Reduction
High (Low Incentive)				
(N = 7)	Chosen	4.07	+.34 *	
	Rejected	2.57	−.26	
				+.60
Low (High Incentive)				
(N = 10)	Chosen	4.94	−.05	
	Rejected	3.52	+.05	
				−.10

* A plus value indicates increased attraction.

TABLE 17

TASK RATING CHANGES AS A FUNCTION OF DISCREPANCY OF INFORMATION
UNDER CONDITIONS OF HIGH VOLITION

Task Assigned	Task Rated	Initial Rating	Change
Preferred			
(N = 8)	Preferred	3.78	+.34 *
	Nonpreferred	2.41	+.08
Nonpreferred			
(N = 6)	Preferred	4.86	−.44
	Nonpreferred	3.29	+.09

* A plus value indicates increased attraction.

Although the major results of this experiment support the notion that volition affects the magnitude of dissonance resulting from a subsequent choice, some minor effects turned out in a completely unexpected way. Referring again to Tables 16 and 17, one can see that there are relatively large differences between conditions in the initial level of liking for the tasks. The differences in Table 17 are not statistically reliable and are apparently a chance effect. But the differences in Table 16 are reliable and presumably are due to the volition manipulation, that is, to the offer of either 6 or 12 credit points for participation. But though one might expect that from the choice to participate there would be greater dissonance and initial liking in the 6-point condition than the 12, the obtained effects are exactly opposite. This outcome is apparently inconsistent, not only with the theory but also with the results of several other experiments. What, then, might account for it?

We wish to mention two possible factors that might account for this effect.[10] The first is that the tasks to which the subject committed himself were not particularly negative in character. Thus the reluctance on the part of subjects to participate was probably due largely to the length of time involved in the task rather than to the unpleasantness of the tasks *per se*. Since even in the High Volition condition the subjects were to be given a normal amount of credit for the time they would have to put in, there probably was not very much dissonance aroused in conjunction with the commitment to participate. Hence liking for the tasks could easily be affected by processes other than attempts to reduce dissonance. If there is some kind of direct effect of rewards on liking for things that are instrumental in obtaining these rewards, then the operation of that effect could easily have been responsible for the results in this experiment.

The second factor that may have operated to produce a reversal of the normal "forced-compliance" dissonance effect is the order in which the relevant factors occurred. The typical paradigm in forced-compliance experiments is for both consonant and dissonant cognitions to be created at the same time, or for the dissonant cognitions (e.g., those concerning the unpleasantness of the task) to be introduced prior to the consonant (the inducing rewards, justifications, etc.). However, in the present study the reward was mentioned before the subject had been given much information about what he was to get the reward for. Hence it would be possible for the reward to create a positive reaction, which in turn could have a direct effect (rather than a dissonance effect) on the subject's liking for the instrumentality that would get him the reward.

These two factors, then, either individually or in interaction, could account for the positive effect of the incentive manipulation on initial liking for the tasks. Needless to say, the empirical establishment and theoretical elaboration of either of these possible direct effects of reward on liking would indicate an interesting and significant qualifi-

[10] These factors were suggested by Gerald Leventhal.

cation of the statement of conditions under which dissonance occurs. One further possible explanation of the reversal effect may be noted before we move on. It is that the subjects may have felt it necessary to demonstrate to the experimenter, through high liking for the tasks, that they would be good subjects. The greater the reward offered, the greater would be their tendency to say they liked the tasks. However, this explanation is not entirely plausible, for the subjects had already signed up to participate before they made their first ratings of the tasks. We mention it, therefore, only because we cannot completely rule it out as a possibility.

In summary, the results of this experiment are consistent with the hypothesis that dissonance is a direct function of volition. Where commitment and information inconsistent with that commitment provide the conditions under which cognitive elements are dissonant (one follows from the obverse of another), the magnitude of dissonance, or motivational tension, is controlled by the degree of volition. *The greater the degree of volition involved in the occurrence of dissonant cognitions, the greater the magnitude of dissonance.*

SOME IMPLICATIONS OF THE CONCEPTS OF COMMITMENT AND VOLITION FOR THE INTERPRETATION OF DATA

We have tried to show that commitment is a necessary condition for the arousal of dissonance and that the magnitude of dissonance is a direct function of the degree of volition involved in the occurrence of the dissonant relationship. If these assumptions are different from the original formulation of the theory, then they should have some consequence for the interpretation of data assumed to bear on the theory. In this section we shall try to point out some differential consequences.

The interpretation of empirical data depends on both the independent conditions and the dependent effects. Almost all of the research we have reviewed has been explicit in regard to both the independent and dependent sides of the experimental paradigm. In a few cases, however, special assumptions are needed in order for the studies to be understood in terms of our propositions concerning commitment and volition. We shall therefore discuss some important examples requiring such special assumptions.

THE NECESSITY FOR SPECIAL ASSUMPTIONS

As we mentioned, it is possible to interpret some studies as relevant to dissonance theory only if certain assumptions are made. Where

the assumptions are plausible, the interpretation in terms of dissonance theory is plausible, though it may not be the *only* plausible
interpretation.

Two kinds of assumptions may be necessary: one concerning *commitment*, the other concerning *volition*. The interpretation of each study
requires that a commitment be identified in order for there to be a
clear case of dissonant cognitions. Once a commitment is identified,
and assuming the existence of one or more important cognitions
discrepant with that commitment, the degree of volition will control
the magnitude of dissonance, at least in part. Where the degree of
volition is low, the magnitude of dissonance will necessarily be small.
Where the degree of volition is high, the magnitude of dissonance will
be large and will vary as a function of other factors such as the general
importance of the relevant cognitive elements, and the ratio of dissonant to cognitive elements. Let us, then, inspect some examples of
studies in which the role of commitment or volition or both is unspecified.

A relatively early example of a study in which neither commitment
nor volition is specified is that by Zimbardo (1960). His experiment
showed that opinion change increases as a function of discrepancy
size between the communicator and communicatee, and as a function
of the importance of the issue. The conditions under which he made
this demonstration allow his study to be interpreted plausibly in
terms of dissonance theory. First of all, the communicator and communicatee were pairs of good friends, sufficiently good friends to sign
up together to participate in his study. Thus *each communicatee was
interpersonally committed to the communicator.* Furthermore, the
element of volition was provided by the subjects' volunteering to
participate in the study. In this case, the subjects came from a girls'
school in which studies were infrequently done, and thus there was no
standard "norm" or expectation for students to participate in research,
nor was there any arrangement for students to receive "credit points"
or other rewards for their participation. Hence the *pairs of friends got
themselves into the situation in which they found themselves in disagreement.* It was under these conditions that Zimbardo was able to
show that the amount of opinion change was a function of degree of
disagreement and importance of the issue.

A second example is the previously described study by Adams
(1961), in which mothers were asked to listen to a tape-recorded talk
on the importance of either environmental or hereditary factors in
child development. The mothers, who had all expressed the opinion
that child behavior was due mostly to environmental factors, were

asked if they were interested in hearing another talk on one side or the other of the issue and, if so, on which side. It was assumed that mothers who heard the talk opposing their own position, that is, the talk concerning the importance of hereditary factors, would experience dissonance and would, in order to reduce it, volunteer to hear the talk on environmental factors, which supported their initial position. However, from our own point of view, the conditions of this study *do not* clearly fulfill what is necessary for the arousal of dissonance. Although it is true that the mothers were asked to listen to the tape-recorded speech and therefore presumably had some degree of volition, their commitment to the issue is not at all clear. It seems highly doubtful that the issue of learned versus hereditary factors in child development is anything but academic for mothers of young children. If that is true, then their opinions on the issue are presumably more of a judgmental nature or a result of automatically assimilated available social norms than they are a commitment. Thus we would hold that no clear dissonance prediction is possible under these conditions. As the reader may recall, the results of this study are, in fact, at variance with the simple dissonance theory prediction of selective volunteering to hear the speech supporting the initial view. If our analysis is correct, this set of evidence cannot be considered negative evidence for the theory.

A third example is Gerard's experiment (1961), in which subjects were led to believe that they were or were not conforming in an Asch-type of conformity situation. He found that "conforming" subjects who had previously been led to believe they had high ability in judgment on a task similar to that used in the conformity situation subsequently showed high attraction to the group and high subsequent conformity. It is quite possible to interpret these effects in terms of dissonance between one's perception of the physical stimulus and one's knowledge about one's own conforming behavior. In this case, the subject is committed by virtue of making the discrepant response himself or so he is led to believe. And since these subjects were college students who were completely voluntary in their participation, we may also assume a relatively high degree of volition was engendered. Thus it seems likely that this experiment did arouse dissonance where subjects were made to feel that they behaved in a manner contrary to their perception of the physical stimulus.

A fourth example, not unlike the above, was the study conducted by Bramel (1962), described in Chapter 9. After giving college students information designed to raise or lower their self-evaluation, he led them to believe that they were making homosexual responses. He found that those whose self-evaluation had been raised, tended, under these conditions, to project homosexual tendencies on others. This interpretation in terms of dissonance theory seems plausible if we can make an assumption similar to that used in the Gerard experiment discussed above. That is, we must again assume that the subjects got themselves into this dissonant situation through their own volition. This assumption seems fairly reasonable in that the subjects were volunteer college students who did not have to participate in this particular project. Thus the interpretation in terms of dissonance theory is quite plausible.

While these four studies can plausibly be interpreted in terms of dissonance theory, it should be clear that they have not made explicit provision for the role of commitment and/or volition. If our analysis is correct, then the obtained relationship between the dissonance-arousing and -reducing variables in each of these studies could be increased by insuring commitment and by magnification of the degree of volition or could be eliminated by reduction in the degree of commitment or volition. It would be interesting, for example, to replicate the Gerard or the Bramel study under conditions of high pressure to participate in the study. It is possible that such a replication would reveal little or none of the "dissonance-reduction" effects obtained.

DISSONANCE THEORY AND OTHER THEORETICAL AND EMPIRICAL MODELS IN PSYCHOLOGY

part IV

Dissonance, balance, and incongruity

— 12

Our aim in this part of the volume is to discuss the place of dissonance theory with regard to aspects of research and theory in the psychology of cognition, motivation, attitudes, and social interaction. In so doing, we hope to be able to be more specific about just where the present theory, as we view it, is different from other widely held conceptions in psychology and where it is similar. We shall attempt, wherever possible, to clarify the basic assumptions of the theory vis-à-vis other conceptions and also to indicate where dissonance theory might make unique predictions to a range of empirical events dealt with by various theoretical and research emphases current in psychology.

In the present chapter we shall discuss the relation of dissonance theory to other theories of inconsistency and incongruity. The increasing stream of research growing out of these models makes advisable an attempt to separate the elements that we take to be particular to dissonance theory and those that we feel reside in the other theories.

We shall also discuss (Chapter 13) dissonance theory as it relates to decisional processes. In the course of this discussion, we shall take up the Lewinian formulation of decision stabilization, the conflict model growing out of learning theory, and a paradigm for analyzing decisional conflicts, put forth by Janis.

Finally, in Chapter 14, we shall attempt to deal with other notions of social influence and communication, such as those growing out of Asch's research, work on communication and persuasion, and studies of small group interaction and influence. We shall also touch on the question of personality and persuasibility. In each case we shall try to show how the dissonance formulation might cope with issues and problems raised by these various research emphases.

These particular problems and issues were selected for discussion because, on the one hand, they represent important theoretical issues and problem areas in current psychological research on motivation and social psychology, and, on the other, because we feel that dissonance theory is particularly appropriate for understanding various of their facets.

Cognitive dissonance is regarded by Festinger (1957) as a motivational state because it has behavioral properties in common with other motivational states, especially the so-called homeostatic drives. When homeostatic drives are aroused, the organism engages in behavior that is directed to reducing drive tension. Cognitive dissonance is included among a psychologist's inventory of drives or motives because its arousal always elicits behavior that is (successfully or unsuccessfully) directed to returning the organism to a state in which the drive is at a lower level of arousal or is entirely quiescent. Motivational states, in general, have other properties than these drive-reducing ones but the question of the extent to which cognitive dissonance shares attributes with other motives has received only incidental attention in research on dissonance theory. Thus far "drive character" has been the emphasized common quality. Otherwise, inclusion or exclusion of cognitive dissonance from a list of motives would be of little strategic importance to dissonance theory.

In considering the relationship of dissonance theory to other theories of balance or incongruity, a major issue concerns the motivational one: Just what pushes the organism to reduce inconsistency between the various cognitions or between cognitions and behavior, and so forth? This question has to do with the kinds of pressures that set the process of resolution going, that make for tension which must be reduced by various paths or balanced states.

In general, most incongruity theorists conceive of the need to reduce inconsistency as a general motive; this, therefore, accounts for its drive value. Even such a physiological determinist as Hebb (1955) can speak of the "immediate drive value of cognitive processes without intermediary" (p. 252). Although he relates such processes to "basic motives," he does discuss the feedback from cortical functioning which "makes intelligible the equating of anxiety aroused by threat of pain and the anxiety aroused by cognitive processes related to idea of the self" (p. 251). For cognitive theorists, the specification of the discrepancy-reduction notion as a drive is even more explicit.

Heider (1958), for example, takes the most classical Gestalt position on this matter, locating the idea of incongruity in the stimulus field. For him, imbalance is completely encapsulated in the stimulus field and thus inconsistency is motivating in itself. For Heider, as for Jordan (1953), who states this in terms of pragnanz, there is no reason whatsoever to make any assumptions about underlying motives. In attempting to explain the development and stabilization of interpersonal perceptions, Heider stresses the fact that the sentiment (or affect) characterizing one's response toward some object will tend toward a balanced relation with a person having some relationship to that object. A simple consequence of a person experiencing an unstable interpersonal cognition is that there will be further cognitive work attempted by the person until changes occur that make the cognition balanced and therefore stable. Osgood (1960, p. 345) characterizes Heider's theory as one in which "if a person likes another person, and desires a certain object X, it is fitting (i.e., 'balanced') that he strive to be with the other person and acquire the object, that he assume the other person also likes him, and that the object is of value intrinsically, that he assume the other person also finds the object desirable, and so forth." States of imbalance might be created when P, for example, finds that the O he admires does not like X the way he does. Such a state of imbalance produces stress and tension, and it is these stresses that generate cognitive change. In effect, Heider assumes a "preference for balanced states," and in so doing he adopts a position widely accepted by Gestaltists that people need to organize their experience as meaningfully as possible and that the dynamics of such a need are not motivational ones but stimulus field dynamics.

Both Osgood and Festinger speak of cognitive inconsistencies as motives analogous to other drive states like hunger, thirst, sex, and anxiety, though they are purely cognitive in origin. Osgood, Suci and Tannenbaum (1957) equate "cognitive elements" with the meaning of signs and claim that congruity exists when the evaluative meaning of interacting signs are equally polarized or intense, either in the same or opposite evaluative directions. In the process of cognizing these signs, any incongruity that exists because of differences in polarization must be resolved, and therefore cognitive changes ensue.

Festinger's view is that cognitive dissonance is a need that has much the same motivating characteristics as other needs. He assumes that the simultaneous existence of cognitions which in one way or another do not "fit together" (dissonance) leads to effort on the part of the person to somehow make them fit better (dissonance reduction). For Festinger (1957, p. 3), as we have seen, the existence of nonfitting cognitions is a motivating factor in its own right; in place of dissonance one could conceivably substitute other notions like "hunger," "frustration," "disequilibrium," and so forth. Cognitive elements are said to be dissonant when one implies the obverse of the other. The degree to which there are dissonant elements determines the degree to which psychological tension having drive character is said to exist, making for the stress toward cognitive modification.

It should be understood that neither of these latter theorists necessarily makes the Gestalt assumption about the tendency to maintain consistency as part of the widely operative motivation toward the elaboration and stabilization of ordered forms. In effect, they do not necessarily lean on the conventional Gestalt emphasis on unlearned autochthonous determination. All these theorists, except for Heider, of course, assume that the need for resolution of inconsistency has its origins and motivational dynamics in much the same processes as other needs. Thus, through child training history with its long record of trials in "conflictlike" situations resulting in the elimination of competing and incompatible responses, a state of consistency between cognitive, affective, and behavioral responses toward objects will itself become a gratifying state of affairs. In effect, it will become a stable, learned motive or, as Allport (1937) puts it, an autonomous motive. Thus an encounter with any inconsistency will be painful in itself and will activate the individual's learned responses or reorganization toward consistency (see Hovland and Rosenberg, 1960, p. 225).

The other possible basis for the strain toward resolution of inconsistency, is, of course, in direct and deliberate social training. Most overtly in formal educational procedures, and more subtly in the demands that parents and the structured nature of the world of things make from earliest years, the child is subject to the constant requirement that he endow his responses with some consistency, with varying immediate rewards and punishments for compliance and failure. Thus, although none of the present incongruity theorists takes a position on which of these two mediational processes is responsible for motivation toward resolution of inconsistencies, either sequence is consistent with their assumption of a general motivating tendency resulting from incongruity.

It seems to us, however, that it is not too useful to speak of dissonance or incongruity reduction as a *general* motive. First of all, it simply adds to the plethora of need states postulated by psychological theorists to account for any given response tendency. We feel that psychology would benefit from an attempt to specify the conditions under which responses occur in as economical a fashion as possible without adding a new need every time some new and puzzling behavior is isolated. Secondly, the present and increasing unclarity of the motivation concept itself would seem not to encourage the addition of some new general motive to the present list. As Cofer (1959, p. 194) says, motivation apparently "has no automatic response indicators," and on the antecedent side "the rejection of homeostatic drives as sufficient to motivation also makes insufficient the deprivation operation in the control of motivation."

Furthermore, we feel that the specification of dissonance or incongruity or imbalance as a general motive rests on a theoretical confusion between motives and motivational states. Motives themselves are generally thought of as states of chronic arousal. They refer to the "energizing of behavior and especially to the sources of energy in a particular set of responses that keep them temporarily dominant over others and account for continuity and direction in behavior" (Hebb, 1955, p. 244). Drives, or motivational states, deal with a more specific conception about the way in which this occurs; drive is an hypothesis of motivation that "makes the energy a function of a special process distinct from those S-R or cognitive functions that are energized" (Hebb, 1955, p. 244). Motivational or drive states are tied to specific arousal through discrepancies between motives and their satisfaction. The point is that the discrepancies between other motives and their satisfaction result in behavior in the interests of discrepancy reduction; such behavior is not necessarily simply due to the fact that two stimuli or cognitions are "inconsistent" with one another.

In one of his major theoretical writings, Osgood appears to take this position, though he does not appear to do so explicitly in other places. In his Nebraska symposium paper (1957) he brings in the reticular formation as the physiological basis of the immediate drive value of cognitive processes, but he takes the position that when meaning is blocked because of incongruity, there is drive-producing tension largely because there has been some effect on rewards and punishments or their anticipation, with regard to a possible host of primary and social needs. In sum, it may be reward and punishment related to other needs that makes inconsistency motivating.

However, in the experimental work that has come out of his laboratory, Osgood does not deal explicitly with the idea of the blockage to the satisfactions of other needs or motives that discrepancy produces. His major focus is on semantic incongruities; on the basic dimensions of verbal meaning. In his experimental work he has tried to show that incongruities centering around inconsistencies along the dimensions of evaluation, potency, and activity motivate cognitive change. Thus inconsistency reduction takes place largely as a result of logical inconsistencies along the evaluative dimension that serves as a crucial focus for the assignment of other cognitions. When liked persons were associated with disliked objects, incongruities were assumed to have been created. Osgood et al. (1955, 1957) then bring to bear their general "principle of congruity" and expect that the evaluations of the person and the object will regress in the direction of a common value; the liked person when associated with the disliked object becomes less liked and the disliked object when associated with the liked person becomes less disliked.

To return to our main concern, we feel that cognitive dissonance involves more than what Festinger has explicitly prescribed in his theoretical statement. This has to do with the sources of relevance or psychological implication. It should be apparent from the review of evidence that each experimenter generally knows intuitively just which elements are likely to be relevant and which elements are likely to be irrelevant. But what are the conditions which produce relevance independently of an experimenter's familiarity with his society? One answer to this question is *other motives*. Motives are capable of implying that certain elements should exist and that certain other elements should not exist. The cognition corresponding to smoking ("I am smoking") and the cognition corresponding to reading about lung cancer and smoking ("Smoking causes death from lung cancer") are relevant to one another because obvious motives interact, viz., "gain pleasure from smoking" and "avoid painful death," in addition to many others. As Festinger points out, the cognitions "hot weather is good for corn" and "letters take two weeks to go from New York to Paris" might become relevant if the individual who entertained these cognitions was motivated to earn money by speculating on the American corn crop at the Paris exchange. This kind of analysis has enabled us to elaborate cognitive dissonance in a way not explicitly stated by Festinger in his theory: *Cognitive dissonance is a general "motivational state" that always occurs when there is some prior motive associated with the cognitions that are dissonant.* Although a dissonant relationship is defined more broadly, we are not confident that other forms of psychological implication would in fact provide the conditions necessary to the arousal of dissonance. It is true that other motives which are currently being studied, such as n Achievement, or n Affiliation, and so forth, can be reduced to "simpler" or more "basic" tendencies and drives, but they are not defined in a way that makes this elaboration essential to a complete explanation. Cognitive dissonance, however, must necessarily be defined in such a manner because of the *relevance* criterion.

We have implied earlier that relevance is usually determined in an *a priori*, common sense fashion by the experimenter. Through his experience with the culture in which he is conducting his research, the investigator knows what behaviors, beliefs, values, and so on, have something to do with one another and what stands will be discrepant with what motive satisfactions. Since relevance of cognitions is essential to the production of dissonance, only the outcomes of experiments can show that the investigator has been correct in his *a priori* analysis of relevance. If cognitions were not relevant, no dissonance would occur and the predicted effect of dissonance would not be obtained. It is presumably impossible to produce dissonance between cognitive elements that are irrelevant to one another.

It is in exactly this sphere that the distinctive advantage of dissonance theory with regard to the motivation of discrepancy resolution becomes apparent. In the other incongruity theories, a general residual motive is always assumed to get behavior going. This, we feel, leaves a general undifferentiated state always responsible for cognitive change or behavior and makes difficult the prediction of specific courses of resolution unless some "regression hypothesis" (Osgood et al., 1957) or some "least effort principle" (Rosenberg and Abelson, 1960) is introduced. The point is that while Festinger in his theoretical statement takes the same general position and speaks of a general motive, *because of the relevance criterion and because most of the specific experiments generated by dissonance theory explicitly trade on the frustration of other motives*, the theory is a powerful one. Thus in the gambling experiments, the choice experiments, the coercion experiments, the communication experiments, the hunger, thirst, and avoidance experiments, and so forth, *some prior motivation is always considered*. In effect, what we are saying is that the strong effects of the dissonance manipulations in the various experiments dealt with in the present volume are in fact due to the *commitment on the part of the person to a behavior that has implications for the frustration of important motives*. Every experiment evokes another motive whose instrumental connection to inconsistency produces drives toward the resolution of inconsistency. Basic to the arousal of dissonance appears to be the incompatibility introduced by the individual's commitment to behave in some way, presumably out of some strong motive, such as pleasing the experimenter, which frustrates another strong motive.

Dissonance theory, we have seen, is in part a theory of *postdecision* behavior, and it is the process of the decision to behave in a way that may frustrate motive satisfaction that links motivation to the resolution of inconsistencies. In any one of the experiments mentioned, the simple existence of inconsistency has not been shown to be enough to motivate behavior; in each case the person has arrived at a state of dissonance as a consequence of some prior commitment that has consequences for satisfaction of important needs.

This gap between Festinger's theoretical statement and the actual experiments that have been generated by it is reflected in Osgood's (1960, p. 349) comment that Festinger's theory fails to give explicit recognition to the need for cognitive elements to be brought into some relation with one another if they are to interact and produce cognitive modification. However, Osgood does make the same point we are making: "The implicit recognition of the need for linkage in some unit" appears in the design of dissonance experiments. Thus dissonance only occurs "when a person is forced to make a choice to behave in some way that is discrepant from his cognitions or if a prior choice that he has made has led to a situation of cognitive discrepancy." Dissonance is aroused by the process of decision which has some negative consequences for the individual and which therefore creates a discrepancy between some prior state (or the cognitions which would lead him to maintain that state) and the present behavior he engages in.

A second way in which dissonance theory is different from other models of cognitive inconsistency is in its specification of resistance *to change*, especially through *commitment*. For if we assume that a given inconsistency of cognitive elements arouses a motivational state, a problem remains about which consequences will ensue. This problem is handled in dissonance theory by appeal to the notion of differential resistance to change of the relevant cognitive elements. Those elements that are least resistant to change will tend to be those which do in fact change in order for dissonance to be reduced. Since decisional or behavioral commitment contributes to resistance to change, commitment tends to result in the "fixing" of one of the important relevant elements. Hence dissonance tends to be reduced by change in cognitions other than those involved in the commitment. The net result is that where dissonance is aroused in conjunction with a commitment, its effects are more limited (and specifiable) than where the incongruity has nothing to do with commitment (or other forms of resistance to change).

Another relevant issue here concerns the extension made by some incongruity theorists like Newcomb (1953) and especially Cartwright and Harary (1956) from interpersonal perception to interpersonal relations. The latter attempt a formal definition of balance in Heider's system in terms of the mathematical theory of linear graphs. While there may be tremendous advantages in such specification, as Osgood (1960, p. 346) points out, it causes some confusion in conceptualizing the notion of cognitive change. Cognitive dynamics, he says, transpire within the nervous systems of individuals, and the representations we make of them reflect relationships as *the individual perceives them*. However, it seems that Newcomb and Cartwright and Harary shift too easily from the subjective cognitive interactions within individuals to the objective issues of group structure and dynamics. While it is possible that the laws governing the resolution of incongruities within the cognitive structures of individuals can be transferred to interactions between people and within groups of people, such transformations remain to be proven and tested, and the new mediating assumptions necessary to go from one set of issues to another must be clearly specified. It is clear, however, that Festinger and Osgood are quite aware of this restriction of their systems. It is also possible that a good deal of predictive looseness enters a system that is based on the pressures to resolve incongruities between aspects of an individual cognitive structure and yet attempts to be specific with regard to interactions between individuals.

In summary, we may say that discrepancies or inconsistencies, especially as they appear in the experiments deriving from the dissonance formulation, produce a drive toward their resolution *because of motive states, insofar as discrepancy has some instrumental relationship to their satisfaction or frustration.*

Dissonance and decisional

processes

— 13

DECISION STABILIZATION

The dissonance formulation generally holds that dissonance is a necessary consequence of choice between alternatives or choice to engage in some discrepant behavior. The amount of dissonance and subsequent attempts at resolving it are coordinated to the host of variables mentioned in Part II: importance, attractiveness, and so forth. Thus, for example, the more evidence there is that a person has made a "wrong decision" (i.e., the greater the dissonance), the more he will like and seek support for his original decision until, as dissonance reaches its limit, he revokes his decision or changes his behavor (see Festinger, 1957, pp. 126–131, 162–176, and Cohen, Brehm and Latané, 1959). We also assume that as a result of being chosen a number of times, an item might finally be chosen over an even more attractive alternative, simply as a function of postdecisional dissonance reduction. Thus the theory is concerned with new experiences with the chosen object that may follow after its choice as well as with the imminent consequences of choice. Deutsch, Krauss and Rosenau (1962) argue that such a process may be maladaptive in that it leads the person to distort the evidence surrounding him in his environment. They claim that while it is possible that the decision process contains a maladap-

232

tive mechanism in order to facilitate the "freezing" of decisions, it is not necessary to posit dissonance reduction as the mechanism by which decisions are stabilized or frozen.

Such a view of the maladaptive quality of dissonance resolution tendencies stems from a Lewinian point of view with regard to the decisional process. In Lewin's (1947) view there can be no postdecision tension because of the unresolved pull of unchosen alternatives or because of forces related to the predecision situation. There can be some forced choice, but any *true* decision will presumably have resulted from a prior resolution of the relationship between the approach and avoidance gradients of the competing alternatives. Thus the act of decision does not mean merely that the forces toward one alternative become stronger than those toward the other alternative. As Lewin says, "If this were the case, the resultant force should frequently be extremely small. A decision rather means that the potency of one alternative has become zero or is so decidedly diminished that the other alternative and the corresponding forces dominate the situation." He goes on to say that: "If the opposing forces in a conflict merely change so that the forces in one direction become slightly greater than in the other direction, a state of blockage or extremely inhibited action results rather than that clear one-sided action that follows a real decision" (1947, p. 336). Thus there should be no postdecision dissonance and no consequent attempt to stabilize a decision after choice.

An alternative explanation to the dissonance formulation is that a decision becomes stabilized when the activities in the pursuit of the chosen alternative are such that they either enhance the subjective probability of the occurrence of the chosen as compared with the unchosen alternative or they change the situation confronting the individual in such a way that new additional consequences become associated with the chosen and unchosen alternatives (see Deutsch et al., 1962). Thus, if an individual decides to do something, his decision becomes stabilized as a result of activities in connection with the decision or nonactivity in pursuits inconsistent with the decision, which therefore reduce the subjective probability that he can engage in other pursuits. The general assumption of this point of view, as stated by Deutsch et al., is that it is not necessary to deprecate the other pursuits or to enhance the value of the chosen alternative for the decision to become stabilized. Moreover, if the subjective probability of the nonchosen pursuits becomes zero after the person decides on the chosen pursuit, presumably its effective "valence" (expected utility) becomes zero, and there should be no dissonance.

More specifically, according to one reasonable interpretation of this point of view,[11] an individual's evaluation of an item (an object, event, person, etc.) reflects two factors: its valence and its potency. The valence is the degree of inherent attraction or aversion of the item in terms of the person's values, preferences, and so on and is presumably stable for any given person over time and across situations. The potency is the salience or attention-holding power that the item has for the individual and is, by definition, constantly changing and not necessarily (or at least not wholly) determined by the attributes of the item itself. Valence and potency are said to operate in combination, such that their product determines the item's *effective* valence for the individual and thus his evaluation of it. In other words, if one item is "liked" more than another, it may be because the former is more valent but equally potent, or because the former is equally valent but more potent, or because it is both more valent and more potent.

If an individual is given a number of objects and asked to rate them in terms of how much he "likes" them, Lewinian theory attributes differences in ratings to differences in actual valence, because the potencies of all the objects are presumably equal in such a case. If, then, one of the objects is chosen, its potency will increase, and, since the total potency of any situation will always be equal to 1, the potency of the unchosen objects will decrease accordingly. (If the choice is irrevocable, the chosen alternative might then have a potency of 1 and the other alternatives a potency of 0.) Thus the *effective* valences of all the objects will be changed, although their *actual* valences remain unaltered. (Theoretically if the choice could be eliminated or "destroyed" so that the potencies would revert to equality, the effective valences would also return to their original prechoice values.) If, after the choice, the relative potency of the unchosen item could be increased, its effective valence should increase and that of the chosen one decrease accordingly.

Clearly some of the predictions involved are in direct contradiction to those that would arise from dissonance theory. For example, if after choice the relative potency of the rejected alternative is increased by introducing information elaborating its positive features and advantages, dissonance theory would predict that such information would increase dissonance and lead to an increase in the evaluation of the chosen alternative and possibly to a decrease in the evaluation of the rejected one. A Lewinian prediction, however, is that as a result of such information, the relative potency of the rejected alternative would

[11] See Rosenau, Norah. Decisional importance, dissonance and information. Unpublished manuscript, New York University, 1961.

increase and that of the chosen one decrease. In addition, the actual valence of the rejected alternative might be heightened slightly as a direct consequence of the informational content. Thus the effective valence of the chosen alternative should decrease somewhat, as reflected in evaluations of it, and the effective valence of the rejected alternative should increase by a greater amount.

On the other hand, predictions from the two theories concerning the effects of positive information about the chosen alternative would not necessarily be opposed. With respect to negative information about the chosen alternative, however, the distinctions between the two theories are not very clear because, from the Lewinian point of view, the changes in potency of the alternative that is directly affected would be in a direction opposite to the changes in valence. Thus any specific prediction would depend on the particular strength of the manipulations used in an actual situation. It is interesting to note, nevertheless, that if a single assumption is made in this respect, both Lewinian and dissonance theories lead to the same empirical predictions in the one case of which a number of studies done within the dissonance framework are examples. As Rosenau points out, if negative information about the chosen alternative is introduced, dissonance theory would predict that dissonance would increase and lead to an increase in the evaluation of the chosen alternative and a decrease in the evaluation of the rejected one. The Lewinian interpretation would be that the information would decrease the actual valence of the chosen alternative somewhat but increase its relative potency and decrease the relative potency of the rejected alternative. If we assume that the direct effect on actual valence will not be as great as the changes in relative potencies, then the Lewinian prediction would also be that the evaluation of the chosen alternative would increase and that of the rejected alternative decrease.

The general decisional formulation growing out of the Lewinian background is for the most part extremely unspecified, and before one could begin to test its implications experimentally, the theoretical model would have to be elaborated to a great extent. This would necessitate extensive clarification of such concepts as "subjective probability," "valence," "salience," "potency," and so forth. Since such a task is obviously not within our present framework, we leave as an open question the utility of the Lewinian model for understanding the consequences of decisions. Although we have pointed to some differential predictions, we know of no data testing the general utility of the Lewinian model or crucially testing the differential implications of these alternative formulations.

DISSONANCE AND CONFLICT THEORY

Another possible theoretical model for understanding the consequences of choice among alternatives is that of *conflict theory*. Like Lewinian decision theory, conflict theory might claim that cognitive revaluation occurs *before* choice as a consequence of the need to change the relative approach-avoidance gradients so that a choice of one alternative or another can in fact be made. Thus the necessity to discriminate between alternatives in order to choose might be responsible for revaluation rather than postdecisional revaluation as a consequence of dissonance reduction. At this point it is not possible to evaluate the contribution of such competing processes to revaluation; one can only begin to indicate some of the conditions under which one or another of these processes might be expected to occur and to indicate some general research directions.

First of all, we may examine whether the same principles that apply to postdecisional behavior are applicable to predecisional behavior, that is, do they apply to the entire decision process? As has been noted, the best-known and best-accepted body of propositions that apply to predecisional behavior is contained in conflict theory (Lewin, 1931, 1935, 1951; Miller, 1944, 1959; Brown, 1957; Berlyne, 1960). Briefly, the conflict model assumes that conflict creates psychological tension. The tension will increase as the average magnitude of the opposing tendencies increases. This tension would thus be greatest where the opposing approach and avoidance tendencies were exactly equal in magnitude and where both tendencies were very strong. An individual may reduce this tension by changing the approach and avoidance tendencies so that they are less equal in strength or so that their average magnitude is less. Conflict theory assumes that the tension and consequent attempts to reduce it occur during the period leading up to the choice (or possession of the goal). Dissonance theory, on the other hand, assumes that the tension and reduction processes occur only after the individual has committed himself in one way or another, that is, has anticipated obtaining the goal.

Thus it would appear at first glance that conflict theory and dissonance theory refer to different processes. But is dissonance theory applicable to predecisional behavior? Suppose we assume for the moment that any prechoice change in the relative or absolute magnitude of a gradient is actually a kind of decision.[12] If we could take "snap-

[12] We are indebted to Timothy Brock for his aid in clarifying this analysis of the decisional process.

shots" of an individual in conflict, we would have a series of views, in no two of which the disposition of the gradients would be exactly the same. If the period immediately before a "snapshot" is taken is assumed to have involved a decision, then the disposition of the gradients in the "snapshot" should be predictable from the principles governing postdecisional behavior. According to this point of view there would be no need to arbitrarily dichotomize the decision process into pre- and postdecisional phases. One of the "snapshots" taken of the process might follow a decision that is more irrevocable or consummatory than the others, but to label this step "THE decision" may be to misrepresent the actual process and emphasize the inadequacy of the psychologists's observations.

From this point of view it would seem that the same general principles could apply to the entire decision process. In terms of possible research stemming from this point of view, let us imagine an individual who has never seriously thought about buying an automobile. This individual, through a completely unexpected "windfall," is suddenly financially capable of buying a car and wishes to do so. If he is limited by the sum of money to a particular price range, he needs information bearing on the various cars in this price range. Let us assume, too, that for some reason this person must make up his mind very quickly. If an experimenter were lucky enough to capture an individual in this state, he might begin by presenting the individual with communications that are negative and positive with respect to the qualities of a particular car. This would constitute independent manipulation of approach and avoidance gradients. After the subject indicates his comprehension of these initial communications, more communications might be made available, and their direction would be described to the subject. Then the subject would be asked to select from among these communications the ones he wished to read next. The subject would choose communications on the basis of his initial approach and avoidance gradients and his over-all motivation to purchase *the best car* in his price range. The subject could choose among further combinations of communications that have a known effect on the relative and absolute strength of his gradients or no effect at all. The simplest prediction is that where the initial communications induced approach and avoidance gradients of equal height and magnitude (maximal dissonance), the subject would choose further combinations of communications that promised to alter the strength of the gradients rather than a combination of communications that promised to maintain the equal strengths of the gradients. This repeated process of presentation, comprehension, and choice of further communications seem to be characteristic of the predecisional process. At each step of the process, dissonance principles could conceivably be applied.

With this general background of the complex interrelationship between dissonance and conflict notions in mind, let us consider more formally the possibility that conflict could serve as an alternative explanatory concept to dissonance in "free-choice" situations. In so doing, we shall indicate some specific research directions. As we saw in our review, most experiments demonstrating an effect of dissonance have utilized either approach-avoidance or double approach-avoidance conflict situations. It would appear, therefore, fairly easy to construct an alternative explanation that these various effects are due to some motivational characteristics of conflict. Conflict, however, as we have said, has traditionally referred to what happens *prior* to a choice or commitment, while dissonance refers to what happens *after* a choice or commitment. Thus it might be possible to set up a relatively "crucial" experiment to test between these alternative explanations. Two hypotheses may be stated with reference to a person in a choice situation: (1) Conflict prior to commitment will produce revaluation of the choice alternatives; and (2) Dissonance after commitment will produce revaluation of the choice alternatives. It is to be understood that revaluation from conflict should occur *before* commitment while that from dissonance should occur *after* commitment. In each case the revaluation is such as to enhance the chosen alternative relative to the unchosen.

An unequivocal test of the dissonance hypothesis is possible by measuring changes in evaluation of alternatives after *an overt and irrevocable commitment to one of the alternatives*. Thus the experimental test might consist of having individual subjects: (1) rate the attractiveness of a variety of objects; (2) choose overtly between two; (3) rate the objects again immediately after the choice; and (4) rate them one final time at least several minutes later but preferably a day or so later. To insure that any obtained changes are a function of dissonance, the initial magnitude of dissonance could be manipulated by varying either the relative or the average attractiveness of the choice alternatives (by selection of the alternatives according to the initial ratings).

If dissonance affects revaluation of the alternatives, then changes between the immediate and postponed *after*-choice ratings should be greater for high than for low dissonance choices. A conflict theory that highlighted, for example, discriminations before choice would presumably find it difficult to explain any such changes occurring from immediate-after to postponed-after ratings.

It is more difficult to make an unequivocal test of the conflict hypothesis because subjects cannot be prevented from making covert choices before the overt choice is known. Thus it is difficult to determine at what point a rating will reflect the effects of conflict but not those of dissonance. The following procedure might yield relatively unequivocal information about the effects of conflict prior to choice. After various objects have been initially rated by the subject, two might be selected for choice. They would be selected so as to be fairly unequal in attractiveness. The subject would, however, be asked to postpone his choice, since he is to be given some further information about the objects. Items of information would then be given one by one to the subject. Each item should tend to reduce the difference in attractiveness of the alternatives, thus increasing amount of conflict involved in deciding between the two. The subject would be asked to rate the alternatives after each new piece of information. Five or six items of information could be used. In a control condition, subjects matched for initial ratings of the choice alternatives would receive the same informational items but without having to make a choice.

If conflict motivates revaluation of choice alternatives in such a way as to minimize the conflict, then the information should produce less reduction in the difference between the ratings of the two alternatives in the choice condition than in the no choice condition. Failure of support for the dissonance hypothesis could result from inadequate methods as well as from a wrong hypothesis. Thus the experimental techniques must be very carefully worked out if negative results are to be convincing. Whether or not the dissonance hypothesis is supported, if the conflict hypothesis is supported, then much of the evidence collected for dissonance theory is subject to this alternative explanatory effect. Positive results would thus have important implications for the validity of the theory and its supporting evidence.

It is also possible that "conflict theory" may be used to describe the situation of induced behavior or "forced compliance" where the person has chosen to participate in some discrepant behavior. For most of the experimental situations described in the present volume, an approach-avoidance conflict model would be appropriate. We could coordinate the reward to the approach tendency, and the dislike of the task, for example, eating food, to the avoidance tendency.

This model assumes that conflict creates psychological tension. The magnitude of this tension will increase as the opposing approach and avoidance tendencies become equal in magnitude. The tension will also increase as the average magnitude of the opposing tendencies increases. The tension would thus be greatest where the approach and avoidance tendencies were exactly equal and where both tendencies were very strong. An individual experiencing this tension will try, in proportion to its magnitude, to reduce or eliminate it. He may do so by changing the opposing approach and avoidance tendencies so that they are less equal in strength or so that their average magnitude is less.

Now let us see how this model would apply to one of the experiments described earlier. Consider, for simplicity, only the approach tendency created by the promised reward and the avoidance tendency created by dislike for eating the vegetable in Brehm's experiment on commitment to unpleasant behavior (Brehm, 1960a). Let us assume that the approach tendency is always stronger at the goal (agreement to eat and obtainment of the reward) than the avoidance tendency. When the subject is told that he will be given the reward if he eats a certain amount of the vegetable, he will experience conflict tension to the extent that the opposing tendencies thus created are equal and high in strength. If the accompanying tension motivates the individual to try to reduce the conflict, we would find signs of this in his attempts to increase the magnitude of the approach tendency or to reduce the magnitude of the avoidance tendency. The strength of such attempts should be proportional to the magnitude of conflict created by the initial tendencies.

In line with the experiment in question, let us ignore any attempts to change the approach tendency and simply inspect the attempts that would be concentrated on the avoidance tendency. In general, we might say that to reduce the conflict, the individual may change anything that contributes to the strength of the avoidance tendency. Thus he could increase his liking for the vegetable or he could decrease the amount he would eat. The amount is, in this case, controlled, so that the only way in which the individual could reduce the avoidance tendency is to increase his liking.

The first of the two independent variables in this experiment was the amount of eating required. It is clear that the greater the amount of required eating, the stronger would be the tendency to avoid the goal and, consequently, the stronger would be the conflict prior to choice. Drawing from our above discussion, one would thus say that the more the amount of food required to be eaten, the greater would be the increase in liking for the food.

It should be noted that while the predicted changes in liking are consistent with dissonance theory, the assumed intervening process differs. Conflict theory assumes that the tension and consequent attempts to reduce it occur during the period leading up to choice (or possession of the goal). Dissonance theory, on the other hand, assumes that the tension and reduction process occur only after the individual feels committed one way or the other—for example, has attained the goal.

With this in mind, let us look at the second manipulation in the vegetable experiment. The reader will recall that it consisted of giving subjects information to the effect that the vegetable had either very high or very low food value. The low food value information would presumably increase the magnitude of avoidance of eating while the high value information would presumably increase the approach tendency. It should be noted, however, that this information was given only after the subject had agreed to eat the stipulated amount of food in order to get the prize.

With no further choice to be made, there would presumably be neither conflicting tendencies nor conflict tension created by the information. On the other hand, dissonance theory assumes only that the person has chosen to commit himself to a discrepant situation on some prior occasion in order for *further* inconsistent information to create additional dissonance and attempts to reduce it. Since the results of the experiment indicated that the information, in conjunction with the amount of eating, did indeed affect changes in liking for the food, it would seem that dissonance theory is more applicable to these data than is this particular conflict model.

A further possibility, however, is that the low food value information created a new avoidance tendency and thereby had the psychological effect of reopening the choice. In other words, it could be said that regardless of the overt commitment made by the individual, when he receives the information consistent with eating, he *feels* that he must again choose whether or not to take the goal.

Since the vegetable experiment or any of the others presented does not furnish information that would help us choose between the latter formulation of conflict theory and dissonance theory, numerous new experiments might be suggested. Their general goal would be to vary feelings of choice and the magnitude of dissonant cognitions independently of each other in order to assess their individual effects on attitude change. However, it may be said in connection with the conflict model, also, that because there exists no one conflict theory and because one would have to be constructed in order to test its explanatory power vis-à-vis dissonance theory, major tests of the differential implications of these alternative formulations would be very difficult. In effect, what general conflict theory exists (e.g., Miller, in Hunt,

1944) has not laid the groundwork for the application of reinforcement principles to the effects of choice among alternatives or commitment to discrepant situations.

DECISIONAL CONFLICTS

An analysis of the consequences of decisions within the framework of a psychoanalytically-oriented behavior theory about conflict has been presented by Janis (1959a, 1959b). For Janis (1959a, p. 200), the term "decisional conflict" is used to refer to "opposing tendencies within an individual which influence the way in which the alternatives are formulated, the consistency and intensity with which any alternative is accepted, and the degree to which the decision is subsequently carried out." This definition is, at least in part, readily assimilable to the dissonance formulation; the two models appear to be in some conceptual agreement about the meaning of postdecisional conflict.

Janis has identified four main types of conflict. These arise from: (1) utilitarian loss to self, (2) utilitarian loss to others, (3) social disapproval, (4) disapproval from self. Three sources of motivation in these conflict types are identified: (1) verbally mediated incentive values regarding conscious goals, (2) preconscious affective charge, (3) unconscious affective charge. Six determinants of mode of resolution are: (1) perceived status, (2) personality factors, (3) effortfulness of mode of resolution, (4) institutionalized patterns and traditions, (5) availability of postdecisional information, (6) advance warnings and predictions. In addition to this set of concepts Janis emphasizes the centrality of the construct "work of worrying," especially in connection with the sixth determinant of mode of resolution. We will not attempt to describe this schema in detail here.

Janis makes distinctions among factors that most of the researchers mentioned in our review assume either to be of equal weighting for their subjects or that they assume are distributed among their subjects in a random fashion so that they have no systematic influence. An example of this is Janis' division of sources of motivation into conscious, preconscious, and unconscious charges.

Since unconsciously motivated conflicts are more resistant to solution via corrective information, social pressures, and so on, more extreme modes of resolution of such conflicts are apt to occur. Dissonance theory obviously does not take explicit account of these different sources of motivation in formulating propositions about the mode of reduction of postdecisional dissonance. In general, it might be said that the problem of choice of mode of dissonance reduction has not been specified in a careful manner in the theory, though in each experimental test of the theory conditions that block off modes of dissonance reduction other than the ones deemed relevant by the experimenter are set up. And there is, of course, a good deal of experimental intuition involved in setting dissonance going in the first place.

Festinger's determination of mode of resolution is as a direct function of the resistance to change of relevant cognitive elements. Festinger could analyze any given decisional situation and organize corresponding cognitive elements in terms of their probable degree of resistance to change. Cognitive elements corresponding to actual environmental reality (such as the location of a room one visits every day) are highly resistant to change, whereas cognitions corresponding to a person's likes (such as his distaste for spinach) are less resistant to change. The notion of reality-anchorage provides a criterion for deciding *a priori* the degree of resistance to change of relevant dissonant elements. But Janis might argue that distaste for spinach, for example, may be rooted in a series of traumatic childhood feeding experiences so that this ostensibly simple food preference might be maximally resistant to change, even more resistant to change than one's cognitions concerning the location of his school lunchroom where spinach is often served. In effect it is precisely the nonreality-based (unconscious) cognitions that might be most resistant to real change. This reasoning suggests cautiousness in employing reality-anchorage alone as a criterion of resistance to change and also highlights the possible importance of taking account of the different sources of motivation that Janis specifies.

The type of motivational source and the determinants of mode of resolution may all be viewed as variables that affect the resistance to change of elements in dissonance. The value of Janis' scheme would be displayed in an experiment in which preferred mode of resolution was not predictable from an analysis of relevant elements in terms of resistance to change. Without being too explicit on this point, dissonance theory implies that the mode of postdecisional conflict resolution will always follow the cognitive elements that are least resistant to change. If Janis can show that taking account of motivational source in conjunction with one or several of his determinants enables him to predict a preferred mode of resolution in which cognitive elements relatively *highly* resistant to change are altered, this would force a considerable extension and revision of dissonance theory insofar as it can be applied to postdecisional behavior.

Of course, from the standpoint of a good theory, there are disadvantages: Janis' six determinants are not exhaustive, and one might go on endlessly listing qualitatively different modes of resolution. Whether or not such schema-building is worthwhile will be demonstrated by experiments in which the outcomes are not predictable from the relatively more modest and more abstract set of concepts developed by Festinger. It is empirically possible to identify: (1) the relevant considerations (cognitive elements) that are involved in a decision, (2) the affective sign or direction of the motivational charge, and, finally, (3) the resistance to cognitive and/or affective modification of the dominant considerations. It remains to be shown that Janis' scheme has some advantage over an analysis in terms of dissonant and consonant cognitions and their respective resistances to change.

Dissonance, attitude change, and social influence

— 14

A number of very general differences exist between the approach to attitude change and social influence taken by dissonance theory and that taken by other theoretical approaches. The dissonance approach may be distinguished from the approach of, for example, the Yale program of research on communication and attitude change directed by Carl Hovland. The Yale program has been one of the major sources of research on the determinants of attitude change, and it is therefore instructive to use some central aspects of this work as a reference point for evaluating the distinctive contributions of dissonance theory. We shall discuss this under three headings: (1) research on communication discrepancy and attitude change, (2) research on improvisation and attitude change, and (3) self-esteem and attitude change. Another set of research issues has grown up around the problem of (4) conformity and social influence. This research is best represented by small group research on social influence and by some of Asch's research.

COMMUNICATION DISCREPANCY AND ATTITUDE CHANGE

A good deal of experimental evidence exists which shows that the more extreme an attitude or opinion, the more difficult it will be to produce change in that attitude (e.g., Hovland, Harvey and Sherif, 1957). On the other hand, it has also been shown (e.g., Goldberg, 1954; Hovland and Pritzker, 1957) that the greater the discrepancy between the subject's position and the opinion advocated, the greater the opinion change toward the advocated position. In an attempt to assess such diverse findings, Hovland (1959) has proposed some empirical principles that specify in greater detail the relationship between communication discrepancy and attitude change. However, the typical determinants, such as whether or not the communication presented is in the subject's latitude of acceptance or rejection, whether or not the communication is ambiguous, or the communicator is seen as credible, are hardly more than descriptive or common sense guidelines to variables that have to be conceptually revaluated in each new experimental setting. At the most, they are loosely related in a *post hoc* fashion to a very general social learning theory (Hovland, Janis and Kelley, 1953) or to a set of broadly interpreted judgmental categories (Hovland, Harvey and Sherif, 1957). In effect, we may say that much of the research in this area growing out of the Yale tradition has not made clear the theoretical conditions that govern the relationships between communication discrepancy and attitude change, and it has therefore been difficult to relate the two on other than an empirical basis.

Dissonance theory, however, takes a fairly unequivocal stand on this question. It attempts to provide a particular conceptualization of the relationship between communication discrepancy and attitude change via its assumption of the tension created by engaging in attitude-discrepant commitment. It assumes that when such tension is created, the person will strive to resolve it, and the more the tension, the more he will attempt to resolve it. It assumes most basically that strong either-or effects can occur when there is such tension and that people may go from one extreme to another in their attitudes in order to reduce the tension.

Dissonance theory does not necessarily make predictions about when a person will or will not engage in the discrepant behavior. When, however, conditions are such that the person is confronted with a communication or behavioral potential that is contrary to his attitude position, but he nevertheless engages in the discrepant behavior, dissonance is produced. When a person involves himself in some way with a contrary communication, when he advocates it, when he works over it, when he agrees to expose himself to it, and so forth, dissonance arises and may be reduced by coming to accept the advocated contrary position.

The most broadly stated attitude theory would say that the stronger the prior attitudes, the more will the individual want to act in a fashion consistent with those attitudes. However, dissonance theory would say that under conditions where the person agrees to engage in attitude-discrepant behavior, we are led to quite opposite expectations. It says that the greater the communication discrepancy (i.e., the stronger the forces toward attitudinal maintenance, away from discrepant behavior), the more dissonance is experienced on discrepant commitment. The greater the dissonance, the more the person must reduce it and, therefore, the greater may be the consequent change in his attitudes to conform with the discrepant stand. Under such conditions we arrive at a prediction that goes counter to most generally accepted assumptions about the effects of extremity of attitude.

The most general derivation that can be made from dissonance theory is that the more an initial attitude would lead one *not* to commit oneself to discrepant behavior (deprivation, unpleasantness, counter-propaganda), the greater the dissonance and consequent revaluation of one's own attitude. In line with this, as we have noted, Cohen (1959b), Cohen, Terry and Jones (1959), and Zimbardo (1960) have shown that subjects most extreme in their negative attitudes toward an issue changed most to agree with the attitude issue as a result of commitment to a dissonance-producing situation. Brehm (1959) has found that, keeping motivation not to eat disliked food constant, the more disliked is the food one is committed to eat, the greater is the dissonance and consequent revaluation so that the disliked food is now liked better. These experiments show that the magnitude of dissonance and consequent attitude change increase as the amount of inconsistency between attitude and commitment increases.

It should be noted that such a proposition depends on the fact that a strong commitment to accepting the communication as credible is introduced. More generally, alternative modes of dissonance reduction like derogating the communicator, rejecting the information, "uncommitting" oneself, and so forth, must be made difficult. In Zimbardo's (1960) experiment, for example, the subject could not repudiate the communicator, for she was a close friend, even though the friend communicated an opinion that was clearly in the subject's "latitude of rejection." Similarly, an attempt was made to induce the subject to feel that she would not be able to influence her friend in turn after the experimental session. In an experiment by Aronson, Turner and Carlsmith (in press) subjects were exposed to a persuasive communication by a highly credible source, others by a mildly credible source. The extent of the discrepancy between the subject's opinions and that of the communicator was also varied. The subjects were then asked to give their opinions a second time. The results show that for the highly credible source, the amount of opinion change increased with increasing discrepancy. For the mildly credible source, opinion change decreased with increasing discrepancy, and subjects in the large discrepancy condition who did not change disparaged the communicator.

These results confirm the notion that dissonance in these communication situations is introduced by some "commitment," whether the commitment be to exposure, eating, a friend, or a highly credible communicator. Once such limits to dissonance reduction through repudiation are introduced, there results a clear relationship: The greater the discrepancy, the greater the dissonance and the greater the resulting amount of attitude change toward support of the commitment.

Thus, under conditions where the person is committed to a discrepant situation, predictions emerge that are different from those derived from the research on communication and attitude change (Hovland, Janis and Kelley, 1953; Hovland, 1959). From the latter, we might assume that the more strongly held an initial position, the less is the attitude change. The reasoning in the present section suggests that the stronger the forces (i.e., the more the involvement in one's own attitude position) *against* a person's being committed to a discrepant situation (e.g., involvement with a contrary communication), the greater the dissonance and the *greater* the consequent revaluation of his attitudes when he does commit himself.

DISSONANCE VERSUS IMPROVISATION

A good deal of the theory and research growing out of the Yale program has been concerned with the conditions under which the probability of giving a certain response to a certain stimulus could be changed. In general, it was thought that reinforcing the individual's discrepant response to the stimulus would decrease the probability of his making the original response when the stimulus was again presented. These notions grow out of the position that an attitude can be conceptualized as a "repertoire of responses" about a given issue. Attitudes can be changed by having the person incorporate new statements into his response repertoire. The general question posed by the Yale group was, "What conditions will reinforce a discrepant response to an attitude question?"

An answer has been proposed by Kelman (1953). According to him, the probability of making a given response can be increased by inducing the person to make the response along with implicit "supporting" responses or it can be decreased by inducing the person to make the response along with implicit "interfering" responses. A supporting response is an ". . . implicit response made by the individual (usually a self-verbalization), which provides arguments in favor of the overt response he makes; which produces further motivations in the direction of the overt response; or which relates the overt response to other stimulus situations." An interfering response is ". . . any implicit response made by the individual which provides motivations against the overt response he makes; which limits the stimulus situations to which the overt response is applicable; or which is generally irrelevant (such as aggressive or distracting response)" (Kelman, 1953).

Thus Kelman asserts that if an individual can be induced to say something he ordinarily would not say, the probability of his making the induced statement again will be a function of whether or not the response was accompanied by implicit supporting or interfering responses. Whether the accompanying responses for any given overt response will be supporting or interfering depends in turn on the conditions under which the overt response is elicited. To induce a person to say something he ordinarily would not, one may use "response restriction." Response restriction will tend to produce supporting responses ". . . when the communication is perceived favorably, when the restriction is in line with the subject's own needs, and when it enhances the subject's feeling of choice; response restriction would tend to produce interfering responses, and hence impede (attitude) change, when the communicator is perceived unfavorably, when the restriction frustrates the subject's own needs, and when it creates an atmosphere of high pressure" (Kelman, 1953).

To collect evidence on his theoretical notions, Kelman conducted an experiment in which junior high school students were asked to write an essay either in support of a comic book they favored (for the reading of younger children) or in support of one they disfavored. Differential restriction of their responses to writing in support of the disfavored book was induced by different offered rewards. Low restriction of response was obtained by a moderately attractive prize for writing in support of the favored book and, at the same time, a competitive chance (the best five essays) for a very attractive prize for writing in support of the disfavored book. High restriction was obtained by offering the moderately attractive prize for either kind of essay but additional highly attractive prizes to all who would write in support of the disfavored book. Thus, for low restriction, writing in support of the disfavored book meant giving up the moderately attractive prize in order for a small chance of getting the high attraction prize, whereas for high restriction it meant getting both the moderately and highly attractive prizes and giving up nothing. Attitude change was measured by asking subjects to indicate on a five-point scale, both before and after writing the essays, how good or bad they thought each of 12 different comic books representing both favored and disfavored types were.

The data of interest are the attitude change scores for those subjects who wrote in support of the initially disfavored book. They engaged in counter-attitudinal persuasion. The change scores showed that these subjects' attitudes became more favorable toward the initially disfavored book. In addition, subjects who were in the low restriction condition showed greater favorable change than those in the high restriction condition. It is apparent, then, that at least under the stipulated experimental conditions, a person induced to argue against his private attitude will tend to change his attitude toward the position for which he argued. Furthermore, if it can be assumed that Kelman successfully manipulated response restriction, then the lower the amount of response restriction, the greater the amount of change in the direction of the discrepant position supported.

Since some subjects chose to support the favored side, some the disfavored side, and since the proportion supporting the disfavored side was different in the high and low restriction conditions, some of these effects could be due to the problem of sampling bias (subject self-selection). It seems likely, however, that at least some of the effects are due to the discrepancy between persuasion and initial attitude and to the differential types of inducement used to obtain the discrepant persuasion. As it has turned out, Kelman's results are consistent with later findings.

Kelman offered three alternative explanations for his results but found that the data did not wholly support any of them. He did conclude, however, ". . . that conditions favorable to change are those in which conformity is accompanied by implicit supporting responses, and conditions unfavorable to change are those in which conformity is accompanied by implicit interfering responses" (Kelman, 1953). Since Kelman's explanation of the results was *post hoc* and no further work has been done on it, it remains at the hypothetical level.

A similar approach to understanding the consequences of discrepant persuasion was adopted by Janis and King (1954, 1956). They were interested in the attitudinal consequences of role playing. In their first study (1954), they had college students present, as sincerely as possible, a speech from a prepared outline or listen to a speech given by another student. In all cases the position of the speech disagreed with the initial position of both the speaker and listener. A questionnaire was used to measure opinions both before and after the experimental inductions. The opinion change scores indicated that speech givers tended to show more change toward the discrepant position upheld by the speech than did the listeners. Differences between replications indicated that those speech givers who showed most change also tended to have engaged in greater improvisation in their talks and to have been more satisfied with their performances in giving the talks.

A second study (King and Janis, 1956) was designed to gather evidence on the separate effects of improvisation and satisfaction in producing opinion change. Again each subject (college student) was given a speech upholding a position discrepant from his private opinion. In the first group he was asked to read the speech silently; in the second, to read it aloud; and in the third, to read it silently and then give it aloud as would an impromptu speaker. Answers to a post-experimental questionnaire showed that subjects who gave the improvised speech were less satisfied with their performance than were those who simply read the speech aloud. Thus, if improvisation increases attitude change from discrepant persuasion, then the improvisation group should show more change, whereas, if satisfaction increases change, then the nonimprovisation group should show more. The opinion change scores showed a greater net percentage of subjects changing in the direction of the speech in the improvisation condition. There was no difference in amount of opinion change between the nonimprovisation group and a control in which the speeches were silently read. The investigators suggested that the crucial aspect of improvisation in producing opinion change is "invention." Arguments invented by the individual are more likely to convince him, and, in addition, the individual inventing arguments is less likely to have interfering responses.

In summary, the research by Kelman and by Janis and King indicated that counter-attitudinal persuasion tends to result in attitude change in the direction of the assumed or induced position. Second, Kelman's low restriction condition produced more attitude change than did his high restriction condition. Third, the results of the experiments by Janis and King demonstrated that the discrepant persuasion requiring improvisation produces more attitude change than discrepant persuasion without improvisation. Finally, these investigators failed to find evidence that satisfaction with performance in giving discrepant persuasion has any effect on amount of attitude change. The improvisation hypothesis is clearly supported by the data.

As mentioned earlier, the definition of a discrepancy between an attitude and a behavior can be considered a special case of the defining statement of a dissonant relationship. We have said that whenever an individual engages in a behavior that his attitude would lead him not to engage in, he will experience dissonance and will attempt to reduce or eliminate it. Thus an individual will tend to change his attitude so that it would more nearly lead to, or be consistent with, the behavior in which he engaged.

According to dissonance theory, engaging in discrepant verbal behavior will tend to result in attitude change toward the discrepant position to the extent that the initial attitude was strong, the discrepant behavior was strong, and the inducing force was weak. The experiments by Janis and King (1954, 1956) and Kelman (1953), cited earlier, supported the hypothesis that the amount of attitude change toward the discrepant position is a direct function of the amount of improvisation required in the discrepant persuasion. At the same time, clear support has been given to the derivation from dissonance theory that the amount of positive attitude change will be an inverse function of the magnitude of the force that induces the discrepant persuasion. Questions arise, then, as to how these theoretical notions and empirical phenomena fit together. Do they agree, disagree, or complement each other?

Before delving into this comparison, we should note that the concept of improvisation is not yet well defined either conceptually or empirically. Although the effects of improvisation are said to be self-persuasion through "good" arguments and reduced resistance to change through suppression of interfering responses, such as feelings of doubt and guilt, the conditions that produce such improvisation have not been clearly stated.

In comparing the improvisation concept with dissonance theory, let us first ask if the former notion, improvisation, can be used to explain data supporting the latter. On the theoretical side, it is difficult to see how the improvisation hypothesis can predict the differential effect of the inducing force. At best, one might predict that the amount of improvisation and consequent attitude change would increase as the magnitude of the inducing force increased. This prediction is, however, precisely opposite to that from dissonance theory and to the empirical findings. Thus, unless it is true that a low inducing force tends to produce relatively more improvisation, the improvisation hypothesis seems incapable of explaining the data supporting dissonance theory. Data relevant to this possible exception are available.

These data come from the experiments by Festinger and Carlsmith (1959) and by Cohen, Brehm and Fleming (1958). In the former study, the discrepant persuasion given by the subjects was tape recorded and then coded for various indices of strength, including persuasiveness of arguments, variety of arguments, over-all strength of persuasion, and time spent on relevant verbalization. Although there was no attempt to get subjects offered $20.00 to give stronger persuasion than subjects offered $1.00, it was reasonable to expect that the former would tend to try harder than the latter because of this difference in incentive value. Analysis of the various indices of strength confirmed this expectation, showing for each index an unreliable tendency for subjects in the $20.00 condition to make the discrepant statement more strongly than did subjects in the $1.00 condition. If these differences can be considered to reflect a like difference in amount of improvisation engaged in by these two groups, then improvisation cannot account in a straightforward manner for the differences in amount of attitude change, for the amount of attitude change was greater in the $1.00 than in the $20.00 condition. This does not say that improvisation was not operating in this experiment, for it may have been counteracting the dissonance-reduction effect. All it says is that the amount of improvisation engaged in by the subjects does not seem to account for the results in any simple manner.

Cohen, Brehm and Fleming (1958), in their study, attempted to measure the intervening processes assumed to vary with improvisation. Using a postexperimental questionnaire, they measured the perceived pressure to write the discrepant essay, the extent to which the subjects were self-motivated to write the discrepant essay, and the extent to which subjects reported awareness of interfering responses. In line with the manipulation of amount of justification, subjects given high justification felt more pressure than subjects given low justification. Furthermore, subjects exposed to high justification were less self-motivated and reported more interfering responses than did those given low justification. Thus the obtained difference in amount of attitude change, which was greater for the low than for the high justification condition, is consistent with both dissonance theory and the improvisation concept.

The latter study raises some additional questions about our ability to compare the two theoretical notions. Dissonance theory is not stated in terms of "self-motivation" and "interfering responses." Nor is it clear how such terms or the operations for them might be incorporated into the theory. Self-motivation, for example, could be, under some conditions, an index of the amount of dissonance being experienced by an individual (or of the amount of dissonance reduction accomplished). The same may be said for "interfering responses" where the direction of the relationship is reversed (or the sign of the index changed). To put it more generally, at least some aspects of improvisation may be considered indices of dissonance or dissonance reduction. With such overlap and ambiguity in terminology and measurement, the relationship between the two theoretical notions must be carefully worked out. What we must press for is a sufficiently clear statement of the independent conditions and consequent attitudinal changes so that crucial comparisons can be made at both the conceptual and empirical levels.

Further evidence on the effect of improvisation *per se* comes from the Rabbie, Brehm and Cohen (1959) study. The purpose of this study, as we noted, was to see whether or not verbalization of a discrepant stand had any effect on attitude change above and beyond the effect of dissonance. College students were individually asked to write an essay against intercollegiate athletics. Half of them were given high, half, low justification for writing the counter-attitudinal persuasion. To determine the effect of actually making the discrepant persuasion (which had to be completely improvised by the subject), half of each justification group was given the attitude measure *before* writing the essay, while the other half was given it *afterward*. A postexperimental questionnaire check on the justification manipulation indicated it was successful.

As we saw earlier, dissonance theory leads to the prediction that attitude change toward the discrepant position will tend to be greater with low justification (low force to comply) than with high. Since the theory indicates that the commitment to take the discrepant stand should be sufficient to produce the attitude-changing dissonance, we would expect that subjects whose attitudes were measured *before* writing the essay would show more positive attitudes toward the discrepant position if they had been given low justification than if they had been given high. This expectation was confirmed by the mean difference in attitude between the two justification conditions. If, on the other hand, improvisation increases the amount of attitude change toward the discrepant position, then subjects whose attitudes were measured *after* they wrote the essay should have more positive attitudes than those whose attitudes were measured before. Comparison of the mean attitude scores failed to confirm this expectation. Mean attitudes after verbalization were not different from those measured before. However, where attitudes were measured after writing, the justification manipulation failed to produce a significant effect on attitudes, apparently due to higher variation in attitudinal response under these conditions. Such an increase in variability of response would indicate that though there was no *general* increase in attitude change from improvisation, there were individual cases of both increase and decrease in amount of change. We may conclude, therefore, that improvisation increases the variability of attitudinal response to dissonance created by a decision to take a discrepant behavioral position. Until further explored, this generalization should be limited to the conditions of the present experiment, that is, an initial attitude of high strength and presumably a relatively high magnitude of dissonance from the decision to take the discrepant stand. Where the force to comply is great compared to the resisting force from the initial attitude (as appears to be the case in the studies by Janis and King, 1954, 1956), improvisation still may have a direct effect on attitudes as hypothesized. As we shall see, however, a direct effect of improvisation under these conditions would be predicted by dissonance theory as well.

Two additional pieces of evidence are relevant to the dissonance versus improvisation argument. The first concerns the data from the study by Cohen and Latané on choice and attitude change (see Table 6, Chapter 7). It will be remembered that in this experiment, those subjects in the low choice condition changed their attitudes more, the more they felt that they had made a "sincere, organized, and convincing speech" against their own position. These results are consistent with both the dissonance and improvisation arguments. However, under conditions of high choice, results quite inconsistent with the improvisation argument were obtained; the better the perceived quality of their speeches, the *less* attitude change was obtained. Such data, while clearly unexplainable by the improvisation notion, can perhaps be fitted into a dissonance formulation. Here we would stress the dissonance produced upon mere commitment to a discrepant stand and the possibility of discrepant self-persuasion behavior as a mode of reducing that dissonance. To the degree that the improvisation hypothesis leans on the subject's self-feelings and his perception of his sincerity in actually fulfilling his discrepant commitment, these data would appear to be inconsistent with the improvisation hypothesis.

Another set of data more in accord with a dissonance than an improvisation interpretation comes from the unpublished effort experiment by Zimbardo. It will be recalled that in this experiment the hypothesis was that the greater the effort involved in taking a discrepant position with regard to a contrary communication, the greater the dissonance and consequent attitude change toward that discrepant stand. Zimbardo manipulated effort by having subjects read discrepant communications into a tape recorder with a delayed auditory feedback apparatus attached. Half the subjects received a 0.3 second delay (high effort), half received a 0.01 second delay (low effort). It was found that the greater the effort (greater delay) the subject experienced in reading the communication in a sincere, convincing, and compelling manner, the greater the attitude change toward the discrepant position. Now, if we assume that the crux of the improvisation hypothesis is the necessity for the subject to sincerely convince himself much as an external communicator would, it is difficult to see how it can be applied to these data. Under conditions of delay, a good deal of disorganization of speech and thought occurs, making it difficult for the subject to do a good job in reading the discrepant report and thus persuade himself. However, even though there is greater disruption of speech and thought in the high effort condition, there is greater attitude change, a result clearly derivable from dissonance theory. Although it is true that this experiment does not provide the most ideal test of the improvisation hypothesis, since the subject read a report rather than freely improvised, the condition under which he had least opportunity to persuade himself was the one that produced most attitude change. Such a result would certainly not seem consistent with even the most broadly conceived improvisation hypothesis.

In summarizing the data in support of dissonance theory, it may be said that the concept of improvisation can alternatively explain some of it but not all. We turn, then, to the complementary question of whether or not dissonance theory can explain data supportive of the improvisation concept.

It will be recalled that, with the initial attitude strength and inducing force held constant, the greater the strength of discrepant verbal behavior, the greater will be the magnitude of dissonance and consequent attitude change. If it can be assumed that an increase in improvisation represents an increase in strength of verbalization, then the magnitude of dissonance and consequent attitude change will be a direct function of the amount of improvisation. It is clear, therefore, that the results of the experiments by Janis and King (1954, 1956) and Kelman (1953) can be explained by dissonance theory in a direct and simple manner. Thus, at the theoretical level, the improvisation effect may be a special case of dissonance theory.

However, it may be premature to close the issue in favor of dissonance theory, since the experiments supporting dissonance theory may be explained in other ways by making certain assumptions about the effects of the experimental conditions in question. In defense of dissonance theory, it has been seen in preceding pages that a variety of derivations in this general problem area have been supported by experimental results. One need not, however, appeal to less relevant evidence in order to settle this question: Theoretical differences are easy to find and amenable to test. Consider, for example, the case in which the counter-attitudinal arguments are prepared for the individual and he is induced to repeat them. According to the notions involved in the improvisation hypothesis, the stronger the arguments involved or the greater the number of such arguments (or both), the greater should be the interfering responses and, consequently, the less should be the amount of attitude change toward the discrepant position. If this derivation is somewhat shaky, it can at least be said that the improvisation hypothesis would not predict *greater* attitude change with increased strength of furnished arguments. On the other hand, dissonance theory implies that increased strength of arguments (or more arguments) will increase the magnitude of dissonance and consequent attitude change toward the discrepant position.

While the problems discussed may well lead to clarifiying research, there is another set of data at least as provocative. It is the *within* condition relationship between strength of discrepant persuasion and amount of attitude change. As we noted in Chapter 7, in some experiments (e.g., Cohen, Brehm and Fleming, 1958) increased attitude change is directly associated with number of original arguments given, as would be expected from the improvisation hypothesis, while in others (e.g., Festinger and Carlsmith, 1959; Rabbie, Brehm and Cohen, 1959) the same variables are inversely related.

Since the positive relationship between strength of verbalization and attitude change can be explained by both improvisation and dissonance concepts, the interesting problem is the negative relationship. It suggests several leads for further research. The first assumes that the discrepant verbalization itself has dissonance-reducing effects. The study by Rabbie, Brehm and Cohen (1959) showed that the decision to make the discrepant persuasion is sufficient to create dissonance and consequent attitude change. Since the decision is to "make discrepant persuasion," it is possible that any behavior consistent with it will tend to reduce the consequent dissonance. Thus the stronger the actual discrepant persuasion effected by the individual, the more consistent is his behavior with his decision and the less will be the magnitude of dissonance (from the original decision). Note that this would occur only where the attitude-changing dissonance was consequent to the initial decision. Under conditions that do not produce dissonance from the decision, the magnitude of dissonance may vary *directly* with the strength of the discrepant persuasion.

A second possible lead, also in terms of dissonance theory, assumes that there are large individual differences in perception of the magnitude of the inducing force. The higher is the perceived force, the greater will be the motivation to comply and the greater, presumably, will be the strength of the compliant behavior. At the same time, however, increased (perceived) force will result in decreased dissonance and consequent attitude change. Thus individual variation in the perceived magnitude of the inducing force will tend to produce a negative correlation between strength of discrepant persuasion and amount of attitude change toward the discrepant position. If this explanation were correct, one would want to state the conditions that promote or inhibit individual variation in the perceived magnitude of the inducing force.

A third possible lead for research comes from an explanation similar to that just discussed. Where that explanation assumes variations in the perceived magnitude of the inducing force, this explanation assumes variations in perceived "credibility" of the inducing force. If, for example, the inducing force is a prize of high value, then some persons may believe they will get it, while others may to some degree doubt that they will actually get it. The more doubt an individual experienced, the less motivated he would be to comply and, consequently, the less strong would be his discrepant persuasion. But as the perceived credibility decreased and reduced the force to comply, the magnitude of dissonance consequent to compliance would increase. Thus decreased perceived credibility will tend to result in decreased strength of discrepant persuasion and increased attitude change toward the discrepant position.

Finally, it should be noted that from the point of view of the improvisation concept, a negative relationship between the strength of verbalization and the amount of attitude change toward the discrepant position would tend to occur where interfering responses were positively related to strength of discrepant persuasion. Individual variation in perceived pressure could, for example, be positively related to strength of verbalization and also extent of interfering responses.

In summary, the evidence on counter-attitudinal persuasion supports the following empirical generalizations: The amount of attitude change toward the discrepant position will be (1) generally a direct function of the strength or degree of improvisation of the discrepant persuasion and (2) an inverse function of the magnitude of the force inducing the discrepant persuasion. While both generalizations are consistent with dissonance theory, only the first is consistent with the improvisation hypothesis.

SELF-ESTEEM AND SOCIAL INFLUENCE

We may note that the dissonance formulation also has implications for the body of research on self-esteem and attitude change. In their volume *Personality and Persuasibility* (1959), the Yale group has presented a number of studies dealing with the impact of persuasive communications on persons of high and low self-esteem; Janis (in Hovland, Janis and Kelley, 1953, and Hovland and Janis, 1959) and Cohen (1959a) have summarized the results of these studies. Briefly, these studies indicate that persons of high self-esteem are less susceptible to persuasion presented by the mass media, by individual communicators, and in face-to-face situations. The personality predisposition of self-esteem is a complex and many-sided variable containing components of social withdrawal, feelings of inferiority and inadequacy, and so forth. In general, however, it can be regarded as encompassing some dimension of ego-strength and resistance to vulnerability. When self-esteem is viewed in this light it becomes amenable to a dissonance theory analysis which leads to derivations regarding the relationship between self-esteem and influence running directly counter to those made by the Yale group. Thus we might say that in situations where persuasive communications are directed at the individual, or in a forced-compliance situation, the person of high self-esteem *who agrees to consider contrary information or who complies* should experience more dissonance than the person of low self-esteem who behaves in such a fashion. In effect, high self-esteem is a cognition that does not support the acceptance of influence or compliance; the person of high self-esteem is accustomed to thinking of himself as having integrity and of his opinions as correct and true more than the low self-esteem person. Thus persons of high self-esteem may, of course, comply less, everything else being equal. Although dissonance theory is irrelevant to the determinants of compliance, it does, however, say that when, for whatever reasons, the person *does* comply, he should experience some dissonance and consequent attitude change toward the new information or situation. A low self-esteem person has characteristically been shaken in his convictions and had his opinions questioned; when induced to expose himself to counter-propaganda or to adopt a discrepant stand, he should experience less dissonance and consequent attitude change. We might expect, therefore, that the higher the self-esteem, the more the dissonance on being influenced and the stronger the pressure on the person to reduce those tensions, everything else being equal, by justifying his stand more, being more certain that his new position is the correct one and being less responsive to counter-communications.

The general point that can be made here is that any personality construct that would lead the person not to perform a discrepant act or respond to a persuasive communication contrary to his initial attitudes will produce more dissonance and consequent attempts at dissonance reduction when he does so. We may say, then, that under conditions where the person commits himself to some discrepant experience like involving himself with some situation or information that is counter to his values or attitudes or that is unpleasant, the relationship between self-esteem and attitude change will be different from that suggested by the existing body of work on communication and attitude change.

Although self-esteem is generally viewed as a chronic state, it would seem reasonable to assume that at least some of the major components constituting it could be manipulated experimentally; personality theorists do not usually qualify their formulations by stating that variables have effects only when chronic. Given a clear and precisely stated dimension along which the personality construct operates, it should always be manipulable and result in more precise determinations of its effects through experimental procedures. Recalling Gerard's (1961) experiment on ability and conformity, we can see a direct confirmation of our line of reasoning regarding the effects of self-esteem. It will be remembered that the high ability subjects who were made to feel that they had complied (in their "real impulse") conformed to the group more on a second conformity task and were more attracted to the group than the low ability subjects who conformed. Thus high ability subjects experienced more dissonance on compliance than low ability subjects, and in order to reduce that dissonance (i.e., make consistent their cognitions about their ability and their compliance) they became more attracted to the group and modified their behavior in the direction of the group on a subsequent series of trials.

Bramel's (1962) homosexuality experiment also bears on the present argument. His data showed that subjects who were made to believe that they experienced homosexual arousal experienced dissonance and greater consequent attribution of homosexuality to others, the more favorable their self-evaluations. In this experiment, high self-esteem is clearly dissonant with believing that one has experienced homosexual arousal. The lower the self-esteem, the less dissonance produced by this particular discrepant commitment.

In summary, both Gerard's and Bramel's experiments provide evidence strongly confirmatory of our line of reasoning regarding the direct relationship between self-esteem and attitude change where dissonance is produced through discrepant commitment.

SOCIAL INFLUENCE AND CONFORMITY STUDIES IN THE LIGHT OF DISSONANCE THEORY

One of the most significant areas of research in social psychology over the past decade or so has been that of conformity and social influence. This line of research has attempted to parcel out the various group and individual determinants of conformity. It appears that dissonance theory may lead to a somewhat different view of the conformity process than is suggested by much of this research. We shall discuss this issue with reference to (1) research on communication and social influence and (2) research on group factors in conformity.

COMMUNICATION AND SOCIAL INFLUENCE

A large and impressive body of interrelated research on the processes of social influence is represented by the program of research carried out originally at the Research Center for Group Dynamics at Michigan by Festinger and his associates. This work is best summarized in Festinger's articles on informal social communication (1950) and social comparison processes (1954), in which a number of propositions relating communication, group factors, and social influence are set forth. Among the most important of these propositions are those dealing with the effects of group cohesiveness on the acceptance of influence on the part of a group member. In general, research has shown that when cohesiveness is increased (i.e., when people's attraction to a group to which they belong increases), people are more subject to social influence. In sum, people change their opinions more to conform with those of others in their group, the more cohesive the group.

In all these experiments, cohesiveness is manipulated experimentally by means of prior inductions, and in some public fashion, subjects are shown that they are deviant. Thus, under presumed group pressure, they change their opinions to conform with those of the group and they do so the more they are attracted to the other members of the group (i.e., the more cohesive the group). However, it is reasonable to view the situation of public conformity to an initially disagreed-with position as one of forced public compliance; as a response to forces emanating from the group, the person takes a public stand that is counter to his initial attitude position. Once we view the social influence studies in this light, they become susceptible to a dissonance analysis that leads to somewhat different conceptions about the influence process than that given by the usual small group studies.

If we apply our analysis of the forces for and against taking such a discrepant stand (i.e., changing one's opinions to comply with the group stand), we can see that such a behavior, in the terms of the present discussion, produces dissonance. We may then ask: What are the factors in this situation controlling the magnitude of dissonance and therefore the magnitude of true private attitude change? In other words, What will determine the degree to which the subject experiences dissonance because of the necessity to take a public stand against his opinions and therefore what will be the degree to which he changes his true opinion to conform with the public stand? The force analysis is obviously applicable here. According to dissonance theory, the more the cognitions against taking a discrepant stand, the greater the dissonance and consequent attitude change toward that position when one does take the stand. We may view the issue of cohesiveness within this framework: High cohesiveness would make for relatively more supporting cognitions. There is more support for making a public discrepant commitment in response to a group to which you are more attracted than to one to which you are less attracted. We should therefore expect greater dissonance, the less the cohesiveness.

The social influence position would predict greater public conformity the higher the cohesiveness. The dissonance formulation would not necessarily take a stand on who conforms, but it would predict that *for those people who did conform or comply, there would be greater true private attitude change, the less the cohesiveness.* Under conditions where the subjects' adherence to the new attitude position was measured (e.g., under conditions of counter-communication or with measures of certainty), the low cohesive group should show stronger resistance to counter-communications, a demonstration of their greater true private attitude change. It is clear that the dissonance analysis leads to the expectation of an inverse relationship between public conformity and true private attitude change: There should be less public conformity (i.e., discrepant commitment) where there is less cohesiveness but more "true" attitude change toward the publicly complied with stand.

In summary, we may say that the present discussion also serves to indicate that dissonance theory can lead to predictions that go counter to obvious or common sense interpretations of the uniform superiority of a cohesive group or, for example, a likable communicator in inducing social influence or communication acceptance (see Smith, 1961). In this sense, firm adherence to dissonance canons of discrepant commitment leads to seemingly paradoxical, though testable, effects.

In a widely cited series of experiments Asch (1951) found that when a naive subject is asked to judge the length of a line after having heard confederates pretending to be naive subjects, he may give an obviously wrong but unanimous judgment about the same line. It was generally found that where three or more confederates agree on the "wrong" judgment, approximately 30 to 40% of the naive subjects will agree with this "social reality" and give the "wrong" judgment. It was also found that increasing the number of confederates giving the "wrong" judgment up to 10 made no difference in the absolute number of subjects conforming with them. Now, the physical situation and the instructions are so clear, however, that when this social pressure is absent—that is, when the naive subject alone makes judgments—about 100% of judgments and subjects will be "right." And, according to the reports of Asch and others, a subject confronted with the wrong judgments of the confederates will tend to stick with his own first judgment, whether "right" or "wrong" on subsequent trials. In other words, if the naive subject agrees with the confederates on the first judgment trial, he will tend to agree with them on all subsequent trials. If he disagrees with them on the first trial, then he will tend to stick with "physical reality" on all subsequent trials.

If we adopt a point of view consistent with dissonance theory, we are able to present a relatively differentiated picture of the Asch situation. Such a point of view would assert that there is a strong conflict in this situation between agreeing with physical versus social reality. If this is true, the individual placed in this situation presumably decides on these alternatives on the first or second judgment he has to make. However, once he has made this decision, he must justify it to the extent that he is aware of information (the physical reality or confederate's judgments) that would indicate he decided wrongly. In dissonance terms, once having decided to conform, for example, the greater the number of confederates exerting pressure toward conformity, then the stronger the cognitions supporting compliance, and the less the dissonance and consequent need to justify his decision once the subject does comply. Thus we might expect that the naive subject who conforms (i.e., shows discrepant commitment) when three confederates are present will experience more dissonance and will therefore have more need to justify his decision as a means of reducing that dissonance than the subject who conforms when there are ten confederates against him. And to the degree that the amount of confidence in the correctness of one's judgment reflects the justification process, there should be more confidence regarding the conforming response among those subjects who have fewer confederates to face initially. Thus, while the Asch situation as it stands makes no distinctions among those who conform under large numbers of confederates and those who do so under small numbers, a dissonance analysis that views conformity as compliance to a stand discrepant from one's attitudes or opinions would distinguish between these subjects with regard to their real acceptance of the new stand they have taken. In line with this we should expect that where there were communications representing counter-conformity pressures on a second trial, fewer of the subjects who conformed under smaller numbers would regress back toward their initial position than those who conformed under larger numbers.

Conversely, we have those subjects who decide to stay with "physical reality" in the face of confederates who give the "wrong" judgment. Here we might expect the reverse, namely, the more confederates against him, the fewer are the number of cognitions supporting his action and thus presumably the greater the dissonance and consequent need to justify his decision. However, nonconformers may easily repudiate the others and consequently experience little or no dissonance from disagreeing with them. In summary, it would appear that an analysis in terms of forces supporting and disconfirming discrepant behavior growing out of the dissonance formulation could lead to certain predictions that are neither obvious nor easily arrived at in a conventional Asch-type formulation of the conformity process.

Gerard's (1961) experiment on manipulated conformity and ability provides an excellent illustration of the utility of the dissonance formulation in illuminating the conformity situation. His experiment demonstrates the effects of cognitive dissonance on attitudes (attraction to the group) and, more importantly, on behavior (conformity to judgments made by other group members). It also illustrates the fact that the dissonance formulation does have implications for behavioral change as well as for cognitive realignments.

In this part of the volume we discussed what we believe to be some of the critical differences between dissonance theory and other models of incongruity reduction, decisional conflict, attitude change, conformity, and social influence. In many cases we have indicated where dissonance theory would lead to expectations that appear to go counter to those derived from other models of the processes discussed. This particular virtue of dissonance theory, that is, its specification of predictions that are nonobvious insofar as they are not derivable from either empirical considerations, intuition, common sense, or straightforward assumptions about learning or motivation, is one we wished to highlight.

We hoped, in this discussion, to point out some of the problems involved in comparing dissonance theory to other theories and to indicate some possible guidelines in effecting crucial tests between dissonance and other formulations. It should be clear that in sharp distinction to most of the other models we discussed, dissonance theory, as we view it, gains its power primarily from its specification of commitment, the ratio of dissonant to consonant cognitions, and of the possible modes of dissonance reduction.

IMPLICATIONS AND CONCLUSIONS

part V

Applications of dissonance
theory to social problems
— 15

In the foregoing chapters we attempted to present the evidence relevant to the dissonance formulation, to evaluate the theory in the light of this evidence and to indicate some possible extensions of the theory and its relationship to other theoretical and empirical models in psychology. As a final comment on the generality and predictive usefulness of the theory it might be valuable to look at it from the point of view of its applicability to some important social issues. The question we shall be trying to answer is: *Can the application of the dissonance formulation to these social problems help to shed some light on the psychological processes underlying these problems and provide some guidelines for social action?* Our intention here is not to use these social issues as tests of the theory or as evidence for support of the theory; rather we hope to explore the problem areas we have chosen in terms of whether or not some of the phenomena known to be important can be coordinated to the propositions of the theory. To the degree that they can be so coordinated, insights about the social problems may be uncovered and suggestions about research and social action stimulated.

The two problem areas we have selected for discussion are those of desegregation and indoctrination. The former is, of course, a major social issue in our time, and the uncertainty, ambivalence, and conflicts centering around it would appear to make worthwhile an appraisal from the dissonance theory standpoint. Certainly such an appraisal could only help to highlight some of the dimensions of this problem. The indoctrination problem (or "brainwashing" as it has been widely called) was an extremely salient issue at the time of the Korean War, and even though it appears to be a less immediate issue today, the general problems of thought control and the manipulation of men's loyalties that remain with us make it an interesting focus for the application of the dissonance formulation.

A DISSONANCE ANALYSIS OF DESEGREGATION AND INTEGRATION

One of the most pressing social issues facing America and the world today is the changing status of nonwhite groups in their relationship to the dominant white population. Racial desegregation in the United States is a crucial aspect of this worldwide pattern of change, and the magnitude and complexity of the problem make it imperative that social scientists attempt some understanding of the dynamics of this aspect of social change.

A major stumbling block in understanding the dimensions of the problem involves the confusion between desegregation and integration. Whenever public authorities make statements to the effect that there is a "need for time" and that we cannot hope to "change men's hearts and minds overnight," they demonstrate that they do not understand the difference between desegregation, an objective social, legal, and political process, and integration, a subjective attitudinal process. *Desegregation* involves a pattern of changes in the organization of social institutions; it has been defined (Clark, 1960) as change from "a system of organization in terms of separate facilities for whites and Negroes, exclusion of Negroes, or a deliberate restriction of the extent or area of participation of Negroes, to a system wherein distinctions, exclusion, or restriction of participation based on race no longer prevail." Desegregation, in effect, denotes a change in behavior; it is the social, political, legal, judicial, administrative, or community process by which racial barriers to the enjoyment of full and equal civil rights are removed. Inherent in the term *"integration,"* on the other hand, is the process of attitudinal change toward the removal of fears and hatreds, stereotypes and superstitions. Clark's (1960) position is that there can be no integration before desegregation. He goes on to say that objective situational changes (in our terms, behavioral changes) are necessary antecedents to attitudinal changes in the minds of men.

If we accept this distinction between desegregation and integration and the position advanced by Clark that "in the process of social change, situational and behavioral changes precede and probably govern affective and attitudinal changes," we can see the immediate relevance of dissonance theory. As we have noted many times, dissonance theory deals with just such a range of issues: It concerns the process of attitudinal transformation which takes place as a necessary consequence of discrepant behavioral commitments. Dissonance theory attempts to understand the conditions under which behavioral commitments produce cognitive and attitudinal realignments in persons. Given the extensive preoccupation of dissonance theory with this issue, it might be valuable to explore its potential applicability to the desegregation and integration processes. Such an attempt might provide a great deal of insight into the dynamics underlying these processes, uncover some clues as to why, when, and how they work, and indicate some of the directions future social action might take in order to ensure successful integration.

It should be clear that we are not arguing that the many social, political, economic, and demographic factors generally assumed to be important in understanding desegregation and integration are irrelevant to an understanding of these processes. We recognize, of course, that such factors as the rural-urban ratio, the Negro-white ratio, the traditionalism of the community, the socio-economic status of the white residents, the area of the South, and so forth (see Pettigrew and Cramer, 1959) have all been shown to be highly related to the schedule of desegregation. However, we shall assume all these factors to be given, and, within them, attempt to bring the dissonance formulation to bear on desegregation and integration.

In an important article in which he thoroughly appraises the evidence regarding desegregation, Clark concludes that the "hypothesis that attitudinal and other subjective changes are necessary antecedents to behavioral changes is not supported by the empirical data examined in this survey. On the contrary, these data suggest that situationally determined behavioral changes generally preceded any observable attitudinal changes" (1953, p. 72). He goes on to discuss the fact that neither time nor opportunity for preparing the public for change nor the gradualness of desegregation seem to be necessarily related to the "effectiveness" of the desegregation process. In addition, it appears that the success of desegregation, that is, the degree to which it is accompanied by little active resistance or violence, is not necessarily dependent on the degree of expressed racial prejudice among the whites prior to desegregation. It appears that prejudiced whites can accommodate to a changed social situation as well as less prejudiced whites. In effect, the evidence suggests that determinants of the success of desegregation must in fact be sought elsewhere than in the prejudiced attitudes of whites (see Pettigrew, 1961) or in the suddenness or gradualness of desegregation. It would seem that a dissonance theory analysis in terms of the conditions under which forced compliance occurs and has effects on attitudinal realignments might throw some light on the desegregation process.

THE AROUSAL OF DISSONANCE

For a variety of reasons we may expect that most white persons who enter the desegration process experience dissonance arousal. Usually they have some general anti-Negro attitudes so that their behavior in committing themselves to interacting with Negroes constitutes a discrepant act. As we have seen throughout this book, the irrevocability of the commitment is one basic determinant of the degree to which the person changes his attitudes so as to become more favorable toward the discrepant situation. Thus, under conditions where the white person involved in a desegregated setting has most invested in remaining where he is, or where public policy demands that the interracial policy will not change, or where the person commits himself to some irrevocable public interracial housing policy (Clark, 1953; Pettigrew, 1961), it should be expected that the white person will be most likely to reduce dissonance by succumbing to a range of effects that serve to make cognitions consistent with behavior. In effect, we expect that, among other things, the dissonance reduction process should result in a more favorable perception of the social climate shared with Negroes and a change toward more favorable attitudes toward Negroes. Thus, everything else being equal, commitment to an irrevocable interracial policy should result in at least some change in attitudes toward the Negroes: Forcing a person to behave in a fashion discrepant from what he believes can result in a change in private opinion. According to the dissonance theory analysis, behaving in a manner contrary to one's attitudinal position creates dissonance, which can be reduced by changing one's attitudes so that they become more consistent with the behavior engaged in.

As Clark puts it in reviewing the evidence on desegregation: "When the structure of a situation is changed in assumed opposition to previous or existing attitudes and motivation, the initial modification of the behavior of individuals and the eventual compatible changes in their attitudes and motivation are likely to take place" (1953, p. 75).

While the direction of attitude change resulting from interaction with Negroes can be thus understood, what, according to dissonance theory, are some of the factors controlling the magnitude of the dissonance experienced and therefore the magnitude of consequent attitude change? One obvious controlling factor is the extent of contact with Negroes: The greater the contact, in terms of intensity (proximity, intimacy, frequency, duration), the greater the dissonance and the greater the efforts to reduce dissonance. In other words, the more severe is the discrepant behavioral commitment, the greater is the dissonance and consequent favorable attitude change toward Negroes.

A second determinant of the amount of dissonance and attitude change in the desegregation situation concerns the choice involved in the commitment: The more a person is compelled to make the commitment, the less will be the dissonance created by taking it and the less the attitude change. Thus, the more the individual experiences some choice in interacting with Negroes, the greater the dissonance and the greater the resulting attitude change toward Negroes.

Another factor concerns the initial attitude position. We have previously seen that the more unfavorable are persons toward a position or an event, the more dissonance and consequent attitude change they experience on commitment to that event. Thus we should expect that whites, who through some exercise of choice, have become committed to interaction with Negroes, would change their attitudes toward Negroes more in the favorable direction, the more unfavorable they were to begin with.

Most of the instances of desegregation on record involve situations of forced compliance. Such compliance generally occurs in public housing which constitutes the majority of interracial housing situations. Since prevailing norms encourage the growth of racially homogeneous neighborhoods, only some firmly established public policy can result in the establishment of an interracial housing project. The causes underlying this circumstance are not our concern here; they are adequately described in the report of the Commission on Race and Housing, entitled "Where Shall We Live?" (1958), as well as in other sources. At present we are concerned *mainly* with the forced-compliance aspects of situations arising in housing, where white individuals are engaged, more or less without personal involvement, in making the decision to desegregate. The aspects of the situation that deal with the individual's personal choice will be discussed later.

Two studies that were done on housewives in public housing projects (Deutsch and Collins, 1951; Wilner, Walkley and Cook, 1955) produce findings which appear to be consistent with the dissonance formulation. The housing setting seemed to these two groups of investigators to be a useful one for studying the effects of personal association between the members of different racial groups. Public housing was studied because of the scarcity of private interracial housing and also because it had existed for more than 10 years and had a chance to develop standard patterns and variations with respect to racial occupancy. The variations in patterns provided a natural social experiment for the investigators in which they could examine the effects of interracial contact in a reasonably controlled manner. The study by Deutsch and Collins examines the impact of integrated interracial patterns (where families are assigned to apartments without consideration of race) and the segregated biracial pattern (Negro and white families live in the same project but are assigned to different buildings or to different parts of the project). The Wilner et al. study was carried out in four different projects in separate cities, all of which had quite a small proportion of Negroes. Here the segregated projects took the form of scattered Negro and white buildings rather than separate areas. Thus Wilner et al. could examine more closely the influence of physical proximity over and above the official designations of the projects, since some whites in the building-segregated projects lived closer to Negroes than some whites in the integrated projects.

Both studies reported (1) more favorable attitudes toward Negroes, the greater the proximity to Negroes in the housing projects and (2) greater likelihood of favorable attitude change, the more unfavorable the initial attitude. The first of these findings, however, is more clearly brought out in the Wilner et al. study, which actually determined relative proximity to the Negro tenants. Deutsch and Collins' data showed that "more people in integrated than segregated projects respect Negroes and desire to be friendly with them" (p. 84), as well as being "more favorably disposed toward Negro people in general" (p. 90). With regard to attitude *change*, the study notes that, "It is clear . . . that no matter what her original attitudes were, a house-wife in the integrated project, if she changes them as a result of her experiences in the project, will most likely change them in a more favorable direction. Relatively, she is more likely to change, however, *if her original attitudes were unfavorable*. In the segregated projects, if the housewives' attitudes are unfavorable or neutral, attitude change is also more likely than not to be reported in a favorable direction. This cannot be asserted unequivocally for those in the latter type of project who were originally favorably disposed toward Negroes" (p. 97).

This is borne out in Table 18 (adapted from Deutsch and Collins, p. 98). In this table we can see that though the integrated communities show more absolute favorable change toward Negroes, within each project those who are initially least favorable become the most favorable.

TABLE 18

NET GAIN IN PER CENT IN FAVORABLE ATTITUDE CHANGE FOR TWO INTE-
GRATED AND TWO SEGREGATED HOUSING PROJECTS AMONG HOUSEWIVES,
BASED ON SELF-REPORTS OF PRIOR AND PRESENT ATTITUDES
(ADAPTED FROM DEUTSCH AND COLLINS, 1951)

ORIGINAL ATTITUDE	Integrated		Segregated	
	I *	II	III	IV
Highly prejudiced	71	78	26	19
Moderately prejudiced	46	61	18	2
Favorable	13	28	15	−18

* Roman numerals refer to particular housing projects.

Similarly, Wilner et al., who analyzed their data with regard to perceived social climate, extent of contact, and proximity of location conclude that—concerning favorable attitude change—"Contact and perceived social climate tend to reinforce each other when their influence operates in the same direction, and to cancel each other out when their influence works in the opposite direction" (p. 106).

It should be mentioned that if one were to be entirely consistent in adopting a thoroughgoing dissonance theory position, it would be expected that there would be more favorable attitude change, the more unfavorable the social climate. However, we should make it clear that in any natural situation there will be reasonable limits to the theory, which common sense tells us should not be pushed too far. A range of other competing factors conspire to rule out the possibility of ever obtaining unconditional forces producing relatively irrevocable commitment to desegregation. Thus it is reasonable to expect that good social climate and positive contact will themselves have a direct effect on attitude change toward Negroes. We can say, though, that desegregation always occurs in a situation where there is some coercion and some choice at the same time; it is their interaction that should determine the direct effects of contact and social climate on attitude change.

Table 19 demonstrates that attitude *change* varies directly with amount of proximity (defined as having a Negro in the same building in an integrated project or in the same court in a segregated project) and initial unfavorableness of attitude (adapted from Wilner et al., p. 93).

TABLE 19

RELATION BETWEEN PROXIMITY AND FAVORABLE CHANGE IN ATTITUDE TO-
WARD NEGROES BASED ON SELF-REPORTS OF PRIOR AND PRESENT ATTITUDE
IN TERMS OF NET GAIN IN PER CENT

	Integrated				Segregated			
	I		II		I		II	
INITIAL ATTITUDE	Near	Far	Near	Far	Near	Far	Near	Far
Unfavorable	82	39	52	19	79	40	86	47
Favorable	24	10	11	0	13	7	−3	9

The data in Table 19 give the figures on favorable change toward Negroes for both integrated and segregated projects. However, since it was possible for the people in this study to live close to a Negro in another building (segregated-near) or far from a Negro in an integrated building, the data are grouped in terms of integrated-segregated, near-far. The data show that whether the project is integrated or not, the people who live near Negroes become more favorable toward them. Also, it is clear that within any project or degree of proximity to Negroes, the people who were initially least favorable toward them become, after moving into the projects, most favorable.

Thus, in both the Deutsch and Collins and the Wilner, Walkley and Cook studies, the evidence is strongly supportive of the generalization that the greater the proximity to Negroes and the more unfavorable the prior attitude toward them, the more positive attitude change toward them occurs.

ATTITUDES TOWARD DESEGREGATION

In both the Deutsch and Collins and the Wilner et al. studies there was a tendency on the part of the respondents to prefer the type of occupancy they had experienced; thus the white housewives who had lived in integrated housing units preferred to remain in this kind of occupancy and were more likely to recommend it as public policy than those who had lived in segregated units. However, the data are not analyzed with regard to proximity, perception of social climate, or extent of contact to determine their relationship to attitudes with regard to future desegregation. Nor do we know whether there is any relation between favorable attitude change toward Negroes and favorable attitude change toward further desegregation.

All these attitudinal data appear to be consistent with the dissonance formulation: They show that for the most part whites become favorable toward Negroes when they have been initially unfavorable and when they have been thrown into close proximity with Negroes. It was impossible to compare directly the effects of segregated versus integrated housing projects because of the possibility that each project has its own peculiarities and the fact that the restricted sampling of projects prevented the assumption of random factors. Nevertheless, given commitment to a housing policy, factors we previously assumed to produce greater dissonance, namely, proximity and initial unfavorableness, seem to have led to greater attitude change. However, we should interpret these results with some caution. First, the data on initial attitude position are not statistically controlled for regression and may not represent precise change data. We may assume attitude change from the data, but, in fact, the respondents *reported* the change, opening the data to other interpretations. Then, again, we do not know if the respondents who were favorable to begin with simply did not have any more distance left to change, making the result a spurious effect of possibility to change. Without control over the potential distance to change, we must evaluate these data as most inconclusive. Furthermore, the near-far differences could just as easily be attributed to a simple effect of experience with Negroes. In the present case one does not know whether greater contact with Negroes could have resulted in more positive attitude change, irrespective of the presence of dissonance reduction. On the other hand, it is true that the data on simple contact are equivocal (see Saenger, 1953) and that there is no necessary assurance that contact always leads to positive attitudes. Therefore it is our best guess, since contact is so indeterminate, that dissonance reduction may supply some of the motivating force in the present situation for people to seek out positive qualities of the Negro co-residents in order to reduce the dissonance occasioned by their own behavior. In this case dissonance reduction would be responsible, though indirectly, for positive attitude change.

CHOICE

It was pointed out previously that dissonance effects would be greater, the more the person chooses to engage in the contact situation.

If this contact is made voluntarily (though, of course, within the context of the general forced-compliance situations of the public housing project), one may expect *greater* favorable attitude change as a result of the experience than if the experience were solely the result of a *fait accompli* in which the individual suddenly found himself.

Although there are no real data on this point, it would certainly seem that severe attempts to force compliance or *faits accomplis* without some prior choice in commitment would not accomplish maximum positive attitude change; in fact, they might often produce boomerang effects, consistent with the whites' initial resistance. On the other hand, eliciting compliance from the person and imparting to him some choice in and control over his decision to desegregate should have positive implications for the integration process. Thus those whites whose compliance to the desegregation process is elicited rather than forced should, everything else being equal, show more dissonance on commitment and more positive attitude change toward Negroes as a mode of reducing that dissonance.

Of course, in the desegregation situation it is not often true that everything else is equal. As stated before, the amount of irrevocability in the decisional process is a critical issue. Under conditions where the person knows that the situation is an open one and that he can leave the situation any time he so desires, effects opposite to those predicted by the dissonance formulation may result. Thus boomerang effects resulting in the strengthening of the person's anti-Negro attitudes may result if compliance is too weak or if the number and importance of discrepant cognitions are not anchored strongly enough to force some cognitive revaluation.

While some perception of choice is certainly necessary if dissonance and large consequent attitude change are to be produced, it is also necessary to obtain firm compliance to the desegregation situation so that boomerang effects are prevented from occurring. This, of course, demands a clear and unequivocal public policy. Where boomerang effects, violence, and active resistance have occurred in the desegregation process, they appear to have occurred when there was an ambiguous public policy, ineffective police action, or a conflict between competing government authorities or officials. According to Clark (1953, p. 54), the accomplishment of successful desegregation with a minimum of social disturbance depends at least on

1. A clear and unequivocal statement of policy by leaders with prestige and other authorities.
2. Firm enforcement of the changed policy by authorities and per-

sistence in the execution of this policy in the face of initial resistance.

3. A willingness to deal with violations, attempted violations, and incitement to violations by a resort to the law and strong enforcement action.

4. A refusal of the authorities to resort to, engage in, or tolerate subterfuges, gerrymandering, or other devices for evading the principles and the fact of desegregation.

It is within these general constraints forcing the desegregation process that variations in degree of volition can affect the degree to which positive attitude change in line with desegregation results. Such a perspective may aid in clarifying a seeming contradiction pointed out by Cook (1957). Cook cites a personal communication from Taylor, who did a study of white residents in a block into which Negroes had moved. In contrast to the *public* housing situation dealt with previously, this is an area of *private* housing. In the former, there is a greater commitment on the part of resident whites who presumably want to stay in a project where the formal and explicit policy commits them to interaction with Negroes. In the latter, however, people are free to come into and go from a neighborhood as they please; no commitment to an overt policy of interaction with Negroes exists. Thus, in the private housing study, those who were relatively more favorable toward Negroes at the time the first Negro was about to move in became *more favorable* after the Negroes had been living there a few weeks; those who were initially most unfavorable had become still *more unfavorable.* These latter generalizations appear to be consistent with a straightforward self-selective effect of motivation and attitude; the conditions of dissonance arousal are not met in such a situation. (The potential economic losses many whites feel they suffer is, of course, relevant here.) Thus, central to the applicability of the dissonance formulation in this area is control over the direction of the decision. In effect, in desegregation, commitment to interaction has to be relatively unequivocal before integration can occur. Thus public housing which requires some physical desegregation will more certainly be a locus for dissonance arousal and reduction via favorable attitude change toward Negroes than will private housing.

In line with this, Mayer (1957), studying a Detroit suburb where private housing predominates, finds that *all* white residents move, even those who profess belief that the Negro and white can live together amicably. The most extremely prejudiced move first, however. In an illuminating review of the desegregation process, Pettigrew (1961) along with Clark also points out that violence and rejection of desegregation have generally occurred in localities where at least some of the authorities gave prior hints that they would gladly return to segregation if disturbances occurred; peaceful desegregation has generally followed firm and forceful leadership (p. 105). In effect, where "uncommitment" is possible, dissonance may not be clearly operating and positive attitude change will not ensue.

Another factor obviously central to the application of the dissonance formulation to the desegregation process is the normative environment surrounding the individual. Dissonance theory is nonspecific with regard to the mode of dissonance reduction used by the individual after dissonance arousal. Most experimental studies have dealt with very restricted aspects of the environment and have generally attempted to control to some degree the avenues of dissonance reduction used. In the present situation, the social pressures surrounding the individual will determine in part whether or not he uses attitude change as a means of reducing the dissonance occasioned by desegregation. Thus positive attitude change may take place provided that the cost of such a cognitive change (measured in terms, for example, of social disapproval or ostracism) is not too severe for the individual. This seems to have been the pattern in public housing. This factor may introduce considerations of the relative risk of engaging in one or another mode of dissonance reduction in a given situation. Anchoring a person's attitudes to a strong and pervasive set of social norms embodying negative attitudes toward Negroes makes it difficult to change one's attitudes toward Negroes as a means of making one's behavioral commitment consistent. In such a case, dissonance reduction could well take the form of, e.g., increase in feelings of obligation to commit oneself or leaving the field.

On the other hand, as both Pettigrew and Clark point out, these same considerations of relative risk can be brought to work for successful desegregation. Clark says, "Opposition and overt resistance to desegregation are decreased, if not eliminated, when the alternative for the whites is the complete loss of a desired public facility or the imposition of a direct economic burden or some other important stigma" (1953, p. 53). The other important stigmas can, of course, refer to the conformity pressures in the environment. Pettigrew's discussion makes the issue of conformity more salient than any personality or demographic issues; he feels that prestigeful community members who take the lead in working for desegregation can always serve to hold people within the desegregation situation and thereby allow the process of dissonance reduction and consequent attitude change to proceed along socially sanctioned lines.

If, however, the individual has *no* commitment to engage in the interracial situation, either voluntary or forced, and has prior unfavorable attitudes, selective judgment or perception may lead to an increase in the intensity of these attitudes and/or leaving the vicinity of Negroes. As we have said, this seems to have been the case in private housing. Here, even those with favorable attitudes may leave, simply because of response to social pressures and norms. In settings such as private housing or clubs, then, it is clear that the conditions of dissonance arousal are not met and that we should rarely expect consequent positive attitude change toward Negroes.

Some of the factors involved in obtaining the commitment crucial to the arousal of dissonance and to its reduction by positive attitude change are discussed by Clark (1953), Tumin (1958), and Pettigrew (1961). Tumin finds that people of higher social class and prestige in the community are most likely to feel guilty and disturbed as a result of lower-caste treatment of Negroes and would be most active in bringing about a positive change. (Vander Zanden [1960] finds, however, that this is by no means true for all communities.)

A study of a group of "influentials" in a southern community (Deutsch and Steele, 1959) shows that while 88% of the sample believed that school integration would inevitably come very soon, 79% believed in segregation and favored closed schools. This discrepancy between the wishes and beliefs of these influential members of the community is indicative of a great deal of cognitive inconsistency. In effect, the study showed that a great majority of respondents were thinking about problems of race relations in terms of change and Negro progress. It should thus be clear that the policy of forced compliance in accepting desegregation can take advantage of this attitudinal inconsistency. Clark (1953) notes this and says that the "conflicts and ambivalences inherent in the original attitudinal and motivational pattern are exploited and those which are compatible with the new pattern of behavior are reinforced and strengthened by external pressures and force. Those which are in opposition are weakened, made ineffectual or eliminated" (p. 56).

People of lower educational status and class, on the other hand, may have more unfavorable attitudes toward Negroes. For such people there may be a need for greater external pressures in order to effect initial commitment. But, Pettigrew (1961) points out that deviates on *other* social dimensions (i.e., radicals, out-groupers, members of ethnic groups, members of special sects, etc.) are *less* anti-Negro than conformers. This highlights such variables as class and status as determinants of the risk involved in succumbing to dissonance effects that lead to favorable attitude change in the face of a potentially hostile environment. These factors are mentioned, also, by Deutsch and Steele (1959).

Other results consistent with the dissonance formulation are the following: (1) Favorable attitude toward the Negro was correlated with the belief that other white women in the neighborhood approved of associating with Negroes (Wilner et al.); (2) Behavior tends to change more readily than attitudes; more housewives in all projects knew Negroes well than desired friendly relations with them (Deutsch and Collins).

The findings, in general, suggest that the desegregation-integration situation may be viewed as a two-step process in dissonance reduction. Individuals who are committed to being in close proximity to Negroes may reduce their initial dissonance by first (1) interacting with them. The additional dissonance that may be caused by interacting with individuals about whom one still has unfavorable stereotypes may be further reduced by (2) changing the stereotypes, that is, by favorable attitude change toward them. (3) The third possible link—the generalization to more favorable attitude change toward Negroes as a group—comes still more slowly (for example, see Deutsch and Collins, p. 90).

The desegregation-integration situation seems characterized by the fact that favorable attitudes are at first directed toward those with whom the individual is in most immediate interaction. This has been stressed by Cook (1957), who cites studies by Harding and Hogrefe (1952) and Minard (1952) (studying department-store employees and miners, respectively). These particular studies also demonstrate that favorable attitudes and behavior toward the Negro are limited to the expectations of the work situation. Thus white employees in the department stores studied expressed willingness to have Negroes as co-workers but not as friends; white miners in West Virginia would work with Negroes amicably below ground but they separated above ground. Similar evidence is also presented in the study by Stouffer et al. (1949) of Negro platoons in combat companies during World War II.

Also consistent with dissonance formulation are the studies concerning the relation between predisposition to behavior and actual behavior, when people are forced into contact with a disliked minority group. Lapierre (1934), Kutner, Wilkins and Yarrow (1952), and Saenger and Gilbert (1950) found that white individuals who have on another occasion previous to the "test" situation displayed a predisposition *not* to interact with a minority group, did in fact interact with them when presented with the *fait accompli* of association with members of the minority group. It is not known, however, whether such behavior resulted in a more favorable attitude change toward a Negro in these studies, though the dissonance formulation would imply that it might, so long as the previously mentioned conditions of choice and commitment were salient.

In conclusion, we may say that a good part of the desegregation and integration process can be clarified if one adopts a perspective growing out of dissonance theory. From such a perspective, which highlights the interplay between behavior and subsequent attitudes, the integration process must be seen as an on-going process and one that demands a longitudinal view. The results of desegregation should therefore be seen in changes in attitudes over a long-time period, as people strive to make their attitudes consistent with their current behavioral situation *if* they are in the midst of the desegregation process. Individuals may comply with a desegregation situation when their attitudes are discrepant from it for a variety of reasons ranging from inertia to financial incentives and the need to conform to powerful agents. While it is necessary to have a minimum of these extrinsic motivations in order to obtain compliance to a desegregated situation, the strength of any of these forces beyond the minimum obviously makes a great deal of difference in ultimate attitude change. The more compelling such forces are, the less should dissonance be aroused; the more the forced compliance can be elicited under minimal extrinsic incentive conditions, the more dissonance and resultant attitude change there will be. Obviously there is a need to explore the social and administrative possibilities that will provide *the best compromise between getting the person into the desegregation situation and giving him some perception that he has been responsible for his commitment.* In effect, social policy must always attempt to maximize the person's perceived choice in entering and committing himself to the desegregation situation.

However, once having gained commitment to the desegregation process, the issue of irrevocability of the decision becomes central. If authorities make it clear that no undoing of the process is possible, people must of necessity come to terms with it some way and to one degree or another. The manner in which people reduce this dissonance occasioned by compliance will be a function of the situational bounds that facilitate or block one or another mode of dissonance reduction. Where the social environment is firm and harsh in its anti-Negro attitudes, perhaps other modes like dissociation or even stronger anti-Negro attitudes will develop. The latter possibility can serve as a dissonance reducer in that it may reduce the proportion of cognitions in conflict with prior attitudes (see Cohen, 1962). Thus, where community leaders can be mobilized to give legitimate social sanction to favorable changes in attitudes toward Negroes, we might expect that dissonance reduction will occur through positive attitude change rather than through moving or negative attitude change. And, in fact, as Pettigrew points out, many Southerners faced with what appears to be a solid unanimity of attitudes favoring segregation rarely change toward favorableness to Negroes. But, as he says, "When even one respected source—a minister, a newspaper editor, even a college professor—conspicuously breaks the unanimity, a dramatic modification is achieved in the opinions of many conforming Southerners" (p. 109).

In summary, when the forces on people (their needs, extrinsic rewards, coercions, etc.) are minimally strong enough to propel them into commitment to a situation where desegregation exists, such as public housing or a job situation, and the interracial policy in such a setting is firm and irrevocable, dissonance will result to the extent that they feel they have had a choice in committing themselves (i.e., the forces are relatively weak), and will be resolved via positive attitude change toward Negroes to the degree that such positive attitudes are socially sanctioned. Thus, the most favorable climates for integration via dissonance arousal and reduction would appear to be job settings and public housing where there is some choice in entering the desegregation situation. On the other hand, the school setting, characterized by a relative absence of choice, might be expected to present unusual difficulties in progress toward integration.

It should be clear from the above discussion that the problem of successful integration requires a very subtle analysis and demands a careful and cautious choice between the social and political constraints necessary to bring about desegregation and keep people in it and the need for them to experience some personal choice with regard to their commitment to desegregation. It is understandable that Clark and other persons are committed to the view that formal and official desegregation must precede any attitude changes because of the dearth of evidence showing that desegregation comes about with attitudinal changes over time. However, such a position can be fruitful only when it is understood that the *conditions* under which this formal, physical desegregation takes place are major determinants of the degree to which integration is successful (i.e., the degree to which it will result in favorable attitude and behavioral change toward Negroes). It is true that many of the advocates of desegregation feel that it does not matter *what* people's attitudes are or *how* they react so long as desegregation, and therefore racial equality, is brought about. But, if one is oriented toward the long view, and takes the position that desegregation is after all the first step toward integration, he should examine thoroughly the conditions under which desegregation takes place. While one might be committed to the process of physical desegregation, there is no reason why, within the process, one cannot isolate the factors in its implementation that will allow successful integration to follow efficient desegregation. Through the present dissonance theory analysis we have attempted to indicate some of the determinants of attitude change once the forced compliance making for desegregation occurs.

In any case, the degree to which dissonance and consequent attitude change may occur seems to be determined in part by the range of factors we have discussed earlier. Beginning with the assumption that there must be some compliance and commitment to the desegregation situation, we have mentioned at least three factors (for two of which there appears to be evidence) in connection with the success of desegregation and resulting integration. These are the subjective feeling of choice in entering the desegregation process, the degree of proximity to Negroes, and the initial attitude toward Negroes. It should be obvious that the many other factors we have discussed as relevant to dissonance and consequent attitude and behavior change, such as effort and active participation, would also be relevant for understanding the desegregation problem.

If there were some consistent attempt to explore the desegregation situation from such a point of view as this, we feel that a good deal of progress in understanding the determinants of integration would take place. The emphasis in dissonance theory on the attitudinal consequences of behavioral commitments seems to be a model *par excellence* for analyzing certain aspects of the desegregation process. Since the evidence seems to suggest that there has been no clear instance of desegregation wherein the objective social and situational changes came as a consequence of subjective individual and attitudinal changes, it would seem worthwhile to approach the problem from the point of view of the effects of behavior on attitudes. Given the fact that desegregation authorities must perforce be committed to a policy that stresses the need for unequivocal, immediate physical desegregation, dissonance theory could conceivably contribute to its success through its specification of the conditions under which attitudinal changes result from behavioral commitment.

DISSONANCE THEORY AND THE PSYCHOLOGY OF INDOCTRINATION

"Brainwashing" has become one of the most widely discussed and confusing of social problems since the Korean War brought to the general public the news that American military and civilian personnel were being manipulated in some frightening way by the Communist Chinese. The term was originally used to describe Chinese indoctrination techniques and then quickly applied to just about anything that Communists did anywhere. It included everything from years of intensive Russian and Chinese efforts to extract false confessions, to thought reform among the Chinese, to collaboration and synthetic bacteriological warfare confessions on the part of American POWs. As Lifton (1961) says, behind this web of semantic confusion lies an image of "brainwashing" as "an all-powerful, irresistible, magical method of achieving control over the human mind." Nothing, it would seem, could produce such results other than a combination of the "theories of Dr. I. P. Pavlov and the wiles of Dr. Fu Manchu" (Bauer, 1957).

We may reserve the term "brainwashing" for the extreme forms of thought control or "ideological reform" produced by the most intensive and extended attack against the individual target. This should be distinguished from the methods of indoctrination used against American prisoners of war. The elemental thought reform programs that were applied to small numbers of civilian prisoners, missionaries, and many Chinese intellectuals and students, were much more comprehensive and powerful than the modifications applied to POWs in Korea. Nevertheless, on close study it seems that the extreme brainwashing procedures themselves contain nothing highly mysterious or fearful and that the effects obtained can be understood in terms of current psychological notions at the level we now conceive of them (Schein, Schneier and Barker, 1961). Extreme thought control consists essentially of confession and re-education, brought about by a combination of a great variety of methods like social isolation, extreme physical deprivation, stimulus deprivation, sleep deprivation, complete milieu control, inculcation of a sense of guilt and shame, group analysis and sanction, emotional appeals, aims of ego-breakdown, attempts to stimulate religious conversion processes, and a goal of complete change in role behavior and personal identity. Lifton, in his book on thought reform (1961), recalls his unforgettable first encounters with an elderly European bishop so shaken by the power of the prison thought reform program he had been through that he could only denounce it as an "alliance with the devil," and the young Chinese girl, shaken from the group hatred that had been directed against her at a university in Peking, yet wondering if she had been "selfish" in leaving.

In the present section we are assuming that such "brainwashing" can only be understood by taking into account a range of complex psychological processes that involve intellectual, emotional, and physical elements and that demand study of such issues as guilt, shame and confession, the effects of physical and sensory stimulation and deprivation of all sorts, the effects of group pressures, and techniques for controlling the environment (Schein et al., 1961). However, we assume that the results of the application of fewer and weaker pressures on American POWs can be understood as essentially the use of "group indoctrination" procedures and that the effects of these processes can at least be partly illuminated by the application of dissonance theory to the indoctrination process.

Throughout the following discussion we will be referring to the great bulk of American POWs—Army prisoners. A number of Air Force personnel were captured also, and in the attempt to extract germ warfare confessions from them for the purposes of international propaganda, they were subjected to somewhat more intensive coercion than the Army POWs and were the targets of a more comprehensive indoctrination program aimed at "training them to lie," among other things.

In the present discussion we are adopting the position that dissonance theory can be fruitfully applied to the Chinese indoctrination program as an aid in understanding, at least in part, its effects on the Army POWs. Certainly the evidence regarding the relevance of other obvious factors is very ambiguous. The results of a large-scale study of Army POWs (Schein, Hill, Williams and Lubin, 1957) argue against any simple interpretation of resistance or collaboration and their effects in terms of easily measured personality or background variables; a series of biographical questions, intelligence scales, and personality inventories failed to distinguish between the reactions of different men to the POW situation. Of course, it is probably reasonable to assume that with further, more intensive research, the complex interaction of learning, physiological, motivational, cognitive, and social factors will ultimately account for a large portion of the observed effects. Nevertheless, the present lack of any clear-cut relationships between behavior in the indoctrination situation and personality and background provides some rationale for our attempt to shed some light on the indoctrination program and its effects, using assumptions derived from the dissonance formulation. In pursuing this aim we shall necessarily ignore a number of significant psychological processes that were undoubtedly operative in the program; instead we shall simply assume that many such factors were involved and concentrate on exploring the utility of dissonance constructs alone.

We have been saying that actual "brainwashing" is a prolonged psychological process in which the efforts of many are directed against an individual. To be successful it requires, among other things, that the individual be isolated from his normal associations and environment. However, it is obvious that such a time-consuming process could not be employed against such a sizable group as the Army POWs. An exhaustive government study failed to reveal even one conclusively documented case of actual "brainwashing" of an American prisoner in Korea; in the opinion of the investigating committee, the POWs were subjected to "group indoctrination," not "brainwashing" (see Report of Committee on Government Operations, 1957). In Korea the aims of the Chinese appeared to be twofold: (1) They wanted to obtain as much collaboration as possible from American troops as part of their general propaganda aims, and, in so doing, (2) they wanted to produce some change in the basic attitudes and behavior of the prisoner and to sow some doubt, confusion, and ideological uncertainty. In effect, they seem to have been trying to get control—moral control—of American troops.

In attempting to assess the indoctrination program directed against the POWs, we are immediately led to the proposition that it is possible for peoples' beliefs to be affected and changed as a function of coercion. No one, as Bauer (1957) says, is amazed that confessions can be produced under coercion, but the unique issue in the indoctrination program is that peoples' beliefs appear to be susceptible to change. Coercion can obviously affect behavior, but what can induce a man to change his beliefs? Scrutiny of the Communist techniques of indoctrination shows that coercion and persuasion, belief and behavior, tend to become indistinguishable. The central question that has been asked by Bauer and other interested observers is: When coercion or the threat of coercion is applied, does the individual's motivation to accommodate make him a willing collaborator in attempting to persuade himself? Bauer concludes that the most important issue to understand is how the prisoner, who responded to a situation in which he saw no viable alternative but to participate, not only controlled his behavior but also began to control his attitudes. Once we examine the indoctrination process within this framework, we can see the potential fruitfulness in the application of the dissonance formulation.

As we have seen throughout the present book, the adoption by the individual of a stand discrepant from his attitudes can produce dissonance and consequent attitude change toward that stand. Once having engaged publicly in such discrepant behavior and being unable to repudiate it, the person can reduce the dissonance by, among other avenues, coming to agree with the new stand. We have seen that at least some of the determinants of the amount of dissonance and consequent attitude change are: (1) the amount of inducement (rewards, pressure or degree of coercion), (2) the amount of discrepant behavior engaged in, (3) the degree to which the subject is confronted with his discrepant behavior, and (4) the strength of his prior attitudes. Let us examine the experiences of the American POWs in these terms.

It seems clear that when the range of reports on the Korean experience are studied, the general conclusion one must draw is that relatively few severe coercions were used to extract confessions and collaborative behavior from the troops. No drugs were used, no torture, no pulling out of fingernails. In distinction to the behavior of the North Koreans and contrary to the expectations of the American troops, their Chinese captors welcomed the prisoners "with open arms." The Chinese tried to create an atmosphere of leniency and friendliness, and after the troops had made the long and debilitating march back to the permanent camps, their conditions were relatively tolerable.

It is true, of course, that the general situation of the POW was one in which he felt a great deal of constraint and pressure to behave in the direction required by his captors. Ordinarily such a feeling would be expected to result in little dissonance and consequent attitude change over any discrepant act. However, the immediate and apparent difference between the POWs' expectations about the terrifying and brutal treatment they would receive at the hands of the Chinese and the "reasonable" treatment that, considering the circumstances, they actually received may well have produced in them some perception of personal volition. This perception of lessened pressure, viewed against the background of expected terror and torture, may well have produced a modicum of dissonance for the POW when he did comply and also may have caused him to be more susceptible to Chinese-directed avenues of dissonance reduction.

We are interested first in the factors behind compliance with the requests of the Chinese for confessions and information. POWs were induced to comply, it seems, by a multiplicity of factors. The immediate issue is the obvious one of the amount of general pressure put on the men in a situation where they were partly debilitated. Here a range of possibilities can be examined: (1) trivial demands were enforced, (2) omnipotence of the captors was demonstrated, (3) rewards and indulgences were given, (4) threats of punishment were made, (5) degrading experiences were applied, (6) perceptions were controlled,

(7) prisoners were isolated, and (8) exhaustion and debility were induced (West, 1957). In the very large majority of instances, the latter methods were less often applied; most of the pressures on the POWs were in the form of trivial demands, indulgences, threats, and the demonstration of the omniscience of the Chinese. In effect, it was the materialistic rather than the ideological or physical considerations that made the difference in collaboration, that is, it was the captors' inducements of preferential treatment. Rewards, it would seem, were quite real for those who paid the price. We know from much research evidence that such compliance situations produce more dissonance than those that use extreme pressure, and therefore that the POW who agreed to collaborate under such circumstances might have experienced relatively great change in his attitudes toward the Chinese and their ideology.

Within this general pressure, leaders were segregated from other prisoners; informational support and ties from home were systematically broken; men were made to distrust their buddies through the use of informers; group life was available only in Communist-inspired activities, and one man's collaboration was used to get others to comply as a demonstration of the uselessness of resistance (Schein, 1956).

Given these general conditions and pressures, the men who collaborated appeared to do so for a number of discernible reasons: (1) There were POWs with "weak egos" who were motivated by fear, were unable to withstand the rigors to which they were subject, who complied with authority figures, and who were susceptible to blackmail; (2) There were opportunists who had no stable group identification and were interested only in material benefits; (3) For those who could not withstand the pressure, a convenient rationalization was that they were infiltrating the Chinese ranks for intelligence purposes; (4) Some POWs were low-status, poorly educated persons who were receptive to Communist ideology; and (5) Some few were Communist sympathizers (Schein, 1957a).

It is obvious that among those who collaborated, both the general pressures applied to them and the particular individual reasons for complying could have affected the amount of dissonance experienced on compliance and the amount of subsequent attitude disruption. The assumption we are making here is that the determinants of compliance in the indoctrination program were such that they made for relatively great dissonance and attitude change. The POWs knew that rewards would be given if they paid the price; the alternatives of "coming across" and getting off easily or resisting and taking the "consequences" were quite real. What was unclear were the conditions the Chinese placed on the pleasures of preferential treatment. The papers and talks the POWs engaged in were potent weapons in the enemy's propaganda arsenal and could have served to change some of the POWs ideological position (Segal, 1957).

We may raise the question, however, of the meaning of the rewards to the POWs. We have been assuming that the rewards of food, soap, cigarettes, small clothing, and so on were very minor in the face of the demand for a seemingly "treasonable" act of collaboration. The general context was one of reasonably tolerable treatment that generated little hatred for the Chinese, for they would never do anything that incurred the resentment of the mass of POWs; the Chinese carefully avoided hostile acts that would cement the group of prisoners into a unit. In the context of such over-all treatment, the man who complied for minor luxuries would appear to have subjected himself to dissonance and laid himself open to ideological conversion. However, it is conceivable that even such apparently minor indulgences loomed very large in a situation where troops feared death, were isolated, could not tolerate the food given them because of American soft habits about food, and so forth. To the degree that these rewards were seen as great incentives, there would be less dissonance and consequent attitude change to be expected on collaboration.

In general, then, to the degree to which the personal motives and group pressures can be viewed as compelling compliance, there would be less dissonance on compliance. One further issue can be noted here. The more differentiated and anti-Communist was a man's ideology, the more dissonance he would have experienced on compliance, everything else being equal. However, it is possible that a number of the troops, particularly the poorly educated teen-agers, had no particularly differentiated prior attitude toward communism and very little information about the subject. For such prisoners, collaboration would not produce much dissonance, and therefore we would expect less attitudinal shake-up over time. We may say, therefore, that the stronger the subjects' attitudes regarding the evils of communism and the more negative his attitudes toward collaboration in general, the greater the dissonance and consequent attitudinal effects on compliance. Although there are no explicit data from studies of POWs bearing on this point, such a generalization is entirely consistent with the research on communication and attitude change growing out of dissonance theory (see Brehm, 1960b; Cohen, 1960).

We have stressed throughout this book that the basic dissonance-producing situation is the one where the individual actively engages in discrepant behavior of some sort. It would appear that this device was one of the main procedures used by the Chinese. In general, they tried to get intelligence information through written and oral interrogations. They tried to engage the prisoners in propaganda activities, including false confessions, peace petitions, special broadcasts and recordings, writing special kinds of letters home, and so forth. And they tried to get the prisoners to participate in indoctrination sessions with a view toward influencing them to accept Communist ideas. In such sessions men discussed the material, and at the end of the discussion, squads had to provide written answers to questions handed out, answers that had been given in the lectures. Thus, discussing the lecture meant rationalizing the predetermined conclusions (Schein, 1956).

The Chinese always paced their demands, starting with trivial demands and then increasing the amount and kind of compliance. But what is most important, *they always demanded constant participation from the POW. It was never enough for the prisoner to listen and absorb; some kind of verbal or written response was always demanded.* Even if the POW would not give original material, he would be made to copy something. The Chinese apparently believed that if they could once get a man to participate, he was likely to continue and that eventually he would accept the attitudes that the participation expressed (Schein, 1956). This would certainly seem to be a policy entirely consistent with the most basic assumptions of the dissonance formulation.

In general, for propaganda purposes, the Chinese wanted men to cooperate in specific ways without caring whether they accepted communism or not, although their general assumption seems to have been that a man would change in the process. Another effective technique for getting men to lose confidence in their own beliefs was to make them confess publicly to nonexistent wrongdoings and to criticize themselves. They were required to go through these rituals over and over again, no matter how trivial or far from reality the supposed offense. This self-criticism before his fellow prisoners had to be analyzed in terms of the wrong thoughts that lay behind the deed (Schein, 1956). Such public expression of discrepant behavior is certainly one of the main determinants of dissonance and consequent attitude change.

Furthermore, later in the program, some men were asked to participate on a voluntary basis; these prisoners were called "self-study pros." Such free choice to participate in a discrepant act can only be viewed as an important determinant of dissonance and attitude change in the light of a number of studies mentioned earlier in Part II. Men were also asked to write out answers to questions voluntarily. If they refused, they were asked to copy them from notebooks. Then the information the man copied would be shown to another as evidence of collaboration by volition. This could then be used to persuade the second man, but, more importantly, to blackmail the first man. Also, when the men who did collaborate in posing for pictures, appearing publicly at peace conferences, and so forth, came back to their prison units, the hostility of others regarding their behavior and the rewards they received often caused them to collaborate even further. Such collaboration was supported by rationalization that they were not harming the UN, were infiltrating the Chinese, and so forth. These experiences can be viewed in dissonance terms as confrontation by the POW of his discrepant behavior and the meaning and consequences of his collaboration. Viewed in the light of Brock's (1962) experimental results, such a procedure of facing the subject with his own behavior should increase the dissonance occasioned by compliance and result in greater potential change in attitudes.

In the Army's terms, a man who collaborated because he wanted a cigarette was as much a collaborator as one who did so because he wanted to further the communist cause. From the point of view of dissonance theory, all participation produces some dissonance, but such initial differences in motivation to comply can be factors in the degree to which dissonance is experienced through compliance and in the amount of subsequent attitude change.

It has been estimated that at least 70% of American POWs contributed to communist psychological efforts in that they committed at least one act of collaboration. However, only some 10 to 15% of the men chronically collaborated (see Report of Committee on Government Operations, 1957). The dynamics of their response, of course, are very complex. It is clear, however, according to dissonance theory, that the number of acts of compliance and collaboration and the degree of involvement in such collaboration ought to be significant determinants of the amount of postcompliance dissonance and attitude change. Whatever the criterion used by the Army for determining collaboration, in terms of the present argument—everything else being equal— there should have been an increase in the amount of dissonance from those 70% who collaborated only once to those 12% or so who chronically collaborated to those very few who were the most active collaborators.

It should also be pointed out that within any given act or number of acts of compliance, the POW could comply in many different ways (West, 1957). He could *comply defensively* by such behaviors as making a statement of "objective guilt," that is, that the results were criminal irrespective of the motives; making a statement that the crime was unwittingly committed; making ambiguous statements containing no explicit admissions but that constituted a confession by implication; agreeing to comply but failing to carry through, for example, writing a confession but refusing to sign it; making an obviously unacceptable, sabotaged confession; making an incomplete and unconvincing confession; making compromise deposition bargains with interrogator; and alternately confessing and retracting. The prisoner could also show *active compliance:* he could confess to criminal tendencies, that is, say that his attitude was as criminal as if he had actually committed the alleged crime; he could make subtly sabotaged confessions, that is, make veiled communications to outsiders while at the same time making the confession acceptable to the interrogator; he could completely cooperate in all explicit demands and pretend to accept guilt; and he could strive to please his captor, anticipate demands, and pretend repentance. Finally, the prisoner could show *complete compliance* by accepting the objective truth of his guilt, showing involuntary symptoms of remorse, and making behavioral choices indicative of complete identification with and commitment to the captor. We may therefore say that greater dissonance and attitude change would result the more complete the compliance: Those POWs showing defensive compliance should have experienced less dissonance than those showing active compliance, who should have showed less dissonance than those engaging in complete compliance.

All these specific factors should have produced more or less dissonance and consequent attitude change, depending on their severity. It should be clear from the theory that those POWs who were treated well, who completely complied for small rewards when they had strong anti-communist attitudes, and who were made constantly aware of their collaboration in the pressure for further collaboration, should have experienced the most dissonance and the most consequent shake-up of their ideological position. The next task is to attempt to evaluate exactly how effective the Chinese Communists were in their indoctrination program.

It would seem that by disrupting social organization and by the systematic use of rewards and threatened punishments the Chinese were able to elicit a considerable amount of collaboration. This is not surprising when one considers the tremendous effort they made to discover the weak points in individual prisoners and the unscrupulousness with which they manipulated the environment (Schein, 1956). However, a number of authorities seem to believe that the Chinese methods were, after all, quite unsuccessful. Citing the fact that only

10 to 15% of the POWs were active collaborators and accepted their captors' ideological teachings to any degree, and that among those who did, more than half came away with only a mild affinity toward communism, Segal (1957) and Schein (1956, 1957b) cast doubt on the effectiveness of the Chinese program. Furthermore, they report that on repatriation only 45% of those who participated showed some sympathy toward communism as a way of life; among these 45%, only half accepted their captors' teaching and only a very few came away extremely sold. Schein says that "one can only conjecture, of course, the extent to which prisoners began to believe in communism . . . and the degree to which repatriates are now, as a result of their experience, predisposed to find fault with a democratic society if they cannot make a go of it." The question turns on whether the process of collaborative behavior is itself sufficient to initiate the process of ideological change and whether a person who has committed acts consonant with a new and negative ideology might be forced to adopt this ideology in order to "rationalize" his behavior (reduce dissonance). Schein (1957a) reasonably feels that "rationalizations will not acquire the permanence of beliefs unless supported by social reinforcements." Thus prisoners who came home found no support or need to rationalize their beliefs. And Hinkle and Wolff (1956) say that these methods produce only variable changes in attitudes and behavior. They say, "Changes in attitude and behavior are of much smaller degree than is usually supposed. They are relatively transient. After a period of months the prisoner reverts to former attitudes, though the changes that did take place initially are understandable in terms of the experiences the prisoners went through."

It seems to us that the assessment of the effectiveness of the Chinese can only be made in terms of the aims of the Chinese. If one assumes that the Chinese were really trying to make Communists of our troops and that they wanted converted Americans to remain in Korea, the lack of explicit and strong effects on the ideology of the great majority, and the fact that only 21 Americans chose to remain, indicates that the indoctrination program was a failure. Thus Schein, West, and the various government agencies who studied the problem are skeptical of the power of the Chinese program. But, if one makes the assumption that the Chinese aim was primarily to obtain collaboration for propaganda purposes and in the process to produce ideological effects on American troops and create doubts in their mind as to the validity of the American way of life, they can be considered very successful indeed. The dissonance formulation would lead to the position that such a shake-up of initial attitudes is a result of forced compliance under a number of conditions ranged along the dimension of relative number of cognitions supporting and disconfirming the collaboration. Thus *the effect of the indoctrination program would have to be evaluated not only in terms of active collaboration and lasting ideological change but also in terms of the production of apathy, withdrawal, doubt, and a generally more permissive and understanding orientation toward China and communism.* Such a weakening of and lessening of confidence in old attitudes and values constitutes some form of attitude change; the dissonance formulation would assume that not only is active advocacy of the new position an indication of the operation of dissonance but also that such a general "shaking loose" is also a meaningful effect of dissonance.

When one once considers the Chinese program in this light, the peculiar behavior of many repatriates becomes quite comprehensible. When first interviewed, the vast majority of the returning POWs did not express fear of the Chinese or rage against them. This attitude contrasted markedly with the feelings about the Japanese shown by American prisoners of the Japanese during World War II; in the latter case the POWs showed violent animosity against the Japanese. Also, POWs who did collaborate in Korea would say typically that they did not like communism for the United States, but that it might do a lot of good in backward areas.

This view of the effectiveness of the indoctrination program through the medium of dissonance reduction processes is highlighted in the case history presented by Santucci and Winokur (1955). They describe a patient who in the course of indoctrination received rewards for singing communist songs, making procommunist statements, and writing procommunist essays. In their terms, which can easily be translated into dissonance terms, "If in the beginning the patient did not believe in his statements and activities, there would inevitably have been an internal conflict between his motor and speech responses as opposed to his thinking." The patient could have avoided dissonance by outwitting his captors or by suffering punishment. But, once collaborating, he could have started to resolve the dissonance by "thinking in favor of his captors." From the clinical material presented by Santucci and Winokur, the latter is what he did. And the proof for this is that he was sent to a camp for more intensive indoctrination, a step that might never have taken place had he not been viewed as at least in part indoctrinated. The authors go on to say that after repatriation there was a strong conflict between his thinking and the opinions and beliefs current at home. He met with hostile attitudes toward collaborators, and "this produced in him symptoms of confusion and a fugue state." In effect, after returning, the patient, although not necessarily advocating communism in the face of a nonsupportive environment, was confused, disrupted, and had ideological conflicts, testifying perhaps, to the dissonance-producing characteristics of the indoctrination program.

In a review of Milocz's *Captive Mind*, a book about the ideological conversion of Polish intellectuals under the Communist State, Kecskemeti (1953, pp. 275–278) gives a revealing and compelling descriptive account of extreme effects that can partly be attributed to the processes of dissonance arousal and reduction. He says that early in the Communist regime, professional personnel and artists were invited to produce; the new state showed an encouraging interest in creative work. Creative work was organized; it was no longer a hit-and-miss individual affair. The intellectuals "suddenly found themselves part of the big machine, and they found that they could produce only by adapting themselves to the rhythm of the machine. The artist's own creative impulse was now psychologically combined with the type of responsibility which the executive of a big state-owned industry must accept for output in terms of the specifications worked out in advance at the highest levels of policy making. Obviously noble, individual gestures are ridiculous in this sort of situation; it is ridiculous for the individual to insist that the production plan must take account of his individual tastes or ideas. It is his problem how he can square the requirements of the position with his own personal values. This could be done only by learning to think the thoughts of the system; otherwise creative work became impossible." And so, confronted with the choice of either working according to specifications or not at all, many intellectuals helped to transform themselves. Thus, in this case, neither brute coercion nor narcotics achieved the "subjugation" of some of the intellectual community; they found that they were being transformed from within.

The general picture that emerges from consideration of the indoctrination program, as well as from the experimental data we have presented on the centrality of choice and commitment, is that the traditional clichés of the "free spirit" struggling against external oppression are quite inadequate. These general effects on attitude and ideology point up clearly the significance of *the individual's own efforts to reduce the psychological tension he has helped to create by his own discrepant behavior and the necessity to look within the individual's cognitive and motivational systems* in order to increase our understanding of thought reform. Such added insights can certainly aid us in evolving defenses against systematic manipulation of the individual.

It should be clear that the dearth of concrete and reliable data on the desegregation and indoctrination situations makes it impossible to apply the dissonance formulation unequivocally to these areas or to use them as unequivocal sources for support of the validity and generality of the theory. We also wish to state that we do not intend to convey the impression that even if satisfactory data were available, the dissonance formulation could alone explain the complex phenomena involved in the desegregation and indoctrination situations. Obviously many additional social, psychological, political, and economic factors are intimately involved.

What we have tried to do in the present chapter is to show how the dissonance formulation, as we have thought of it, is potentially applicable to aspects of these important social problems. Central to our discussion, implicitly and explicitly, were the notions of choice and commitment. In both the desegregation and the indoctrination settings, the major focal point for analysis was seen to be the interplay between the environmental constraints forcing behavior and the individual volitional processes involved. In both cases we attempted to show that the strongest effects on attitudes, ideology, and subsequent behavior are produced when careful thought is given to the conditions under which people are forced to comply with the demand that they do something they do not want to do. Changes in attitudes, and so forth, away from an initial position one has held, toward a new and originally unpleasant position, depend certainly on first arranging the social conditions that elicit the new and recalcitrant response. However, it is the manner in which the environment is organized in getting the person into the new situation, or arranged once he is in it, that determines how well he will adjust to it by accepting it, incorporating it, rationalizing it, and, finally, even proselytizing for it. Real changes in peoples' attitudes and behavior, as well as how good they feel about such changes, will result to the degree that social policy maximizes their sense of choice and responsibility when it forces them to engage in discrepant behavior.

Summary and perspective

— 16

CONCEPTUAL SUMMARY

Throughout this book we have attempted to present some idea of the scope and generality of dissonance theory. In discussing experimental tests of the theory, in indicating the directions of its extension, in comparing and evaluating it with regard to other theoretical models, and in illustrating some of its social applications, we have shown the range of phenomena to which the theory can be applied.

It should be evident by now that the theory is different in its essential nature from most other theoretical models in psychology. Where the major concern in other theories has been largely with the guidance of behavior—that is, with what leads to a given behavior or commitment—dissonance theory deals, at least in part, with the *consequences* of a given behavior or commitment. It suggests that some aspects of the modification of behavior can be best understood in terms of post-commitment factors rather than in terms of instrumental and/or reinforcement factors.

We have given many illustrations of this connection between commitment and subsequent change in perception, cognition, and motivation. We have shown that the theory has predictive power with regard to free choice, forced compliance, and exposure situations.

A central kernel of dissonance theory, as we have attempted to illustrate, is the notion that *a person will try to justify a commitment to the extent that there is information discrepant with that commitment.* It seems to us that this "insight" has never before been formally stated in psychology and that on it is based much of the power and versatility of the dissonance formulation. Commitment provides a specification of the conditions under which one cognition follows from the obverse of another, or, as we have expanded the basic defining statement of dissonance, when one cognition follows from any variation from another in the direction of being obverse. Hence the concept of commitment helps to specify the point at which a dissonant relationship occurs. The addition of the notion of volition may perhaps allow for the further provision of the exact point at which a dissonant relationship will create a psychological tension of some consequence. It is in this sphere that we can clearly distinguish dissonance theory from such notions as instrumental learning, adjustment, or hypothesis-testing. In the latter cases, the confrontation of discrepant information by the individual does not necessarily produce dissonance for him. It simply presents the occasion for a compromise solution between his existing cognitive structure and the new information. However, under conditions where commitment is present, dissonance does clearly occur and produce its effects on cognition and, perhaps, on perception or behavior.

Beginning with the theoretical discussion in Chapter 1, we have tried to show that *commitment* may be a unique aspect of dissonance theory and that the addition of volition may perhaps enable a clear specification of dissonance arousal. We have not, however, offered a formal theoretical statement to show precisely how these variables operate in the arousal of dissonance. At this point we may speculate further about these processes.

The definition of a dissonant relationship remains unchanged: A dissonant relationship exists when one cognitive element follows from the obverse of another. A consonant relationship exists when one element follows from another. In addition, elements can be unrelated to each other.

What gives particular psychological meaning to one element following from another or from its obverse is *commitment.* Knowledge that one has or will have certain need satisfactions (those associated with the commitment) "follows from" the commitment. Knowledge that one must give up certain need satisfactions follows from the obverse of the commitment. Knowledge concerning need satisfactions unaffected by the commitment is irrelevant.

As Festinger (1957) has stated, these bits of knowledge or cognitive elements must be weighted according to their importance to the individual. Although the evidence on the importance variable is not completely supportive, we assume that the lack of support may be due to lack of understanding of other factors (such as volition). While it may be true that importance operates only as a self-relational variable and not in terms of extrinsic, instrumental value (e.g., in terms of money), it is premature to draw this conclusion. Even considering these limitations, it is adequate to say that the magnitude of dissonance created by a dissonant relationship is a direct function of the importance of the relevant cognitive elements.

Another significant aspect of Festinger's formulation is that the magnitude of dissonance associated with a given cognition ". . . will depend on the proportion of relevant elements that are dissonant with the one in question" (1957, p. 17). This statement is the basis of much of what is "nonobvious" in the theory. For example, it is the major assumption involved in the derivation that the *less* the reward for saying something discrepant with one's private attitude, the *greater* the amount of attitude change. This assumption, then, says that the magnitude of dissonance (and consequent attempts to reduce dissonance) is greatest where the weighted dissonant and consonant cognitions are equal in magnitude. Hence, under some conditions, reductions in consonant (need-satisfying) factors will tend to increase the magnitude of dissonance and consequent attempts to reduce it. Thus, whether reduction takes the form of attitude change, object revaluation, information seeking, proselyting, or what-have-you, it may increase in magnitude as rewards or benefits decrease.

Perhaps no less important in the dissonance formulation is the implicit assumption that relevant cognitive elements are interchangeable and additive. That is, any relevant cognition can serve in either the arousal or reduction of dissonance and the effect of any given element is added to that of any other element. If a person commits himself to saying something discrepant with his private belief, money for doing so reduces his dissonance, but so can the perception that he was interpersonally obligated, the judgment that he will become a "better man," the judgment that his compliance will help science (or any other "good" cause), interpersonal attraction to whomever made the request, a change in his private belief, and so on. It is noteworthy that these various factors, which can affect the magnitude of dissonance, are not necessarily related in any way other than through their relevance to the dissonance in question. Consequently, *seemingly* unrelated factors can be interrelated. In the above example of a person who says something discrepant with his private belief, the less money he receives for this commitment the more dissonance he will experience, and, at least under some conditions, the more scientifically valuable he will consider his behavior. Our point, then, is that the assumption that dissonance is controlled by a ratio of dissonant to consonant factors that may be independent and are additive allows a particularly powerful way of analyzing complex human behavior.

A final factor that may perhaps control the magnitude of dissonance is the degree of volition involved in the occurrence of the dissonant relationship. It should be clear that the volitional aspect can enter in regard to either side of a dissonant relationship and have the same effect on the magnitude of dissonance: There need not be volition in regard to both sides of the dissonant relationship.

The significant aspect of volition may be to denote that the individual has voluntarily gotten himself into a general situation or set of circumstances. Then, if that situation includes aspects that follow from the obverse of getting into it (by virtue of some commitment), the individual will experience dissonance. It may be that volition is implicit in any situation of unequivocal dissonance arousal.

THE SCOPE OF THE THEORY

It may be illuminating to review the studies we have cited and presented throughout in terms of the propositions they have tested, the behaviors they have utilized to test those propositions, and the phenomena to which they have predicted. Such a summary of all the extant research evidence should serve to point up: (1) the wide range of issues with which research in dissonance theory has been concerned; (2) the variety of settings, subjects, and materials that have been dealt with by investigators in order to put the theory to empirical test; and (3) the multiplicity of actual situations to which the theory is potentially applicable.

In presenting this summary we shall follow in major outline the distinction made earlier between the factors controlling dissonance arousal and the possible modes of dissonance reduction. In connection with each proposition we shall cite the research evidence relevant to it. Wherever we make a statement about the particular phenomena studied in a given piece of research, the reference to the research will follow immediately. While we do not distinguish between studies that have used male subjects, those that have used females, and those that have used both, it should be mentioned that the studies are divided approximately equally in this respect.

The most general proposition asserts that *the magnitude of dissonance aroused is greater*

1. *The more attractive the rejected alternative when the person
   chooses between attractive alternatives.* This has been shown with
   regard to
   ——college students choosing between appliances and other consumer articles (Brehm, 1956).

2. *The more negative the characteristics of the chosen alternative
   when the person chooses between two courses of action.* This has
   been shown with regard to
   ——college students choosing between gambling strategies (Festinger, 1957, pp. 162–176; Cohen, Brehm and Latané, 1959).
   ——college students deciding to become engaged (Cohen, pp.
   78–81).

3. *The greater the number of rejected alternatives when the person
   chooses between attractive alternatives.* This has been shown with
   regard to
   ——grade school children choosing between toys (Brehm and
   Cohen, 1959a).
   ——adult car owners in a midwestern metropolis who have pur-
   chased cars (Ehrlich et al., 1957).

4. *The less the cognitive overlap between attractive alternatives.* This
   has been shown with regard to
   ——grade school children choosing between toys (Brehm and
   Cohen, 1959a; Brock, in press).
   ——nursery school children choosing between toys and crackers
   (Brock, in press).

5. *The more recent the decision to choose between attractive alternatives.* This has been shown with regard to
   ——adult car owners in a midwestern metropolis who have pur-
   chased cars (Ehrlich et al., 1957).

6. *The more important the relevant cognitions surrounding a decision.*
   This has been shown with regard to
   ——college students choosing between gambling strategies
   (Cohen, Brehm and Latané, 1959).
   ——college students assessing a delinquent's case history about
   which they have disagreed (Zimbardo, 1960).
   ——clerical employees in a large office indicating their preferences
   for various jams (Deutsch, Krauss and Rosenau, 1962).

7. *The less the amount of positive inducement for commitment to discrepant behavior*, that is,
   (a) *the smaller the financial incentives or prizes for commitment.* This has been shown with regard to
       ——college students appraising a negative task positively to another person (Festinger and Carlsmith, 1959).
       ——college students agreeing to go without food for a substantial period of time (Brehm, pp. 133–136).
       ——college students agreeing to go without water for a substantial period of time (Brehm, pp. 137–143).
       ——college students writing essays in favor of the behavior of a local police force after a brutal police incident (Cohen, pp. 73–78).
       ——grade school children induced to cheat (Mills, 1958).
   (b) *the less the justification for commitment.* This has been shown with regard to
       ——college students writing essays against their positions on a salient attitude issue (Cohen, Brehm and Fleming, 1958; Rabbie, Brehm and Cohen, 1959; Brock and Blackwood, in press; Cohen, pp. 97–104).
   (c) *the more negative the characteristics of the inducing agent.* This has been shown with regard to
       ——Army reservists at a training camp who agreed to eat grasshoppers (Smith, 1961).
8. *The greater the choice in commitment to discrepant behavior.* This has been shown with regard to
   ——college students delivering electric shock to another person (Brock and Buss, in press).
   ——college students agreeing to write essays in favor of a religious position to which they do not adhere (Brock, 1962).
   ——college students making a public speech against their own positions on a salient attitude issue (Cohen and Latané, pp. 88–91).
   ——college students agreeing to expose themselves to a communication known to be counter to their own positions on a salient attitude issue (Cohen, Terry and Jones, 1959).
   ——college students communicating a negative evaluation of a stranger to the stranger (Davis and Jones, 1960).
9. *The less the coercion applied in order to induce discrepant commitment.* This has been shown with regard to
   ——nursery school children giving up an attractive toy (Aronson and Carlsmith, in press b).

————college students agreeing to spend three hours copying tables of random numbers (Brehm, pp. 84–88); Brehm and Cohen, 1959b).

10. *The less the person's ability or self-esteem would lead him to perform a discrepant act.* This has been shown with regard to

————college students judging stimuli in a conformity situation modeled after Asch's experiment (Gerard, 1961).

————college students judging others' homosexual arousal in an interpersonal assessment situation (Bramel, 1962).

11. *The more the person has to engage in the negative behavior (i.e., the more discrepant behavior to which he is committed).* This has been shown with regard to

————college students undergoing initiation into a sex discussion group (Aronson and Mills, 1959).

————college students fishing for unseen containers holding money (Aronson, 1961).

————college students receiving shock for expressing nonbelief in ESP (Raven and Fishbein, 1961).

————junior high school students eating disliked foods (Brehm, 1960a).

————college students working over a communication known to be counter to their positions on a salient attitude issue (Cohen, 1959b; Zimbardo, 1960).

————college students agreeing to participate in an auditory feedback task on which they anticipate failure (Cohen and Zimbardo, pp. 143–151).

————college students memorizing a difficult list of symbolic definitions in preparation for an aptitude test they might not have to take (Yaryan and Festinger, 1961).

12. *The more negative information the person has about the discrepant situation to which he is committed.* This has been shown with regard to

————college students agreeing to spend 3 hours copying tables of random numbers and learning that others, not themselves, are to receive money for this (Brehm and Cohen, 1959b).

————junior high school students eating disliked vegetables and reading that the vegetables are not very nutritious (Brehm, 1960a).

————college students confronted with the essays they had written in favor of a religious position to which they do not adhere (Brock, 1962).

————college students learning that instead of successfully influ-

Summary and Perspective / 305

encing another person to accept their positions on a salient attitude issue, they had caused the others to become even more intransigent in their own positions (Cohen, 1962).

This listing covers the range of dissonance-arousing situations that have been investigated by the present authors and others concerned with dissonance theory. We may now turn to a summary of modes of dissonance reduction that have been cited in the preceeding pages.

MODES OF DISSONANCE REDUCTION

Since the tension associated with dissonance arousal has been conceptualized as an intervening variable, it may only be observed in terms of the effects on certain specifiable psychological processes. In this section we shall list the specific dependent variables measured in the experiments discussed and cite the evidence relevant to each one.

1. *Attitude change.* In this category we include all the changes in evaluation, belief, and opinion that reflect the cognitive realignments resulting from the pressure to reduce existing dissonance.
   (a) *Opinion change.* Here we may mention the various opinion dimensions that have been employed, ranging from moderately involving issues to highly salient ones. Opinions on the following issues have been studied in the experiments deriving from the dissonance formulation:
   ——the behavior of a local police force (Cohen, pp. 74–78).
   ——the institution of a compulsory religion course at a large university (Cohen and Latané, pp. 88–91).
   ——the adoption of undergraduate coeducation at a male college (Cohen, Brehm and Fleming, 1958; Cohen, 1962).
   ——a tuition rise at a large university (Brock and Blackwood, in press).
   ——the abolition of all intercollegiate athletics at a large university (Rabbie, Brehm and Cohen, 1959; Cohen, pp. 97–104).
   ——the advisability of young men marrying by the age of 23 (Cohen, Terry and Jones, 1959).
   ——belief in ESP (Raven and Fishbein, 1961).
   ——the adoption of a numerical grading system at a major university (Zimbardo, 1960).
   ——the advisability of punishment for children cheating (Mills, 1958).
   ——the minimum age for teenagers' driving (Allyn and Festinger, 1961).

———reasons for becoming a Catholic and sympathy and understanding for someone who had become a Catholic (Brock, 1962).

———the advisability of foster homes for juvenile delinquents as an aid in curbing delinquency (Cohen, 1959b).

(b) *Evaluative change.* In the studies discussed, dissonance was seen to have implications for change in the following:

———*Liking for persons*

———a target of one's derogation (Davis and Jones, 1960).

———a communicator of discrepant information (Allyn and Festinger, 1961).

———one's fiancee (Cohen, pp. 78–81).

———*Attraction to groups* (Gerard, 1961; Aronson and Mills, 1959)

———*Preference for objects*

———toys (Brehm and Cohen, 1959a; Aronson and Carlsmith, in press b; Brock, in press).

———appliances and other consumer articles (Brehm, 1956).

———*Valuation of activities*

———a boring and time-consuming task (Festinger and Carlsmith, 1959; Brehm and Cohen, 1959b; Brehm, pp. 84–87; Levanthal and Brehm, pp. 210–217; Cohen and Brehm, pp. 206–209).

———*Food preferences* (Brehm, 1959, 1960a; Deutsch, Krauss and Rosenau, in press; Smith, 1961; Brock, in press).

———*Sensory characteristics*

———preference for colors (Aronson, 1961).

———judgment of weights (Brehm and Leventhal, pp. 192–198).

———*Subjective experiences*

———rating of pain from electric shock (Brock and Buss, in press).

———cognition of hunger (Brehm, pp. 133–136).

———cognition of thirst (Brehm, pp. 137–142).

———*Assessment of a case history* (Zimbardo, 1960)

2. *Exposure to information.*

———selective exposure to and avoidance of a graph purporting to show the true cumulative probabilities of winning or losing in a gambling situation (Festinger, 1957, pp. 126–131, 162–176; Cohen, Brehm and Latané, 1959).

———selective exposure to information relating to an important impending examination (Mills, Aronson and Robinson, 1959; Rosen, 1961).

———selective exposure to information regarding child-rearing practices (Adams, 1961).

———selective exposure to automobile advertisements (Ehrlich et al., 1957).

3. *Recall of information.*

———selective recall of information concerning ratings about oneself or about one's favorite TV personality (Brehm, pp. 92–97).

4. *Perceptual distortion.*

———judgment of the degree to which the person feels he has been compelled to commit himself to discrepant behavior (i.e., feelings of obligation) (Brock and Buss, in press; Cohen, pp. 97–104; Cohen and Zimbardo, pp. 143–151).

———projection of one's own "experience of homosexual arousal" on to another person (Bramel, 1962).

———belief in the likelihood of occurrence of a possible future event (an intelligence test) that might not occur (Yaryan and Festinger, 1961).

5. *Behavioral change.*

———the ordering of food items (Brehm, pp. 133–136).

———drinking water (Brehm, pp. 137–142).

———productivity on a job (Adams and Rosenbaum, 1962).

———change in performance so as to make for failure (Aronson and Carlsmith, in press a).

———conforming to a group norm in an Asch-type situation (Gerard, 1961).

———changing strategies after a gambling sequence (Festinger, 1957, pp. 126–131, 162–176; Cohen, Brehm and Latané, 1959).

———setting a dial on an auditory apparatus so as to increase the possibilities of failure on a new trial (Cohen and Zimbardo, pp. 143–151).

The foregoing review demonstrates that many of the major derivations of the theory have been tested and supported. Some of the supported derivations concerning the arousal of dissonance in a "free-choice" situation are that: (1) A choice between attractive alternatives creates dissonance; (2) Dissonance arising from a choice is proportional to the attractiveness of the rejected alternative; (3) Dissonance arising from a choice is proportional to the qualitative dissimilarity of the choice alternatives; and (4) Dissonance arising from a choice is proportional to the importance of the choice. Supported derivations concerning the arousal of dissonance in a "forced-compliance" situation include: (1) Dissonance from commitment to comply decreases as rewards, incentives, or justifications for compliance increase; (2) Dissonance from commitment to comply decreases as coercive forces to produce compliance increase. In regard to studies of "exposure," the following additional derivations—among others—have been supported: (1) The amount of dissonance consequent to exposure to discrepant information is a direct function of the importance of the issue; (2) Dissonance in the communicatee is a direct function of the difficulty or effort involved in exposure to the discrepant information. Evidence has also supported the contention that dissonance is a direct function of choice in both "free-choice" and "forced-compliance" situations.

Evidence on the *effects* of dissonance has shown that it bears on: (1) opinions on various issues, (2) evaluations of persons, groups, and activities, (3) salience of information, (4) recall of information, (5) acceptance of information, (6) seeking of and voluntary exposure to information, (7) perceptual distortion, (8) change in behavioral commitment, and (9) motivation.

In short, the theoretical statement has shown itself to be very powerful in the understanding and prediction of a variety of behavior in a variety of situations. It is this very power that would seem to demand the continued elaboration and refinement of the theory.

ASSESSMENT OF THE THEORY

This volume presents the contribution of ourselves and others to dissonance theory. We have done research on the theory, have generally interpreted the results as supportive of the theory, and are convinced of the utility of the theory in understanding behavior. However, we are not necessarily satisfied with much of the work that has been done, including our own, and we would like to point out what we feel are important issues in scrutinizing the work in dissonance theory. In the present section our discussion will focus on the question of general guidelines for evaluating the theory.

While the previous section served to indicate the scope and generality of dissonance theory, we may raise here the question of just how well and unequivocally tested is the theory. Can we assess the quality of support for the theory and measure the firmness of the ground it stands on at this point? Such a question brings into focus the relationship between specific experiments bearing on a theory and a theory as a general body of propositions. That is, what is the relationship between the adequacy, rigor, and compellingness of any particular experiment or series of experiments and the power and validity of the theory they bear on? We do not, of course, pretend to be able to answer these general philosophical questions in any definitive way, nor even to arrive at any firm conclusions with regard to the present body of work, but there are some guidelines we can indicate for evaluating the support for dissonance theory.

A strong position would be that though any given experiment might have methodological inadequacies and be open to numerous alternative explanations, the fact that together they all seem to be consistent with the theory is enough to establish the validity of the theory. At the other extreme, it might be said that while the theory has not been clearly supported because of inadequacies in each specific experiment, at the very least the experiments have served to indicate the broad empirical outlines of the theory and the specific directions of definitive tests.

There is, however, a more reasonable middle course, which we think it prudent to follow. This point of view suggests that the theory is built on a series of interrelated propositions that have received more or less support. Therefore one must perforce examine the evidence bearing on the propositions of the theory. Some propositions have been tested by relatively few studies, some by numerous studies; for some propositions the evidence is inconclusive because of methodological and conceptual difficulties, for others there exist extremely rigorous tests. In evaluating the general structure of the theory, it is clear that the relationship between the number of studies, the kind of support, and the excellence and unequivocality of the particular studies must be carefully examined.

Some idea of the extent and diversity of support the theory has received can be gleaned from the preceding section where we attempted to present a conceptual summary of the material. It can be seen that some propositions, noticeably those having to do with the amount of positive inducement, the amount of choice, the amount of negative behavior engaged in, and the amount of negative information received, have been given a good deal of attention. Others having to do with, for example, cognitive overlap and coercion have been relatively neglected.

However, examination of the diversity of support is surely not enough for a thorough assessment of the theory. It is also necessary for the critic to look carefully into each of the studies, to evaluate the methodological and conceptual problems encountered in each, and to get some feeling for the adequacy of the study as it stands by itself. Such an evaluation or series of evaluations must be weighed against the extent and kind of evidence for one or another proposition of the theory before any definitive assessment can be made.

We have not taken such an explicit and detailed assessment as our goal in the present book. To have taken up each experiment, those of others and our own, in terms of methodological and conceptual problems, alternative explanations, misapplications of the theory, and so forth, would have meant an inordinately detailed and cloudy narrative. In our published work and in the new experiments given here, we have attempted wherever possible to indicate the theoretical and methodological difficulties we have encountered. We have assumed that other extant research will be susceptible to such systematic evaluation by the critical reader.

We can, however, indicate here our general evaluation regarding the adequacy of the dissonance formulation. What can we say in the theory's favor?

1. First of all, there have been few outright disconfirmations of the theory, either from experiments explicitly designed to test the theory or from relevant evidence from other theoretical sources.

2. The dissonance experiments we have discussed were all performed explicitly to test the theory, and the theory has by and large *predicted* the results of these experiments.

3. It would certainly seem that methodological artifacts cannot alone account for a diversity of outcomes, all consistent with the general theory. Even assuming a good deal of methodological unclarity in some experiments, it is difficult to see how that could account for the fit between the theory and all of the data collected.

4. While each experiment or at least a number of experiments can be explained in alternate ways, there appears to be no theory that at present can more easily explain the phenomena dealt with by all the dissonance experiments.

5. The alternative explanations that have been offered in connection with one or another specific experiment bearing on the theory too often are based on other hypotheses that themselves are untested (e.g., "expectation" hypotheses for the "forced-compliance" experiments).

What, on the other hand, can we say against the theory?

1. For one thing, it is clear that there are certain kinds of imprecisions in the theory, such as the degree to which choice is a necessary condition, the role of commitment, and the delineation of a cognitive element.

2. Some important propositions have received far too little attention and await more compelling tests.

3. There is one apparent disconfirmation of the theory, dealing with the avoidance of dissonant information.

4. It is clear that a number of the experiments bolstering the theory are open to alternative explanations, some of which are as compelling and perhaps more grounded in common sense than the dissonance formulation.

5. The adequacy of the theoretical statement can be better and better assessed, the more attempts there are on the part of people with diverse interests to test the theory. So far only a relatively small group of researchers have attempted to put the theory to test.

In summary, while it seems to us that the theory has been extremely successful in predicting to a wide range of phenomena and that its major propositions have been supported many times over, we do feel that critical evaluations of the experiments are necessary at any point for evaluating the success of the theory. The mere existence of methodological and conceptual inadequacies in experiments should cause us to look at the theory with an ever-critical eye.

THEORETICAL AND CONCEPTUAL ISSUES

We have endeavored throughout to point out where dissonance theory is unclear at conceptual or operational levels. However, three general issues may require a little further discussion.

The first issue concerns the use of dissonance theory to "explain" well-known phenomena. There is no reason, of course, why the theory should not be applied to any data that happen to fit. But it seems to us that such application of the theory does little to further our general understanding of psychological phenomena unless it leads to implications that other interpretations do not. These further implications could then be put to empirical test to see whether or not the use of dissonance theory in regard to the phenomenon in question was fruitful. But it should be clear that empirical demonstration of further implications does not necessarily mean that dissonance theory accounts for the original phenomenon, for other psychological processes may work in parallel ways. An example of this issue is seen in the application of dissonance theory to the phenomena of attitude and opinion change, a detailed discussion of which was presented in Chapter 7.

A second issue bears on the conceptualization of the "forced-compliance" paradigm. An assumption generally made is that the inducing force used to obtain compliance varies from just barely adequate to much more than adequate. But what constitutes an adequate stimulus may be very complex indeed, although this has not been clearly analyzed in "forced-compliance" experiments. Suppose, for example, that the smaller monetary reward is not "adequate" in a "forced-compliance" experiment. However, at the experimenter's request to comply, the subject may wish to avoid saying no to the experimenter; therefore, *in order to comply*, he may try to mobilize motivations consistent with compliance. With a higher monetary inducement, there would be much less need to mobilize other motivations in order to comply. This kind of process could result in effects similar to those derived from dissonance theory. Hence we are suggesting that future research might well look more closely into the assumption of what is adequate to provide compliance.

A final issue is that the frequent difficulty of specifying modes of dissonance reduction, and which mode will most likely be used, leads to ambiguities in the interpretation of experimental outcomes. Before the running of an experiment, the possible and likely modes of dissonance reduction require careful attention and specification. Those that are uninteresting must be blocked off in order that those which are interesting and are to be measured will be used. But it will still frequently happen that, after the experiment is over, anything that occurred can be interpreted as dissonance reduction, whether or not it was seen as a possible mode beforehand. What is obviously needed to cope with this problem is a much better understanding of the factors that control dissonance reduction.

FUTURE PERSPECTIVES

Since most of the major conceptual derivations that have been made have been tested and supported, it is well to ask the question, "What next?" The possible answers are multitudinous, and we will limit ourselves to mention of a few major issues.

First of all, the conditions necessary and sufficient for the arousal of dissonance are still not absolutely clear. We have speculated that *commitment* and *volition* are necessary conditions and that they, together with discrepancy and importance of cognitions, constitute the sufficient conditions for the creation of dissonance. However, events outside the individual's control may still conceivably affect dissonance differently from events over which he has some control; and, in addition, other as yet unidentified variables could affect dissonance. We do not intend that there should be a proliferation of conceptual variables involved in the arousal of dissonance; we do intend that the theoretical statement concerning the arousal of dissonance continue to receive critical appraisal. A great deal still remains to be done on such problems as the definition and specification of cognitive elements, the logical relationship between them, and the exact locus of psychological tension in a dissonant relationship.

The main virtue of dissonance theory is that its use permits so much understanding. It points to many nonobvious sources of tension. But we may continue to ask if there are not dissonance-arousing conditions, other than the ones we have discussed, that have been overlooked. Situations that are not obvious at first sight should surely be searched for and shown to be amenable to experimental test. This has, in part, been done with many of the variants of discrepancy, but there is no doubt that more work is needed along these lines.

A number of problems still remain in regard to the reduction of dissonance. Too little is known about how dissonance will be reduced, including the determinants of resistance to change of cognitions and, in particular, the effects of commitment on resistance to change. Nor is it clear how or when two or more channels of dissonance reduction may interact: When will separate channels be positively related and when will they be unrelated or perhaps even negatively related?

Another issue that presented itself throughout concerns the place of personality variables in the theory. This issue is important over and above the problem of whether or not dissonance theory has anything to say about the study of personality. Here we speak of the use of personality dimensions that have been isolated, conceptualized, and accepted by psychologists as constructs intervening between the arousal and reduction of dissonance. Such specification of personality variables in the dissonance process could help to identify more clearly the conditions that arouse dissonance and the manner in which it may be reduced.

Other problems concern extrapolation to parameter values not covered by previous research. These problems are particularly relevant and important to the use of dissonance theory in the analysis of real-life situations. Only by extending empirical tests to increasingly significant problems of human behavior can we gain some confidence in its applicability to major problems of our times, such as racial integration and "brainwashing." What is needed, then, is replication of laboratory tests, but perhaps in field settings.

It would be premature to say that the main outlines of the theory have been entirely proven and that no more tests need be made. Understanding and successful application of the theory still depend in large part on the intuition of the individual investigator. For any given empirical test, numerous assumptions must be made about the relevant operational variables, that is, how they relate to the conceptual variables, how they relate to each other, and how they relate to other ways of understanding human behavior, such as "field theory," "learning theory," psychoanalytic theory. Although certain simple paradigms, such as "forced compliance," might at first appear to need no further replication, common sense tells us that we do not yet know all there is to be known.

Consider, for example, the relationship between instrumental objects and goal objects. Peak (1958) and others have theorized that the affect associated with the instrumental object is a function of the valence of the goal and the object's instrumental value for attaining that goal. An implication of such a view is that positive affect associated with the instrumental object will increase as the goal object becomes more valuable. While the experimental evidence for this proposition is not overwhelmingly supportive, it appears to be inherently plausible. However, it seems to be contradictory to the derivation from the dissonance formulation that increased liking for a task varies inversely with the amount of reward for performing the task. Further research can help to clarify the conditions under which direct relationships and inverse relationships between evaluations of instrumental objects and goal objects obtain.

Another instance of the remaining unclarity in, for instance, the forced-compliance paradigm is suggested by our speculations on the role of volition in dissonance arousal and the observed changes in perceived obligation as a mode of dissonance reduction. The issue here involves whether or not dissonance can be reduced in any situation, no matter what the source of arousal, by changes in obligation. That is, can the individual picture himself as having been forced into a situation, as having little responsibility for his plight, even if the dissonance is not aroused with regard to any explicit inducing force? Or is this change in obligation specific to dissonance aroused by some force to comply? The implication of this question concerns whether volition as a variable is ever completely eliminated in the dissonance process.

Another point has to do with the assumption that there are special implications of the theory, such as those we have pointed out in relation to the general issue of motivation. Whenever such implications come to light, they must, of course, be put to empirical test.

A final point concerns the salience issue. It will be recalled (pp. 92–94) that evidence for the salience of dissonant cognitions immediately after choice was judged to be a puzzling phenomenon for the theory. It should be clear that the theory is stated in terms of dissonance arousal and reduction. However, it is interesting to consider that there may be effects of dissonance other than those centering around the way that the person tries to reduce dissonance. This may perhaps be the reason that derivations from the theory regarding salience of cognitions are not as easily made as derivations about modes of arousal and reduction. It is not at all certain what the conceptual issues are or how these processes come about, but there may be other effects of dissonance that have to be discovered rather than deduced. Salience may be one of these effects. Further research on this issue is certainly necessary, for, if salience is an important issue and we cannot derive it from the theory, it means that our grasp on the fundamental processes involved in dissonance is not a strong one. To the extent that other nonderivable effects of dissonance turn up, a way may be pointed toward a more fundamental formulation of the relevant psychological processes in dissonance theory.

It is clear, then, that while major facets of the theory have been tested and supported, there are numerous directions for further investigation. It is our hope that by summarizing the present evidence and by reporting several new experiments, by speculating on a modification of the theoretical statement, and by discussing some implications of the theory, we will stimulate further interest in, and research relevant to, this approach to the understanding of complex human behavior.

As research evidence accumulates, the special insights to be obtained from dissonance theory become more and more a part of our general fund of knowledge about human behavior. At the same time we inevitably gather increasing amounts of information that are either not encompassed by or are inconsistent with the theory. Thus the very process of firmly establishing a theory assists in the replacement of the theory by a more general formulation that integrates other theoretical notions.

We wish to conclude by underscoring the value of building a theoretical model on the basis of an important insight and establishing the validity of the insight. But new insights are demanded, then, in order to generate more powerful models and to stimulate further new research. Insofar as the basic notion of dissonance theory is concerned, it appears to be firmly established by the present data. There seems to be little point in demonstrating the same thing over and over again in future research. What is needed is, of course, a new, more general insight to stimulate new, interesting research. By this we do not mean that research on dissonance theory necessarily demands a new series of insights or that the elaborating and strengthening of the major insight of the theory are not important goals in themselves. What we do mean is that new and different research into such problems as, for example, subjective probability, the effects of choice, adaptation to discrepant environments, the influence of expectations, and the effects of coercive power might require more than even the most expanded and rigorously stated dissonance formulation could provide. In order to stimulate the investigation of such problems, it may be necessary to integrate the insights provided by dissonance theory with those of other notions into a broader theoretical formulation. We hope that task will be aided by the present volume.

References

Ackerman, N. W. and Jahoda, Marie. *Anti-Semitism and emotional disorder: a psychoanalytic interpretation.* New York: Harper, 1950.

Adams, J. S. Reduction of cognitive dissonance by seeking consonant information. *J. abnorm. soc. Psychol.*, 1961, **62**, 74–78.

Adams, J. S. Toward an understanding of inequity. General Electric Company, 1961.

Adams, J. S. and Rosenbaum, W. B. The relationship of worker productivity to cognitive dissonance. *J. appl. Psychol.*, 1962, **46**, 161–164.

Allport, G. W. *Personality: a psychological interpretation.* New York: Holt, 1937.

Allyn, Jane and Festinger, L. The effectiveness of unanticipated persuasive communications. *J. abnorm. soc. Psychol.*, 1961, **62**, 35–40.

Anderson, N. H. and Hovland, C. I. The representation of order effects in communication research. In C. I. Hovland (Ed.). *The order of presentation in persuasion.* New Haven: Yale University Press, 1957.

Aronson, E. The cognitive and behavioral consequences of the confirmation and disconfirmation of expectancies. Application for Research Grant submitted to the National Science Foundation. Harvard University, 1960.

Aronson, E. The effect of effort on the attractiveness of rewarded and unrewarded stimuli. *J. abnorm. soc. Psychol.*, 1961, **63**, 375–380.

Aronson, E. and Carlsmith, J. M. Performance expectancy as a determinant of actual performance. *J. abnorm. soc. Psychol.* (in press a).

Aronson, E. and Carlsmith, J. M. The effect of severity of threat on the devaluation of forbidden behavior. *J. abnorm. soc. Psychol.* (in press b).

Aronson, E. and Mills, J. The effects of severity of initiation on liking for a group. *J. abnorm. soc. Psychol.*, 1959, **59**, 177–181.

Aronson, E., Turner, Judy and Carlsmith, J. M. Communicator credibility and communication as determinants of opinion change. *J. abnorm. soc. Psychol.* (in press).

Asch, S. E. Effects of group pressure on the modification and distortion of judgments. In H. Guetzkow (Ed.), *Groups, leadership and men.* Pittsburgh: Carnegie Press, 1951.

Atkinson, J. W. Motivational determinants of risk-taking behavior. *Psychol. Rev.*, 1957, **64**, 359–372.

Bauer, R. Brainwashing: psychology or demonology? *J. Soc. Iss.*, 1957, **13**, 41–47.

Berkowitz, L. The judgmental process in personality functioning. *Psychol. Rev.*, 1960, **67**, 130–142.

Berlyne, D. E. *Conflict, arousal and curiosity.* New York: McGraw-Hill, 1960.

Bramel, D. A dissonance theory approach to defensive projection. *J. abnorm. soc. Psychol.*, 1962, **64**, 121–129.

Bramel, D. Selection of a target for defensive projection. *J. abnorm. soc. Psychol.* (in press).

Brehm, J. W. Post-decision changes in the desirability of alternatives. Unpublished doctoral dissertation, University of Minnesota, 1955.

Brehm, J. W. Post-decision changes in the desirability of alternatives. *J. abnorm. soc. Psychol.*, 1956, **52**, 384–389.

Brehm, J. W. Increasing cognitive dissonance by a fait-accompli. *J. abnorm. soc. Psychol.*, 1959, **58**, 379–382.

Brehm, J. W. Attitudinal consequences of commitment to unpleasant behavior. *J. abnorm. soc. Psychol.*, 1960a, **60**, 379–383.

Brehm, J. W. A dissonance analysis of attitude-discrepant behavior. In C. I. Hovland and M. J. Rosenberg (Eds.), *Attitude organization and change.* New Haven: Yale University Press, 1960b.

Brehm, J. W. Motivational effects of cognitive dissonance. In M. R. Jones (Ed.), *Nebraska Symposium on Motivation.* Lincoln: University of Nebraska Press, 1962.

Brehm, J. W. and Cohen, A. R. Re-evaluation of choice alternatives as a function of their number and qualitative similarity. *J. abnorm. soc. Psychol.*, 1959a, **58**, 373–378.

Brehm, J. W. and Cohen, A. R. Choice and chance relative deprivation as determinants of cognitive dissonance. *J. abnorm. soc. Psychol.*, 1959b, **58**, 383–387.

Brock, T. C. Cognitive restructuring and attitude change. *J. abnorm. soc. Psychol.*, 1962, **64**, 264–271.

Brock, T. C. Effects of prior dishonesty on post-decisional dissonance. *J. abnorm. soc. Psychol.* (in press).

Brock, T. C. and Blackwood, J. E. Dissonance reduction, social comparison and modification of others' opinions. *J. abnorm. soc. Psychol.* (in press).

Brock, T. C. and Buss, A. H. Dissonance, aggression and evaluation of pain. *J. abnorm. soc. Psychol.* (in press).

Brown, J. Principles of intrapersonal conflict. *J. conflict Resol.*, 1957, **1**, 135–154.

Cartwright, D. and Harary, F. Structural balance: a generalization of Heider's theory. *Psychol. Rev.*, 1956, **63**, 277–293.

Clark, K. B. Desegregation: an appraisal of the evidence. *J. Soc. Iss.*, 1953, **9**, 2–76.

Clark, K. B. Desegregation: the role of the social sciences. *Teachers College Record*, 1960, **62**, 1–17.

Cofer, C. Motivation. In *Annual review of psychology*. Stanford: Annual Reviews, Inc., 1959.

Cohen, A. R. Some implications of self-esteem for social influence. In C. I. Hovland and I. L. Janis (Eds.), *Personality and persuasibility*. New Haven: Yale University Press, 1959a.

Cohen, A. R. Communication discrepancy and attitude change: a dissonance theory approach. *J. Pers.*, 1959b, **27**, 386–396.

Cohen, A. R. Attitudinal consequences of induced discrepancies between cognitions and behavior. *Publ. Opin. Quart.*, 1960, **24**, 297–318.

Cohen, A. R. A dissonance analysis of the boomerang effect. *J. Pers.*, 1962, **30**, 75–88.

Cohen, A. R., Brehm, J. W. and Fleming, W. H. Attitude change and justification for compliance. *J. abnorm. soc. Psychol.*, 1958, **56**, 276–278.

Cohen, A. R., Brehm, J. W. and Latané, B. Choice of strategy and voluntary exposure to information under public and private conditions. *J. Pers.*, 1959, **27**, 63–73.

Cohen, A. R., Terry, H. I. and Jones, C. B. Attitudinal effects of choice in exposure to counter-propaganda. *J. abnorm. soc. Psychol.*, 1959, **58**, 388–391.

Communist interrogation, indoctrination and exploitation of American military and civilian prisoners. *Report of the Committee on Government Operations of the Permanent Subcommittee on Investigations of the United States Senate.* Washington: U.S. Government Printing Office, 1957.

Cook, S. W. Desegregation: a psychological analysis. *Amer. Psychologist*, 1957, **12**, 1–13.

Davis, K. and Jones, E. E. Changes in interpersonal perception as a means of reducing cognitive dissonance. *J. abnorm. soc. Psychol.*, 1960, **61**, 402–410.

Day, C. R. Some consequences of increased reward following establishment of output-reward expectation level. Unpublished M. A. thesis, Duke University, 1961.

Deutsch, Martin and Steele, Kay. Attitude dissonance among Southville's intellectuals. *J. Soc. Iss.*, 1959, **15**, 44–52.

Deutsch, Morton and Collins, Mary. *Interracial housing: a psychological evaluation of a social experiment.* Minneapolis: University of Minnesota Press, 1951.

Deutsch, Morton, Krauss, R. and Rosenau, Norah. Dissonance or defensiveness? *J. Pers.*, 1962, **30**, 16–28.

Edwards, A. L. *Experimental design in psychological research*. New York: Holt, Rinehart and Winston, 1960.

Ehrlich, Danuta, Guttman, I., Schonbach, P. and Mills, J. Post-decision exposure to relevant information. *J. abnorm. soc. Psychol.*, 1957, **54**, 98–102.

Festinger, L. Informal social communication. *Psychol. Rev.*, 1950, **57**, 271–282.

Festinger, L. A theory of social comparison processes. *Hum. Relat.*, 1954, **7**, 117–140.

Festinger, L. *A theory of cognitive dissonance*. Stanford: Stanford University Press, 1957.

Festinger, L. and Bramel, D. The reactions of humans to cognitive dissonance. In A. Bachrach (Ed.), *The experimental foundations of clinical psychology*. New York: Basic Books, 1962.

Festinger, L. and Carlsmith, J. M. Cognitive consequences of forced compliance. *J. abnorm. soc. Psychol.*, 1959, **58**, 203–210.

Gerard, H. B. Inconsistency of beliefs and their implications. Paper read at American Psychological Association, New York, September, 1961.

Goldberg, S. C. Three situational determinants of conformity to social norms. *J. abnorm. soc. Psychol.*, 1954, **49**, 325–329.

Guetzkow, H. and Bowman, P. H. *Men and hunger*. Philadelphia: Brethren Publishing House, 1946.

Harding, J. and Hogrefe, R. Attitudes of white department store employees toward Negro co-workers. *J. Soc. Iss.*, 1952, **8**, 18–28.

Hebb, D. O. Drives and the C.N.S. (conceptual nervous system). *Psychol. Rev.*, 1955, **62**, 243–254.

Heider, F. *The psychology of interpersonal relations*. New York: Wiley, 1958.

Hinkle, L. E. and Wolff, H. G. Communist interrogation and indoctrination of "enemies of the state." *Arch. Neurol. and Psychiat.*, 1956, **76**, 115–174.

Hovland, C. I. Reconciling conflicting results derived from experimental and survey studies of attitude change. *Amer. Psychologist*, 1959, **14**, 8–17.

Hovland, C. I., Harvey, O. J. and Sherif, M. Assimilation and contrast effects in reactions to communication and attitude change. *J. abnorm. soc. Psychol.*, 1957, **55**, 244–252.

Hovland, C. I. and Janis, I. L. (Eds.). *Personality and persuasibility*. New Haven: Yale University Press, 1959.

Hovland, C. I., Janis, I. L. and Kelley, H. H. *Communication and persuasion*. New Haven: Yale University Press, 1953.

Hovland, C. I., Lumsdaine, A. A. and Sheffield, F. D. *Experiments on mass communication*. Princeton: Princeton University Press, 1949.

Hovland, C. I. and Mandell, W. An experimental comparison of conclusion-drawing by the communicator and by the audience. *J. abnorm. soc. Psychol.*, 1952. **47**, 581–588.

Hovland, C. I. and Pritzker, H. A. Extent of opinion change as a function of amount of change advocated. *J. abnorm. soc. Psychol.*, 1957, **54**, 257–261.

Hovland, C. I. and Rosenberg, M. J. (Eds.). *Attitude organization and change.* New Haven: Yale University Press, 1960.

Janis, I. L. Decisional conflicts: a theoretical analysis. *J. Conflict Resol.*, 1959a, **3**, 6–27.

Janis, I. L. Motivational factors in the resolution of decisional conflicts. In M. R. Jones (Ed.), *Nebraska symposium on motivation*. Lincoln: University of Nebraska Press, 1959b.

Janis, I. L. and King, B. T. The influence of role playing on opinion change. *J. abnorm. soc. Psychol.*, 1954, **49**, 211–218.

Jordan, N. Behavioral forces that are a function of attitudes and of cognitive organization. *Hum. Relat.*, 1953, **6**, 273–287.

Kecskemeti, P. Review of The Captive Mind, by C. Milosz. *Commentary*, 1953, **16**, 275–278.

Kelman, H. Attitude change as a function of response restriction, *Hum. Relat.*, 1953, **6**, 185–214.

King, B. T. and Janis, I. L. Comparison of the effectiveness of improvised vs. non-improvised role-playing in producing opinion changes. *Hum. Relat.*, 1956, **9**, 177–186.

Kutner, B. C., Wilkins, C. and Yarrow, P. R. Verbal attitudes and overt behavior involving racial prejudice. *J. abnorm. soc. Psychol.*, 1952, 47, 649–652.

LaPiere, R. T. Attitudes vs. actions. *Soc. Forces*, 1934, 14, 230–237.

Lewin, K. Environmental forces in child behavior and development. In C. Murchison (Ed.), *A handbook of child psychology*. Worcester, Mass.: Clark University Press, 1931.

Lewin, K. *A dynamic theory of personality*. New York: McGraw-Hill, 1935.

Lewin, K. Group decision and social change. In T. M. Newcomb, and E. Hartley (Eds.), *Readings in social psychology*. New York: Holt, 1947.

Lewin, K. *Field theory in social science*. D. Cartwright (Ed.), New York: Harper, 1951.

Lewin, K., Dembo, Tamara, Festinger, L. and Sears, Pauline. Level of aspiration. In J. McV. Hunt (Ed.), *Personality and the behavior disorders*. New York: Ronald, 1944.

Lifton, R. J. *Thought reform and the psychology of totalism*. New York: Norton, 1961.

Mayer, A. Russel Woods: change without conflict. *Special research report to the commission on Race and Housing*, February 1957, mimeographed.

Miller, N. E. Experimental studies of conflict. In J. McV. Hunt (Ed.), *Personality and the behavior disorders*. New York: Ronald, 1944.

Miller, N. E. Liberalization of basic S-R concepts: Extension to conflict behavior, motivation and social learning. In S. Koch (Ed.), *Psychology: A study of a science*. Vol. 2. *General systematic formulations, learning and special processes*. New York: McGraw-Hill, 1959.

Mills, J. Changes in moral attitudes following temptation. *J. Pers.*, 1958, 26, 517–531.

Mills, J., Aronson, E. and Robinson, H. Selectivity in exposure to information. *J. abnorm. soc. Psychol.*, 1959, 59, 250–253.

Minard, R. D. Race relations in the Pocahontas coal field. *J. Soc. Iss.*, 1952, 8, 29–44.

Newcomb, T. M. An approach to the study of communicative acts. *Psychol. Rev.*, 1953, 60, 393–404.

Osgood, C. E. Motivational dynamics of language behavior. In *Nebraska symposium on motivation*. Lincoln: University of Nebraska Press, 1957.

Osgood, C. E. Cognitive dynamics in the conduct of human affairs. *Publ. Opin. Quart.*, 1960, 24, 341–365.

Osgood, C. E., Suci, G. J. and Tannenbaum, P. H. *The measurement of meaning*. Urbana: University of Illinois Press, 1957.

Osgood, C. E. and Tannenbaum, P. H. The principle of congruity in the prediction of attitude change. *Psychol. Rev.*, 1955, 62, 42–55.

Peak, Helen. Psychological structure and person perception. In R. Tagiuri and L. Petrullo (Eds.), *Person Perception and Interpersonal Behavior*. Stanford: Stanford University Press, 1958.

Pettigrew, T. F. Measurement and correlates of category width. *J. Pers.*, 1958, 26, 532–544.

Pettigrew, T. F. Social psychology and desegregation research. *Amer. Psychologist*, 1961, 16, 105–112

Pettigrew, T. F. and Cramer, M. R. Demography of desegregation. *J. Soc. Iss.*, 1959, 15, 61–71.

Rabbie, J. M., Brehm, J. W. and Cohen, A. R. Verbalization and reactions to cognitive dissonance. *J. Pers.*, 1959, **27**, 407–417.

Raven, B. H. and Fishbein, M. Acceptance of punishment and change in belief. *J. abnorm. soc. Psychol.*, 1961, **63**, 411–416.

Rosen, S. Post-decision affinity for incompatible information. *J. abnorm. soc. Psychol.*, 1961, **63**, 188–190.

Rosenberg, M. J. and Abelson, R. P. An analysis of cognitive balancing. In C. I. Hovland and M. J. Rosenberg (Eds.), *Attitude organization and change.* New Haven: Yale University Press, 1960.

Saenger, G. *The social psychology of prejudice.* New York: Harper, 1953.

Saenger, G. and Gilbert, E. Customer reactions to the integration of Negro sales personnel. *Intl. J. Opin. Att. Res.*, 1950, **4**, 57–60.

Santucci, P. S. and Winokur, G. Brainwashing as a factor in psychiatric illness. *Arch. Neurol. Psychiat.*, 1955, **74**, 1–6.

Schein, E. H. The Chinese indoctrination program for prisoners of war. *Psychiat.*, 1956, **19**, 149–172.

Schein, E. H. Reaction patterns to severe, chronic stress in American Army prisoners of war of the Chinese. *J. Soc. Iss.*, 1957a, **13**, 21–30.

Schein, E. H. Patterns of reactions to severe chronic stress in American Army prisoners of war of the Chinese. In *Methods of forceful indoctrination: observations and interviews.* New York: Group for the Advancement of Psychiatry, 1957b.

Schein, E. H., Hill, Winifred, F., Williams, H. L. and Lubin, A. Distinguishing characteristics of collaborators and resisters among American prisoners of war. *J. abnorm. soc. Psychol.*, 1957, **55**, 197–201.

Schein, E. H., Schneier, Inge and Barker, C. H. *Coercive Persuasion.* New York: Norton, 1961.

Segal, J. Correlates of collaboration and resistance behavior among U.S. Army POWs in Korea. *J. Soc. Iss.*, 1957, **13**, 31–40.

Sherif, M., Taub, D., and Hovland, C. I. Assimilation and contrast effects of anchoring stimuli on judgments. *J. Exper. Psychol.*, 1958, **55**, 150–155.

Smith, E. E. The power of dissonance techniques to change attitudes. *Publ. Opin. Quart.*, 1961, **25**, 626–639.

Stouffer, S. A., Suchman, E. A., DeVinney, L. C., Star, Shirley, A., and Williams, R. M., Jr. *Studies in social psychology in World War II.* Vol. I. *The American soldier: adjustment during army life.* Princeton: Princeton University Press, 1949.

Tumin, M. M. *Desegregation: resistance and readiness.* Princeton: Princeton University Press, 1958.

Vander Zanden, J. The Klan revival. *Amer. J. Soc.*, 1960, **65**, 456–462.

West, L. J. United States Air Force prisoners of the Chinese Communists. In *Methods of forceful indoctrination: observations and interviews.* New York: Group for the Advancement of Psychiatry, 1957.

Where shall we live? *Report of the Commission on Race and Housing.* Berkeley: University of California Press, 1958.

Wilner, D. M., Walkley, Rosabelle and Cook, S. W. *Human relations in interracial housing: a study of the contact hypothesis.* Minneapolis: University of Minnesota Press, 1955.

Yaryan, Ruby and Festinger, L. Preparatory action and belief in the probable occurrence of future events. *J. abnorm. soc. Psychol.*, 1961, **63**, 603–606.

Zajonc, R. The process of cognitive tuning in communication. *J. abnorm. soc. Psychol.*, 1960, **61**, 159–167.

Zimbardo, P. G. Involvement and communication discrepancy as determinants of opinion change. *J. abnorm. soc. Psychol.*, 1960, **60**, 86–94.

Author Index

327

Subject Index

Alternative(s), attractiveness of and magnitude of dissonance, 6, 61ff
  attributes of, 22–23
  in forced-compliance situation, 21–22
  in free-choice situation, 21
  manipulated importance of, 62
  valence of, 233–235
Attitude, change, *see* Change (attitudinal)
  definition, 16–17
  discrepancies in, 14ff
Attribute, *see* Cognition

Balance, theories of cognitive, 17, 224ff
Behavior, cognitive change concerning, 69
  discrepant, through forced compliance, 21–22
  discrepant and attitude change, 291–292
Boomerang, 55
Brainwashing, 286

Change, attitudinal, and the boomerang effect, 55ff

Change, attitudinal, and commitment, 107ff
  and perceived obligation, 103, 104
  as function of arousal of dissonance, 7, 15–16
  as function of commitment to discrepant behavior, 9–10
  as function of expended effort, 29ff, 255–256
  as function of initial attitude, 273ff
  as function of number of rejected alternatives, 36–37, 38–39
  following choice, 45
  following discrepant behavior, 24–25, 42, 44
  following interpersonal interaction, 273ff
  following threat of punishment, 41–42, 84ff
  following voluntary exposure to information, 44
  in evaluation of subjective experience, 32–34
  behavioral, to reduce dissonance, 69
  in beliefs following coercion, 288ff
  motivational, as mode of dissonance reduction, 132